UNDERSTANDING AND TREATING ALCOHOLISM

Volume 2

Biological, Psychological, and Social Aspects of Alcohol Consumption and Abuse

UNDERSTANDING AND TREATING ALCOHOLISM

Volume 2

Biological, Psychological, and Social Aspects of Alcohol Consumption and Abuse

JILL LITTRELL
Arizona State University

LAWRENCE ERLBAUM ASSOCIATES, PUBLISHERS

1991   Hillsdale, New Jersey   Hove and London

Lawrence Erlbaum Associates, Inc., Publishers
365 Broadway
Hillsdale, New Jersey 07642

Library of Congress Cataloging in Publication Data

Littrell, Jill.
    Understanding and treating alcoholism / Jill Littrell.
        p.   cm.
    Includes bibliographical references and indexes.
    Contents: v. 1. An empirically based clinician's handbook for the
treatment of alcoholism — v. 2. Biological, psychological, and
social aspects of alcohol consumption and abuse.
    ISBN 0-8058-0872-8 (set). — ISBN 0-8058-0870-1 (v. 1).
    ISBN 0-8058-0871-X (v. 2)
    1. Alcoholism–Treatment.   2. Alcoholism.   I. Title.
    [DNLM: 1. Alcohol, Ethyl—adverse effects.   2. Alcoholism—
genetics.   3. Alcoholism—psychology.   4. Alcoholism—therapy.
5. Risk Factors. WM 274 L 782u]
RC565.L57   1991
616.86′106—dc20
DNLM/DLC
for Library of Congress   90-15725
                                                           CIP

Printed in the United States of America
10 9 8 7 6 5 4 3 2 1

Contents

Preface

In 1981, after having completed my Ph.D. in clinical psychology, I entered the field of alcoholism. I spent a year at the Veteran's Administration Hospital in Phoenix working exclusively in the Alcohol Dependency Department. After this training experience, I went to work in the Alcohol and Drug Dependency Department at CIGNA Health Plan.

While beginning my work, I was impressed by the amount of "factual" information which was voiced by my colleagues and my patients. Having been trained as a scientist, I wondered whether there was research to support the "facts" which seemed to be coin of the realm, and, if there was such research, whether the research justified the conclusions which everyone seemed to believe. I made inquiries of my mentor, Fred Obitz Ph.D., who directed me to empirical sources. The next eight years were spent pursuing these sources.

These volumes are the result of my Odyssey through the empirical literature on alcoholism. In organizing the chapters and selecting the material, I have attempted to provide persons in the field with all the information I wished someone had organized for me before I started. Hopefully, as a result of these volumes, professionals will have a good understanding as to which of the factual statements about alcohol and alcoholism are supported by data and some of the empirically validated ways to proceed with treatment.

I wish to thank my mentor and friend, Robert Cialdini Ph.D. for support and an introduction to empirical work; my clinical supervisor and friend, Fred Obitz Ph.D. for introducing me to this field; my brother, Jordan Tappero M.D. for answering my endless questions about medicine; and my husband, Gus Levine Ph.D. Without the support, patience, enthusiasm, statistical consultation, and conceptual input of Gus Levine this project would not have been attempted.

God grant me the serenity
to accept the things I cannot change,
Courage to change the things I can,
And wisdom to know the difference.

HEREDITY IN ALCOHOLISM: RESEARCH METHODS, BOTTOM LINES, AND WHAT IT MIGHT MEAN

Introduction

Twin and adoption studies, as well as familial association studies provide strong suggestion of a hereditary contribution in the development of alcoholism. This section begins with a chapter reviewing twin and adoption studies. Bottom lines are offered about what the research has established and where questions still remain. Although it is clear that some form of alcoholism is probably inherited, it is less clear that alcoholism which is inherited is the primary variety and not the primary sociopathy/secondary alcoholism type. Further, although the case for male inheritance is sturdy, conclusions for women are more obscure.

Establishing that alcoholism is inherited raises numerous questions. Different research methodologies have shed light on a variety of questions. Chapter 2 addresses the question of association between alcoholism and other psychiatric disorders. Investigators have attempted to discern whether inheriting alcoholism might be linked to inheritance of some other psychiatric disorder. Some bottom lines are available.

There are other ways to investigate the nature of the syndrome that constitutes inherited alcoholism. Some researchers have contrasted various types of alcoholics. By comparing alcoholics who have an alcoholic parent with alcoholics who have no alcoholism in their family background, researchers have identified a syndrome which seems to describe those alcoholics who are more likely to have inherited their alcoholism. Interestingly, when researchers divide alcoholics according to any trait represented in the syndrome, the rest of the syndrome seems to emerge as descriptive of the group. That is, the same cluster of traits seems to hang together in association with a positive family history for alcoholism. This area of research is discussed in chapter 3.

Another way, although a bit more round about, to approach the nature of what might be inherited is to examine the childhood characteristics of alcoholics. Of course retrospective recall is always suspect. Fortunately, a number of good longitudinal studies have been conducted. These studies have allowed for bottom lines as to the childhood characteristics that are most often descriptive of future alcoholics. Although the methodology of the longitudinal studies does not allow inferences regarding whether precursor traits are part of an inherited syndrome, some of the traits that emerge as precursors have been demonstrated to be in part themselves determined by genetics. Chapter 4 in this section concerns the findings from longitudinal studies.

A final research paradigm that yields findings relevant to what might constitute the syndrome of inherited alcoholism, has been the examination of children of alcoholics. Offspring of alcoholics, many of whom will probably develop alcoholism later in life, but are too young to have experienced serious alcohol involvement, have been scrutinized and compared to controls on a variety of characteristics. The same traits that emerge in the longitudinal studies are reflected in the studies of offspring of alcoholics. There is a wealth of information available on temperament, hormonal and neurochemical traits, as well as responses to alcohol. Findings from this area of research are discussed in chapter 5.

All of these diverse research methodologies suggest rather similar conclusions. There is consistency in the data. The last chapter in this section presents some global theories that have attempted to integrate findings across research methodologies. Some of these theories propose rationale for why alcohol might be more compelling for those at risk. In the last chapter of this section, global theories are reviewed. Major unanswered questions are discussed.

1 Twin and Adoption Studies

UNCONTROLLED CORRELATIONS

Although the majority of male alcoholics (47–87%) do not have an alcoholic parent, the lifetime risk for alcoholism among children of alcoholics is 20–30% whereas it is 5–10% in the general population (Cotton, 1979). The incidence of alcoholism among first degree, male (sibling or parent) relatives of identified alcoholics is 25%, which is higher than the population parameter of 5–10%. The incidence of alcoholism among first degree, female relatives of identified alcoholics is 5% vs. the population parameter for female alcoholism of 1% (Winokur, Reich, Rimmer, & Pitts, 1970).

TWIN STUDIES

Major support for a genetically mediated diathesis (tendency or disposition) toward alcoholism is provided by two types of studies: twin studies and adoption studies. The methodology employed in the twin studies has been to compare concordance rates for drinking between identical and fraternal twins. The argument assumes that sibling pairs of identical and fraternal twins are equally likely to share a similar environment. If environment is the only causative factor in determining drinking behavior, then concordance rates should be the same for both types of twins. If concordance rates are greater for identical than fraternal twins then major differences between dizygotes vs. monozygotes must account for the difference. Dizygotes twins share on average only half their genes, whereas identical twins are the same on all of their genes. Any obtained concordance differences are attributable to genes, that is a hereditary component. A difference in concordance rates between the two twin types supports the genetic case.

There have been a large number of twin studies conducted in a number of different countries. Most of these studies have supported the genetic hypothesis. Partanen, Bruun, and Markkanen (1966) examined fraternal and identical twin pairs. They found differences in concordance rates between identical and fraternal twins on frequency and amount of drinking but not on number of problems created by drinking. Younger twin pairs, as opposed to older twin pairs, exhibited greater differential concordance between monozygotic vs. dizygotic pairs on drinking frequency and subjective loss of control. Jonsson and Nilsson (cited by Goodwin, 1979) studied 7500 Swedish twin pairs and found greater concordance for monozygotes than dizygotes on quantity of alcohol consumed but not on adverse consequences from drinking. Kaij (1960) reported a concordance rate for alcoholism (defined as 2 or more symptoms from the categories of consistent black outs, craving, or withdrawal symptoms) among monozygotic pairs of 54.2% vs. 31.5% for dizygotic twins. Further, the concordance rate discrepancy between monozygotic and dizygotic twins increased when only severe cases of alcoholism were examined (p. 36). Concordance for alcoholism was independent of concordance for other diagnoses. Hrubec and Omenn (1981) found a concordance rate for alcoholism (criteria having been met by diagnosis of alcoholism at time of VA hospital claim) of 26.3% among monozygotes, which was significantly greater than the 11.9% concordance rate for the dizygotes. There was also support for heritability of alcoholic cirrhosis and alcoholic psychosis beyond the contribution attributable to the heritability of alcoholism.

In a study of 879 male monozygote twin pairs and 1940 male dizygote twin pairs, Kaprio et al. (1987) found that type of zygosity enhanced that prediction of one sibling's drinking by the other sibling's drinking, thus suggesting that concordance was greater among monozygotes than dizygotes. The authors were sensitive to a possible nongenetic confound to the genetic variable differentiating monozygotes from dizygotes. In this study, it was found that monozygote twins vs. dizygote twins live together until an older age and subsequent to that have more weekly contact with each other. The authors tested the contribution of types of zygosity in predicting drinking behavior after removing the effect of social contact. After removing the effect of social contact, the difference in concordance between the monozygotes and the dizygotes remained significant. The authors suggested that their analysis supported the genetic case. There was a problem with the analysis, however. Careful scrutiny of the report suggests a further, probably critical problem. Removing the effect of social contact prior to testing the predictive utility of type of zygosity will provide a valid test of genetic effects, only if social contact does not interact with type of zygosity in predicting drinking behavior. The authors preliminary analyses suggested that such an interaction does occur. That is, social contact is more important in predicting concordance for drinking habits among the monozygotes than among the dizygotes. Such being the case, the legitimate test of genetic contribution would have been to test the predictive utility of type of zygosity in determining one twin's drinking from the other twin's drinking after the interaction of social contact with type of zygosity had been removed. Such a test was not provided and thus legitimate conclusions cannot be drawn.

Findings from the prior adult twin studies have been consistent in supporting greater concordance for problem drinking among monozygotes vs. dizygotes, although there has been some inconsistency in the dependent variables upon which the greater concordance has been demonstrated. Some researchers have examined twin samples asking about additional variables in youthful samples. In a sample of youth taking the National Merit examination, Loehlin (1972) found support for greater concordance among monozygotes vs. dizygotes for hangovers and heavy drinking. Heath and Martin (1988) and Heath, Jardin, and Martin (1989) compared concordance between monozygote vs. dizygotes pair on amount consumed per week (a continuous variable encompassing normal drinking levels), age of onset of drinking, and the dichotomous category of drinking or abstention as a teenager. Greater concordance was observed among 20 to 30-year-old monozygotes as compared to dizygotes of both sexes for current level of consumption (Heath & Martin, 1988). Age on onset of drinking in adolescence manifested greater concordance for female monozygotes than female dizygotes, although difference in twin types were not observed among boys (Heath & Martin, 1988). There were differences in concordance rates between monozygotes and dizygotes of both sexes on the dichotomous variable of abstention or not during adolescence (Heath & Martin, 1988). A study by Heath, Jardine, and Martin (1989) suggested that for females, being married or unmarried also moderates the degree of concordance between twin pairs. The differential in concordance between monozygotes and dizygotes was greatest in female unmarried twins. In the Heath, Jardine, and Martin (1989) study looking at females only, there was no correlation between concordance between twin pairs and the amount of social contact between the twin pairs. That is, more social contact between the monozygote girls than the dizygote girls could not account for differences between twin type pairs in concordance of drinking. In total, then these studies with younger populations are consistent with the genetic case for problem drinking and possibly other drinking events (age of onset, consumption levels) as well.

In contrast to the bulk of twin studies that have found greater concordance between monozygotes than dizygotes, is a study by Gurling, Murray, and Clifford (1981), which reported negative results. Monozygotes displayed a concordance rate of 21% for alcohol dependence vs. 25% in the dizygotes, a nonsignificant difference. Unlike some of the earlier studies specifically examining alcoholism as the dependent variable, Gurling et al.'s sample was unusual in that a large number of female twin pairs were included. As is discussed later, the case for inheritance of alcoholism in females is less clear. Further, Murray, Clifford, and Gurling (1983, p. 34) remarked that their sample was recruited from a psychiatric hospital. They may have tapped into populations of alcoholics whose alcoholism was preceded by depression. As will be discussed later, the case for inheritance among primary depressed/secondary alcoholics may be weaker than for other forms of alcoholism.

Comment.   A number of researchers have provided caveats with regard to extrapolating findings from twin studies to the general population. Twins are distinguished from the larger population by unique characteristics. Twins tend to have more birth defects, be born to older mothers, and develop more slowly than nontwins (Alterman & Tarter, 1983). It is possible that these unique characteristics may in some way modify inherited factors predisposing to alcoholism and thereby distort conclusions regarding the potency of genetic factors in influencing the development of alcoholism in the general population.

There are data suggesting that the basic premise allowing inferences regarding genetic contribution from the twin study methodology is flawed. Kapirio et al. (1987) established that monozygotes reside in a common residence longer than do dizygotes and they also spend more time together after establishing separate residences. Time spent together is a predictor of concordance of drinking habits between pairs, this factor being more important for the male monozygotes than for the male dizygotes. There is a real flaw in the twin study methodology which has been recruited to examine the importance of heredity in determining a characteristic. This may explain why identical twins are found to be similar on most characteristics, whether the characteristic is known to be genetically controlled or not (Gabrelli & Plomin, 1985). Twin studies do not totally eliminate the confounding of genetic and environmental influences.

Beyond a flaw in the basic logic of methodology, individual twin studies on alcoholism probably have their own unique problems. One study that was particularly flawed was the one executed by Kaij. The Kaij (1960) examination of monozygote vs. dizygote samples was part of a larger study on other issues. Kaij spent more time interviewing monozygotes than dizygotes, thus there was more opportunity to establish concordance for the monozygote twins than for the dizygote twins (Murray et al, 1983). A further telling criticism of the Kaij study was the failure to ensure the blindness of the investigator categorizing the drinking behavior of the subject (Murray et al, 1983).

Despite the flaws in the methodology of individual studies and flaws in the basic assumptions of twin study methodology, the twin research is of value. The methodology does offer the opportunity to rule out the hypothesis. Hypothesis consistent findings offer tentative support for the hypothesis, particularly when the findings are consistent with the observations from other approaches. As we shall see, supportive findings from other research avenues have suggested the genetic case.

THE HALF-SIBLING METHODOLOGY

Schuckit, Goodwin, and Winokur (1972) examined a population of half siblings of identified alcoholics. The half siblings were categorized according to whether they did or did not have an alcoholic biological parent and whether they were or were not raised by a parent who was alcoholic. (There were four groups, all comprised of half siblings of an identified alcoholic proband.) A major result of this study was that having an alcoholic biological parent was the variable that contributed to alcoholism in the half sibling. Being raised in a home with an alcoholic parental figure did not influence the incidence of alcoholism in the half sibling. A further comparison made possible by the interesting design in this study was between those half siblings who had been raised with the alcoholic sister or brother, and those half siblings who did not share a childhood environment with the alcoholic sister or brother. Presumably the environment in which the identified alcoholic proband had been raised was more "alcohologenic" in terms of nurturance. There was no difference between the incidence of alcoholism in the half sibling when they were raised with a to be alcoholic than when they were raised in an environment apart from the alcoholic half sibling.

There were some factors in this half sibling study that limit generalizability of results. Over half the subjects in this study were Black and there was a high incidence of broken homes in all groups, thereby diminishing the representativeness of the findings. Further, the authors did not report the sex ratios of the four groups of half siblings. Because sex strongly influences incidence of alcoholism, confounding on this variable could result in erroneous conclusions. Despite these caveats, the clever design of this study and the consistency of the results with other findings makes this one more study suggesting that the hereditary strongly influences the development of alcoholism.

ADOPTION STUDIES

A second type of study shedding light on the genetic contribution to alcoholism has been the adoption study method. Adopted out children of alcoholic parentage (Family History Positives) are compared to adopted out children of normal parentage (Family History Negatives). The methodology assumes that adoptive home placements do not differ as a function of biological parentage and some authors (Cloninger and colleagues; Goodwin and colleagues) have empirically validated this assumption on their particular data bases.

Roe's study

The earliest adoption study was reported by Roe (1944). Roe detected no difference in the rate of alcoholism between those with and without alcoholic parents (Roe, 1944). A crucial flaw in the Roe study was pinpointed by Cloninger, Bohman, and Sigvardsson (1981). Sixty-seven percent of Roe's family history positive adoptees were raised in rural environments where the incidence of alcoholism is low. Only 28% of the family history negatives were raised in rural environments. In light of subsequent studies, it is probably reasonable to conclude that this confound may have masked a genetic contribution.

Goodwin et al.'s Studies

Goodwin, Schulsinger, Hermansen, Guze, and Winokur (1973) compared Danish adult male adoptees whose biological parent had been hospitalized for alcoholism with Danish adult male adoptees whose biological parents suffered from psychosis or displayed no apparent mental illness. Goodwin et al. (1973) did not report on whether the alcoholic biological parent suffered from primary alcoholism as opposed to alcoholism associated with sociopathy. The researchers did have access to police records. Sixteen of the 55 biological alcoholic parents had been arrested for public intoxication. (The reason for this distinction becomes clear in later discussion.) No differences were detected in the quality of the adoptive home environment.

The 55 family history positives and 78 controls were all interviewed to assess their drinking practices. Goodwin et al. reported a significant increase in the incidence of alcoholism among the family history positives (18%) compared to the incidence among family history negatives (5%). Data from the study did support the genetic case for alcoholism. The authors looked at inheritance for other traits as well. No significant increase in character disorders among the FHP group was detected. The adoptees in the FHP group were more often divorced regardless of drinking status. Although there were no differences between the FHPs and FHNs on police records, both populations were surprisingly high on this variable. Fourty-four percent of the adoptees in the biological FHP group and biological FHN groups had police records.

A closer look at how alcoholism was defined in the Goodwin et al. (1973) study, suggests a more refined conclusion. Alcoholism was defined as having experienced problems in at least three life areas once a criteria for heavy drinking was reached. The criteria for heavy drinking was relatively conservative (6 drinks per occasion twice per month). When Goodwin et al. distinguished adoptees who were heavy drinkers from those who were not heavy drinkers without regard to problems, family history positives did not differ from family history negatives. The incidence of heavy drinking in the FHP group was 49% whereas it is 55% in the FHN group. Unfortunately, the Goodwin et al. study did not test whether those FHP who reach criteria for heavy drinking, consume in greater quantities than FHNs who have also reached criteria. The study's results do suggest that among those drinking up to quantitative criterion, the heavy consumption of the FHPs more often ramifies into problems effecting many life areas.

Some (Murray et al., 1983; Peele, 1986) have criticized the Goodwin et al. study on the grounds that the genetic case is only established when alcoholism is defined as heavy drinking and problems in at least 3 life domains. Goodwin et al.'s definition of alcoholism may fail to capture alcoholism. Perhaps heavy drinking with fewer than 3 problems also captures the essence of alcoholism. Critics argue that using an alternative definition of alcoholism, perhaps a genetic hypothesis would not be supported. There is a counter argument to the argument of the critics, however. Any definition of alcoholism will be somewhat arbitrary. There is good reason to believe that Goodwin et al.'s definition constitutes a good way to separate alcoholism from modal drinking. Survey data in the United States (Cahalan & Cisen, 1968; Schuckit, 1986) suggest that heavy drinking and a limited number of problems created by drinking are well within the limits of social drinking. That is, Goodwin et al.'s criteria probably did differentiate alcoholism from heavy drinking. The finding of more FHPs in the alcoholic category and fewer FHP in the heavy and circumscribed problem drinking categories, with the converse for FHNs does support the genetic inheritance hypothesis. It should be noted that other researchers have also found that the concordance between offspring and parent alcoholism will vary as a function of the definition of alcoholism. Parker and Harford (1988) report an association between paternal alcoholism and nonadopted offspring's dependent drinking, but no association between paternal alcoholism with nonadopted offspring's problem drinking without dependence.

Goodwin and associates reexamined their data base exploring additional issues. In a second study, Goodwin, Schulsinger, Moller, Hermansen, Winokur, and Guze (1974) investigated the impact of being raised in an alcoholic home in conjunction with being a biological "child of." FHP adoptees were compared with their biological brothers who had not been placed for adoption. The findings suggested that being raised in an alcoholic environment did not contribute to the development of alcoholism. The incidence of alcoholism in the adoptees (25%) did not differ significantly from the incidence in the family history positives raised at home (17%). The results of this study also suggested that a severely alcoholic biological parent confers greater liability to the offspring than a mildly alcoholic parent. In this study FHPs were categorized according to the severity of the alcoholism in the biological drinking parent. Those children born to alcoholics who had been hospitalized 4 or more times for drinking, drank more and displayed more problems due to their drinking than did those children born to alcoholics who had only been hospitalized once for their drinking.

Goodwin and associates reported two studies examining data from female adoptees (Goodwin, Schulsinger, Knop, Mednick, & Guze, 1977a, 1977b). Findings from these studies failed to suggest that daughters of alcoholics were at increased risk for alcoholism. The FHP female adoptees did not differ from the FHN female adoptees on any of the drinking dependent variables. Goodwin et al. cautioned against concluding that FHP females are not a genetic risk. The incidence of alcoholism in the control group was unusually high. Further, the subjects in the studies were in their middle and late 30s when they were interviewed. Since women do not surpass the age of risk for developing alcoholism until their 40s, differences between the populations might be expected to emerge in later years.

The Goodwin et al. studies represent very good early efforts to establish the genetic case. The case was supported for men but not for women. The high incidence of police records in the adopted out men raises concern about whether alcoholism associated with sociopathy rather than primary alcoholism was being investigated.

Cadoret et al.'s Iowa Studies

Cadoret and associates examined adoptees from Iowa (Cadoret, Cain, & Grove, 1980; Cadoret & Gath, 1978; Cadoret, O'Gorman, Troughton, & Heywood, 1985; Cadoret, Troughton, & O'Gorman, 1987). Data on biological parents were obtained from adoption records and public records when available. In the Cadoret and Gath (1978) study, the authors remarked on the sex of the biological alcoholic parent. In the Cadoret and Gath (1978) publication, the authors remark that in no case was the biological mother alcoholic. In subsequent reports, the authors did not specifically report the sex of the biological alcoholic parent. In the Iowa studies, adoptees were selected for having biological backgrounds of either alcoholism or antisocial personality (ASP). Control group adoptees were selected such that matching occurred on age, sex, and biological mother's age at time of adoption, and in the 1978 and 1980 studies, amount of time spent in foster care. Results were the following. In all studies, alcoholism in the biological parent predicted primary alcoholism in the adoptee. The one negative finding was that biological parent alcoholism failed to predict alcoholism secondary to depression in the adoptee in the Cadoret and Gath (1978) publication. In Cadoret and Gath's (1978) study, there was further support for the genetic case in that alcoholism in the extended biological family of the adoptee predicted alcoholism without regard to primacy at the .006 level, N = 84. (Associations with ASP are discussed in a later section.) Support for the inheritance of alcoholism in women was reported in the 1985 study, although sex of alcoholic parent was not analyzed as a variable in this study. It becomes clearer in later discussion that sex of the biological alcoholic parent is particularly relevant in women.

Swedish Adoption Studies

Cloninger and colleagues have reported a number of adoption studies analyzing a data base collected from the records of Swedish adoptees of alcoholic, biological parents (Bohman, Cloninger, Sigvardsson, & von Knorring, 1982; Bohman, Cloninger, von Knorring, & Sigvardsson, 1984; Cloninger, Bohman, & Sigvardsson, 1981; Cloninger, Sigvardsson, von Knorring, & Bohman, 1984; Sigvardsson, Cloninger, Bohman, & von Knorring, 1982; Sigvardsson, von Knorring, Bohman, & Cloninger, 1984). Based on statistical analyses of their sample, the authors have advanced the notion that there are two separate types of inheritance for alcoholism: milieu limited alcoholism and male limited alcoholism. In a later publication (Schuckit, Li, Cloninger, & Deitrich, 1985), Cloninger speculated on a third inheritance pathway, although this third pathway has not been discussed elsewhere in the literature. In later publications, Cloninger has not mentioned it further.

According to Cloninger and colleagues, milieu limited alcoholism and male limited alcoholism are distinguished in the following ways. Both males and females can develop milieu limited type of alcoholism. Its onset occurs later in life (over 30). It is less often associated with antisocial, criminal activity. Without the proper environmental factors, the genotype for milieu limited alcoholism will not develop into excessive drinking. Milieu limited alcoholism contrasts with male limited alcoholism. Male limited alcoholism only is manifested in males. In females, the genotype is expressed as somatization. The onset of male limited alcoholism occurs early in life (late adolescence or early adulthood). Excessive drinking is usually associated with antisocial behavior. Environment factors do not influence whether this type of genotype will manifest as excessive drinking.

The hypothesis regarding two distinct pathways for alcoholism emerged from a discriminate analysis analyzing data on male adoptees (Cloninger et al, 1981). In this analysis, alcoholic adoptees were graded in terms of severity according to the number of occasions they had been brought to the attention of the Swedish authorities for misconduct related to drinking. Those in the severe group had sometimes received treatment for alcoholism. In the 1981 Cloninger et al. analysis, the authors asked the question: What composite of weighted background variables would distinguish adoptees who are not alcoholic, adoptees who are severely alcoholic, adoptees who are moderately alcoholic, and adoptees who are mildly alcoholic? The background variables which the computer lumped together to differentiate the groups suggested to the authors that the severe and mild alcoholic adoptees were similar in background and different from the moderate alcoholic adoptees. Both clusters differed from those adoptees who were not alcoholics. The Cloninger et al. (1981) study was the study in which the variables discriminating the groups were identified.

The methodology employed to derive conclusions regarding separate inheritance patterns has received criticism (Littrell, 1988). The authors did not perform t-tests to determine whether those background variable which supposedly distinguish between severe alcoholic adoptees, moderate alcoholic adoptees, and mild alcoholic adoptees differed statistically between the groups. It would have been possible in the data analysis to construct a new dependent variable from the discriminate function (the weighted set of background variables) such that a group mean for each of the four groups would have been generated. In the authors' publications, it was not even clear that the milieu-limited and male-limited groups differed significantly on the discriminate functions.

Before it can be assumed that specific background variables are associated with different patterns of alcoholism in the offspring, some evidence of statistical association is needed. Assuming that the authors could produce evidence of statistical significance, there is another problem in deriving the inferences that were drawn. It must be remembered that Cloninger et al. studies represent correlational findings. This caveat becomes particularly relevant when considering maternal background variables. If we assume that a form of alcoholism in the father is passed on, or causes, a particular form of alcoholism in the son, there are problems with knowing how to interpret information on the mother. Take the case for those adopted out children of alcoholics who became moderately severe (defined according to the 1981 study's definition) alcoholics. Severely alcoholic, criminal fathers did more often sire moderately alcoholic adopted away sons. In this group, the rate of alcoholism in the mother was low. What can be made of this finding? Do findings regarding the mother, suggest that moderately alcoholic males never inherit their alcoholism through a gene which can be expressed in females? Or do the findings tell us about the type of women that anti-social/alcoholic men are likely to marry? Similar questions can be raised about the less severe alcoholism in the father and alcoholism in the mother which is related to the milieu limited form. To determine what is happening, cases should be restricted to one alcoholic parent married to a normal individual. In the real world, variables such as paternal alcoholism are confounded with various type of maternal variables. This creates difficulties in drawing inferences.

Despite problems with the speculative separate pathways of inheritance, the Swedish data base analyses present strong evidence for the general picture of a genetic contribution to alcoholism which is associated with socially disruptive conduct. The support for inheritance was found for both males and females. However, the association between alcoholism in female adoptees was limited to alcoholism in the biological mother and did not reach significance among those with biological fathers who were alcoholic (Bohman, Sigvardsson, & Cloninger, 1981). Unfortunately, there is no way to know whether the association between daughter's alcoholism and mother's alcoholism, reflects prenatal environment or genetic contributions. There was also some suggestion in the data that paternal alcoholism predisposes adopted away daughters to somatization. Additional findings from the Swedish studies are discussed in other chapters in this section.

CRITICISM OF THE ADOPTION AND TWIN STUDIES

The adoption and twin studies have been criticized by Murray et al. (1983), Peele (1986), and Saunders and Williams (1983). Despite relevant criticism specific to individual studies, the conclusion of all review articles, save Peele's, is that the data support inheritance. There are generic issues which can be raised.

There are some subtle issues that have not been resolved. It has been recognized that there are various forms of alcoholism. Schuckit (1980c) has been a proponent of distinguishing between primary alcoholism and secondary alcoholism. Secondary alcoholism is alcoholism that has been preceded in time by another primary disorder such as antisocial personality (ASP) or depression. In order to ensure that the genetic case for primary alcoholism has been supported by the twin studies, it would be necessary to establish that in the twin studies concordance for primary alcoholism had been demonstrated. In fact, none of the twin studies examined type of alcoholism. In the Kaij study, Murray et al. (1983) commentary suggests that primary sociopathy/secondary alcoholism was investigated. Given the lack of attention to the type of alcoholism under investigation and the fact that the Kaij study probably examined primary sociopathy, no conclusions from the twin studies as to the type of alcoholism that is inherited can be stated with any confidence.

In the adoption studies, researchers have varied in whether they had attended to the primary and secondary alcoholism distinctions. Goodwin et al. (1973) examined primary alcoholism in the adoptee but did not mention the variable in the parent. The Swedish studies were sensitive to the differentiation in the adoptee. However, registration with the Temperance Board, a criterion for particular degrees of severity of alcoholism in the adopted away offspring, suggests that Cloninger and colleagues were examining a socially disruptive variety of alcoholism, if not alcoholism, which was preceded in time by socially disruptive behavior. (The primary vs. secondary distinction rests on temporal differentiation.) Criminal activity in the father emerged in the backgrounds in both the milieu limited and male limited pathways suggesting that primary sociopathy was a possibility. Hence in the Goodwin et al. and Cloninger et al. studies, the type of alcoholism for which inheritance was established is unclear.

Cadoret and colleagues were the only investigators who attempted to distinguish primary vs. secondary alcoholism in the adoptee and the biological parent. The extent to which they were able to arrive at veridical temporal distinctions in the biological parent on the basis of adoption records in unknown. Further, Cadoret and colleagues did not attempt to distinguish primary from secondary alcoholics in the biological extended families of adoptees. Given the confusion as to the primary/secondary issue across studies, firm conclusions cannot be drawn regarding which type of alcoholism is inherited from the twin and adoption studies.

A critical issue for the establishing heritability is whether confounding genetic liability with mother's drinking during gestation or mother's drinking during the nursing period occurred. Had mother's drinking during the gestational or lactation period been confounded with genetic heritage contributed by either parent, findings might be attributable to the effect on the fetus or infant of exposure to alcohol. At least for the male adoptees, the case can be made that mother's drinking probably cannot account for the positive findings. Data on mother's drinking status was reported in many adoption studies. In Goodwin et al.'s study (1973) in 15% of the cases the alcoholic parent was the mother. No data were reported as to whether the mother drank during the gestational period. It could be that the 15% of maternal alcoholics were all drinking during gestation and can totally account for the increased rate of alcoholism in the FHP adoptees, but this is unlikely. The Goodwin et al. study probably demonstrates the impact of heredity. In all cases (males and female adoptees were lumped together) reported in the Cadoret and Gath study (1978), the alcoholic parent was the father and data were available ruling out alcoholism in the mother. The case for genetics without an maternal environmental confound was established by this study. In the Swedish studies (specifically the Cloninger et al, 1981 study), the mother's drinking status was measured and entered as a variable in the discriminant analyses that were performed. The rate of maternal alcoholism among the male, moderate alcoholics was low. Thus paternal genetic factors, rather than gestational influence can be assumed to have accounted for the increased rate of alcoholism among the male adoptees in this study. Across studies, the case for a genetic contribution to the risk for alcoholism in males is well established.

Ruling out the possibility of a confound of genetic contribution with mother's drinking during gestation or lactation is more equivocal in the investigations of female adoptees. It should be recalled that Goodwin et al.'s data failed to find increased risk of alcoholism among female adoptee of alcoholic biological parents. Cadoret, O'Gorman, Troughton, and Heywood (1985) found that the risk of alcoholism among female adoptees was increased by alcoholism in the biological parent, although sex of parent was not reported or analyzed. In the Swedish adoption studies, biological mother's alcoholism increased the rate of alcoholism in the female adoptee although biological father's alcoholism did not (Bohman et al, 1981). In the Swedish study, mother's genetic contribution may have been confounded with maternal environmental influences (e.g., nursing or gestational environment). In the Bohman et al. (1981), some additional data on the mothers of female alcoholic adoptees were reported. The relatively shorter hospital stay after birth (not tested for statistical significance) among the alcoholic female adoptees probably mitigates against a confound of maternal drinking during gestation. The occurrence of a significant weighting on a discriminant function of extended postnatal stay with the biological mother after birth among those females who developed alcoholism, allows for the possibility of greater exposure to a drinking, nursing mother among those females who later became alcoholic. Hence, the Swedish studies fail to firmly establish the case for inheritance in women.

Some bottom lines can be proffered examining all the studies investigating the case for inheritance of alcoholism in women. Because those studies yielding positive findings for an association between parental alcoholism and female adoptee alcoholism did not rule out maternal drinking during the critical periods of nursing and gestation, an unequivocal case for inheritance in the development of female alcoholism is presently not available. Whether a genetic contribution increases the risk of alcoholism in females is as yet unknown.

A final issue concerns the magnitude of effect (usually assessed as proportion of variance accounted for) of inheritance in causing alcoholism. Most prior reviews of the adoption and twin studies have concluded that genetics exert a definite but small effect on the development of alcoholism (Murray et al., 1983; Saunders & Williams, 1983). Although effect size has been reported in some studies (viz., the Swedish studies), the meaning of such reports is obscure. The problems inherent in estimating effect size have been well articulated. It is agreed that any legitimate estimate should be based on a huge N. Further, the range of the dependent variable represented in the study will greatly alter the statistic (Glass & Hakstian, 1969). Since there have been few huge N studies and there has been little attempt to ensure a random selection of the entire range of deviant drinking behavior, conclusions regarding the magnitude of the genetic impact are premature.

SUMMARY

A number of twin studies have provided findings consistent with the case for the inheritance of alcoholism. Of course, there is a crucial flaw in the twin methodology. The environment of monozygote twins is more similar than the environment of dizygote twins. Hence, findings from twin studies are not definitive. The adoption studies have been consistent in their support of inheritance. There is still a questions about what type of alcoholism is inherited, the primary type or the type associated with criminal, socially disruptive behavior. Although the case for male inheritance emerges from the studies, the case for inheritance of female alcoholism is less clear.

2 What Else is Inherited Along with Alcoholism: Studies of Familial Association

Another big question in the literature has been which additional psychiatric diagnoses share inheritance risk with alcoholism. The first avenue of inquiry has been to establish concordance patterns in families. There have been a number of investigations identifying those pathological conditions co-occurring in families that have a high incidence of alcoholism. Researchers have approached the question in two complementary ways. Some have selected alcoholic probands and then assessed the relatives of the probands to determine which pathologies occur at rates greater than would be expected in control populations. Others have selected probands with particular afflictions and then assessed the incidence of alcoholism among family members. Such studies have yielded the following results.

RAW ASSOCIATIONS

When alcoholic probands are selected, higher rates of depression, particularly among female relatives are found (Pitts & Winokur, 1966; Winokur et al, 1970). Only one study found alcoholism elevated in the family members of depressed probands (Winokur, Cadoret, Dorzab, & Baker, 1971); other studies did not find this association (Gershon et al, 1982; Merikangas, Leckman, Prusoff, Pauls, & Weissman, 1985; Weissman et al, 1984). Similar inconsistency has been found in the study of bipolar depressives. James and Chapman (1975), Reich, Clayton, and Winokur (1969), and Gershon et al. (1982) did not find an increase in alcoholism among the family members of bipolar depressives, although Cassidy, Flanagan, Spellman, and Cohen (1957) found an increased rate of alcoholism in the family members of bipolars who increase their own drinking during episodes of illness.

Higher rates of antisocial personality (ASP) and hyperactivity are found in the male relatives of alcoholic probands than in control populations (Amark, 1951; Merikangas, et al., 1985). Others have found that the higher rates of ASP among family members is greater among the family members of sociopathic alcoholics than the family members of primary alcoholics (Winokur, Rimmer, & Reich, 1971). (Primary alcoholic is the term used for alcoholics with no other major psychiatric diagnosis or psychiatric condition which temporally precedes the alcoholism.) This finding raises the question of whether the increased risk for sociopathy in FHPs is specific to relatives of sociopathic alcoholics.

Hyperactive children and adult attention deficit disorder patients have increased rates of familial alcoholism, ASP, and hysteria (Cantwell, 1972; Morrison & Stewart, 1973; Wender, Reimherr, & Wood, 1981). Female hysterics have high rates of familial alcoholism (Arkonac & Guze, 1963; Guze, 1975; Woener & Guze, 1968). Sociopaths have high rates of familial alcoholism and hysteria (Guze, 1975; Guze, Goodwin, & Crane, 1969). Increased alcoholism has been found among the relatives of schizophrenics, psychoneurotics and personality disorders (Pitts & Winokur, 1966; Winokur & Pitts, 1965). Female borderlines have higher rates of alcoholic relatives than do female bipolar depressives and female schizophrenics (Loranger & Tulis, 1985). Bulimics have increased familial alcoholism rates (Bulik, 1987). Finally, some have found that agoraphobics have higher rates of familial alcoholism when compared to persons with specific phobias or nonanxious controls, although there are contradictory reports (Harris, Noyes, Crowe, & Chandhry, 1983; Munjack & Moss, 1981).

Potential Explanations for the Raw Associations

Positive findings from familial association studies are consistent with the hypothesis that the genes for alcoholism and particular disorders might be transmitted concomitantly. Nongenetic explanations for familial association are, however, available. These explanations are reviewed here.

It is known that particular cultural attitudes and practices found in some ethnic groups are associated with increased rates of alcoholism (Vaillant, 1983). It is possible that particular subcultures might inculcate values and learned behavior which predispose to both alcoholism and certain pathologies. Common cultural training would then be the explanation for the association.

It is known that assortive mating, the coupling of particular pathological types, does occur. Alcoholic and sociopathic men marry hysterical women more often than would be predicted on the basis of chance (Guze, Goodwin, & Crane, 1970; Woener & Guze, 1968). Given assortive mating, one would expect a familial clustering of particular disorders. No genetic explanation would be required. Hysterical mothers might transmit hysteria to children via modeling or genetic contribution. Alcoholic fathers might transmit to sons through learning or through genetic pathways. In this way, alcoholic fathers would not be implicated in the transmission of hysteria, and hysterical mothers would not be implicated in the transmission of alcoholism.

It has been speculated that sometimes people develop alcoholism in response to psychological problems in themselves or their family members. Rimmer, Reich, and Winokur (1972) estimate that 32% of any alcoholic population are alcoholics who have developed their abusive drinking subsequent to and perhaps in response to depression. There is evidence that depression is hereditary (Cadoret, 1978a). Those primary depressives with secondary alcoholism could be expected to transmit their depression to their offspring through a genetic mechanism. The transmission of a hereditary, primary condition to offspring in secondary alcoholics would contribute to a familial association between alcoholism and the primary condition. The hereditary mechanism would obtain for the primary condition rather than the alcoholism. No genetic mechanism would link the association between the primary condition and the alcoholism. A similar argument can be adduced for ASP (Schuckit, 1973).

A related explanation to the previous possibility is that alcoholism might create all manner of disorder in family members. Being raised in a home disrupted by alcoholism is likely to create some behavioral disturbance in children and other relatives. Family members responding to the trauma of the alcoholism would result in a statistical association between the alcoholism in the proband and a wide variety of mood and behavioral disturbances among family members.

All prior explanations for the familial association findings are possible. Focusing now on the explanation of a shared genetic pathway between alcoholism and other afflictions, there are some additional findings that would be expected were the shared genetic pathway valid. First, any condition that is purported to be genetically inherited in association with alcoholism should itself be inherited. Second, the association between the two afflictions should be found (a) when alcoholic probands are selected and family members are assessed for the associated affliction, and (b) when probands exhibiting the particular affliction are selected and then their relatives are assessed for alcoholism. The results of the research findings previously cited permitting such tests lead to the conclusion that depression, and ASP coupled with hyperactivity, are the disorders which satisfy the initial conditions expected with genetic linking.

THE NOTION OF THE DEPRESSIVE SPECTRUM

Winokur et al. (1971) have advanced the notion of depressive spectrum disease to explain the familial associations between depression, alcoholism and antisocial personality (ASP). Raw data has established that regardless of whether an alcoholic proband is selected first or a proband with the associated disorder is selected first, depression and alcoholism seem to covary in families. A more refined methodology is required to further pursue the genetic association. Adoption study findings are germane. If the genes for a particular condition and alcoholism have a high probability of concomitant transmission, then it would be expected that the adopted out offspring of the biological parent with alcoholism should display higher rates of the condition which is hypothesized to be genetically linked. Conversely, adopted out offspring of the biological parent with a particular genetically linked disorder should display higher rates of alcoholism.

In the main, adoption studies fail to support an association between depression and alcoholism. Von Knorring, Cloninger, Bohman, and Sigvardsson (1983) found no increased depression among the biological parents of alcoholic adoptees. Increased alcoholism was noted among the biological mothers of depressed adoptees, however. Von Knorring et al. caution that their criteria for depression was stringent and hence, real relationships may have been obscured. For the positive finding a caveat is required. An alternative explanation to the genetic one for the association of maternal alcoholism and adoptee depression, is that alcoholic intrauterine environment predisposes to depression.

Several other adoption studies have failed to find an association between depression and alcoholism. Goodwin et al. (1973) failed to find increased depression in the adopted away sons of alcoholics. Goodwin et al., (1977b) examined adopted and nonadopted out daughters of alcoholics. The adopted out daughters displayed no elevation in depression compared to a control group of adoptees with normal biological parents. Those daughters of alcoholics raised at home were more likely to be depressed. This suggests that environment has a role in depression, although the possibility of the necessity of a dual contribution of genetics and environment can not be ruled out. In an adoption study by Cadoret et al. (1985) biological parental mental illness (which included depression) was not associated with adoptee ASP or alcoholism. The preceding studies then, do suggest genetic independence of alcoholism and depression.

A study by Mullan, Gurling, Oppenheim, and Murray (1986) employed an unusual methodology. The study examined the concordance rates for alcoholism in twin pairs and the concordance rates for neurotic depression (symptoms of anxiety and dysphoria) in the same twin pairs. The results were that concordance between twins of the two conditions (alcoholism and depression/anxiety) were independent. (The correlation between a concordance index for alcoholism and a concordance index for depression/anxiety was not significant.) The authors concluded that alcoholism and depression/anxiety are not inherited together. This study is sometimes cited in advancing the case of the genetic independence of alcoholism and depression/anxiety (Schuckit, Irwin, & Brown, 1990).

Winokur and colleagues have focused on identifying a subclass of unipolar depressed individuals whose relatives are more likely to be alcoholic or to display antisocial personality disorder. Winokur et al. (1971) found that persons (both sexes) developing depression prior to age 40 have more alcoholism and antisocial personality in their male relatives than males developing depression after age 40. There was no elevation in the incidence of alcoholism and ASP among the relatives of male, late-onset depressed compared to the general population. Winokur (1979) and Winokur, Behar, VanValkenburg, and Lowry (1978) have further described their subclass of depressed individuals who had an alcoholic or antisocial personality familial background (i.e., were manifesting depressive-spectrum disease). These individuals were characterized by an early but gradual onset of their depression, less recidivism, a trend toward hypochondriasis, more sexual and marital difficulties, and more irritability than those without a familial background of alcoholism and ASP.

The fact that there is an early onset of depression with less subsequent recidivism in the depressive-spectrum depressed is suggestive. The findings lead to the conclusion that depression is a response to the family of origin rather than a constitutional problem. Given that the symptomology found in the depressive-spectrum depressed is so diffuse, the explanation of a protean stress response to living in an alcoholic family of origin environment is implied. Environment may account for the familial aggregation of depression and alcoholism.

ANTISOCIAL DISORDER SPECTRUM

While Winokur et al. have included alcoholism under the rubric of depressive spectrum disease, other authors have posited an antisocial disorder spectrum (Cadoret, 1978b). The familial association studies suggest that alcoholism, hysteria, and ASP tend to aggregate in the same families (Guze, 1975; Cloninger, Reich, & Guze, 1975). The familial association studies are bolstered by the frequent co-occurence of dual diagnoses within individuals of alcoholism and antisocial personality (Lewis, Rice, Helzer, 1983; Lilienfeld, VanValkenberg, Larntz, & Akisal, 1986) and alcoholism and hysteria (Lewis, Helzer, Cloninger, Croughah & Whitman, 1982; Lilienfeld et al., 1986). Other studies suggest that childhood hyperactivity is also part of the spectrum. Hyperactivity and acting out are precursors to female hysteria (Cantwell, 1972; Guze, Woodruff, & Clayton, 1971) and male antisocial personality disorder (Cantwell, 1972; Gittleman, Mannuzza, Shenker, & Bonagura, 1985). Male alcoholics often have a dual diagnosis of attention deficit disorder, a residual of childhood hyperactivity (Wood, Reimherr, Wender, & Johnson, 1976; Wood, Wender, Reimherr, 1983). According to one variant of the spectrum notion, the disorders of alcoholism, ASP, hysteria, and childhood hyperactivity may all be expressions of the same genetic liability.

Looking to adoption studies to untangle nature from nurture has redounded in some support for genetic associations among the disorders of alcoholism, ASP, hysteria, and hyperactivity. Particular adoption studies have examined genetic associations between (a) hyperactivity and alcoholism, and (b) hysteria and alcoholism. Adopted out hyperactive children have high rates of alcoholism and

ASP in their biological backgrounds (Cadoret & Cain, 1980; Cadoret et al, 1976a). No adoption study has measured the incidence of hysteria in the biological mothers of adoptee alcoholics. Biological parent predictors of adoptee hysteria have been examined. Cadoret et al. (1978b) found that parental ASP predicted somatization in female adoptees. Alcoholism associated with criminality in biological fathers is associated with increased somatization, a cardinal feature of hysteria, in adopted away daughters (Cloninger, Sigvardsson, von Knorring, & Bohman, 1984).

A large number of adoption studies have examined the link between ASP and alcoholism. The studies in which support for the association has been adduced have not, however, attempted to establish whether the type of alcoholism under investigation was associated with antisocial activity unrelated to drinking. Cloninger et al. (1981) have identified alcoholism and criminality in the background of alcoholic adoptees whose own alcoholism was established by virtue of socially disruptive behavior (registration with the Swedish authorities). When psychopathic adoptees are selected, a biological family background of alcoholism, psychopathy, criminality, and drug abuse has been identified (Schulsinger, 1972). Cadoret (1978b) and Cadoret, Cunningham, Loftus, and Edwards (1976a) found that a biological parental background of alcoholism or ASP predicted severity of antisocial symptomotology in adult adoptees.

There are negative findings regarding the link between parental alcoholism and adoptee antisocial personality disorder. Goodwin et al. (1974) found no increase in ASP among adopted away sons of alcoholics, although the study established an association between alcoholism in the biological parent and alcoholism in the adopted away son. Cadoret and Gath (1978) found no increase in childhood conduct disorder (a precursor to ASP) among the adopted away sons of alcoholics. Cadoret et al. (1985) failed to find an association between ASP in the biological parent and alcoholism in the adopted away offspring or alcoholism in the biological parent and ASP in the adopted away offspring. Crowe (1974) found no increase in alcoholism in the adopted out children in incarcerated mothers.

In some studies, investigators have attended to the type of alcoholism under study in the parent and the offspring. Attempts to discriminate alcoholism that is not associated with antisocial conduct vs. alcoholism associated with antisocial conduct have occurred. Winokur et al.'s (1970, 1971) familial association studies found no increase in antisocial personality among relatives of alcoholics who did not themselves display antisocial behavior. In an Iowa adoption study by Cadoret, Troughton, and O'Gorman (1987) the obtained correlation between alcoholism in the biological parent and ASP in the adoptee disappeared when the link between ASP and alcoholism in the offspring was partialed out. These studies have suggested the independence of alcoholism unassociated with antisocial manifestations and antisocial personality.

In recent research there has been an attempt to unconfound the variables of alcoholism and criminality, breaking populations into crime unassociated with alcoholism, alcoholism unassociated with crime, and alcoholism associated with crime. Bohman (1978) had access to the Swedish adoption records as well as other official documents from which it was possible to determine the health statuses of biological parents and adult adoptees. Bohman (1978) eliminated from his analysis of the Swedish data base those biological parents who were both alcoholic and criminal, leaving the categories of alcoholism without criminality and criminality without alcoholism. Results suggested independence of pure criminality from pure alcoholism. Alcoholic fathers had offspring with a higher rate of pure-alcoholism but not pure criminality. Pure alcoholism in fathers also was significantly related to alcoholism associated with crime in the adoptees. Fathers who were pure criminals were not associated with increased risk for alcoholism in adoptees whether associated with crime or not, although in a subsequent study (Bohman et al. 1982), it was found that they more often sired adopted away sons who were pure criminals.

In a 1982 study, Bohman et al. included an additional category of biological father, viz. those who were both alcoholic and criminal. The findings of the 1978 study were essentially replicated. An additional finding was that the biological fathers who were both alcoholic and criminal were significantly related to alcoholism unassociated with crime in their adopted away sons. The finding that pure criminality (i.e., criminality unassociated with alcoholism) in the parent is independent from alcoholism in the adopted out offspring replicated the earlier Crowe (1974) study.

The Bohman study (1978) and Bohman et al. study (1982) suggested that there may be a form of criminality that is not associated with alcoholism. Further delinination of the characteristics of the type of criminality unassociated with alcoholism is found in the Bohman et al. (1982) study. Through discriminant analysis, the characteristics of biological fathers of pure criminals (those criminals who are not alcoholic) were identified. Bohman's biological fathers of pure criminals (those criminals without alcoholism) were characterized by petty crime with little violent crime. Although there was teenage alcohol abuse, adult alcohol problems were not a prominent characteristic in the biological fathers of the pure criminals.

Related information is available. The characteristics of criminal who are alcoholics vs. criminals who are not alcoholic have been investigated. Bohman et al., (1982), find that criminals who abuse alcohol compared to criminals who do not abuse alcohol are more recidivistic, have longer jail terms, and have more convictions for violent crimes. The alcohol abusing criminals have fewer property crime offenses than the criminal nonalcoholics. (Note, this does not mean that property crimes are not high among alcoholic criminals.) Goodwin, Crane, and Guze (1971) and Guze, Tuason, Gatfield, Stewart, and Picken (1962), who did not eliminate those with a dual diagnosis of ASP, report similar findings. Criminals who are alcoholic vs. those who are not alcoholic display more prison misconduct, experience an earlier onset of criminal problems, experience more arrests, report more fighting and wanderlust, and display more trouble with depression and suicidal incidents. Among criminals over the age of 30, the percentage of alcoholics was increased, suggesting that whereas nonalcoholic criminal remit with maturity, alcoholic criminals continue to sustain problems as long as they drink.

The above findings are suggestive of two possible varieties of criminality. One type is associated with alcoholism. Such criminal alcoholics are most likely to be convicted of violent crime. This type of criminality would predispose to alcoholism in the offspring and also similar types of criminal activity in the offspring. The second type of criminality would not predispose to alcoholism in the offspring. Such a criminal would be more likely to be convicted of petty crimes, to display less recidivism, and to exhibit fewer problems behind the walls.

ASSOCIATION BETWEEN THE INHERITANCE OF ALCOHOLISM AND LIVER DISEASE IN NONALCOHOLIC FEMALES

In a study by Arria, Tarter, Williams, and Van Thiel (1990) suggestion of possible genetic linkage between alcoholism and susceptibility to develop nonalcoholic liver disease in females emerged. These authors compared nonalcoholic persons with documented liver disease who did and did not have a family history of alcoholism. (The family history of alcoholism was established on the basis of social rather than health indicators of alcoholism.) The group of liver disorder patients who were FHP had developed their liver disorders at a younger age than did FHN patients, although this association was only found among the females. There was also suggestion that the early development of liver disease in the FHPs was associated with the presence of HLA B8 halotypes. The authors of this study did remark upon the confound of FHP status and age in their study. The cohort of FHP liver disease patients were younger than the FHN liver disease patients. In the general population, it may be that younger persons have a tendency to label more of their relatives as alcoholic which might account for the findings. (That is, the younger patients just had a prediliction to label relatives as alcoholic, regardless of the validity of the label.) Although the authors comment upon the tentative nature of the bottom line from their research, the findings will undoubtedly stimulate additional research in this area.

It should be recalled that in a study by Hrubec and Omenn (1981; see Chapter 1) results suggested that alcoholism and cirrhosis were inherited independently. The fact that the Hrubec and Omenn study was conducted on male subjects, whereas the association between inheritability of liver disease and alcoholism was particular to females in the Arria et al. (1990) may explain the discrepancy.

SUMMARY OF TESTS OF SPECTRUM HYPOTHESES

Studies addressing the question of which disorders tend to co-occur in the same families, especially when offspring are adopted out, do allow for conclusions regarding hereditary transmission. The depressive-spectrum hypothesis of genetic transmission is not supported by the adoption studies (Schuckit, 1986). The antisocial spectrum including hyperactivity, hysteria, and alcoholism is supported by familial association studies and adoption studies.

The issue of whether alcoholism and ASP are linked genetically will be further discussed Chapter 6. The Cadoret et al. findings, Goodwin et al. (1973) study, and Crowe (1974) study suggest genetic independence of ASP and alcoholism. However, conclusions regarding independence of ASP and alcoholism may be premature. Some investigations examining temperament of children of alcoholics have yielded findings suggesting a temperament similar to the findings reported in investigations of sociopaths. There are other interpretations of the independence of alcoholism and ASP reported in the Cadoret et al. studies and Goodwin et al. (1973) studies. These comments are left to Chapter 6.

In addition to indicating which pathologies might be genetically linked, the spectrum studies recommend refinements in extant nosology. The depressive-spectrum studies suggest unipolar depressives can be fruitfully subdivided into early onset types vs. late onset types. The studies investigating associations between alcoholism and ASP suggest that there are meaningful subcategories within criminal populations. The criminal, who is not an excessive drinker, and does not have a family history of alcoholism, can be expected to follow a different course in his criminal career than the alcoholic criminal.

3 Are There Types of Alcoholics Whose Drinking is More Likely to be Inherited?

A large literature has developed in which alcoholics are subdivided on some dimension, and then comparisons are made between the two types of alcoholic groups along a number of characteristics. Much of this work keeps turning up the same basic dichotomy: those alcoholics who have a family history vs. those alcoholics who do not have a family history of alcoholism. For the most part, the same clustering of variables seems to appear across studies. Particular subtypes are associated with increased frequency of alcoholism in the family history as well as particular drinking patterns and sober behavior. Some of the research differentiating subtypes is reviewed here.

FAMILY HISTORY POSITIVES VS. FAMILY HISTORY NEGATIVES

Researchers have divided alcoholic populations according to whether or not alcoholic subjects have a family history of alcoholism. Differences between the two alcoholic populations have been found. Alcoholics with a family history develop their drinking problems at a younger age, display a more rapid progression, and experience more alcohol induced problems (Hesselbrock, Hesselbrock, & Stabenau, 1985b; McKenna & Pickens, 1981; Penick, Read, Crowley, & Powell, 1978; Schaeffer, Parsons, & Errico, 1988; Schuckit, 1983b, 1984c; Volicer, Volicer, & D'Angelo, 1983); although Vaillant (1983, p. 69) failed to detect a relationship between family history and age of onset and others have found that the earlier onset among FHP alcoholics may be attributable to the higher incidence of ASP alcoholics in the FHP group (Hesselbrock et al.,

1985b). Alcoholics with a family history are less likely to be improved at follow-up (Frances, Bucky, & Alexopoulous, 1984; Goodwin et al., 1971), however, if the follow-up period is sufficiently long (20 years) then differences are not detected (Vaillant, 1983). FHP alcoholics are more likely to report childhood conduct difficulties or problem behaviors during childhood(Alterman, Petrarulo, Tarter, McGowan, 1982; Frances, Timm, & Buckey 1980; Schaeffer et al., 1988; Schuckit, 1983b; Sher & Mc Crady, 1984); although group differences have not reached significance in some studies (Alterman, Tarter, Baughman, Bober, & Fabian, 1985; Tarter, McBride, Buonpane, & Schneider, 1977). FHP alcoholics are more likely to have been hyperactive children (Alterman et al. 1982), although there are failures to reject the null (Alterman et al., 1985). They score higher on the mania scale of the MMPI (Alterman et al., 1982). When the FHP have alcoholic fathers who are binge drinkers, they have an increased incidence of siblings with alcohol problems (Amark, 1951). FHP alcoholics vs. FHN alcoholics report higher rates of ASP among male relatives and higher rates of somatization/hypochondriasis among female relatives (Penick et al., 1987). Differences on amount consumed have not been detected (Schaeffer et al., 1988) nor on measures of alcohol dependence (Hasin et al., 1988).

In a factor analytic study, Brooner et al. (1990) note that similar associations emerged between a positive family history for alcoholism and the traits in the alcoholic. The syndrome of essential alcoholism (including early onset) was associated with alcoholism in the nuclear family. The personality trait of extroversion was associated with alcoholism in the extended family.

ANTISOCIAL PERSONALITIES VS. NONANTISOCIAL PERSONALITIES

Those alcoholics who are also antisocial personalities are more likely to report a family history of alcoholism (Hesselbrock et al., 1985b; Lewis et al., 1983; Lewis et al., 1987; Schuckit, 1985b; Schuckit & Morrissey, 1979). They are more likely to develop alcohol problems at an early age (Cadoret, Troughton, & Widmer, 1984; Hesselbrock et al., 1985; Lewis et al., 1983; Lewis et al., 1987; Winokur et al., 1971). They report more drug abuse (Cadoret et al., 1984). Antisocial personality alcoholics are more likely to have made suicide attempts (Schuckit, 1985b). They are found to manifest more global difficulty at follow-up (Schuckit, 1985b).

A further differentiation of ASP alcoholics was offered by Gilligan, Reich, and Cloninger (1988). These researchers examined the alcoholic styles in male alcoholic brothers of early onset, plus antisocial male alcoholics vs. late onset, no ASP feature alcoholics. The alcoholic brothers of the early onset, ASP alcoholics were more likely to display early onset, social problem drinking themselves.

EARLY ONSETTERS VS. LATE ONSETTERS

Those alcoholics with the early onset syndrome have more alcoholic relatives (Buydens-Branchey et al., 1989a; Templer, Ruff, & Ayers, 1974; von Knorring, Bohamn, von Knorring, & Oreland, 1985); although differences in the Tarter et al. 1977 sample failed to reach significance. Those alcoholics with early onset who have never experienced a period of controlled drinking test higher on the mania scale of the MMPI while appearing less pathological than other alcoholics on other MMPI scales (Tarter et al., 1977). The early onsetters are also more likely to recall childhood daydreaming, impulsivity, not working up to ability, poor peer relationships, not being able to sit still, and having a low tolerance for frustration (Tarter et al., 1977) as well as other hyperactivity/minimal brain dysfunction symptoms (De Obaldia & Parsons, 1984). Those with early onset perform less well on tasks requiring persistent attention (Alterman et al., 1982). They perform less well on vocabulary and abstract reasoning tests (DeObaldia & Parsons, 1984; Pishkin, Lovallo, Bourne, 1985); although differences are less pronounced when differential levels of education are controlled (DeObaldia & Parsons, 1984). They are more likely to have attempted suicide, to have displayed aggression problems, and less likely to have ever married (Buydens-Branchey et al., 1989a).

In other studies, early vs. late onset has been operationalized differently. Von Knorring, Palm, and Andersson (1985) observed that those alcoholics with onset of alcohol problems prior to 25 who displayed diversity in their social problems, reported more drug abuse, more boredom and thrill seeking behavior, and have lower monoamine oxidase (MAO) than late onset alcoholics or nonalcoholics. The early onsetters with diverse social problems score more highly on Zuckerman's sensation seeking scale and more extroverted on the Eysneck scale (Von Knorring, Bohman, von Knorring, & Oreland, 1985). Early onset of problem drinking is associated with the greater severity of problem drinking (Lee & DiClimente, 1985).

Atkinson, Turner, Kofed, and Tolson (1985) have examined the early vs. late onset dichotomy in an older sample (age 53–72). Dichotomizing early vs. late onsetters by the criteria of onset before or after age 40, they found the early onsetters experienced more frequent relapses, displayed more elevation on the pathology scales of the MMPI, and reported more alcoholic family members (Atkinson et al., 1985). There is a finding that suggests that after a sufficient age is reached, differences between early and late onset alcoholics may be less pronounced. Kofoed, Tolson, Atkinson, Toth, and Turner (1987) failed to observe a relationship between age of onset and duration in treatment in a population of older (>55) alcoholics.

YOUNG VS. OLD ALCOHOLICS

Regardless of whether subgroups of alcoholics are selected for early age of onset, history of ASP, or a family history of alcoholism, an association is noted among the three variables. The family history positive alcoholics are those with the early onsets, the higher frequency of antisocial personalities, the poor prognoses in studies with short follow-up intervals, and the more dramatic symptomotologies.

By examining young vs. old alcoholics, a pure early onset population is compared to a mixed onset population. A number of studies have addressed differences between old and young alcoholics, but most have failed to include age-matched control groups. It therefore cannot be determined whether the identified differences are unique to alcoholic populations or whether the differences reflect characteristics of age or cohort differences in the general population. Despite the failings of these studies for independent inferential purposes, these studies are consistent with other data. The identified differences between the old and young alcoholics capture the findings obtained in the contrast between the early onsetters and the late onsetters, with the same composite clusters emerging.

Many studies have reported that young alcoholics more often report alcoholic parentage or alcoholic relatives than do older alcoholics (Gomberg, 1982; Jones, 1972; Rosenberg, 1969; Schuckit, Rimmer, Reich, & Winokur, 1970; Yamane, Katoh, and Fujita, 1980). Younger alcoholics more often have personality disorders and trouble with the police (Abelsohn & van der Spuy, 1978; Foulds and Hassall, 1969; Rosenberg, 1969; Schuckit et al., 1970; Yamane et al. 1980). They report more drug involvement (Gomberg, 1982; Rosenberg, 1969). They have made more suicide attempts (Hassall, 1968; Rosenberg, 1969; Yamane et al., 1980). They report more childhood hyperactivity (Gomberg, 1982).

TYPOLOGY RELATED TO DRINKING PATTERN

Most of the studies reviewed in this chapter have not examined differences in drinking patterns that might be associated with particular types of alcoholics (family history positives, early onsetters, primaries, etc.). There are, however, a few suggestive studies in the literature examining drinking pattern. Parker (1972) found that female binge alcoholics were more likely to have alcoholic fathers than the nonbinge types. Schuckit, Rimmer, Reich, and Winokur (1971) found that male binge alcoholics were more likely to have alcoholic children. It would seem that a binge pattern is associated with higher incidence of familial alcoholism.

The case is advanced in the personality chapter that binge drinking reflects an failed attempt to maintain sobriety in those alcoholics with severe trouble limiting their intake on any one occasion. The binge pattern can be expected to emerge later in life after a protracted history of drinking problems. The binge pattern would not be anticipated among younger drinkers who might eventually become bingers. Hence, although FHPs or early onset alcoholics might eventually display a binge pattern, a different pattern would be observed in young adulthood. There are data that speaks to this issue. Glatt and Hills (1968) and Hassal (1968) report that solitary drinking is characteristic of young alcoholics. McCord (1988) found that FHP alcoholics vs. FHN alcoholics were more often daily drinkers. Further, whereas FHN alcoholics were members of social clubs, FHP alcoholics were characterized by low rates of social participation. These findings suggest that the early onset, positive family history alcoholics may be daily drinkers as well as more often solitary drinkers.

Alterman, Tarter, Baughman, Bober, and Fabian (1985) looked at alcoholics who had displayed hyperactivity in childhood. The suggestion of more severe alcohol dependence among the hyperactive emerged in this study. Those who were hyperactive more often reported drinking to alter their mood, required more external control to stop drinking, reported more difficult withdrawal symptoms, and reported more drug use (Alterman et al., 1985).

SUMMARY

Findings from studies examining types of alcoholics are fairly consistent. The variables of family history positive status, antisocial personality, childhood hyperactivity or attention deficit problems, early onset of problem drinking, more pronounced alcohol dependence, all seem to cluster. A few variables have emerged as related to the cluster although fewer studies have examined these variables. Low MAO, sensation seeking, higher scores on the mania scale of the MMPI have been reported. The next chapters discuss longitudinal studies and then research on children of alcoholics. The same characteristics that appear as part of the cluster descriptive of early onset, FHP alcoholics emerge as precursors to adult alcoholism in the longitudinal studies. In studies in which children of alcoholics are observed, these traits are identified as well. There is remarkable consistency in the data.

4 Longitudinal Studies

Another avenue of research has been the longitudinal study. In this type of research individuals are observed throughout the lifespan and categorized along a number of dimensions at significant stages in their lives. Some individuals develop alcoholism whereas others do not. Those persons who have not developed adult alcoholism are compared with those who have developed alcoholism, in terms of their childhood characteristics.

The present purpose of examining the longitudinal studies is to identify the nature of the inherited temperament that predisposes to alcoholism. In this chapter, only those longitudinal studies examining childhood precursors to adult alcoholism are considered. There have been some longitudinal studies of the impact of adolescent/early adult drinking in predicting later adult drinking. These studies are discussed in Chapter 1 of Volume I. Since these latter studies speak more to the issue of the natural history of alcoholism and less to the issue of what might be the nature of inherited drinking, these studies are not discussed in this chapter.

There have been several longitudinal studies that have tracked youth through adulthood. A study by Vaillant (1983) and by McCord and McCord (1962) recruited samples from lower class neighborhoods. A study by Robins (1966) sampled children from a child guidance clinic. A study by Monnelly, Hartl, and Elderkin (1983) recruited from a residential treatment center for youth with behavior problems. A study by Jones (1968) was an exception to the practice of sampling from areas with high base rates of problems. Jones' subjects were predominantly middle class. All studies have been relatively consistent in their findings.

THE FINDINGS FOR MALES

Robin's Child Guidance Project

Robins, (Robins, Bates, & O'Neal, 1962) began with a cohort of children seen at a child guidance clinic. Another group of children from the same neighborhood was also included in the sample. There were 503 individuals who survived to age 25 in the clinic group and 99 who survived to age 25 in the community sample. Each individual in the sample was interviewed 30 years after their selection. Alcoholism was established on the basis of personal interview with the subject or a relative, use of death certificates, hospital, police, or VA records. The criteria for chronic alcoholism were: death from acute alcoholism; or medical complications of drinking; or diagnosis of alcoholism in the army, hospital, or prison; or arrests, loss of job, absenteeism, fights, serious family complaints along with chronic unemployment; or five or more arrests for drinking within the last 5 years. Probable alcoholism was established by self-report of inability to control drink or arrests, loss of job, absenteeism, fighting, or family complaints without the occurrence of chronic unemployment. Heavy drinking required drinking at least three times per week at least 3 drinks per occasion or drinking 7 drinks per sitting. Persons classified as exhibiting no excess in drinking had never fulfilled the requirements for heavy drinking over an extended period of time.

The final sample that was followed included 437 men of whom 24 were classified as alcoholic. There were 170 women of whom 8 were alcoholic. More of the clinic population became alcoholic than did those in the control group. The authors also remarked upon the fact that there were better childhood data available for the clinic attenders. As in other studies, ethnicity was predictive of future alcoholism (high among the Irish; low among the Jews). Being on welfare as a child or being supported by parental criminal activity was also predictive of future alcoholism. Once a criteria of heavy drinking was met, more of those in the lowest status SES group met the criteria for problem, alcoholic status. Parental inadequacy (neglect or being flagrantly antisocial) also related to future alcoholism. Childhood characteristics predictive of adult alcoholism included a broad range of antisocial behavior (running away, theft, assault). Future alcoholics were not distinguished by mood disturbances, restlessness, or seclusiveness. Childhood antisocial behavior was related to future alcoholism after controlling for parental neglect and social status.

The Robins study was part of a larger project examining the roots of sociopathy and mental illness. In the 1962 summary, alcoholics were not differentiated as to their own sociopathy. It is unclear whether the roots of primary rather than secondary alcoholism were being investigated. In the 1966 report (Robins, 1966), Robins excluded those individuals who were both alcoholic and sociopathic. The same antisocial childhood behavior predicted both adult alcoholism and adult sociopathy, although the future sociopaths exhibited a broader range of acting out behavior.

McCord and McCord's Cambridge–Sommerville Youth Project

McCord and McCord (1960, 1962) and Joan McCord (1972, 1981, 1988) have reported results from a project initiated in 1939. Two hundred and fifty-five boys and their families from the urban Boston area were selected. Some were included on the basis of needing counseling although others who were not viewed needing help were included in order to round out the sample. Some of the sample participants received counseling during their youth as part of the project. All of the sample was interviewed in their homes by social workers over an initial 5-year interval. The subjects were between the ages of 9 to 15 at the beginning of the study. Subjects were followed through age 43 to 53. Official records regarding arrest and welfare information were available. Thirty eight persons could be described as definitely alcoholic. (Alcoholism was established on the basis of having received treatment, having been arrested 3 times for public drunkenness, or driving while intoxicated, or having self-described as alcoholic). Sixty-one men satisfied some of the criteria for alcoholism. One hundred and thirty-two men met none of the criteria for alcoholism. Across reports, the subjects included in analyses have varied slightly due to having been eliminated on one or another bases such as not having data available, not having been raised by natural parents, not including more than one sibling per family, etc.

In the original report (1960, 1962), characteristics that were found to distinguish the future alcoholics were: elevated self-confidence, being less disturbed by normal fears, having been more aggressive, increased hyperactivity, and increased masculine activity. There was a tendency toward more sex fears and sadism among the prealcoholics. They did not differ in terms of degree of solitary vs. group activity; inflated sense of self-importance (grandiosity); oral activities such as thumb sucking, or physical complaints. In the 1960 and 1962 analyses, alcoholics were not differentiated as to those who were also criminals vs. those who were not for the purpose of identifying precursor traits.

In a 1981 and 1988 report, McCord differentiated the background of those who became criminal but not alcoholic; those who became alcoholic but not criminals, those who were both alcoholic and criminals, and those who were neither alcoholic or criminal. The pure alcoholics and alcoholic/criminals were distinguished by having evidenced self-confidence, by being rated as aggressive by their teachers. In the 1988 report, McCord indicated that shyness was low in those who were to become criminal or alcoholic, although a combination of both shyness and aggression, especially when the father was alcoholic, was predictive of alcoholism. Those who were both alcoholic and criminal had resented authority the most as youngsters, although the pure alcoholics had resented authority the least of the four groups. The two criminal groups (pure criminals and alcoholic/criminals) were distinguished from the noncriminal groups by having received less parental affection, having less often been supervised after school, having had an aggressive parent, and having had few standards of behavior imposed upon them as children.

Like Vaillant, McCord (1972) did find that certain aspects of the parental environment distinguished the family of origin homes of future alcoholics. (In the 1972 report, McCord did not report the extent of criminal involvement among those classified as alcoholics, although the 1960 book did.) Homes associated with future alcoholism manifested more illegitimacy, incest, maternal employment, attenuated open display of maternal affect and more maternal ambivalence toward the son, more inconsistent supervision, more multiple caretakers in the parental role, and more mutual dissatisfaction between the parents with regard to their roles (McCord, 1972). In the 1960 publication, the lack of parental demands on the offspring was found to relate to future alcoholism. With regard to the offspring's reaction to the childhood environment, it had previously been noted that prealcoholics were also found to express less favorable attitudes toward their mothers and siblings (McCord & McCord, 1962).

In the original publication (McCord & McCord, 1960), the variable of maternal encouragement of son's dependency did not differ among future alcoholics versus the rest of the sample; maternal restrictive behavior was low among those who became alcoholic. In the 1988 report, McCord did consider some interactions between variables. A lack of maternal control over the son was predictive of son's alcoholism when the father was not alcoholic, but was less so when the father was alcoholic. When the father was alcoholic and the mother held him in high esteem, the son was especially likely to develop alcoholism.

It should be noted that the McCords had a bias toward the theory that conflict over dependency leads to alcoholism. They (see 1960 report) interpreted their finding of heightened aggression and overt self-confidence in future alcoholics as indicative of its opposite, that is, they suggested these traits were a facade. They noted the findings of maternal ambivalence and the findings of fewer parental demands as having a created a condition of role confusion for the alcoholic. Their conclusions suggested a stress reduction role for alcohol in the life of the alcoholic who deeply wanted independence but for whom life had not provided internal resources. Had the McCords' controlled for the effect of paternal alcoholism in the relationship between family of origin environment and alcoholism in the offspring, as did Vaillant, they might have decided that there was no causal link between family environment and future alcoholism. As we discuss next, although the home of origin environments of future alcoholics are distinctive, the environment may be a correlate of paternal alcoholism rather than be a causal factor in the development of alcoholism in the offspring.

Vaillant's Analysis of two Data Bases

Vaillant (1983) examined precursors to alcoholism in two samples: his core city sample and his college sample. The core city (urban poor) sample was comprised of White males selected for an absence of delinquency in junior high school. This sample was to serve as the control group in the Glueck study examining the lives of delinquent boys. Teacher observations were available. The sample was followed until their mid 40s. The final sample yielded 118 alcoholics and 263 asymptomatic drinkers. Alcoholism was established in more than one way. Vaillant employed DSM-III criteria, a composite problem list, and criteria that had been employed by Cahalan. Vaillant tested hypotheses using each of the criteria. In terms of personality predictors to alcoholism regardless of criteria, Vaillant identified hyperactivity and school and truancy problems. Childhood environmental strengths, boyhood competence, childhood emotional problems, IQ were unrelated to the development of alcoholism, although these factors were predictive of later mental health problems. In addition to personality factors as predictors of alcoholism, family history of alcoholism and being raised in a non-Mediterranean culture were related. Being raised in a chaotic environment, parental marital conflict, poor maternal supervision, many moves, poor family cohesiveness, and a lack of close relationship with one's father did relate independently, but were no longer significant in predicting offspring alcoholism after father's alcoholic status was controlled.

Vaillant (1983) also had access to a college sample of 252 White, males who were followed into middle age (over 60). Fifty-eight percent of the 30 alcohol abusers had developed drinking problems after age 45. For this sample, none of the Thematic Apprecaption Test (administered at age 30) results predicted future alcoholism. The future alcoholics described at time of college matriculation were viewed as less shy, less inhibited, less self-conscious, less self-driving, and more lacking in purpose and values than their peers. They were not distinguishable on "oral traits" of pessimism, passivity, self-doubt, or heightened dependency in adult life.

Jones' Oakland Growth Study

Jones (1968, 1981) recruited her sample from the Oakland neighborhood. The sample was all White, American born, urban, and primarily middle class. The children entered the study at 10 years of age and at last follow-up were 38 (as reported in 1968). Jones did not supply precise criteria for each drinking category (problem drinker, heavy drinker, moderate drinker, light drinker, abstainer), although she did provide a subjective description. Of the 66 males for whom records were available, 6 were classified as problem drinkers, 16 as heavy drinkers, 20 were moderate drinkers, 7 were light drinkers, and 3 were abstainers. In their childhood and in junior and senior high school the men had been assessed via the California Q sort. Parent and teacher report and descriptions were also available. The following traits distinguished the problem drinkers at junior high school assessment: undercontrolled, dissociative, direct hostility expression, pushing limits, self-indulgence, negativistic orientation, strong masculinity, and initiating humor. As junior high school students, future problem drinkers were not fastidious, did not display a wide range of interests, and did not reflect upon motives. In high school the descriptors of future problem drinkers were: undercontrolled, pushes limits, manipulative, rapid tempo, expressive, assertive, and masculine. In high school, the future problem drinkers were not: emotionally bland, aloof, or considerate. Despite the variables that emerged as characteristic of future problem drinkers, Jones (1981) suggests that their self-esteem may have been low. On self-report measures there was evidence of feelings of inferiority. However, teacher playground ratings of male future problem drinkers (see Jones, 1981, p. 238) depicted them as displaying leadership qualities, as more assured, as more popular, and more self-accepting, as displaying more good spirits, as more uninhibited, and as appearing to be more self-accepting. If the future problem were low in self-esteem, it was not evident to adults.

The Monnelly et al. Study

Monnelly, Hartl, and Elderkin began with a sample of 200 boys who were tracked between the years of 1939 to 1978. All boys in the sample had been treated in a residential treatment center for youth with behavior problems. There were 38 alcoholics in the final sample. Alcoholism was defined according to the presence of medical, occupational, or behavioral difficulties associated with the use of alcohol. The boys had been assessed on a variety of precursors including body type, although interviewing was not as extensive as in the other studies. Those childhood precursors that distinguished the alcoholics from the rest of the sample were: having left home at an earlier age (lower in the prealcoholics); having been more violent as a youth; and having been slighter of build and having been less coordinated as a youth.

CONCLUSIONS REGARDING MALE ALCOHOLISM
FROM THE STUDIES

All longitudinal studies have found that boys who are gregarious, aggressive, and display rapid tempo are more likely to develop adult alcoholism (Jones, 1968; McCord & McCord, 1962; Robins, 1966; Valliant, 1983). There has been an additional study consistent with earlier data. Cloninger, Sigvardsson, and

Bohman (1988) found in a sample who had either been adopted or whose mother had applied for adoption that the characteristics of sensation seeking and lack of sensitivity to punishment (low harm avoidance) assessed at age 11, predicted alcoholism at age 27.

Across longitudinal studies, there has been a striking absence of data to confirm the hypothesis that childhood depression or neurosis leads to adult alcoholism. No study has found childhood neurotic distress to be predictive of adult alcoholism. There have been, however, some slight refinements regarding how childhood shyness is related to alcoholism. In a later analysis of her data base, McCord (1988) reported that those boys who were both aggressive and shy were most likely to become alcoholic, however, shy boys who were not also aggressive, were most likely to avoid alcoholism and/or criminality. For the most part the data are consistent. The shy, reserved, sad children are not suggested to be at risk for alcoholism. Vaillant (1983) in considering his own data as well as other studies, concludes that early mental health problems may presage later mental health problems but not adult alcoholism.

A problem is presented in the longitudinal research by the fact that alcoholism and sociopathy frequently co-occur within the same person. Such being the case, it is difficult to determine whether childhood precursors to ASP or alcoholism are being identified. The only way to identify precursors for primary alcoholism is to differentiate the adult alcoholic sample into those with and without ASP.

Some researchers have been attentive to the frequent co-occurrence of alcoholism and antisocial personality within the same individual. McCord (1981) distinguished alcoholics without criminal behavior vs. alcoholics with criminal behavior in her adult sample. Childhood defiance of authority was a precursor for one type of alcoholic but not the other. McCord found that only the alcoholics who were also criminals were likely, as children, to have resented adult authority. The adult alcoholics who displayed no adult criminal behavior were less likely than nondeviant adults to have resented adult authority as children. Robins (1966) also tried to ensure that she was studying primary alcoholism and not alcoholism related to antisocial personality. She excluded from her sample those alcoholics who were also sociopathic but nevertheless found that 70% of the alcoholic sample met the minimal criteria for sociopathy. Robins concluded that the same antisocial childhood conduct which predicts adult sociopathy is characteristic of prealcoholics, although the incorrigible behavior of prealcoholics is less broad ranging than that of presociopaths.

The issue of whether secondary alcoholism/primary sociopathy was investigated in the longitudinal studies is particularly suspect for particular data bases. Several of the early studies (viz., McCord and McCord, 1962, Cambridge-Sommerville project and Robins, 1966, child guidance project) recruited their subjects from lower class neighborhoods and included a large number of incorrigible youths in their samples. Fortunately, there are some studies investigating precursors to adult alcoholism in college samples. In these studies, researchers may have been less likely to have tapped into a primary sociopathy/secondary alcoholism population.

Hoffman, Loper, and Kammeier (1974) sampled alcoholics in treatment at a state hospital and a private residential treatment center. Hoffman and colleagues conducted their research in Minnesota, where everyone takes the MMPI at the time of college entrance. Records of MMPIs administered at the time of college matriculation were therefore available. This allowed for comparison of adult alcoholics with nonalcoholics on the basis of college characteristics. Those persons who developed alcoholism later in life were distinguished by higher scores on the MacAndrew scale of the MMPI. (High scorers on the MacAndrew scale are described as aggressive, gregarious, and disinhibited persons who display little concern for future consequences.) In additional investigations of the same type, prealcoholics were found to score more highly on the Psychopathy, Hysteria scales and the Wiggins authority conflict scale of the MMPI than had controls (Loper, Kammeier, & Hoffman, 1973), although alpha inflation due to multiple tests was not controlled. In a third study, on which inferential statistical tests were not conducted, prealcoholics were reported to have achieved means approximately one standard deviation above the standardized mean on the hypomania, psychopathy, and masculine/feminine scales of the MMPI (Kammeier, Hoffman, & Loper, 1973).

The Minnesota MMPI studies were remarkably consistent with each other and with prior findings. They seem to have identified the same syndrome in the middle class sample of prealcoholics as had been identified in the longitudinal studies of blue collar children. The high energy, gregarious, disinhibited types are suggested to be at greater risk.

Vaillant and colleagues (Beardslee & Vaillant, 1984; Vaillant, 1980, 1983) have reported a number of investigations analyzing data from a population selected for essentially normal mental health at the time of college matriculation. The purpose of the studies was to specifically examine whether psychological problems in youth would predispose toward alcoholism. The sample was unusual in that most of those who developed alcoholism did so after the age of 45 (Vaillant, 1980). Some of the precursor traits identified were consistent with prior findings. In terms of precursor traits assessed during college, the prealcoholics were found to be less self-driving, less shy, less inhibited, less self-conscious, more lacking in purpose, more incompletely integrated (Vaillant, 1983, p. 89); and to rely on neurotic denial as a defense mechanism (Vaillant, 1980).

A study by Beardslee and Vaillant (1984) rendered some unusual findings. The only factor that modestly predicted adult heavy drinking in the Beardslee and Vaillant report (1984) was rigidity of superego (i.e., the tendency to be self-punitive). Beardslee and Vaillant also failed to find a relationship between degree of college alcohol use and later alcoholism. The suggestion of self-punitiveness in the Beardslee and Vaillant study represents a deviation from prior findings. It should be noted that the Vaillant college studies may have been investigating late onset alcoholism. There is reason to believe, which will be discussed Chapter 6, that depression may be a precursor to late onset alcoholism. Family history is less heavily associated with late onset alcoholism, perhaps suggesting that genetics and temperament are of less importance in the etiology of this variety of alcoholism. This cannot explain, however, why neurotic personality did not emerge as a predictor of late onset alcoholism in Vaillant's other analyses (see Vaillant, 1983).

There has been an additional report, in which sample selection did not "stack the deck" so heavily in favor of investigating alcoholism associated with sociopathy. Drake and Vaillant (1988) published a later report of an analysis of a subsample from Vaillant's Boston inner city study which has been previously discussed. Drake and Vaillant (1988) reported on predictors of adult alcoholism among FHPs selected for a nondeliquent status in childhood. Predictors of adult alcoholism in this sample were: a greater number of alcoholic relatives, non-Mediterranean ethnicity, school problems, and behavior problems. Childhood chaotic environment was not predictive.

GENERAL COMMENTS ON THE LONGITUDINAL STUDIES

Several caveats are recommended when considering the findings from the longitudinal studies. First, most of the studies were published prior to the advent of the widespread use of multivariate statistics to correct for alpha inflation. Although no particular study corrected for the number of tests performed and the intercorrelations among the dependent variables, the fact that the same childhood characteristics of prealcoholics are identified across studies suggests that these findings are not due to chance. Taken in conjunction with data from other avenues of research, they do allow for inference about the composite of traits that might predispose to alcoholism.

As mentioned previously, firm conclusions regarding the type of alcoholism investigated in the longitudinal studies cannot be derived. Whereas Robins (1966) eliminated from her sample of adult alcoholics who had a primary diagnosis of ASP, others (Jones, 1968; Kammeier & colleagues; McCord & McCord, 1962; Vaillant, 1983) did not. It is difficult to assess whether the identified childhood characteristics are unique to sociopathic alcoholics or pertain to alcoholics in general. The sampling of sociopathic alcoholics is particularly likely to have occurred when the sample was recruited from deviant childhood populations (such as in the Robins study or the McCord Cambridge, Sommerville youth study). The sampling of adult alcoholics from the state hospital and a private residential treatment center who had been to college (such as in the Kammeier et al. studies) or of premorbid college populations (such as in the Beardslee and Vaillant, 1984 and Vaillant, 1980 studies) probably included fewer sociopathic alcoholics. Confidence in the generality of the findings is bolstered by the fact that the same characteristics are identified across samples differing in the proportion of sociopathic alcoholics.

Longitudinal studies, regardless of whether the adult or child population under study was lower class or more affluent, identify a cluster including gregariousness, high energy, nonconformity, and aggressiveness as characteristic of prealcoholics. Longitudinal studies on alcoholism are consistent with the adoption studies in which those who developed adult alcoholism were more likely to have been hyperactive, aggressive, sensitive, and disobedient (Cadoret & Gath, 1978; Goodwin, Schulsinger, Hermansen, Guze, & Winokur, 1975). Longitudinal studies suggest that adult alcoholics were often the energetic, aggressive youths who were moderately incorrigible. These characteristics overlap with the characteristics of hyperactive children.

Given the finding from longitudinal studies of a history of childhood hyperactivity preceding adult alcoholism, it might be expected that if hyperactive children are selected, they will be found to mature into alcoholic adults. There have been longitudinal investigations of hyperactive children observed as young adults. Sometimes elevated rates of alcohol abuse in the hyperactive child population are reported (Hechtman, Weiss, & Perlman, 1984; Mendelson, Johnson, & Stewart, 1971); although this is not a consistent finding (Gittelman et al., 1985). An explanation for the inconsistencies suggests itself. The category of hyperactivity captures a broad spectrum of disorder. Indeed, the diversity of difficulties that manifests as childhood hyperactivity is attested to by the finding that childhood hyperactivity is an associated finding in Gilles de la Tourette's syndrome and adult obsessive compulsive disorder (Lishman, 1987). Perhaps only some proportion of this spectrum of hyperactivity is related to the diathesis for alcoholism, and thus longitudinal studies following hyperactive probands to determine incidence of adult alcoholism would probably be dependent on sample selection, or definition of hyperactivity, for obtaining positive or negative results.

The longitudinal studies tracking hyperactives in total yield an additional conclusion. Although the rates of troubled adult behavior are often higher in the hyperactive group than in the normal control group (Cantwell, 1985; O'Neal & Robins, 1958; Weiss, Hechtman, Perlman, Hopkins, & Wener, 1979) any particular hyperactive child will most likely escape development of alcoholism or ASP (Cantwell, 1985; Weiss et al., 1979) Whereas the relationship between childhood mental health and nondeviant adulthood is strong, the predictive power of childhood problems is weak (Robins, 1978).

THE FINDINGS FOR FEMALES

Jones' Oakland growth study also examined junior high school and high school personality precursors to adult alcoholism (age 38) in females. Recall that Jones' sample was middle class. Like Fillmore (1974, 1975), Jones (1971) found that high school, young adult behavior was not strongly predictive of subsequent adult behavior. Junior high personality was more strongly linked to later adult behavior. For her female sample, Jones found that as youngsters, the adult abstainers and problem drinkers were very similar. They could be characterized as self-defeating, vulnerable, pessimistic, withdrawn, irritable, anxious, guilty, and somatizing. Jones (1981) indicates that the female future problem drinkers were also more unpredictable. Consistent with the Jones findings were those of Block and Haan (1971) whose sample consisted of some of the subjects in Jones sample as well as additional subjects. In Block and Haan's analysis, hyerfeminity, repression, and fearfulness in childhood emerged as predictors of female alcoholism. Jones' (1981) observes that the female future alcoholics are less differentiated from their peers than are male future alcoholics.

Other than the Jones data, there is little longitudinal work on female alcoholism. With few female alcoholics represented in the sample, Robins (Robins et al., 1962) did find that antisocial personality predicted female alcoholism as well as being a male predictor. Wilsnack et al. (1986) did not conduct a longitudinal study, but did query female alcoholics about prior personality. They found that depressive episodes and gynecological problems occurred prior to the development of problem drinking in their sample. When investigating female alcoholism then, depression and anxiety emerge as precursors to drinking.

It is the case that females are more often primary depressives and secondary alcoholics than males (Schuckit, 1985b). The personality predictors emerging in the Jones study may reflect the primary depression. It is known that primary depression, secondary alcoholics develop their alcoholic statuses later in life than do primary alcoholics (Schuckit, 1985b). Future studies in female samples, might attend to this distinction of primary alcoholism vs. primary depressed, secondary alcoholism and/or age of onset of the alcoholism. It would be useful to determine whether childhood personality precursors to primary alcoholism, particularly in female samples, differ from childhood personality precursors to primary depression, secondary alcoholism.

SUMMARY

Longitudinal investigations tracking male adolescent samples through adulthood suggest that the energetic, gregarious, and aggressive are most likely to become alcoholics. Little support for childhood depression as a precursor to male adult, early onset alcoholism has been adduced. Findings from the longitudinal studies are consistent with findings from adoption studies. Hyperactivity, aggressive, and disobedient are traits which emerge in adopted out children of alcoholics. As is discussed in the next chapter, they are also consistent with traits found in nonadopted out children of alcoholics.

Longitudinal investigations of precursors to female alcoholism are quite limited. For females, a depressive/anxious temperament emerges more strongly as a precursor to adult alcoholism. Conclusions are limited by the fact that type of adult alcoholism in females has not been distinguished in the few studies relevant to this issue. Obviously, this is an area in which research is needed.

5 What are the Characteristics of Relatives of Alcoholics?

The research findings from studies comparing family history positives (FHP) with family history negatives (FHN) are organized according to the characteristic on which the two groups were compared. First general findings are discussed. Differential responses of the two groups to alcohol are then presented. Any comparison between FHP and FHN will reflect differences in environment as well as genetics. Not all studies have investigated children of alcoholics. Sometimes siblings and parents were examined by researchers. Because the relative of the alcoholic proband has varied, across studies environmental influences may have varied. Findings will not always reflect the impact of having been raised in an alcoholic home.

In each area to be reviewed there are positive findings as well as negative findings. The reader may be daunted by the inconsistencies. The picture will appear muddled. The conclusion, however, that the findings can be discounted is unwarranted. There are a priori reasons for expecting inconsistencies even when it is assumed that there are robust differences between FHPs and FHNs. Goodwin (1979), whose position is articulated in Chapter 6, has suggested that there are varieties of alcoholism and that they vary in terms of the importance of genetic factors in their etiology. Most researchers have selected for alcoholism in some relative, usually the father. Until recently, the number of alcoholic relatives, whether the alcoholism was primary or secondary to some other disorder, the severity of the alcoholism, time of onset of the alcoholism in the alcoholic proband, have not been considered. The manner in which samples are selected will tap into varying types of alcoholism. Given the lack of consistency in selecting FHP sample, it can reasonably be expected that some FHP samples will, as a group, have very little genetic liability for alcoholism, There is no reason to believe that they should be distinguished from the general population.

A thorough survey of the literature has been attempted. Familiarization with the findings may help the reader to make his/her own assessment. Confidence in any isolated finding should be reserved. Confidence that a trait is a facet of the genetic diathesis for alcoholism is more justified when it is consistent with findings from the longitudinal studies.

DIFFERENCES BETWEEN FHP AND FHN INDIVIDUALS: INTELLECTUAL, BEHAVIORAL, EEG, UTILIZATION OF INTERNAL STIMULI, RESPONSES TO EXTERNAL STIMULI, AND PHYSIOLOGICAL DIFFERENCES

Intellectual

Relatives of alcoholics, as a group, perform poorly on a number of intellectual tasks. Researchers have reported that FHP children performed more poorly on vocabulary tests, the Halstead category test, and Ravens test (Drejer, Theilgaard, Teasdale, Schulsinger, & Goodwin, 1985; Wilson & Nagoshi, 1988) the Stroop test, the Matching Familiar Figures Test (Tarter, Jacob, & Bremer, 1989) and the Porteus Maze Test (Drejer, Theilgaard, Teasdale, Schulsinger, & Goodwin, 1985; Tarter, Jacob & Bremer, 1989a). Tarter, Jacob and Bremer (1989b) found that lower verbal IQ scores was specific to the children of early onset alcoholic fathers. Teachers rate the sons of alcoholics as less verbally proficient (Knop, Teasdale, Schulsinger, & Goodwin, 1985). In Schaeffer, Parsons, and Yohman (1984) laboratory, nonalcoholic relatives of alcoholics were observed to perform poorly on measures of abstracting, problem solving, and perceptual motor skills. These differences obtained whether the alcoholic relative was a sibling or a parent. Tarter, Hegedus, Goldstein, Shelly, and Alterman (1984) and Hegedus, Alterman, and Tarter (1984) found that FHP delinquents performed more poorly on problem solving and achievement tasks than did FHN delinquents. Alterman, Bridges, and Tarter (1986b) examined FHP college students. They found that FHP college students performed more poorly than FHN controls on a group embedded figures task but not on a maze or mirror drawing task. Gabrielli and Mednick (1983) found that children of alcoholics achieved lower verbal IQ scores when compared to children of nonalcoholic sociopaths. Bennett, Wolin, and Reiss (1988) found that young adult offspring of alcoholics scored lower on the Weschler Adult Intelligence Scale. The observed deficits have been attributed by Drejer et al. (1985) and Tarter et al. (1989a) to a reduced capacity for sustained, goal directed attention.

Schandler, Brannock, Cohen et al., (1988) compared FHP, 6- to 11-year-olds with FHN, 6- to 11-year-olds on a task which presumably tapped right brain functioning. A paired associate task requiring the association of a meaningless shape with a particular location was used. The FHP required more trials to reach criterion and made more errors. Their quicker reaction time on error responses suggested a less attentive approach to the task. Schandler et al. interpreted their findings as suggesting an attention/imbalance problem.

Negative results on intellectual tasks have also been reported. Hesselbrock, Stabenau, and Hesselbrock (1985) failed to detect cognitive difference between a sample of nonalcoholic young adult FHPs compared to controls. Tarter et al. (1989a) found higher scorers on an Arithmetic Test for the sons of alcoholics. Tarter et al. (1989a) attributed the superior arithmetic performance to a faster tempo among the FHPs. Hill et al. (1990) could not replicate the difference on the Halstead Reitan category test between FHP and FHNs despite the fact that FHPs had been selected for multiple generations of alcoholism. Johnson and Rolf (1988) caution, based on their negative findings Wechsler Intelligence Scale and the Wide Range Achievement Test, that if FHPs are selected from middle class, nonimpoverished backgrounds, cognitive deficits are not detected.

Behavioral

FHPs have been found to be more impulsive and restless than control children (Aronson & Gilbert, 1963; Knop et al., 1985; Schulsinger et al., 1986). They are more immature, more likely to openly display their anger, and more sensitive to criticism (Aronson & Gilbert, 1963). Jacob and Leonard (1986) found that the only variable off an assessment battery on which FHPs were distinguished from children of depressed was manifestion of high rate of acting out. In older samples, FHPs have recalled more symptoms of minimal brain dysfunction as children (Alterman, Searles, & Hall, 1989; Tarter et al., 1977); although such differences are not found when FHP delinquents are compared to FHN delinquents (Tarter, Hegedus, & Gavaler 1985) and others have failed to replicate (Workman-Daniels & Hesselbrock, 1987; Hesselbrock, Stabenau, & Hesselbrock, 1985; Schuckit, Sweeney, & Huey, 1987). As young adults, FHPs are more likely to display preadult antisocial symptoms (Alterman, Bridges, & Tarter, 1986a). FHPs, particularly those who display problem drinking, are differentiated by low scores on the Socialization scale of the California Personality Inventory (Sher, 1985). Results on the MacAndrew scale, a scale that taps impulsivity, pressure for action, and rebellion, have varied across studies. Saunders and Schuckit (1981) found that FHPs scored more highly on the Mac Andrew, although others have failed to replicate (Alterman, Bridges, & Tarter, 1986a; Newlin, 1985b).

Young adult offspring of alcoholics between the ages of 21 to 25, do exhibit an increased rate of problem drinking. Schuckit and Sweeney (1987) found that the greater the number of alcoholic relatives, the greater the likelihood of alcohol problems. Some have found that among FHP adolescents, there are distinct personality predictors of problem drinking. Chassin et al. (1988) found that problem drinking in FHP adolescents was particularly likely among those scoring low on a measure of self-consciousness. Among those who were both FHP and high MacAndrew scale scorers, the expectation that alcohol would increase feelings of power predicted current alcohol involvement, although this expectancy failed to predict alcohol involvement in other groups.

There are personality traits that do not distinguish FHPs. There have been failures to find differences on Cloninger's Tridimensional Personality measure (De Wit & McCracken, 1990; Moss, Yao, & Maddock, 1989). Negative findings for FHP, college age males have been reported on locus of control, extroversion, neuroticism, anxiety, and assertion (Schuckit, 1982b, 1983a). These findings may be limited to the males of college age. Offspring of alcoholics who are not yet emancipated score as externals on the locus of control (O'Gorman, 1976). Young adult daughters display high rates of depression (Bennett et al., 1988).

EEG

Family history positive individuals vs. children without an alcoholic pedigree have been compared in terms of resting brain wave activity and the evoked potential activity which they display in response to presentation of stimuli. Although many of the alcoholic parents in the sample carried additional diagnoses, Gabrielli, Mednick, Volavka, Pollock, Schulsinger, and Itil (1982) report that FHP boys but not girls, compared to FHNs of like sex, display faster resting EEG activity. Volavka, Pollock, Gabrielli, and Mednick (1985) report a failure to replicate Gabrielli et al.'s particular findings and conclude that the evidence for resting brain wave differential activity in FHPs is equivocal.

Others have examined brain wave activity in response to stimuli. Begleiter, Porjesz, Bihari, and Kissen (1984) report that 7- to 13- year-old sons of alcoholic fathers manifest lower P 300 waves in response to visual task requiring correct lateralization of a figure. Begleiter et al. suggest that P3 waves reflect electrical events in the hippocampus and amygalla. These brain areas mediate memory and orienting to significant stimuli. Whipple, Parker, and Noble (1988) found low magnitude of event related brain potentials in sons of family history positive alcoholics. The brain potentials were correlated with inferior performance on visioperceptual performance (also inferior in the sons of FHP alcoholic group).

Hill, Steinhauer, Park, and Zubin (1990) examined children between 8 and 16. Their FHPs had an alcoholic father, uncle, and grandparent. Less than one-third of fathers were also sociopathic. Mothers were free of diagnosis. Hill et al.

evaluated EEG as subjects performed counting and choice reaction time tasks employing auditory stimuli. The FHPs did differ in particular ways from the FHNs. The N 250 waves were more negative in the FHP groups. For the stimuli that required the most cognitive processing, FHPs displayed P 300s of slightly greater magnitude. As the stimuli decreased in terms of processing required by the task, the P 300 wave amplitudes of FHPs decreased (dropped off) at a steeper rate. In terms of the P 300 latency, for the complex tasks, FHP took longer although their latency was shorter (quicker response) for trials requiring less processing. These results may suggest that when a task is complex, FHP appear to concentrate hard, even harder than FHN, but as soon as difficulty decreases, the FHPs fail to attend. Hill et al. are to be commended for controlling for motivation by paying their subjects money for correct responses.

There have been failures to discern differential brain wave activity during task execution between FHPs and FHNs. These findings are summarized in Polich, Burns, and Bloom (1988b) and Polich et al. (1988c). Hill et al. (1990) question the generalizability of the particular negative findings from the Polich group based on the very liberal criteria of alcoholism for inclusion in the FHP group. Many cases probably had very minimal genetic loading.

Utilization of Internal Stimuli

FHP individuals appear to be less adept at utilizing internal kinesthetic information. FHPs have trouble either discerning or utilizing kinesthetic information in order to maintain their balance. With eyes open or closed, offspring of alcoholics sway more than do control populations (Hill, Armstrong, Steinhauer, Baughman, & Zubin, 1987; Lipscomb, Carpenter, & Nathan, 1979; Tarter et al., 1989); although Schuckit (1985a) sampling a similar population failed to replicate these results. Hegedus, Tarter, Hill, Jacob, and Winsten (1984) found that preteen FHPs swayed more with eyes open but differences with eyes closed failed to reach significance. Aside from the static ataxia data which is equivocal, there is additional suggestion of poor utilization of kinesthetic information in FHPs. FHP have difficulty estimating the extent of their alcohol intoxication (Schuckit, 1980a), although failures to replicate have occurred here too (Lipscomb & Nathan, 1980; Wilson & Nagoshi, 1988). Assuming validity, a deficit ability to evaluate blood alcohol level is consistent with the hypothesis that FHPs may be poor utilizers of kinesthetic information.

Another dependent variable that may tap utilization of kinesthetic feedback is the trait of alexithymia. Those who are alexithymic fail to label or attend to emotional dimensions. Finn and Pihl (1988) compared FHP with an extensive familial pedigree for alcoholism with FHP who only had an alcoholic parent but no other alcoholic relatives. Those with the extensive FHP background were more alexithymic.

Response to External Stimuli

Alcoholics and history positive individuals respond differentially to external stimuli. Petrie (1967) formulated the construct of stimulus augmentation vs. stimulus reduction. Petrie measured augmentation and reducing according to performance on the Kinesthetic Figural After-Effect Test (KFA). Persons were required to estimate the size of a block that they touched with their eyes blind folded. Size estimates were recorded both before and after a person was allowed to rub a stimulus block. Some persons' size estimations increased after rubbing the stimulus block (the augmenters) whereas others decreased their estimates of the test block size (the reducers). Petrie's measure has been criticized for its poor reliability (Herzog & Weintraub, 1982). Although the finding must be regarded cautiously due to problems with the measure, Hennecke (1984) reported that children of alcoholics were more likely to be augmenters on the KFA than were children of normals.

Other measures of augmenting and reducing have been advanced. Given a repetitive, progressively intensified, external stimulus (flash of light, sound, etc.) some individuals will manifest the same magnitude of evoked potential responding, some will augment in the magnitude and others will reduce. On measures of average evoked potential, alcoholics have been found to be stimulus augmenters (Hennecke, 1984). Von Knorring (1976) reports that 85% of alcoholics in his sample were stimulus augmenters whereas 50% of normals or depressives were augmenters.

Responses to Stress

Finn and Pihl (1987) measured those with an extensive FHP background (i.e., those with alcoholism in both first and second degree relatives whose alcoholic father generally had developed alcoholism around age 20) on degree of autonomic responsivity to unavoidable shock. Those with severe family history were more responsive than were those who had only a parent with late onset alcoholism or who were FHN. Finn, Zeitouni, and Pihl (1990) replicated and extended these findings. FHPs responded with greater magnitude of heart rate and digital blood volume amplitude to escapable and unescapable shock. Unlike the FHNs, they failed to habituate to a repeated tone which signaled shock onset. Further, whereas FHNs responded differentially to escapable vs. unescapable shock (displaying an attenuated response to the escapable shock), FHPs did not differentiate between the two.

There is a contradictory finding that does not support the view that FHP are more autonomically responsive. Swartz, Drews, and Cadoret (1987) found that adopted sons and daughters with a biological family history of alcoholism displayed less urinary excretion of epinephrine in response to stress. The stressor employed was a video game taxing perceptual-motor abilities. Although Swartz et al.'s data might reflect differences in stress response, an alternative explanation is that the FHPs are less invested in videogames.

Physiological Measures

Examination of MAO levels in the blood have been made. Monamine oxidase is the enzyme that catabolizes a number of neurotransmitters, viz., norepinephrine, serotonin, and dopamine. Alexopoulous, Lieberman, and Frances (1983) have found significantly lower platelet MAO values in first degree relatives of alcoholics. The same low MAO levels are found in alcoholic populations (Alexopoulous, Lieberman, Frances, & Stokes, 1981; Dolinsky, Shaskan, & Hesselbrock, 1985; Sullivan, Cavenar, Maltbie, Lister, & Zung, 1979; Sullivan, Stanfield, Maltbie, Hammett, & Cavenar, 1978) although additional research suggests that the low MAO values may be peculiar to the early onset, familial type of alcoholism as opposed to the late onset, nonfamilial type of alcoholism (von Knorring et al., 1985). Consistent with these findings, when alcoholics are divided according to whether they display high or low MAO levels, the first degree relatives of those alcoholics who display low MAO values have a more pronounced history of alcoholism compared to first degree relatives of alcoholics with high MAO levels (Major & Murphy, 1978). Schuckit, Shaskan, Duby, Vega, and Moss (1982), whose MAO findings are often cited, did not achieve statistical significance comparing FHPs with FHNs, but the direction of the group means were consistent with the results of previously mentioned studies.

Moss, Guthrie, and Linnoila (1986) matched children of alcoholics with children of nonalcoholics on age and sex. Children who regularly used alcohol or drugs were eliminated. Those in both samples with a family history of affective disorder or schizophrenia were eliminated. All alcoholic parents were FHP alcoholics, although sex of alcoholic parent was not reported. Results indicated an additional biochemical variable which distinguished FHPs. The male family history positives differed from the control males in displaying a higher basal thyrotropin level and a higher peak thyrotropin response to the releasing factor protirelin. No differences were detected among the daughters.

Mueller, Fleming, LeMahieu, Lybrand, and Barry (1988) compared FHP alcoholics with FHN nonalcoholics. These researchers drew blood, mixed the blood with alcohol, and then measured a metabolite of alcohol, phosphatidylethanol. Phosphatidylethanol was elevated in the blood sample from the FHP alcoholics. Mueller et al. suggested that the elevation in the phosphatidylethanol was attributable to the association with FHP status rather than being attributable to the impact of heavy drinking. No correlation between amount consumed and phosphatidylethanol was detected in the study. The authors of the study also remarked upon the fact that there were more smokers in the FHP alcoholic group than in the control group. The authors could not determine whether smoking status related, and could account for, their findings. The authors did not speculate on the behavioral significance of phosphatidylethanol although they suggested that it might be important in identifying persons at risk for the future development of alcoholism.

There have been investigations of genetic markers in the blood and saliva of family members of alcoholics. The technique is to determine which genetic material occurs with greater frequency among FHPs vs. FHNs. Tanna, Wilson, Winokur, and Elston (1988) report an association for the esterase-D marker lodus, although many tests were performed and this was the only positive finding. Hill, Aston, and Rabin (1988) report an association with the MNS blood marker. These authors remark that the chromosome on which the MNS marker is found also contains the gene for alcohol dehydrogenase.

DIFFERENTIAL RESPONDING OF FHP INDIVIDUALS TO ALCOHOL: IMPACT ON BEHAVIOR, ANODYNE EFFECT, SUBJECTIVE PERCEPTIONS, AND BIOCHEMISTRY

In this section, research comparing the response to alcohol of FHPs vs. the response to alcohol of FHNs is reviewed. When differences are found between the groups, the question of those factors that mediate the differential responding becomes important. As will be discussed, FHP do differ from FHNs in their expectations regarding alcohol. It could be that expectations or beliefs rather than a physical difference in responding to alcohol mediates observed differences in behavior. Some studies have included in their designs an alcohol placebo control group. These studies allow for an evaluation of whether the placebo alone (activating expectancies) can redound in group differences. When differences between FHPs and FHNs are found only in response to alcohol and not in response to placebo, a differential response to the pharmacological effect of alcohol rather than expectations is more likely to be the mediator. A chart (Table 5.1) is presented that indicates whether an alcohol placebo condition was included in each particular study. This chart should inform the reader as to where a difference in responding in the FHP group to alcohol could be explained by differential expectations.

Behavior

Diminished Behavioral Impairment

FHPs have been reported to differ in their response to alcohol on measures of static ataxia, cognitive impairment, and P 300 wave activity. Schuckit (1985a, 1988) reported that FHPs displayed less static ataxia than FHNs after imbibing low doses of alcohol. Lex et al. (1988) in a female sample also observed less

TABLE 5.1
Studies in Which the Responses to Alcohol of FHPS Were Compared
to FHNS

Study	Dependent Variable	Control for Expectancy	Result
Schuckit, 1985a	static ataxia	yes-placebo	effect only for alcohol and not for placebo[a]
Schuckit, 1988	static ataxia	yes-placebo	effect only for alcohol and not for placebo[a]
Lex et al., 1988	static ataxia digit symbol substitution	no placebo control	
Lipscomb et al., 1979	static ataxia	no placebo control	
Wilson & Nagoshi, 1988	static ataxia, increased heart rate	no placebo control	
Pollock et al., 1988	Porteus maze	no placebo control	
Baribeau, 1986	recognition of facial expression	yes-placebo	effect only for alcohol and not for placebo[a]
Elmansian et al., 1982	brain waves	yes-placebo	differential responding to alcohol and placebo
Pollack et al., 1983	brain waves	no placebo control	
Volavka et al., 1985	brain waves	no placebo control	
Schuckit et al., 1981	muscular relaxation	no placebo control	
Sher & Levenson, 1982	stress dampening	yes-placebo control	effect only for alcohol and not for placebo[a]
Sher & Walitzer, 1986	stress dampening	yes-placebo control	effect only for alcohol and not for placebo[a]
Finn & Pihl, 1988	stress dampening	no placebo control	
Levenson, Oyama, & Meek, 1987	stress dampening	yes-placebo	effect only for alcohol and not for placebo[a]
Finn, Zeitourni, & Pihl, 1990	stress dampening	no placebo control	
O'Malley & Maisto, 1985	subjective response (intoxication)	yes-placebo	less subjective response for both alcohol and placebo

(*Continued*)

TABLE 5.1 (*Continued*)

Study	Dependent Variable	Control for Expectancy	Result
Schuckit, 1980a	subjective response	no placebo control	
Schuckit, 1984b	subjective response	yes-placebo	effect only for alcohol and not for placebo[a]
Schuckit, 1988	subjective response	yes-placebo	effect only for alcohol and not for placebo[a]
Savoie et al., 1988	subjective response	no placebo control	
Nagoshi & Wilson, 1987	performance, subjective response	no placebo control	
Vogel-Sprott & Chipperfield, 1987	performance subjective response	no placebo control	
Lipscomb & Nathan, 1980	subjective response	no placebo control	
Moss, Yao, & Maddock, 1989	subjective intoxication	yes-placebo	differential responding to both alcohol and placebo
deWit & McCracken, 1990	more rapid perception of high	yes-placebo	effect only for alcohol and not for placebo[a]
Swartz et al., 1987	epinephrine	no placebo control	
Schuckit et al., 1988	ACTH	yes-placebo	effect only for alcohol and not placebo[a]
Schuckit, 1984a	cortisol	no placebo control	
Schuckit, 1988	cortisol	fails to mention placebo data	
Schuckit et al., 1983	prolactin	no placebo control	
Schuckit et al., 1987	prolactin	yes-placebo	the interaction between family history and time post consumption was significant in placebo as well as alcohol condition

[a]indicates that the differential responding between FHPs vs. FHNs is not attributable to expectancies, that is, the differential responding was observed in response to alcohol but not alcohol placebo

static ataxia after imbibing among the FHP. Wilson and Nagoshi (1988) found less static ataxia in young FHP males although not in the rest of their FHP sample. Others have failed to replicate these findings (Lipscomb & Nathan, 1980; Lipscomb et al., 1979; Nagoshi & Wilson, 1987; O'Malley & Maisto, 1985). Schuckit required precise conditions in terms of time after drinking and dosage of alcohol to identify population differences, which could explain failures to replicate.

On a number of dependent variables, FHP have been observed to be less impaired than FHNs following alcohol consumption. Savoie et al. (1988) found that FHPs vs. FHNs of both sexes performed better on a finger tapping test after imbibing, although differences were not detected on a grooved peg board task. Lex et al. (1988) found superior performance among the FHP group vs. FHN group after alcohol consumption on a digit symbol substition task, although De Wit and McCraken (1990) failed to replicate. Schuckit (1985a), citing unpublished data from his own lab, reported that FHPs displayed fewer cognitive deficits than do FHNs after moderate doses of alcohol. Pollock et al. (1986) also found less cognitive impairment for FHPs compared to FHNs on one out of three items pertaining to the Porteus maze performance.

There have been reversed findings as well. Nagoshi and Wilson (1987) found that experimenters rated FHPs more impaired after imbibing, although on objective measures there were no differences between the two populations save on one measure out of 21 measures. Over half the subjects in this study were females and about a quarter of the FHP had alcoholic mothers which might have influenced the results. In other work (e.g., Lex et al., 1988; Savoie et al., 1988), diminished impairment has been found in some studies for both females and males FHPs. However, Schuckit whose finding of less impairment from alcohol in FHPs across studies has been consistent, has only examined male FHPs who qualify on the basis of paternal alcoholism. The phenomenon of a less impairment given alcohol may be more robust among male FHPs and those whose statuses are established on the basis of paternal pedigree.

Nagoshi and Wilson's (1987) are not the only reverse direction findings in the literatures. There have been additional studies in the literature as well. O'Malley and Maisto (1985) found that FHPs were more impaired on a peg board task than were FHNs. O'Malley and Maisto speculated that their findings may have been attributable to the differential motivation among subjects created by the particular design of their investigation. Vogel-Sprott and Chipperfield (1987) also found more impairment in the FHP group on both the ascending and descending limb on measures of bead stringing and hand steadiness. Again, a large percentage (possibly as high as 33%) of the FHP had alcoholic mothers in the Vogel-Sprott and Chipperfield (1987) study. The genetic case is less well established for female alcoholism.

FHPs have also been found to be more impaired in terms of cognitive processing as reflected on EEG findings after drinking. These studies are discussed in the EEG section.

Recognition of Emotions

FHPs may be less adept at labeling feelings in themselves and others when sober. There is suggestion that alcohol may improve FHPs ability to recognize anger. Baribeau, Braun, and Dube (1986) compared the performance of FHPs with FHNs when sober and when drinking moderate amounts on the ability to accurately label facial expressions in photographs. The FHNs performed better on this task for labeling anger when sober but when drinking, the FHPs exhibited superior performance. The experiment unfortunately did not control for alpha inflation resulting from the number of tests performed and the FHNs were probably of a different socioeconomic status than the FHPs. Nevertheless, the results are provocative and deserve replication.

EEG Findings Given Alcohol and Alcohol Placebo

In general, alcohol decreases the amplitude of P 300 waves and increases their latency when people are attending to stimuli. Elmasian, Neville, Woods, Schuckit, and Bloom (1982) reported on the behavior of FHPs who qualified on the basis of father's alcoholism but who were not differentiated as to sex. FHPs were more affected by alcohol on measures of decreased P 300 amplitude and increased latency of P 300 waves. Consistent with these P 300 findings, there was an increased behavioral reaction time, differentially longer in the FHPs than the FHNs after drinking.

There have been investigations of EEG responding following consumption of an alcohol placebo. Elmasian et al. (1982) found the same increased latency of P 300 and decreased amplitude of P 300 in FHPs vs. FHNs after placebo consumption that was observed after alcohol consumption. Polich and Bloom (1988a) failed to find differences between FHP and FHN in P 300 wave responses to a tone discrimination task after placebo consumption. This study failed to replicate the smaller N study findings of Elmasian et al. (1982) in which the FHP were slower on P 300 measures in response after placebo consumption.

Anodyne Effect

Alcohol may provide a more salubrious effect for FHP individuals than for FHN individuals. FHPs display more muscular relaxation given the same dosage of alcohol than do FHNs (Schuckit, Engstrom, Alpert, & Duby, 1981). Pollack, Volavka, Goodwin, Mednick, Gabrielli, Knop, and Schulsinger (1983) and Volavka et al. (1985) report that FHPs responded to alcohol with brain wave activity suggestive of differentially enhanced relaxation which was sustained for a longer period of time after drinking. Spilker and Callaway (1969) report that alcohol decreases stimulus augmentation. Ludwig, Cain, and Wikler (1977) find that stimulus augmenters will work harder for alcohol under laboratory conditions. Previously cited research suggests that FHPs are more likely to be stimulus augmenters. It may be that FHPs are likely to experience alcohol as a stronger reinforcer than FHNs due to its ameliorative impact afforded by alcohol's reduction of stimulus augmentation.

The stress dampening effect of alcohol has also been investigated. The paradigm has consisted of observation of autonomic nervous system responding, usually assessed by the rate of the heart beat, in response to shock. Heart rate occurring after a shock signal is measured in drinking subjects as compared to sober subjects. In sober subjects, signaled shock elicits an increased heart rate, i.e., a stress response. The attenuation in the usual increase in the rate of the heart beat given shock in drinking subjects is referred to as a stress dampening effect.

Indirect evidence of a stress dampening response of greater magnitude in FHP types comes from several sources. Sher and Levenson (1982) compared persons who scored low on the Socialization scale of the CPI (California Personality Inventory) vs. individuals who did not. (It should be recalled that FHP individuals are more likely to be low scorers on this scale.) Sher and Levenson examined heart rate given stress both with and without alcohol. Sher and Levenson found that the alcohol attenuated the heart's stress response. This occurred only for the low CPI scale individuals. The robustness of this finding was called into question by a subsequent study (Sher & Walitzer, 1986) in which a differential dampening of the stress response was almost found ($p<.07$) for high scorers on the MacAndrew and was found for Tarter's minimal brain dysfunction scale but not for high scorers on the So scale of the CPI. Sher and Walitzer concluded that alcohol's differential dampening of stress for individuals who might be at high risk for alcoholism due to their personality characteristics is not a strong differential effect. In fact, a stress dampening response had been found in samples undifferentiated as to FHP status and personality characteristics as well (Levenson et al., 1980).

Subsequent research has divided subjects on the basis of family history rather than personality characteristics. Finn and Pihl (1988) demonstrated a stress dampening effect of alcohol that was particular to FHP vs. FHNs. In their study, Finn and Pihl used a rather strigent criteria for FHP status. They divided the nonalcoholic sons of alcoholics fathers into 2 groups: those with many alcoholic relatives vs. those with only an alcoholic father. Those with the extreme family history were the only group to manifest increased heart rate as a result of drinking during the baseline period. (This finding was replicated by Wilson and Nagoshi, 1988.) In terms of the stress dampening effect, the multiple alcoholic relative subjects only displayed decreased autonomic activity (heart rate measure) when drinking in response to signaled shock. Finn, Zeitouni, and Pihl (1990) replicated these results finding a stress dampening effect for alcohol particular to FHPs under conditions of both escapable and unescapable shock on measures of heart rate, digital blood volume amplitude, and muscle tension.

Levenson, Oyama, and Meek (1987) reported similar results. These researchers compared subjects who were either at risk for alcoholism or were not at risk. Risk status was defined as either exhibiting a positive family history for alcoholism or obtaining a high MacAndrew scores. Results were very similar to the Finn and Pihl findings. Only the at risk manifested an increased heart rate in response to alcohol during the baseline period. Only the at risk had their heart rate stress response dampened by the alcohol in the face of stress. A further refinement was noted in the Levenson et al. study. Among those at risk by virtue of FHP status, alcohol's stress dampening capacity was segregated within those at risk due to paternal but not maternal heritage. Both daughters and sons of alcoholic fathers achieved a greater stress dampening effect. Daughters and sons of alcoholic mothers displayed no stress dampening effect.

Subjective Perceptions

On subjective measures of intoxication, mood measures, measures of physical sensations, measures of self-perceived behavioral impairment, and estimates of amount of alcohol consumed, FHPs have been observed to report less response to alcohol administered in the laboratory (Moss, Yao, & Maddock, 1989; O'Malley & Maisto, 1985; Pollock et al., 1986; Savoie, Emory, Moody-Thomas, 1988; Schuckit, 1980a, 1984b, 1988). One exception has been self-report of anxiety, on which FHP have been found to report a greater decline than have FHNs (Savoie et al., 1988). Several studies have noted that the subjective high from alcohol is experienced at an earlier point in time after alcohol ingestion (De Wit & McCracken, 1990). There have been studies in which differences in magnitude of effect between FHPs and FHNs on self-report measures have not been detected (De Wit & McCracken, 1990; Lex et al. 1988; Rightmyer & Hill, cited by Hill, Steinhauer, & Zubin, 1987; Vogel-Sprott & Chipperfield, 1987; Wilson & Nagoshi, 1988) and a study by Nagoshi and Wilson (1987) in which FHPs reported more subjective intoxication than FHNs. In a study that probably tapped subjective response to alcohol, Lipscomb and Nathan (1980) found no difference between FHP and FHNs in accuracy of blood alcohol level estimates after imbibing.

Subjective perceptions in response to alcohol that individuals are cognizant of imbibing are a function of a number of variables, one of which is expectation. FHPs do differ in their expectations regarding the impact that alcohol will produce for them. Mann, Chassin, and Sher (1987) found that FHPs, especially those who were high scorers on a measure that combined the MacAndrew scale and items off the socialization scale of the California Personality Inventory, expected alcohol to increase personal power, although they anticipate less behavioral impairment. In fact, FHPs expected that alcohol would enhance the cognitive and motor functioning. Others have assessed expectancies on adjective checklists completed just prior to drinking. In some studies differences between FHPs and FHNs have not been detected (Nagoshi & Wilson, 1987; O'Malley &

Maisto, 1985; Schuckit, 1984b); although Wilson and Nagoshi (1988) did find that FHP expected less intoxication. In a study by Schuckit (1988) in which 23 adjectives were examined but there was not statistical control for the number of items tested, difference on 3 of the adjectives were found. FHPs expected alcohol to make them more sad and tired but expected fewer heart palpitations.

Another way to measure expectancy is to examine subjective response to an alcohol placebo. On measures of subjective intoxication after imbibing an alcohol placebo, the findings from different laboratories have not been consistent. Schuckit (1984b) failed to observe differences between FHPs and FHNs in subjective response to placebo. Newlin (1985b) found that FHPs rated themselves as more intoxicated after imbibing an alcohol placebo. O'Malley and Maisto (1985) found that FHPs rated themselves as less intoxicated after imbibing a placebo. The inconsistent findings make it difficult to determine whether FHPs differ from FHNs in subjective response to placebo. Although it is unknown whether FHP display differential subjective responses to alcohol placebo, there is a suggestion that they may rely upon their expectations to a greater extent. O'Malley and Maisto (1985) report that the subjective perceptions of the effects of alcohol of FHPs are better predicted by expectations whereas the subjective perceptions of the FHNs are better predicted by actual blood alcohol levels. A study by Wilson and Nagoshi (1988) in which half the sample was female and half the FHP qualified on the basis of mother's alcoholic pedigree, failed to replicate this finding.

Responses to alcohol placebo are difficult to interpret. The response to placebo will reflect expectancy. It also will reflect conditioned autonomic responses. Newlin (1985a, 1989) has demonstrated that males, but not females, who imbibe socially respond autonomically in a direction opposite the pharmacological effect of alcohol when presented with a convincing placebo substance. Newlin has speculated that the autonomic responding opposite in direction to the pharmacological effect of alcohol reflects conditioning. This conditioned opponent process response may be the mechanism through which tolerance to alcohol develops. Newlin (1985b) has found that FHP who are social drinkers compared to FHN who are social drinkers display a greater heart rate response to alcohol placebo in a direction opposite from the usual effect of alcohol. That is, the FHPs seem to display a more pronounced conditioned opponent process.

Biochemistry

Alcohol Metabolism

An obvious place to look for genetic differences is in the way in which alcohol is metabolized. To review the metabolic process, alcohol is first broken down into acetaldehyde by alcohol dehydrogenase in the liver. The second step in the metabolic process is the conversion of acetaldehyde by acetate aldehyde dehydrogenase. If high blood acetaldehyde levels occur, a flushing response is exhibited.

Differences between FHPs and FHNs in blood alcohol levels have not been detected at any point in time after imbibing (Schuckit, 1981, 1985b; Utne, Hansen, Winkler, & Schulsinger, 1977; Wilson & Nagoshi, 1988). This lack of differences suggests that FHPs and FHNs absorb alcohol and convert alcohol to acetaldehyde in a similar manner.

The second step in the metabolic process, that is the conversion of acetaldehyde to acetate may be different in FHPs vs. FHNs. There are data suggesting that FHPs are less efficient in their metabolism of acetaldehyde. Hence, they can be expected to exhibit higher levels of acetaldehyde after ingesting alcohol. The evidence is the following. Schuckit and Rayses (1979) matched family history positive males with family history negative males on extant drinking habits. They found that the FHP sons produced higher plasma acetaldehyde levels after drinking than did the FHN individuals. Schuckit (1980c) reported a replication of this finding in another sample. However, there has been a failure to replicate, in a study in which there were very few subjects (Behar et al., 1983).

The entire enterprise of measuring acetaldehyde levels is suspect because acetaldehyde breaks down so quickly. Ericksson (1980) advises caution accepting the conclusion that FHPs exhibit higher acetaldehyde levels post alcohol consumption because of the unreliability of acetaldehyde measurement. In response to Ericksson's (1980) caveat, Schuckit (Ericksson, 1980) cogently retorted that measurement unreliability should have made it more difficult to obtain the positive findings. Confidence in the acetaldehyde finding is enhanced by a consistent finding. FHP sons exhibit more intense facial flushing after drinking than do FHN individuals (Schuckit & Duby, 1982). (Facial flushing is probably a function of level of acetaldhyde.)

Assuming the veridicality of the population differences in acetaldehyde levels, one can speculate as to the enzyme mediator. Since there is no difference in blood alcohol levels at any point in time between alcoholics and controls (Schuckit, 1981, 1985b; Utne, Hansen, Winkler, & Schulsinger, 1977), this difference in acetaldehyde values is probably not due to alcohol dehydrogenase differences (the enzyme which catabolizes alcohol) or differences in rate of absorption. It has been attributed to differences in aldehyde dehydrogenase (the enzyme which catabolizes the acetaldehyde) (Schuckit, 1985b).

Attenuated Hormonal Response to Alcohol Among FHPs

Schuckit (1988) has been a proponent of the view that FHPs exhibit less response to alcohol than do FHNs. He contends that this blunted responsivity is exhibited on hormonal responses as well as behavioral responses. Data on urinary epinephrine, the pituitary hormone ACTH, the adrenal hormone cortisol which is regulated by ACTH, and the pituitary hormone prolactin is available.

The Stress Hormones (Epinephrine, ACTH, Cortisol)

Swartz et al. (1987) found that the rise in epinephrine levels in the urine after drinking is diminished among FHPs. The pituitary releasing hormone ACTH is lower in FHP than in FHN after drinking (Schuckit, Risch, & Gold, 1988). Possibly reflecting differences in ACTH, Schuckit (1984a, 1988) observed that FHPs manifested lower cortisol levels after imbibing than do FHNs. Schuckit (1984a) indicated that interpretation of the cortisol data is difficult because differences could reflect differential response to alcohol or differential dirual circadian rhythms. (Cortisol levels follow a circadian pattern.) Further, at the particular dosage of alcohol employed by Schuckit in the 1984a study, it is unclear whether a rise or a fall in cortisol levels should be expected, as dosage of alcohol and cortisol release are curvilinearly related.

Prolactin Response

A 1983 study by Schuckit, Parker, and Rossman and a 1987 study by Schuckit, Gold, and Risch found that FHPs do not differ from FHNs in the magnitude of increased prolactin release immediately after drinking. However, as time elapsed and the blood alcohol levels are decreasing, FHPs manifested lower levels of prolactin than FHNs. Further, in the 1987 study, Schuckit, Gold, and Risch observed a more rapid decline in prolactin (that is, a more rapid return to baseline levels) post drinking among the FHPs. Moss, Yao, and Maddock (1989) were not able to replicate a differential prolactin response to alcohol in FHP males selected for paternal but not maternal pedigree.

Findings Pertaining to DBH

DBH is the enzyme found in norepinephrine neurons that converts dopamine to norepinephrine. Since DBH is released along with norepinephrine when the nerve cell fires, DBH serves as a good index of norepinephrine activity (the firing of norepinephrine neurons). Ewing, Rouse, and Mueller (1974) and Ewing, Rouse, Mueller, and Mills (1975) have found that persons with higher plasma DBH levels report a better mood after drinking, feel less drunk, and under the particular social conditions arranged during their experiment, choose to drink more. The implication of these findings is that perhaps persons who release more norepinephrine will find alcohol particularly attractive.

FHPs have not been found to differ from FHNs in DBH levels. However, a relationship between basal DBH levels and reported typical quantity of alcohol consumed per occasion has been found in FHPs. This correlation between fixed DBH levels and reports of typical number of drinks per occasion is not found if one observes a FHN sample (Schuckit, O'Connor, Duby, Vega, & Moss, 1981). One interpretation of the correlation of drinks typically consumed per occasion and DBH levels in the FHP sample, albeit highly speculative, is that alcohol is rendered attractive for FHPs through its norepinephrine agonist effects. That is, those FHP individuals with unique properties in their catecholamine (nor-epinephrine is a catecholamine) neurons are able to derive more pleasure through drinking alcohol.

Responsiveness to Heavily Drinking Models

FHPs vs. FHNs matched on typical quantity consumed per occasion, have been found to be more heavily influenced by the consummatory behavior of the person with whom they are drinking. In the presence of a heavily drinking model, the FHPs will emulate the behavior of the model to a greater extent than will FHNs (Chipperfield & Vogel-Sprott, 1988).

Criticisms of and Comments on the FHP Studies

Comments relevant to all studies. Before a summary of the way in which FHP individuals differ from FHN individuals, some comments on this type of research are provided. There are numerous reasons why comparisons between FHPs and FHNs may not reflect genetic differences. FHPs can be expected to differ FHNs on a number of critical environmental factors which could account for obtained findings. The following environmental variables seem particularly relevant.

(a)   It is known that sons and daughters of alcoholics are more likely to have experienced head trauma, physical abuse, and prenatal injury than are children in general (Tarter et al., 1984).

(b)   FHP children are much more likely to be raised under chaotic and stressful conditions (Schulsinger et al., 1986).

(c)   There is a suggestion that FHPs are more often abuse drugs than FHNs (Schuckit, 1982a). Schuckit has attempted to control for this contaminating factor by eliminating persons with a history of drug abuse. However, others (e.g., Alexopoulous et al., 1983) have not.

(d)   Most of the research examining children of alcoholics has focused on children of alcoholic fathers rather than alcoholic mothers. It seems possible, however, that women married to alcoholics are more likely to drink during their pregnancy than are women who are not married to heavy consumers.

Before confidence in a hereditary mediator of identified differences between FHPs and FHNs can occur, attribution to the confounding factors would have to be ruled out.

The reader has probably been impressed by the number of failures to replicate. Failures to replicate might suggest that any particular difference between FHPs and FHNs obtained in one or several studies is a less likely marker of an inherited diathesis toward alcoholism. However, there are also reasons why such failures to replicate could be anticipated. First, some studies (e.g., Nagoshi & Wilson, 1987; Wilson & Nagoshi, 1988) have included both male and female FHPs. Whether a genetic mechanism is expressed in the same manner in girls as it might be in boys is unclear. Second, researchers have included children of alcoholic mothers as well as children of alcoholic fathers. There is reason to believe that female alcoholics may less often become alcoholic through a genetic pathway. Hence, those FHPs whose pedigree is established on the basis of mother's alcoholism may not have inherited any risk for alcoholism themselves. Third, in some studies differences between FHPs and FHNs have not been detected on personality measures such as a sensation seeking scale (e.g., De Wit & Mc-Cracken, 1990). Much of the literature suggests that a differential response to alcohol is yoked to differences on personality measures. Hence, a sample of FHPs who do not differ in terms of personality, may be a sample without a genetic risk for alcoholism. Such a sample, would not, for example, be helpful for exploring the nature of a possible unique response to alcohol. Fourth, most studies have not taken into account the type of alcoholism in the family (primary or secondary) in the relative who qualified the FHP for the study. Unless care is taken to ensure the homogeneity of the FHP sample, failures to replicate can be expected.

Comments Specific to Studies Examining Performance Differences

Beyond the general caveats which can be raised for all studies comparing FHPs vs. FHNs, there are specific issues that can be raised for particular classes of findings. Those studies examining performance issues (intellectual and EEG measures) are examined first. In studies finding differences between FHPs and FHNs on EEG and intellectual measures, criticism can be rendered on the grounds that almost no research (save for Hill et al.) has controlled for motivation. In should be recalled that FHPs can be characterized as more irreverent and rebellious. It seems likely that they might be less inclined than FHNs to take an academic task seriously or to stay alert in a sterile environment. Future research should be geared toward teasing apart the various components of intellectual functioning and EEG responding (motivation, actual ability, decreased engagement in the task when the task is viewed as easy) upon which FHPs might differ and which might mediate difference in overall performance.

Comments Regarding Studies Examining Differential Responding to Alcohol.

Those studies that have examined the reactions of FHPs vs. FHNs to alcohol have sometimes been attentive to the issue of factors mediating the effect of alcohol. The possibility that differences in the under-the-influence behavior of

FHP vs. FHN is a function of differential expectations rather than differential pharmacological response to alcohol is important. It is known that FHPs do hold distinct expectations for the effect of alcohol which differ from the expectations of FHNs. Nagoshi (1989, personal communication; Wilson & Nagoshi, 1987) reports that among his subjects he has observed little reliability over time on the individual's autonomic response to alcohol, although expectations and overt behavior are fairly consistent. He believes that for those variables on which differences between FHPs vs. FHNs responding to alcohol has been observed, differing expectations may well account for the findings. Rather than responding physically in a unique manner to alcohol, it may be that FHPs simply hold different beliefs about alcohol which redounds in different patterns of overt behavior and subjective perception. Some of the research reviewed did include placebo control conditions. When difference in behavior in response to alcohol between FHPs vs. FHNs are found, but no difference is observed in response to placebo, differential expectations are less likely explanations for the data.

The reader may refer to Table 5.1 which informs regarding which studies included a control for expectations. Those studies in which differential expectations between FHPs and FHNs are less likely explanations for obtained differences between FHPs and FHNs in response to alcohol are indicated. A perusal of the chart should indicate that the stress dampening effect of alcohol for FHP, attenuated performance impairment of FHP, the impact on emotion identification in others, and the diminished subjective impact on FHPs was demonstrated in response to alcohol but not to placebo. There is evidence then that these differential responses are less likely to have been mediated by expectations.

Whereas the above case is plausible and certainly can be advanced, a problem remains. The possibility of differential expectations accounting for the data cannot be entirely discounted. It is rather difficult to create a convincing placebo. It may be that expectations operate to a greater degree in the given alcohol/told alcohol condition vs. the given inert substance/told alcohol condition. Hence, there may be an expectancy confound that could account for obtained differences in response to alcohol vs. inert substance. In the future, perhaps better placebos will be found that might allow for better research and firmer conclusions.

SUMMARY

Some of the same findings that emerged as precursors to alcoholism in the longitudinal studies are identified as characteristic of relatives of alcoholics. Hyperactivity, problems with sustaining attention, childhood acting out are sturdy findings. The problems in allocating attention may be reflected in the findings suggesting poorer intellectual performance and the EEG data. Some of the hyperactivity could be related to the low MAO enzyme levels (the enzyme which degrades norepinephrine, dopamine, and serotonin) which are identified in relatives of alcoholics.

There is evidence that relatives of alcoholics are less responsive to kinesthetic information. They sway more when they close their eyes. They are less proficient at recognizing emotion in others. They are less able to label their own emotions. Although relatives of alcoholics are less cognizant of or behaviorally responsive to internal changes, the explanation does not seem to be that they are autonomically under responsive. That is, a weak internal signal does not seem to account for the failure to label internally generated information. The Finn and Pihl (1987) data suggests that they are more autonomically responsive to shock. In response to alcohol, they display a more pronounced increase in heart rate. The Newlin data suggests that their conditioned responses to alcohol placebo are of greater magnitude.

The field is rife with failures to replicate, so all statements are tentative. However, behavioral differences among relatives of alcoholics in response to alcohol have been observed. They seem to be less sedated or impaired in terms of their performance. They display a diminished hormonal response to alcohol. In contrast to these attenuated responses, are those findings which suggest that FHPs derive more beneficial effect from alcohol. They seem to derive more relaxation and greater immunity to stress. There is reason to believe that stimulus augmenting of FHPs may be reduced by alcohol. Findings suggesting that relatives of alcoholics are less impaired by alcohol and derive a greater stress dampening effect are consistent with the expectations that children of alcoholics hold for alcohol. They do not expect to be impaired. They do expect their cognitive capacities to be enhanced.

The next chapter considers interpretations of the raw data. There has been speculation regarding why some people exhibiting the temperament characteristic of FHP might be more likely to drink excessively.

6 Integrating Theories

In this chapter an attempt will be made to integrate some of the findings from the longitudinal studies and the findings as to the distinctive traits of relatives of alcoholics. The theories discussed here which integrate research findings have been proffered by major researchers in the field. Tarter and colleagues (Tarter, 1978; Tarter, Alterman, & Edwards, 1985) have proposed the most global theory advancing the idea of a distinct temperament characteristic of alcoholics. They suggest reasons why alcohol might be an attractive drug for individuals possessing this distinctive temperament.

Other researchers in the field have offered less global hypotheses. These hypotheses do not contradict Tarter's theorizing, but rather suggest particular axioms that might be part of the more global picture. Tarter has remarked upon the role of handedness as a component in the development of temperament. Linnoila (1989) has speculated about the neurotransmitter serotonin in mediating temperament. Goodwin (1979) wonders whether an inability to recognize intoxication may predispose to heavier drinking because FHP literally have no way of knowing when to stop. Others have wondered about the significance of having high acetaldehyde levels after drinking. There is evidence that acetaldehyde could make alcohol more attractive.

After presentation of Tarter's global hypothesis regarding temperament and the less global hypotheses, an attempt to tie up loose ends is made. No one ever said that all alcoholism is inherited. Unfortunately, the twin and adoption studies were very imprecise in specifying which type of alcoholism was investigated. The more troubling question is which type or types of alcoholism are inherited. Questions still remain as to whether primary alcoholism is inherited. There are questions about whether the temperament that underlies inherited alcoholism is the same as the temperament that underlies sociopathy. The Iowa adoption studies by Cadoret and colleagues (Cadoret et al., 1985; Cadoret & Gath, 1978) did find some independence between alcoholism and sociopathy. However, another interpretation of these studies can be made which disputes the independence of the two disorders. These issues are discussed later in this chapter.

The final section in this chapter discusses the issue of whether alcoholism in women is inherited. Cloninger's theory regarding two pathways of inheritance is included in this discussion since one of his paths includes inheritance of alcoholism in both sexes, although the other does not.

HOW TEMPERAMENT MIGHT MEDIATE THE DEVELOPMENT OF ALCOHOLISM

The underlying syndrome of sensation seeking, high MacAndrew scale, high activity, and outgoingness suggested by the varied avenues of research could through some biochemical pathway be associated with increased consumption. There is an integrative theory that posits a biochemical basis for the development of alcoholism, i.e., which links temperament to a rationale for alcohol being particularly reinforcing for those with specific temperaments. This integrative theory, proffered by Tarter and colleagues (Tarter, 1978; Tarter, Alterman, & Edwards, 1985; Tarter & Edwards, 1988), allows for the view that the same set of genes may redound in a temperament that could be manifested behaviorally as any one of a spectrum of disorders. This integrative theory rests, in part, on some of the work of Schachter (1971).

Schachter (1971) sought to explain some of the characteristic behavior of sociopaths (the then commonly used term for ASP) viz., the lack of emotional responding and their learning deficiency in an avoidance paradigm. He assessed sociopathic, incarcerated prisoners working at an avoidance task. The avoidance task, avoiding shock, was a latent task embedded in the manifest task of learning how to escape from a maze. Consistent with early data, Schachter found that sociopaths do not learn avoidance tasks well. Prior theorizing attributed this performance deficit to an inability to experience anticipatory anxiety. Contrary to what was previously assumed however, Schachter's data suggested that sociopaths are more reactive autonomically (e.g., on measures of heart rate) than are normals. That is, their heart rates increase to a greater degree when under stress. These findings challenged the extant theory. If sociopaths were emotionally reactive, in fact more reactive than normals, what could account for their inability to learn? The proffered explanation referred to Schachter's earlier work on emotion.

Emotion encompasses an autonomic event, the perception of this event, and the cognitive labeling of the event. The emotional label, based on recognition of an internal event, may be necessary for an emotional reaction to effect volitional behavior. Schachter (1971) adduced evidence that sociopaths are both highly and indiscrimately reactive, just as likely to respond to a little as a big shock. Further, sociopaths take a long time to return to baseline after reacting. Given these facts, Schachter reasoned that if sociopaths react strongly to everything, perhaps sociopaths discount their arousal, never learning to ascribe meaning to it. The effect is, in relevant respects, the same as not being able to experience any reaction at all. Schachter speculated that not all individuals with a noisy nervous system would ignore their highly reactive autonomic activity. Some would learn to attend to and label everything. These persons would develop a different disorder, viz., anxiety neurosis. It does not require much extrapolation to speculate that the same etiology may underlie hysteria. Hysteria or Briquet's is the disorder that keeps emerging in the familial association studies among female relatives of alcoholics.

Schachter's theory offers an explanation for the familial aggregation of two of the antisocial spectrum disorders. The same noisy, poorly regulated autonomic nervous system results in both antisocial personality and hysteria but in different individuals.

It is a big leap to move from the identified shared characteristics of alcoholics and antisocial personalities to the conclusion that alcoholics, like sociopaths, are autonomically overreactive. Additional data is available, however. One study has shown that alcoholics, like sociopaths, do not learn avoidance tasks well (Weingartner & Faillace, 1971). There is evidence that alcoholics, when selected for absence of a history of head trauma, are autonomically overreactive and less well regulated (Chandler, Parson, & Vega, 1975; Lovallo, Parson, & Holloway, 1973; Tarter, 1978). Further, convincing evidence is provided by Finn and Pihl's (1988) study. These researchers adduced evidence that sons of alcoholics with an extensive family history, are more reactive autonomically to shock than were those who only had an alcoholic father.

In Schachter's monograph, he presents data suggesting ways to improve the functioning of sociopaths on avoidance tasks. Given adrenaline, their emotional responses are enhanced. This intensification enables their emotional reactivity to increase above the threshold necessary for recognition. Their performance improves.

Why Might Alcohol Be Reinforcing for Those with Highly Reactive Nervous Systems?

Schachter (1971) found that adrenaline improved the performance of the sociopaths. Childhood hyperactivity, the temperament manifestion that is often a precursor to alcoholism and sociopathy, is improved by adrenergic agonists (ritalin, amphetamines). There is evidence that alcohol shares many properties with adrenaline. Alcohol increases urinary catecholamines and produces an arousal effect on behavior (DeTurck & Vogel, 1982; Matchett & Erickson, 1977).

Alcohol may serve the same function for persons who inherit a noisy nervous system as amphetamine and ritalin (other andrenergic agonist) serves for hyperactive children. If alcoholics have the same noisy nervous systems as do sociopaths, there is reason to believe that they might be in particular need of a drug with arousing properties.

Findings from animal models of alcoholism are relevant here. Rat strains have been bred for alcohol preference. Under baseline conditions these rats are more hyperactive than their nonpreferring counterparts. When given alcohol, the preferrers respond as if alcohol were a stimulant drug. Given a low dose of alcohol, they display more activity. More alcohol is required to induce sedation. Further, the rat perferrers develop tolerance more rapidly to the sedating effects than do the non-preferrers (Li et al., 1989). The picture from the preferring rat strains then is consistent with the data on children of alcoholics. Children of alcoholics display a higher frequency of hyperactivity. They too are more tolerant to alcohol's sedating effects. This consistency may shed light on the subjective effect found in drinking by those who are predisposed to alcoholism.

An Alternative View on How Temperament Might Mediate Alcoholism

The preceding discussion has speculated regarding why persons who are high sensation seeking/high MacAndrew types might find the pharmacological impact of alcohol reinforcing. There is a explanation for linking temperament to increased drinking which does not refer to the pharmacological impact of alcohol. A social explanation is available. It may be that persons with the characteristic prealcoholic temperament are drawn into associating with others possessing similar temperaments. Perhaps the thrill seeking sensation seekers form their own subculture. Perhaps members of this subculture hold positive attitudes and expectations toward heavy drinking. That is, they associate intoxication with positive virtues (virility, bravado, etc.). Were such the case, inherited temperament would mediate the development of alcoholism via a learning/attitudinal route, much in the same way that sex, an inherited trait, predisposes to hair length. Temperament would increase the probability of inculcation of norms and values which would be the direct causal mechanism in the development of alcoholism.

What Might Be the Mediator of Temperament?

If persons at high risk for alcoholism possess a distinctive temperament, the question of the mediator of this temperament follows. A chemical mediator of temperament (e.g., low MAO) seems plausible. Low MAO is associated in the general population with sensation seeking (a construct capturing gregariousness, high energy and attraction to excitement) (Haier, Buchsbaum, Murphy, Gottesman, & Coursey, 1980; Schooler, Zahn, Murphy, & Buchsbaum, 1978;

Zuckerman, Buchsbaum, & Murphy, 1980). Structural pathways to temperament and cognitive styles are also suggested (Gorenstein & Newman, 1980). One hypothesis suggests that sinistrality may be involved.

Left handed alcoholics are more likely to have a positive paternal family history than are right handed alcoholics (London, Kibbee, & Holt, 1985). Further, they experience more relapses before achieving a period of significant sobriety (London, 1985; Smith & Chyatte, 1983). Alcoholics are more likely to be left handed than is the general population (17–39% vs. 10% in general population) (Bakan, 1973; London, 1985; London et al., 1985). Further, alcoholics display increased ambidexterity (Nasrallah, Keelor, & McCalley-Whitters, 1983); and a reliance upon right hemisphere processing strategies (Sandel & Alcorn, 1980).

In the general population handedness is associated with a number of distinctive characteristics. Stuttering, dyslexia, immune dysfunction, and migraine headaches are all increased among the left handed and their family members (Geschwind & Behan, 1982; London et al., 1985). The clustering of left handedness and immune dysfunction found in the general population has been reported in alcoholic populations (London, 1985). The incidence of thyroid dysfunction and migraine headaches is higher among the family members of alcoholics than in the general population (London et al., 1985). FHPs have higher rates of stuttering and enuresis (Haberman, 1966). A possible related finding is that essential tremor, a disorder of unknown origin, is higher among the family members of alcoholics and among alcoholics themselves than among the general population (Schroeder & Nasrallah, 1982).

Geschwind and Behan (1982) have speculated regarding causal mechanisms in the etiology of handedness, brain organization, and associated characteristics. Geschwind and Behan (1982) have hypothesized that high levels of testosterone during gestation may result in more right rather than left brain development and repressed activity in the thymus gland. (The thymus gland is responsible for processing white blood cells and thus has a major role in immune system functioning.) This line of reasoning assigns a causal role to testosterone in the fetus. High testosterone level might be attributable to the genes of the fetus. Alternatively, high testosterone level, which has been documented to be higher in the umbilical cords of the first born (Maccoby, Doering, Jackin, & Kraemer, 1979), could be attributable to the intrauterine environment, more likely a function of the mother's body. Whatever the source of the high testosterone levels, it could cause immune dysfunction, characteristic brain organization, sinistrality, and a predisposition to alcoholism.

Consistent with the testosterone hypothesis is the finding that within alcoholic populations there is an association between being first born and being left handed (London et al., 1985). In terms of the type of alcoholism that high testosterone levels predisposes to, first borns are more likely to be younger onset alcoholics (Yamane et al., 1980). Fetal testosterone, more likely to be elevated among the first born, may be an important factor in contributing to sinistrality, immune disfunction, hemispherisity, and alcoholism, but it cannot explain everything. Inconsistent with a testosterone etiology is the fact that alcoholics, as a group, are more likely to be last born (Blane & Barry, 1973). However, the association with birth order is not a consistent finding and may reflect the impact of other relevant but confounded variables (e.g., SES, ethnicity, religion) (Stagner, 1986).

It would be useful to know whether the cluster of characteristics of FHP left handers also include low MAO and the correlates of MAO (stimulus augmentation, sensation seeking). Such information could suggest whether one etiological pathway could account for all the various findings or whether several etiologies might be required to explain the data.

Dopamine 2 Receptors as a Mediator of Temperament

Blum, Noble, Sheridan, Montgomery, Ritchie, Jagadeeswaran, Nogami, Briggs, and Cohn (1990) report having found a higher frequency of the A1 allele of the dopamine D2 receptor gene in alcoholics vs. controls. Blum et al. related the dopamine D2 system to regulation of reward seeking behavior. This system could underlie temperament as well as drug seeking behavior. Consistent with the role of dopamine in drug seeking behavior are the findings that rodent strains genetically bred to prefer alcohol display lower dopamine levels in particular brain regions under baseline conditions. Alcohol induces greater turnover in dopamine in the preferring rat strains (Modell, Mountz, & Beresford, 1990). Administration of dopamine agonists will also decrease alcohol consumption in rats (Modell et al., 1990).

Serotonin Differences as a Mediator of Temperament and Attraction to Alcohol

Linnoila (1989) has proffered the hypothesis that deficit levels of serotonin may mediate the hereditary propensity to alcoholism. Alcoholics have been found to display low levels of serotonin metabolites in their cerebrospinal fluid (Naranjo et al., 1984). Buydens-Branchey et al. (1989b) found that the deficit serotonin levels (as assessed by plasma tryptophan levels, the precursor to serotonin) were confined to those alcoholics who are early onsetters rather than those who have developed alcoholism later in life. FHPs also display low levels of serotonin levels, although the evidence here is hard to interpret as it was garnered from a depressed population. Those depressed with family histories of alcoholism vs. depressed without family histories of alcoholism were observed to differ in amounts of a serotonin metabolite found in the cerebrospinal fluid (Rosenthal et al., 1980).

Serotonin levels may be related to temperament. This idea emerges due to other populations which also display lower levels of serotonin metabolites. Arsonists and violent criminals have been found to display deficits in serotonin levels (Virkkunen, Nuutila, Goodwin, & Linnoila, 1987).

There is further evidence that low serotonin may be specific to particular types of alcoholics. In a population of criminals, Linnoila et al. (1989) found that those criminals with alcoholic fathers exhibited lower cerebrospinal fluid levels of 5-hydroxyindoleacetic acid (a metabolite of serotonin). They also were more often convicted of an impulsive crime. The findings from this study are difficult to evaluate because, although one group had alcoholic fathers whereas the others did not, the group without alcoholic fathers more often had a history of alcoholism in the male relatives of the mother (who was not herself alcoholic).

Evidence suggesting a role for serotonin in mediating increased attraction to alcohol derives from studies in which procedures increasing serotonin levels have decreased spontaneous alcohol consumption. Giving rats a precursor to serotonin (5-HTP) will induce a tenacious taste aversion to alcohol which does not extinguish (Zabik & Roache, 1983). Giving nondepressed heavy drinkers zimeldine, a drug that blocks serotonin reuptake and hence increases serotonin's activity at the receptor site will decrease their drinking (Naranjo et al. 1984). These studies seem to suggest that increasing serotonin will decrease drinking. However, serotonin receptor site blockers do not impact zimeldine's ability to decrease alcohol consumption (Zabik, 1989). Hence, serotonin circuitry is not necessarily implicated in mediating alcohol preference. There is a further inconsistent finding. Although increasing brain serotonin levels may decrease preference in heavy drinkers, increasing brain serotonin levels, through increasing plasma levels of tryptophan (the precursor to serotonin) has not been found to influence immediate consumption levels in social drinkers (Pihl, Young, Ervin, & Plotnick, 1987).

The idea that those at genetic risk for alcoholism have low levels of serotonin is consistent with the rat research. Alcohol preferring strains of rats vs. nonpreferring strains have found decreased levels of serotonin in the brains of the preferers, although serotonin is only one of the neurotransmitter systems in which the preferers have been found to differ from the nonpreferers (Li et al., 1986).

The serotonin findings are all consistent with the idea that serotonin levels may be associated with temperament. In the animal and human literature, there is evidence that serotonin levels are related to alcohol preference.

WHAT ABOUT ACETALDEHYDE?

Another major thread in the research suggests FHP individuals achieve higher levels of acetaldehyde when they drink. There is a theory that provides rationale for why acetaldehyde might be important in bringing about a more compelling desire to drink. This theory references the TIQs. Acetaldehyde and catecholamines condense to form TIQs (Brown, Amit, & Rockman, 1979). Given higher levels of acetaldehyde, more TIQs should be formed. For rats, both acetaldehyde and TIQs are reinforcing (Amit, Smith, Brown, & Williams, 1982;

Brown, Amit, & Rockman, 1979). Intraventricular injection of THIQs has been found to create an enduring preference for alcohol in rats (Brown et al., 1979; Myers & Oblinger, 1977). These findings have stimulated speculation that elevated accumulation of acetaldehyde might be an important factor in creating alcohol preference in humans.

This speculation may seem puzzling for the reader who has heard the theory on why Orientals have a built in protection against heavy alcohol consumption. Some individuals (viz. particular Orientals) have low aldehyde dehydrogenase which predisposes them to high levels of acetaldehyde when they drink even low doses of alcohol. In fact, in Oriental populations, alcoholics vs. nonalcoholics have been found to less frequently possess the ALDH-2 allele, the gene that predisposes to acetaldehyde accumulation given alcohol consumption (Crabb, Edenberg, Bosron, & Li, 1989). The high acetaldehyde level produces flushing which is believed to discourage heavy alcohol consumption (Schuckit et al., 1985, p. 486). It would seem that FHPs should be discouraged from drinking by their relatively greater acetaldehyde levels. However, the situation is more complex. The complete story seems to be that whereas a lot of acetaldehyde is aversive, a little is reinforcing. Acetaldehyde appears to be sought after and reinforcing at low concentrations and avoided and aversive at higher concentrations. Rats will lever press for intraventricular injections of acetaldehyde, although high peripheral concentrations of acetaldehyde are aversive (Brown et al., 1979). Drinking low quantities of alcohol while taking antabuse, a substance that enhances the accumulation of acetaldehyde, creates a more euphoric alcohol high (Brown, Amit, Smith, Sutherland, & Selvaggi, 1983), thereby promoting the continued consumption of low doses of alcohol. Perhaps the moderate levels of acetaldehyde produced by FHP when they drink, is the optimal level for enhancing the reinforcement value of alcohol.

Future research will hopefully determine whether the accumulation of acetaldehyde is related to any of the other characteristics of FHPs.

DECREASED RESPONSIVENESS TO ALCOHOL AS A CAUSAL GENETIC MECHANISM

Schuckit (1985a) has concluded that FHPs are less responsive to alcohol. Goodwin (1979) has theorized that decreased responsivity could subserve increased consumption in FHPs, as the FHPs may have no mechanism for determining that they should stop drinking. This may be part of the explanation for crapulous consumption.

The reader will recall that many of the findings specific to decreased responsiveness to alcohol among FHPs have not replicated. An interesting report by Schuckit and Gold (1988) lend supportive evidence to the hypothesis of attenuated response to alcohol among the FHPs. These researchers performed a discriminate analysis designed to pick out those responses to alcohol of FHPs which differentiated them from the FHNs. Included in the discriminate function were cortisol levels, prolactin levels, and subjective response. (Unfortunately, the authors did not report mean values so it was impossible to determine the direction of the mean differences from the report.) Using the discriminant function the authors were able to correctly classify 70% of the FHPs and 83% of the FHNs. The authors also attempted to determine those factors that distinguished the FHPs who could be correctly discriminated on the basis of the discriminate function (that is, their response to alcohol) vs. those who could not be correctly classified. Those FHP who were atypical in their response to alcohol, had more depressed relatives than the FHPs who manifested the characteristic response. They also were more likely to have experienced hangovers. The finding on depressed relatives may reflect the fact that the FHPs who did not respond to alcohol as expected, had parents who were secondary alcoholics/primary depressives. Perhaps these atypical responders had not inherited a genetic diathesis toward primary alcoholism.

Perhaps Schuckit is correct in concluding that FHPs are less affected by the intoxicating impact of alcohol. It should also be recalled that FHPs are less responsive to alcohol on some but not all dependent measures. Schuckit has found an attenuation in response in terms of hormones, in terms of behavioral impairment, and in terms of subjective perception of intoxication. However, others have found a greater stress dampening response on autonomic measures and less subjective anxiety. It would seem that FHPs are less responsive in some ways but more responsive in other ways.

SUMMARY

There are hypotheses in the literature regarding how the syndrome that seems to characterize alcoholics and their relatives might lead to excessive drinking. The most global integration has been proposed by Tarter. This theory suggests that alcoholics have an imprecise autonomic nervous system. This particular nervous system has many behavioral implications. Hence, a particular temperament is suggested. For persons of this temperament, alcohol may have an ameliorative impact. Linnoila posits a role for serotonin in underlying temperament and a desire for alcohol. The THIQ hypothesis has not been linked to temperament, although it advances a reason for why alcohol might be highly compelling for some. None of these hypotheses are incompatible. They may all be true, and perhaps true for the same individual. There is little data available as to correlations among the traits (e.g., low MAO, high acetaldehyde when drinking, sensation seeking, left handedness, high MacAndrew scale scores, low serotonin levels) which have been identified in samples of alcoholics and their relatives. Future research may supply answers to whether low MAO is linked to low serotonin levels, whether low MAO predisposes to THIQs, whether the Mac-Andrew scale is associated with THIQs. Such information would help to hone theories.

IS PRIMARY ALCOHOLISM INHERITED?

In the twin and adoption studies precise conclusions as to which type of alcoholism was investigated are difficult to make. Goodwin did examine primary alcoholism in the adoptee. However, 44% of the adoptees had police records, albeit for minor offenses. Whether the parent was a primary alcoholic in the Goodwin et al. (1973) study was not clear. The Cadoret, Iowa studies did distinguish primary alcoholism in the adoptee and the parent, but may have been less successful in making accurate diagnoses in the extended biological family of the adoptee. The Cloninger, Swedish studies and the twin studies seemed to have tapped samples of alcoholics who were also displaying a great deal of publicly disruptive behavior. Based on the twin and adoption studies, there is room for doubt as to the type of alcoholism that was being investigated. Evidence is available from other sources, however. There are reasons to believe that primary alcoholism is inherited.

Schuckit's studies have examined the sons of primary alcoholics. In recruiting subjects, Schuckit has queried regarding family history of mental illness to screen from his sample the sons of sociopaths and depressed persons with secondary alcoholism (Schuckit, 1980b). Schuckit has found differences between FHPs and FHNs on dependent variables that seem more likely influenced by genetics than learning (e.g., static ataxia, cortisol and prolactin response to alcohol). Tarter et al. (1989) recruited sons of alcoholics through the newspaper carefully screening out alcoholic fathers who were also antisocial personalities. Tarter et al. (1989) also found differences on statitic ataxia. These studies suggest that there are distinctive differences between sons of primary alcoholics and the general population. These differences may be related to the set of characteristics which relates to the inheritance of excessive drinking. They do suggest that primary alcoholism is inherited.

DO PRIMARY ALCOHOLICS POSSESS THE SAME GENOTYPE AS SOCIOPATHS?

The familial association research supports the antisocial personality disease spectrum. Antisocial personality, hysteria, childhood hyperactivity, and alcoholism cluster in the same families, and often in the same individual. The notion of a disease spectrum suggests all disorders in the spectrum are inherited together. Two possible explanations suggest themselves. The same sets of genes may predispose to more than one condition. Alternatively, separate sets of genes that are contiguous and therefore more likely to be passed on together may create a correlation between conditions. If alcoholism unassociated with ASP (primary alcoholism) is inherited, the question remains whether its genotype overlaps with the genotype for ASP.

As discussed in the chapter on the twin and adoption studies, the Goodwin et al. (1974) adoption study and the Iowa studies (Cadoret & Gath, 1978; Cadoret et al., 1985; Cadoret et al., 1987) seem to have established independence of the inheritance of alcoholism and sociopathy. However, there is an interpretation that does not dispute the linkage of the genotypes for alcoholism and ASP. In both the Goodwin et al. (1974) study and the Cadoret et al. (1985) study, there was the suggestion that the alcoholism being investigated was mild. The authors of these studies remarked that family members frequently were not cognizant of alcoholism in the relevant family member. Perhaps the prior studies examined a mild form of alcoholism, i.e., a form for which there was only a small genetic loading. Perhaps a high degree of genetic loading is required for flagrant alcoholic symptomotology, for the expression of ASP in conjunction with alcoholism, for familial manifestation of ASP as well as alcoholism, and for an especially high rate of familial alcoholism.

There are studies suggesting that familial alcoholism without familial antisocial personality implies less familial concordance. In the 1985b study by Schuckit, those alcoholics who were primary alcoholics were found to have higher rates of familial alcoholism than the depressed alcoholics, but not as high as the drug abusing and the ASP alcoholics. Other studies, mentioned in the section on ASP alcoholics, suggest these findings are reliable. An implication of these latter studies is that there may be some hereditary contribution to primary alcoholism, but not as great a contribution as for the ASP-alcoholism syndrome.

Moving from familial association studies to investigations of persons at risk (sons of alcoholics), offers additional relevant material. Beyond selecting for those at risk for primary alcoholism, in recruiting FHP subjects Schuckit typically advertises for FHP individuals who are between 21 and 25 and who have not yet developed alcoholism but who are social drinkers. Tarter et al. (1977) finds that primary alcoholics who are characterized by no prior period of social drinking and possibly a more extreme genetic diathesis, report a mean age of onset for alcoholism of 25.9. Schuckit's selection procedure eliminates some of those individuals with the most extreme genetic diathesis (viz., those 21 to 25 who are already alcoholic) (Sher, 1985). Further, Schuckit has not discriminated FHP subjects into those whose parents are early onsetters vs. those whose parents are late onsetters. As noted in the comparison of types of alcoholics research, the evidence suggests that the early onsetters have a stronger inherited diathesis. By lumping together children of early onset and late onset alcoholics, one would expect less extreme findings on genetically determined dependent variables. Despite the fact that Schuckit's recruitment procedures include a great number of subjects expected to have no genetic loading or mild genetic loading, the qualitative characteristics are the same as found in other areas of research. These subjects are the high MacAndrew scale scorers with tendency toward low MAO. These features overlap with the known correlates of ASP, viz., sensation seeking, low MAO, and stimulus augmentation (Zuckerman et al., 1980). It would seem that even those whose genetic loading towards alcoholism is mild, exhibit some of the ASP spectrum characteristics, even if they are not exhibiting an antisocial personality.

The following argument is suggested. The same genes that produce ASP are the ones that produce alcoholism. It may be, however, that a greater genetic loading and perhaps extreme environmental conditions as well are required for the expression of ASP along with alcoholism. It is also consistent with the lower base rate for ASP, than for alcoholism, in the general population. The hypothesis is further consistent with studies finding that different mathematical models predict the development of ASP and alcoholism (Cloninger, Christianssen, Reich & Gottesman, 1978).

A test of the hypothesis would be to determine if two nonsociopathic alcoholic parents, together contributing a high genetic loading, are likely to produce a sociopathic offspring, even when the offspring is adopted away. A study by Hesselbrock et al. (1985) suggests that the incidences of ASP in conjunction with alcoholism (dual diagnoses) increases when there is bilateral pedigree for alcoholism, although there is no such elevation of ASP in conjunction with alcoholism when there is no pedigree or unilateral pedigree. This particular study is hypothesis consistent but not definitive since the authors were not examining adoptees and no attempt was made to assess whether the parental alcoholism was associated with ASP. A study by Earls, Reich, Jung, and Cloninger (1988) found that families with two alcoholic parents have higher rates of children with hyperactivity, oppositional behavior, and conduct disorder than families in which only one parent is alcoholic. This study may have reflected environmental influences. It also may have been tapping genetic precursors to sociopathy. The Hesselbrock et al. and Earls et al. studies suggest that a bilateral, alcoholic pedigree is associated with high rates of sociopathic characteristics in the offspring. Future research may shed additional light on whether these findings reflect genetic or environmental factors.

IS THERE A FORM OF ALCOHOLISM WHICH IS NOT HEREDITARY?

The research reviewed suggests that one hereditary type of alcoholism is exemplified in the individual who is hyperactive in childhood, scores high on the MAC subscale of the MMPI, develops early onset alcoholism, and has a family history of alcoholism. In contrast to this composite picture is the secondary alcoholic with a primary diagnosis of depression. In some studies alcoholics who carry a primary diagnosis of depression have less familial alcoholism than primary alcoholics or sociopathic alcoholics (Schuckit, 1985b; Schuckit et al., 1969; Winokur et al., 1971), although there are exceptions (O'Sullivan, Whillans, Daly, Carroll, Clare, & Cooney, 1983). The depressed alcoholics are unlikely to score highly on the MAC scale (MacAndrew, 1981). They have a later age of onset and fewer social problems (Schuckit, 1985b). Zimberg (1974) made the informal observation that among geriatric alcoholics who develop problem drinking late in life, drinking is often a response to spousal death, retirement, or failing health. It may be that younger depressed individuals also develop problem drinking as a response to external or internally generated problems in life. These individuals may travel a non-genetic road to drinking problems. It should be noted, however, that Cloninger has suggested that his Type I genetic pathway manifests as primary depression/secondary alcoholism.

A RECAPITULATION OF CLONINGER'S TYPES

Cloninger and colleagues have been influential in promoting the possibility of two genetic paths in the development of alcoholism. As discussed in the section on adoption studies, Cloninger has advanced the dichomotomy of Type I and Type II inheritance patterns. The following theory has been advanced. Type I male alcoholics often have mothers who were alcoholics as well as fathers who were alcoholic. The form of alcoholism displayed by the Type Is is believed to be later in onset, less severe, and not as heavily associated with criminal misconduct. Environmental factors will heavily influence whether this type of genotype is expressed in alcoholic drinking. In contrast to Type Is are type IIs. Type IIs do not have alcoholic mothers. This genetic path is believed to be limited to males. The female genotype is expressed as somatization. The form of alcoholism displayed by Type II is severe, early onset, and heavily associated with criminal activity. Environmental factors are less influential in determining whether this genotype will be expressed in alcoholic drinking.

In a later paper, Cloninger (1987a) has attempted to link Type I and Type II with some of the earlier typologies advanced by Jellinek. Cloninger's suggests that Type IIs manifest an inability to abstain. That is, their drinking will be of the daily variety (Jellinek's Delta alcoholics). Cloninger suggests that the Type Is manifest an inability to regulate intake such that loss of control and binging is likely (Jellinek's Gamma or Epsilon alcoholic).

In addition to further speculating on drinking patterns, Cloninger (1987a) has advanced differences in temperament between the two types. He suggests that the Type Is are high in harm avoidance, somewhat neurotic and fearful, high in reward dependence, and low in novelty seeking. Type IIs are thrill seeking and high in novelty seeking, low in reward dependence, and low in harm avoidance.

In his 1987b publication, Cloninger discusses assessment devices for measuring novelty seeking, reward dependence, and harm avoidance, his Tridimensional Personality measure.

In summary, Cloninger's theory contains a number of axioms. The Type I alcoholics are linked with a particular temperament (depression devoid of thrill seeking), an inheritance that can manifest in either male or female alcoholism, and is linked with a loss of control and binging. The type II alcoholics are linked with a unique temperament (gregarious, thrill seeking), an inheritance that can manifest in male but not female alcoholism, and is linked with an inability to abstain.

Comment

Some of the axioms of Cloninger's theory are consistent with the findings of others. For example, Cloninger's dichotomy of temperaments into those who are depressed and neurotic vs. those who are thrill seeking and gregarious conform to the dichotomies which have been advanced elsewhere. Cloninger's theorizing regarding two types of alcoholics does correspond with the findings and thinking of others. In developing his MMPI scale (MacAndrew scale), Craig MacAndrew tapped into a similar dimension as Cloninger's novelty seeking. About 80% of alcoholics conform to a novelty seeking pattern, that is they are identified by their MacAndrew scale scores. In contrast to the high MacAndrew-novelty seekers, MacAndrew found that those alcoholics who were not high scorers on the MacAndrew were depressed, neurotic types, possibly fitting Cloninger's high harm avoidance, Type I pattern (MacAndrew, 1981). Cloninger's dimensions also correspond with Schuckit's categories of primary depression/secondary alcoholism vs. primary alcoholism categories (Schuckit, 1986). Although Schuckit did not describe the temperamental style of the primary alcoholic, he did recognize the uniqueness of the depressive types.

Recognizing that some alcoholics definitely fall into the category of primary depressed, whereas others fall into the high MacAndrew pattern is a less global notion than the network of ideas which Cloninger is advancing. He ties in the types (depressive, high harm avoidance alcoholic vs. novelty seeking alcoholic) with the presumed dichotomy of alcoholics from his adoption study in Sweden. It should be noted that the Swedish adoptees were never assessed on the various personality dimensions. These Swedish adoptees were not assessed on Cloninger's novelty seeking, reward dependence, harm avoidance scales nor on the MacAndrew scale. The hypothesis of linking personality descriptions with clusters of adoptees is intriguing, but cannot be believed unless it is tested.

Cloninger also speculates that daily drinking will be more characteristic of the drinking of the low harm avoidance, high novelty seeking alcoholics (Type IIs). Binging and loss of control will be more characteristic of the drinking of neurotic, high harm avoidance types alcoholics (Type Is). There are very few data relevant to this point. Information on drinking patterns discussed in the chapter on personality (Vol. I, Chapter 4) suggests that binging is a later life adjustment. Primary alcoholics, many of whom are probably high MacAndrew scale scorers, arrive at a point in life, when they decide to quit daily drinking. Their binges represent an unsuccessful attempt to maintain sobriety. There are probably a good number of novelty seeking type alcoholics who eventually arrive at a binge, loss of control style. This is inconsistent with Cloninger's theory. Research should certainly be conducted to determine whether those who are high in harm avoidance, high in reward dependence, low in novelty seeking, who score low on the MacAndrew, and might fit a Schuckit category of primary depressive/secondary alcoholism are more likely to display loss of control or to be bingers than they are to be daily consumers as Cloninger suggests.

Cloninger's theory does address the issue of female alcoholism. The theory links female alcoholism with the Type I temperament, that is the high harm avoidance, high reward dependence, low novelty seeking types. The Type Is conforms to the primary depressed/secondary alcoholics. There are data consistent with aspects of Cloninger's theorizing. Schuckit and Morrissey (1979) has found that the percentage of primary depressives is much greater in female alcoholics than in male samples. It is further known that primary depression/secondary alcoholism develops later in life (Schuckit, 1986). The genetic pathways for primary alcoholism is probably different from primary depression/secondary alcoholism. Hence, the relatives primary depressive/secondary alcoholics are more likely to also be primary depressive/secondary alcoholics than they are to be primary alcoholics. They can be expected to exhibit the features of primary depression/secondary alcoholism, viz., later onset alcoholism.

In comparing relatives of female alcoholics vs. relatives of male alcoholics or comparing female alcoholics vs. male alcoholics may reflect differences between primary depressive/secondary alcoholics and primary alcoholics. In fact a study by Gilligan et al. (1988) found that the male alcoholic relatives of female alcoholics more often exhibit late onset alcoholism with fewer ASP features. The findings from the Gilligan et al. (1988) study in which alcoholic relatives of female alcoholics were compared to alcoholic relatives of male alcoholics may well reflect differences attributable to secondary types vs. primary types.

The fact that primary depression/secondary alcoholism are more likely to be seen in females conforms to Cloninger's theory. However, the critical question is whether there are primary alcoholic women who temperamentally are high MacAndrew scorers, are novelty seekers, and who are low in harm avoidance. Schuckit and Morrissey's (1976) discussion of sociopathic alcoholic females who run afowl of the law and display an early onset pattern suggests that such female alcoholics exist. Research in which the relatives of these women are examined should be conducted. Will the alcoholic male relatives of these sociopathic/alcoholic women conform to the pattern of high harm avoidance/low novelty seeking pattern/high reward dependence or the pattern of the low harm avoidance/high novelty seeking pattern/low reward dependence? Will they display early onset or late onset alcoholism? Will they also display disruptive, illegal activity? These questions should be investigated.

FURTHER COMMENTS ON WOMEN

The twin and adoption studies have not firmly established the case for inheritance of alcoholism in women. In those cases in which there is an association between alcoholism in the parent and alcoholism in the adopted out daughter, the possibility of increased postnatal exposure to a drinking mother was not ruled out.

There is some tentative suggestion that maternal alcoholism, possibly due to gestational drinking, differentially impacts females. Miller and Jang (1977) report that maternal alcoholism seemed to increase the rate of alcoholism in daughters more than sons. Unfortunately no tests of significance were performed in the Miller and Jang study, however. The findings of Bohman et al. (1981) speak against the idea that female offspring will be influenced to a greater extent than male offspring by their mother's alcoholism. The Bohman et al. (1981) study did not find differential sensitivity between the sexes to mother's alcoholism, although daughters alcoholism was not found to increase as a function of father's alcoholism. (Bohman et al., 1981, found that mother's alcoholism increased the risk for alcoholism in females although father's alcoholism did not. For male adoptees, either parents drinking increased the risk for male alcoholism.) The animal literature does, however, suggest that female pups are more heavily impacted by maternal drinking during gestation than are the male pups (Bohman et al., 1981). There has been little specific investigation of how drinking during the gestational period or mother's alcoholism differentially impacts the sexes. It may be that females may be more vulnerable to the impact of particular gestational or post gestational environment than are males. This issue deserves further investigation.

Although inheritance of female alcoholism has not been established, the evidence suggests that female offspring of alcoholics share some of the unique characteristics as their FHP brothers. For example, it has been established that they derive a stress dampening effect from alcohol as do the male FHPs (Levenson et al., 1987). Perhaps they exhibit additional facets of the cluster of traits identified in male offspring of alcoholics. It may be that these traits will advance excessive drinking in the same way in which they mediate excessive drinking in males.

Assuming the case for inheritance of female alcoholism given the same type of genes which predispose in males, some have raised the possibility that women require more genetic predisposition toward alcoholism than men in order to reach a threshold for the expression of alcoholism (Cloninger et al., 1978). To investigate the issue researchers have compared the incidence of familial alcoholism in samples of relatives of female alcoholic probands vs. male alcoholic probands. Some have found that female alcoholics have significantly more extensive family histories than do male alcoholics (Jones, 1972; Lisansky, 1957; McKenna & Pickens, 1981; Rathod & Thomson, 1971; Schuckit et al., 1969). Others have not found significant differences (Cloninger et al. 1978; Dahlgren, 1978; Hoffman & Noem, 1975; Stabenau & Hesselbrock, 1983; Winokur et al., 1970). There is a problem in interpreting these findings. In studies investigating the family history of alcoholics, often the proband is relied upon to report the number of alcoholics relatives in the family. It is known that women, regardless of their drinking habits, report more alcoholic relatives than do men (Midanik, 1983). It seems to be the case that women have a lower threshold for deciding that an individual is alcoholic than do men. As such, those studies in which female alcoholics are found to have a more extensive history than do male alcoholics must be regarded with suspicion. Hence, the familial penetrance data does not strongly support the idea that women require greater genetic liability in order to develop alcoholism.

There is a fact that can be summoned in building the case that women require the *same* rather than greater quantative genetic loading to reach a threshold for the expression of alcoholism as men (Cloninger et al., 1978). Given exposure to heavy drinking, the same percentage of females will become alcoholic as males (Robins, Bates, & O'Neal, 1962). According to Cloninger et al. (1978) this is a reliable finding, although there are exceptions (Lewis et al., 1983). Assuming the reliability of the finding, the attribution of the higher rate of alcoholism in men to differential cultural exposure rather than differential genetic liability is suggested.

Irrespective of whether female alcoholism is inherited, is the question of whether and how mothers transmit alcoholism to their sons. Like the Bohman et al. (1981), Reich et al. (1988) found that there was no difference in the male offspring's risk of developing alcoholism as a function of whether the alcoholic parent was the mother or the father. Cruz-Coke and Varela (1966) advanced the possibility that alcoholism is inherited in an X-recessive gene pattern. Kaij and Dock (1975) have presented evidence ruling out this possibility. The grandsons of alcoholics have the same incidence of alcoholism irrespective of whether their alcoholic grandfather was a maternal or paternal grandfather. Apparently, the Y chromosome from the alcoholic paternal grandfather, passed on to the son, and then to the grandson can serve as a vehicle for alcoholism transmission. The Kaij and Dock study further suggests that women do pass on a genetic contribution to their sons.

SUMMARY

Twin and adoption studies support the inheritance of alcoholism. It is yet unknown whether inheritance occurs for both sexes and whether the alcoholism which manifests without antisocial behavior is also inherited. There is a great deal of evidence that offspring of alcoholics are more likely to be hyperactive as children. As adults they are more likely to be high MacAndrew scorers which captures gregariousness, high energy, and orientation toward adventure. Although there are many unanswered questions about transmission, there is enough information to enable identification of those FHP individuals who are at highest risk. Perhaps knowing which group for whom prevention efforts should be most assiduous, is the more important issue in this research enterprise.

REFERENCES

Abelsohn, D. S., & van der Spuy. (1978). The age variable in alcoholism. *Journal of Studies on Alcohol, 39,* 800–808.

Alexopoulous, G. S., Lieberman, K. W., & Frances, R. J. (1983). Platelet MAO activity in alcoholic patients and their first-degree relatives. *American Journal of Psychiatry, 140,* 1501–1504.

Alexopoulous, G. S., Lieberman, K. W., Frances, R., & Stokes, P. E. (1981). Platelet MAO during the alcohol withdrawal syndrome. *American Journal of Psychiatry, 138,* 1254–1255.

Alterman, A. I., Bridges, K. R., & Tarter, R. E. (1986a). Drinking behavior of high risk college men: contradictory preliminary findings. *Alcoholism: Clinical and Experimental Research, 10,* 305–310.

Alterman, A. I., Bridges, R., & Tarter, R. E. (1986b). The influence of both drinking and familial risk statuses on cognitive functioning of social drinkers. *Alcoholism: Clinical and Experimental Research, 10,* 448–451.

Alterman, A. I., Petrarulo, E., Tarter, R., & McGowan, J. R. (1982). Hyperactivity and alcoholism: Familial and behavioral correlates. *Addictive Behaviors, 7,* 413–421.

Alterman, A. I., Searles, J. S., & Hall, J. G. (1989). Failure to find differences in drinking behavior as a function of familial risk for alcoholism: A replication. *Journal of Abnormal Psychology, 98,* 50–53.

Alterman, A. I., & Tarter, R. E. (1983). The transmission of psychological vulnerability. Implications for alcoholism etiology. *Journal of Nervous and Mental Disease, 171,* 147–154.

Alterman, A. I., Tarter, R. E., Baughman, T. G., Bober, B. A., & Fabian, S. A. (1985). Differentiation of alcoholics high and low in childhood hyperactivity. *Drug and Alcohol Dependency, 15,* 111–121.

Amark, C. (1951). *A study in alcoholism. Clinical, social-psychiatric, and genetic investigations.* Stockholm: Psychiatric Clinic of Korolinska Institutes.

Amit, Z., Smith, B. R., Brown, Z. W., & Williams, R. L. (1982). An examination of the role of TIQ alkaloids in alcohol intake: Reinforcers, satiety agents or artifacts. In F. Bloom, J. Barchas, M. Sandler, & E. Usdin (Eds.), *Beta-carbonlines and tetrahydroisoquinolines* (pp 345–364). New York: Alan R. Liss.

Arkonac, O., Guze, S. B. (1963). A family study of hysteria. *New England Journal of Medicine, 268,* 239–242.

Aronson, H., & Gilbert, A. (1963). Preadolescent sons of male alcoholics. An experimental study of personality patterning. *Archives of General Psychiatry, 8,* 47–53.

Arria, A. M., Tarter, R. E., Williams, R. T., & Van Thiel, D. H. (1990). Early onset of non-alcoholic cirrhosis in patients with familial alcoholism. *Alcoholism: Clinical and Experimental Research, 14,* 1–5.

Atkinson, R. M., Turner, J. A., Kofoed, L. L., & Tolson, R. L. (1985). Early versus late onset alcoholism in older persons: Preliminary findings. *Alcoholism: Clinical and Experimental Research, 9,* 513–515.

Bakan, P. (1973). Left-handedness and alcoholism. *Perceptual and Motor Skills, 36,* 514.

Baribeau, J. M. C., Braun, C. M. J., & Dube, R. (1986). Effects of alcohol intoxication on visuospatial and verbal-contextual tests of emotion discrimination in familial risk of alcoholism. *Alcoholism: Clinical and Experimental Research, 19,* 496–499.

Beardslee, W. R., & Vaillant, G. E. (1984). Prospective prediction of alcoholism and psychopathology. *Journal of Studies on Alcohol, 45,* 503.

Begleiter, H., Porjesz, B., Bihari, B., & Kissin, B. (1984). Event-related brain potentials in boys at risk for alcoholism. *Science, 225,* 1493–1496.

Behar, D., Berg, C. J., Rapoport, J. L., Nelson, W., Linnoila, M., Cohen, M., Bozevich, C., & Marshall, T. (1983). Behavioral and physiological effects of ethanol in high-risk and control children: A pilot study. *Alcoholism: Clinical and Experimental Research, 7,* 404–410.

Bennett, L.A., Wolin S. J., & Reiss, D. (1988). Cognitive, behavioral, and emotional problems among school age children of alcoholic parents. *American Journal of Psychiatry, 145*, 185–190.

Blane, H. T., & Barry, H. (1973). Birth order and alcoholism. *Quarterly Journal of Studies on Alcohol, 34*, 837–852.

Block, J., & Haan, N. (1971). *Lives through Time*. Berkeley, CA: Bancroft Books.

Blum, K., Noble, E. P., Sheridan, P. J., Montgomery, A., Ritchie, T., Jagadeeswaran, P., Nogami, H., Briggs, A. H., & Cohn, M. B. (1990). Allelic association of human dopamine D2 receptor gene in alcoholism. *Journal of the American Medical Association, 263*, 2055–2060.

Bohman, M. (1978). Some genetic aspects of alcoholism and criminality. *Archives of General Psychiatry, 35*, 269–276.

Bohman, M., Cloninger, C. R., Sigvardsson, S., & von Knorring, A. L. (1982). Predisposition to petty criminality in Swedish adoptees I. Genetic and environmental heterogeneity. *Archives of General Psychiatry, 39*, 1233–1241.

Bohman, M., Cloninger, C. R., von Knorring, A. L., & Sigvardsson, S. (1984). An adoption study of somatoform disorders III. Cross-fostering analysis and genetic relationship to alcoholism and criminality. *Archives of General Psychiatry, 41*, 872–878.

Bohman, M., Sigvardsson, S., & Cloninger, C. R. (1981). Maternal inheritance of alcohol abuse. *Archives of General Psychiatry, 38*, 965–969.

Brooner, R. K., Templer, D., Svikis, D. S., Schmidt, C., & Monopolis, S. (1990). Dimensions of alcoholism: A multivariate analysis. *Journal of Studies on Alcohol, 51*, 77–81.

Brown, Z. W., Amit, Z., & Rockman, G. E. (1979). Intraventricular self-administration of acetaldehyde, but not ethanol, in naive laboratory rats. *Psychopharmacology, 64*, 271–276.

Brown, Z. W., Amit, Z., Smith, B. R., Sutherland, A., & Selvaggi, N. (1983). Alcohol-induced euphoria enhanced by disulfiram and calcium carbimide. *Alcoholism: Clinical and Experimental Research, 7*, 276–278.

Bulik, C. M. (1987). Drug and alcohol abuse by bulimic women and their families. *American Journal of Psychiatry, 144*, 1604–1606.

Buydens-Branchey, L., Branchey, M. H., & Noumair, D., S. (1989a). Age on alcoholism onset: 1. Relationship to psychopathology. *Archives of General Psychiatry, 46*, 225–231.

Buydens-Branchey, L., Branchey, M. H., Noumair, D., & Lieber, C. S. (1989b). Age of alcoholism onset: II. Relationship to susceptibility of serotonin precursor availability. *Archives of General Psychiatry, 46*, 231–236.

Cadoret, R. J. (1978a). Evidence for genetic inheritance of primary affective disorder in adoptees. *American Journal of Psychiatry, 135*, 463–466.

Cadoret, R. J. (1978b). Psychopathology in adopted-away offspring of biological parents with antisocial behavior. *Archives of General Psychiatry, 35*, 176–184.

Cadoret, R. J., & Cain, C. (1980). Sex differences in predictors of antisocial behavior in adoptees. *Archives of General Psychiatry, 37*, 1171–1175.

Cadoret, R. J., Cain, C. A., Grove, W. M. (1980). Development of alcoholism in adoptees raised apart from alcoholic biologic relatives. *Archives of General Psychiatry, 37*, 561–563.

Cadoret, R. J., Cunningham, L., Loftus, R., & Edwards, J. (1976a). Studies of adoptees from psychiatrically disturbed biologic parents. II. Temperament, hyperactive, antisocial, and developmental variables. *Journal of Pediatrics, 87*, 301–306.

Cadoret, R. J., Cunningham, L., Loftus, R., & Edwards, J. (1976b). Studies of adoptees from psychiatrically disturbed biological parents: III. Medical symptoms and illnesses in childhood and adolescence. *American Journal of Psychiatry, 133*, 1316–1318.

Cadoret, R. J., & Gath, A. (1978). Inheritance of alcoholism in adoptees. *British Journal of Psychiatry, 132*, 252–258.

Cadoret, R. J., O'Gorman, T. W., Troughton, E., & Heywood, E. (1985). Alcoholism and antisocial personality. Interrelationships, genetic and environmental factors. *Archives of General Psychiatry, 42*, 161–167.

Cadoret, R. J., Troughton, E., & O'Gorman, T. W. (1987). Genetic and environmental factors in alcohol abuse and antisocial personality. *Journal of Studies on Alcohol, 48,* 1–8.

Cadoret, R., Troughton, E., & Widmer, R. (1984). Clinical differences between antisocial and primary alcoholics. *Comprehensive Psychiatry, 25,* 1–8.

Cahalan, D., & Cisin, I. H. (1968). American drinking practices: Summary of findings from a national probability sample. *Quarterly Journal of Studies on Alcohol, 29,* 130–151.

Cantwell, D. P. (1972). Psychiatric illness in the families of hyperactive children. *Archives of General Psychiatry, 27,* 414–417.

Cantwell, D. P. (1985). Hyperactive children have grown up. What have we learned about what happens to them? *Archives of General Psychiatry, 42,* 1026–1028.

Cassidy, W. L., Flanagan, N. B., Spellman, M., Cohen, M. E. (1957). Clinical observations in manic-depressive disease: A quantitative study of one hundred manic-depressive patients and fifty medically sick controls. *Journal of the American Medical Association, 164,* 1535–1546.

Chandler, B. C., Parson, O. A., Vega, A. (1975). Autonomic functioning in alcoholics. A study of heart rate and skin conductance. *Journal of Studies on Alcohol, 36,* 566–577.

Chassin, L., Mann, L. M., & Sher, K. J. (1988). Self-awareness theory, family history of alcoholism, and adolescent alcohol involvement. *Journal of Abnormal Psychology, 97,* 206–217.

Chipperfield, B., & Vogel-Sprott, M. (1988). Family history of problem drinking among young male social drinkers: Modeling effects on alcohol consumption. *Journal of Abnormal Psychology, 97,* 423–428.

Cloninger, C. R. (1987a). Neurogenic adaptive mechanisms in alcoholism. *Science, 415,* 410–416.

Cloninger, C. R. (1987b). A systematic method of clinical description and classification of personality variants. *Archives of General Psychiatry, 44,* 573–588.

Cloninger, C. R., Bohman, M., & Sigvardsson, S. (1981). Inheritance of alcohol abuse. Cross-fostering analysis of adopted men. *Archives of General Psychiatry, 38,* 861–868.

Cloninger, C. R., Christianssen, K. O., Reich, T., Gottesman, I. (1978). Implications of sex differences in the prevalences of antisocial personality, alcoholism, and criminality for familial transmission. *Archives of General Psychiatry, 35,* 941–951.

Cloninger, C. R., Reich, T., & Guze, S. B. (1975). The multifactorial model of disease transmission: III. Familial relationship between sociopathy and hysteria (Briquet's syndrome). *British Journal of Psychiatry, 127,* 23–32.

Cloninger, C. R., Sigvardsson, S., & Bohman, M. (1988). Childhood personality predicts alcohol abuse in young adults. *Alcoholism: Clinical and Experimental Research, 12,* 494–505.

Cloninger, C. R., Sigvardsson, S., von Knorring, A. L., & Bohman, M. (1984). An adoption study of somatoform disorders II. Identification of two discrete somatoform disorders. *Archives of General Psychiatry, 41,* 863–871.

Cotton, N. S. (1979). The familial incidence of alcoholism. A review. *Journal of Studies on Alcohol, 40,* 89–116.

Crabb, D. W., Edenberg, H. J., Bosron, W. F., & Li, T. K. (1989). Geneotypes for aldehyde dehydrogenase deficiency and alcohol sensitivity: The inactive ALDH2 allele is dominant. *Journal of Clinical Investigation, 83,* 314–316.

Crowe, R. R. (1974). An adoption study of antisocial personality. *Archives of General Psychiatry, 31,* 785–791.

Cruz-Coke, R., & Varela, A. (1966). Inheritance of alcoholism. Its association with colour-blindness. *Lancet, 1,* 282–1284.

Dahlgren, L. (1978). Female alcoholics III. Development and pattern of problem drinking. *Acta Psychiatrica Scandinavia, 57,* 325–335.

De Obaldia, R., & Parsons, O. A. (1984). Relationship of neuropsychological performance to primary alcoholism and self-reported symptoms of childhood minimal brain dysfunction. *Journal of Studies on Alcohol, 45,* 386–392.

DeTurck, K. H., & Vogel, W. H. (1982). Effects of acute ethanol on plasma and brain catecholamine levels in stressed and unstressed rats: Evidence for an ethanol-stress interaction. *Journal of Pharmacology and Experimental Therapeutics, 233,* 348–354.

De Wit, H., & McCracken, S. G. (1990). Ethanol self-administration in males with and without an alcoholic first-degree relative. *Alcoholism: Clinical and Experimental Research, 14,* 63–70.

Dolinsky, Z. S., Shaskan, E. G., & Hesselbrock, M. N. (1985). Basic aspects of blood platelet monoamine oxidase activity in hospitalized men alcoholics. *Journal of Studies on Alcohol, 46,* 81–85.

Drake, R. E., & Vaillant, G. E. (1988). Predicting alcoholism and personality disorder in a 33-year longitudinal study of children of alcoholics. *British Journal of Addiction, 83,* 799–808.

Drejer, K., Theilgaard, A., Teasdale, T. W., Schulsinger, F., & Goodwin, D. W. (1985). A prospective study of young men at high risk for alcoholism: Neuropsychological assessment. *Alcoholism: Clinical and Experimental Research, 9,* 498–502.

Earls, F., Reich, W., Jung, K. G., & Cloninger, C. R. (1988). Psychopathology in children of alcoholics and antisocial parents. *Alcoholism: Clinical and Experimental Research, 12,* 481–487.

Elmasian, R., Neville, H., Woods, D., Schuckit, M., & Bloom, F. (1982). Event-related potentials are different in individuals at high and low risk for developing alcoholism. *Proceedings of the National Academy of Science, 79,* 7900–7903.

Eriksson, C. J. P. (1980). Elevated blood acetaldehyde levels in alcoholics and their relatives: A reevaluation. *Science, 207,* 1383–1384.

Ewing, J. A., Rouse, B. A., & Mueller, R. A. (1974). Alcohol susceptibility and plasma dopamine b-hydroxylase activity. *Research Communications in Chemical Pathology and Pharmacology, 8,* 551–554.

Ewing, J. A., Rouse, B. A., Mueller, R. A., & Mills, K. C. (1975). Alcohol as a euphoriant drug: searching for a neurochemical basis. *Annals of the New York Academy of Sciences, 273,* 159–166.

Fillmore, K. M. (1974). Drinking and problem drinking in early adulthood and middle age: An exploratory 20-year follow-up study. *Quarterly Journal of Studies on Alcohol, 35,* 819–840.

Fillmore, K. M. (1975). Relationships between specific drinking problems in early adulthood and middle age: An exploratory 20- year follow-up study. *Journal of Studies on Alcohol, 36,* 882–907.

Finn, P. R., & Pihl, R. O. (1987). Men at high risk for alcoholism: The effect of alcohol on cardiovascular response to unavoidable shock. *Journal of Abnormal Psychology, 96,* 230–236.

Finn, P. R., & Pihl, R. (1988). Risk for alcoholism: A comparison between two different groups of sons of alcoholics on cardiovascular reactivity and sensitivity to alcohol. *Alcoholism: Clinical and Experimental Research, 12,* 742–748.

Finn, P. R., Zeitouni, N. C., & Pihl, R. O. (1990). Effects of alcohol on psychophysiological hyperactivity to nonaversive and aversive stimuli in men at high risk for alcoholism. *Journal of Abnormal Psychology, 99,* 79–85.

Foulds, G. A., & Hassall, C. (1969). The significance of age of onset and excessive drinking in male alcoholics. *British Journal of Psychiatry, 115,* 1027–1032.

Frances, R. J., Bucky, S., & Alexopoulous, G. S. (1984). Outcome study of familial and non-familial alcoholism. *American Journal of Psychiatry, 141,* 1469–1471.

Frances, R. J., Timm, S., Bucky, S. (1980). Studies of familial and nonfamilial alcoholism. *Archives of General Psychiatry, 37,* 564–566.

Gabrielli, W. F., & Mednick, S. A. (1983). Intellectual performance in children of alcoholics. *Journal of Nervous and Mental Disease, 171,* 444–447.

Gabrielli, W. F., Mednick, S. A., Volavka, J., Pollock, J., Schulsinger, F., & Itil, T. M. (1982). Electroencephalograms in children of alcoholic fathers. *Psychophysiology, 19,* 404–407.

Gabrielli, W. F., & Plomin, R. (1985). Drinking behavior in the Colorado adoptee and twin sample. *Journal of Studies on Alcohol, 46,* 24–31.

Gershon, E. S., Hamovit, J., Guroff, J., Dibble, E., Leckman, J. F., Sceery, W., Targum, S. D., Nurnberger, J. I., Jr., Golden, L. R., & Bunney, W. L. S. Jr. (1982). A family study of schizoaffective, bipolar I, Bipolar II, unipolar, and normal controls. *Archives of General Psychiatry, 39,* 1157–1167.

Geshwind, N., & Behan, P. (1982). Left-handedness: Association with immune disease, migraine, and developmental learning disorder. *Proceedings of the National Academy of Science, 79,* 5097–5100.

Gilligan, S. B., Reich, T., & Cloninger, C. R. (1988). Alcohol-related symptoms in heterogeneous families of hospitalized alcoholics. *Alcoholism: Clinical and Experimental Research, 12,* 671–678.

Gittleman, R., Mannuzza, S., Shenker, R., & Bonagura, N. (1985). Hyperactive boys almost grown up I. Psychiatric status. *Archives of General Psychiatry, 42,* 937–947.

Glass, G. V., & Hakstian, A. R. (1969). Measures of association in comparative experiments: Their development and interpretation. *American Educational Research Journal, 6,* 403–414.

Glatt, M. M., & Hills, D. R. (1968). Alcohol abuse and alcoholism in the young. *British Journal of Addictions, 63,* 183–191.

Gomberg, E. S. L. (1982). The young male alcoholic. A pilot study. *Journal of Studies on Alcohol, 43,* 683–701.

Goodwin, D. W. (1979). Alcoholism and Heredity. A review and a hypothesis. *Archives of General Psychiatry, 36,* 57–61.

Goodwin, D. W., Crane, J. B., & Guze, S. B. (1971). Felons who drink. An 8-year follow-up. *Quarterly Journal of Studies on Alcohol, 32,* 136–147.

Goodwin, D. W., Schulsinger, F., Hermansen, L. Guze, S. B., & Winokur, G. (1973). Alcohol problems in adoptees raised apart from alcoholic biological parents. *Archives of General Psychiatry, 28,* 238–243.

Goodwin, D. W., Schulsinger, F., Hermansen, L., Guze, S. B., & Winokur, G. (1975). Alcoholism and the hyperactive child syndrome. *Journal of Nervous and Mental Disease, 160,* 349–353.

Goodwin, D. W., Schulsinger, F., Knop, J., Mednick, S., & Guze, S. B. (1977a). Psychopathology in adopted and nonadopted daughters of alcoholics. *Archives of General Psychiatry, 34,* 1005–1009.

Goodwin, D. W., Schulsinger, F., Knop, J., Mednick, S., & Guze, S. B. (1977b). Alcoholism and depression in adopted-out daughters of alcoholics. *Archives of General Psychiatry, 34,* 751–755.

Goodwin, D. W., Schulsinger, F., Moller, N., Hermansen, L., Winokur, G., & Guze, S. B. (1974). Drinking problems in adopted and nonadopted sons of alcoholics. *Archives of General Psychiatry, 31,* 164–169.

Gorenstein, E. E., & Newman, J. P. (1980). Disinhibitory psychopathology: A new perspective and a model for research. *Psychological Review, 87,* 301–315.

Gurling, H. M. D., Murray, R. M., & Clifford, C. A. (1981). Investigations into the genetics of alcohol dependence and into its effects on brain function. In L. Gedda, P. Parisi, & W. E. Nance (Eds.), *Twin Research 3. Proceedings of the Third International Congress on Twin Studies* (pp. 77–87). New York: Alan R. Liss.

Guyton, A. C. (1981). *Textbook of medical physiology.* Philadelphia: Saunders.

Guze, S. B. (1975). The validity and significance of the clinical diagnosis of hysteria (Briquet's syndrome). *American Journal of Psychiatry, 132,* 138–141.

Guze, S. B. Goodwin, D. W., & Crane, J. B. (1969). Criminality and psychiatric disorders. *Archives of General Psychiatry, 20,* 583–591.

Guze, S. B., Goodwin, D. W., & Crane, J. B. (1970), A psychiatric study of the wives of convicted felons: An example of assortative mating. *American Journal of Psychiatry, 126,* 1115–118.

Guze, S. B., Tuason, V. B., Gatfield, P. ., Stewart, M. A., & Picken, B. (1962). Psychiatric illness and crime with particular reference to alcoholism: A study of 233 criminals. *Journal of Nervous and Mental Disease, 134,* 512–521.

Guze, S. B., Woodruff, R. A., & Clayton, P. J. (1971). Hysteria and antisocial behavior: Further evidence of an association. *American Journal of Psychiatry, 127*, 957–960.

Haberman, P. W. (1966). Childhood symptoms in children of alcoholics and comparison group parents. *Journal of Marriage and the Family, 28*, 152–154.

Haier, R. J., Buchsbaum, M. S., Murphy, D. L., Gottesman, I. I., & Coursey, R. D. (1980). Psychiatric vulnerability, monoamine oxidase, and the average evoked potential. *Archives of General Psychiatry, 37*, 340–345.

Harris, E. L., Noyes, R., Crowe, R. R., & Chaudhry, D. R. (1983). Family study of agoraphobia. Report of a pilot study. *Archives of General Psychiatry, 40*, 1061–1064.

Hassall, C. (1968). A controlled study of the characteristics of young male alcoholics. *British Journal of Addictions, 63*, 193–201.

Hasin, D. S., Grant, B. F., & Endicott, J. (1988). Severity of alcohol dependence and social/occupational problems: Relationship to clinical and familial history. *Alcoholism: Clinical and Experimental Research, 12*, 660–664.

Heath, A. C., Jardine, R., & Martin, N. G. (1989). Interactive effects of genotype and social environment on alcohol consumption in female twins. *Journal of Studies on Alcohol, 50*, 38–48.

Heath, A. C., & Martin, N. G. (1988). Teenage alcohol use in Australian twin register: Genetic and social determinants of starting to drink. *Alcoholism: Clinical and Experimental Research, 12*, 735–741.

Hechtman, L., Weiss, G., & Perlman, T. (1984). Hyperactives as young adults: Past and current substance abuse and antisocial behavior. *American Journal of Orthopsychiatry, 54*, 415–425.

Hegedus, A. M., Alterman, A. I., & Tarter, R. E. (1984). Learning achievement in sons of alcoholics. *Alcoholism: Clinical and Experimental Research, 8*, 330–333.

Hegedus, A. M., Tarter, R. E., Hill, S. Y., Jacob, T., & Winsten, N. E. (1984). Static ataxia: A possible marker for alcoholism. *Alcoholism: Clinical and Experimental Research, 8*, 580–582.

Hennecke, L. (1984). Stimulus augmenting and field dependence in children of alcoholic fathers. *Journal of Studies on Alcohol, 45*, 486–492.

Herzog, T. R., & Weintraub, D. J. (1982). Roundup time at personality ranch: Branding the elusive augmenters and reducers. *Journal of Personality and Social Psychology, 42*, 729–737.

Hesselbrock, V. M., Stabenau, J. R., & Hesselbrock, M. N. (1985a). Minimal brain dysfunction and neuropsychological test performance in offspring of alcoholics. In M. Galanter (Ed.), *Recent Developments in Alcoholism* (pp. 65–82). New York: Plenum Press.

Hesselbrock, V. M., Hesselbrock, N. N., & Stabenau, J. R. (1985b). Alcoholism in men patients subtyped by family history and antisocial personality. *Journal of Studies of Alcohol, 46*, 59–64.

Hill, S. Y., Armstrong, J., Steinhauer, S. R., Baughman, T., & Zubin, J. (1987). Static ataxia as a psychobiological marker for alcoholism. *Alcoholism: Clinical and Experimental Research, 11*, 345–348.

Hill, S. Y., Aston, C. & Rabin, B. (1988). Suggestive evidence of genetic linkage between alcoholism and MNS blood groups. *Alcoholism: Clinical and Experimental Research, 12*, 811–814.

Hill, S. Y., Steinhauer, S., Park, J., & Zubin, J. (1990). Event-related potential characteristics in children of alcoholics from high density families. *Alcoholism: Clinical and Experimental Research, 14*, 6–16.

Hill, S. Y., Steinhauer, S. R., & Zubin, J. (1987). Biological markers for alcoholism: A vulnerability model conceptualization. In P. C. Rivers (Ed.) *Alcohol and addictive behavior: Nebraska symposium on motivation, 1986*. Lincoln, NB: University of Nebraska Press.

Hoffman, H., Loper, R. G., & Kammeier, M. L. (1974). Identifying future alcoholics with MMPI alcoholism scales. *Quarterly Journal of Studies on Alcohol, 35*, 490–498.

Hoffman, H., & Noem, A. A. (1975). Alcoholism among parents of male and female alcoholics. *Psychological Reports, 36*, 322.

Hrubec, Z., & Omenn, G. S. (1981). Evidence of genetic predisposition to alcoholic cirrhosis and psychosis: Twin concordances of alcoholism and its biological end points by zygosity among male veterans. *Alcoholism: Clinical and Experimental Research, 5*. 207–215.

Jacob, T., & Leonard, K. (1986). Psychosocial functioning in children of alcoholic fathers, depressed fathers and control fathers. *Journal of Studies on Alcohol, 47* 373–380.

James, N. M., & Chapman, C. J. (1975). A genetic study of bipolar affective disorder. *British Journal of Psychiatry, 126,* 449–456.

Johnson, J. L., & Rolf, J. E. (1988). Cognitive functioning in children from alcoholic and nonalcoholic families. *British Journal of Addiction, 83,* 849–857.

Jones, M. C. (1968). Personality correlates and antecedents of drinking patterns in adult males. *Journal of Consulting and Clinical Psychology, 32,* 2–12.

Jones, M. C. (1971). Personality antecedents and correlates of drinking patterns in women. *Journal of Consulting and Clinical Psychology, 36,* 61–69.

Jones, M. C. (1981). Midlife drinking patterns: Correlates and antecendents. In D. H. Eichorn, J. A. Clausen, N. Haan, M. P. Honzik, & P. H. Mussen (Eds.) *Present and Past Middle Life.* (pp. 223–243). New York: Academic Press.

Jones, R. W. (1972). Alcoholism among relatives of alcoholic patients. *Quarterly Journal of Studies on Alcohol, 33,* 810.

Kaij, L. (1960). *Alcoholism in Twins: Studies on the Etiology and Sequels of Abuse of Alcohol.* Stockholm: Almquist & Wiksell.

Kaij, L., & Dock, J. (1975). Grandsons of alcoholics. A test of sex-linked transmission of alcohol abuse. *Archives of General Psychiatry, 32,* 1379–1381.

Kammeier, M. L., Hoffman, H., & Loper, R. G. (1973). Personality characteristics of alcoholics as college freshman and at time of treatment. *Quarterly Journal of Studies on Alcohol, 34,* 390–399.

Kaprio, J., Koskenvuo, M., Langinvainio, H., Romanov, K., Sarna, S., & Rose, R. J. (1987). Genetic influences on use and abuse of alcohol: A study of 5638 adult Finnish twin brothers. *Alcoholism: Clinical and Experimental Research, 11,* 349–356.

Knop, J., Teasdale, T. W., Schulsinger, F., & Goodwin, D. W. (1985), Prospective study of young men at high risk for alcoholism: School and achievement. *Journal of Studies on Alcohol, 46,* 273–278.

Kofoed, L. L., Tolson, R. L., Atkinson, R. M., Toth, R. L., & Turner, J. A. (1987). Treatment compliance of older alcoholics: An elderly specific approach is superior to "mainstreaming". *Journal of Studies on Alcohol, 48,* 47–51.

Lee, G. P., & DiClimente, C. C. (1985). Age of onset versus duration of problem drinking on the Alcohol Use Inventory. *Journal of Studies on Alcohol, 46,* 398–402.

Levenson, R. W., Oyama, O. N., & Meek, P. S. (1987). Greater reinforcement form alcohol for those at risk: Parental risk, personality risk, and sex. *Journal of Abnormal Psychology, 96,* 242–253.

Levenson, R. W., Sher, K. J., Grossman, L. M., Newman, J., & Newlin, D. B. (1980). Alcohol and stress response dampening: Pharmacological effects, expectancy, and tension reduction. *Journal of Abnormal Psychology, 89,* 528–538.

Lewis, C. E., Helzer, J., Cloninger, C. R., Croughan, J., & Whitman, B. Y. (1982). Psychiatric diagnostic predispositions to alcoholism. *Comprehensive Psychiatry, 23,* 451–461.

Lewis, C. E., Rice, J., Andreasen, N., Endicott, J., & Rochberg, N. (1987). The antisocial and the nonantisocial alcoholic: Clinical distinctions in men with major unipolar depression. *Alcoholism: Clinical and Experimental Research, 11,* 176–182.

Lewis, C. R., Rice, J., & Helzer, J. E. (1983). Diagnostic interactions. Alcoholism and antisocial personality. *Journal of Nervous and Mental Disease, 171,* 105–113.

Lex, B. W., Lukas, S. E., Greenwald, N. E., & Mendelson, J. H. (1988). Alcohol-induced changes in body sway in women at risk for alcoholism: A pilot study. *Journal of Studies on Alcohol, 46,* 346–356.

Li, T. K., Lumeng, L., McBride, W. J., & Murphy, J. M. (1986). Rodent lines selected for factors effecting alcohol consumption. In K. O. Lindros, R. Ylikahri, & K. Kiianmaa (Eds.) *Advances in biomedical alcohol research.* New York: Pergamon Press.

Li, T. K., Lumeng, L., McBride, W., Murphy, J. M., Froehlich, J., Morzorati, S.(1989). Pharmacology of alcohol preference in rodents. In E. Gordis, B. Tabakoff, & M. Linnoila (Eds.), *Alcohol research from bench to bedside* (pp. 73–86). New York: Haworth Press.

Lilienfeld, S. O., VanValkenberg, C., Larntz, K., & Akisal, H. S. (1986). The relationship of histrionic personality disorder to antisocial personality and somatization disorder. *American Journal of Psychiatry, 143,* 718–722.

Linnoila, M. (1989). Neurotransmitters and alcoholism: Methodological issues. In E. Gordis, B. Tabakoff, & M. Linnoila (Eds.) *Alcohol research: From bench to bedside* (pp. 17–24). New York: Haworth Press.

Linnoila, M., De Jong, J., & Virkkunen, M. (1989). Family history of alcoholism in violent offenders and impulsive fire setters. *Archives of General Psychiatry, 46,* 613–616.

Lipscomb, T. R., Carpenter, J. A., & Nathan, P. E. (1979). Static ataxia: a predictor of alcoholism. *British Journal of Addictions, 74,* 289–294.

Lipscomb, T. R., & Nathan, P. E. (1980). Blood alcohol level discrimination. *Archives of General Psychiatry, 37,* 571–576.

Lisansky, E. S. (1957). Alcoholism in women: Social and psychological concomitants. *Quarterly Journal of Studies on Alcohol, 18,* 588–623.

Lishman, W. A. (1987). *Organic Psychiatry: The psychological consequences of cerebral disorder.* Oxford: Blackwell Scientific Publications.

Littrell, J. L. (1988). The Swedish studies of the adopted children of alcoholics. *Journal of Studies on Alcohol, 49,* 491–499.

Loehlin, J. C. (1972). An analysis of alcohol-related questionnaire items from the National Merit twin study. *Annals of the New York Academy of Science, 197,* 117–120.

London, W. P. (1985). Treatment outcome of left-handed versus right-handed alcoholic men. *Alcoholism: Clinical and Experimental Research, 9,* 503–504.

London, W. P., Kibbee, R., & Holt, L. (1985). Handedness and alcoholism. *The Journal of Nervous and Mental Disease, 173,* 570–572.

Loper, R. G., Kammeier, M. L., & Hoffman, H. (1973). MMPI characteristics of college freshman males who later became alcoholics. *Journal of Abnormal Psychology, 82,* 159–162.

Loranger, A. W., & Tulis, E. H. (1985). Family history of in alcoholism in borderline personality disorder. *Archives of General Psychiatry, 42,* 153–157.

Lovallo, W., Parsons, O. A., & Holloway, F. A. (1973). Autonomic arousal in normal, alcoholic, and brain-damaged subjects as measured by the plethysmograph response to cold pressor stimulation. *Psychophysiology, 10,* 166–176.

Ludwig, A. M., Cain, R. B., & Wikler, A. (1977). Stimulus intensity modulation and alcohol consumption. *Journal of Studies on Alcohol, 38,* 2049–2056.

MacAndrew, C. (1981). What the MAC scale tells us about men alcoholics. An interpretive review. *Journal of Studies on Alcohol, 42,* 604–6625.

Maccoby, E. E., Doering, C. H., Jacklin, C. N., & Kraemer, H. (1979). Concentrations of sex hormones in umbilical-cord blood: Their relation to sex and birth order in infants. *Child Development, 50,* 632–642.

Major, L. F., Murphy, D. L. (1978). Platelet and plasma amine oxidase activity in alcoholic individuals. *British Journal of Psychiatry, 132,* 548–545.

Mann, L. M., Chassin, L., & Sher, K. J. (1987). Alcohol expectancies and the risk for alcoholism. *Journal of Consulting and Clinical Psychology, 55,* 411–417.

Marlatt, G. A., & Rohsenow, D. J. (1980). Cognitive processes in alcohol use: Expectancy and the balanced placebo design. In N. K. Mello (Ed.), *Advances in substance abuse: Behavioral and biological research* (pp. 159–199). Greenwich, Conn.: JAI Press.

Matchett, J., & Erickson, C. (1977). Alteration of ethanol-induced changes in locomotor activity by adrenergic blockers in mices. *Psychopharmacology, 52,* 201–206.

McCord, J. (1972). Etiological factors in alcoholism: Family and personal characteristics. *Quarterly Journal of Studies on Alcohol, 33,* 1020–1027.

McCord, J. (1981). Alcoholism and criminality. Confounding and differentiating factors. *Journal of Studies on Alcohol, 42,* 739–748.

McCord, J. (1988). Identifying developmental paradigms leading to alcoholism. *Journal of Studies on Alcohol, 49,* 357–362.

McCord, W., & McCord, J. (1960). *Origins of Alcoholism.* Stanford, CA: Stanford University Press.

McCord, W., & McCord, J. (1962). A longitudinal study of the personality of alcoholics. In D. J. Pittman, & C. R. Snyder (Eds.), *Society, Culture, and Drinking Patterns* (pp. 395–412). New York: Wiley.

McKenna, T., & Pickens, R. (1981). Alcoholic children of alcoholics. *Journal of Studies on Alcohol, 42,* 1021–1029.

Mendelson, W., Johnson, N., & Stewart, M. A. (1971). Hyperactive children as teenagers: A follow-up study. *The Journal of Nervous and Mental Disease, 153,*273–279.

Merikangas, K. R., Leckman, J. F., Prusoff, B. A., Pauls, D. L., & Weissman, M. M. (1985). Familial transmission of depression and alcoholism. *Archives of General Psychiatry, 42,* 367–372.

Merikangas, K. R., Weissman, M. M., Prusoff, V. A., Pauls, D. L., & Leckman, J. F. (1985). Depressives with secondary alcoholism: Psychiatric disorders in offspring. *Journal of Studies on Alcohol, 46,* 199–204.

Midanik, L. (1983). Familial alcoholism and problem drinking in a national drinking practices survey. *Addictive Behaviors. 8,* 133–141.

Miller, D., & Jang, M. (1977). Children of alcoholics: a 20-year longitudinal study. *Social Work Research and Abstracts, 13,* 23–29.

Modell, J. G., Mountz, J. M., & Beresford, T. P. (1990). Basal ganglia/limbic striatal and thalamocortical involvement in craving and loss of control in alcoholism. *Journal of Neuropsychiatry, 2,* 123–144.

Monnelly, E. P., Hartl, E. M., & Elderkin, R. (1983). Constitutional factors predictive of alcoholism in a follow-up of delinquent boys. *Journal of Studies on Alcohol, 44,* 530–537.

Morrison, J. R., & Stewart, M. A. (1973). The psychiatric status of the legal families of adopted hyperactive children. *Archives of General Psychiatry, 28,* 888–891.

Moss, H. B., Guthrie, S., Linnoila, M. (1986). Enhanced thyrotropin response to thyrotropin releasing hormone in boys at risk for development of alcoholism. *Archives of General Psychiatry, 43,* 1137–1142.

Moss, H. B., Yao, J. K., & Maddock, J. M. (1989). Responses by sons of alcoholic fathers to alcohol and placebo drinks: Perceived mood, intoxication, and plasma protein. *Alcoholism: Clinical and Experimental Research, 13,* 252–257.

Mueller, G. C., Fleming, M. F., LeMahieu, M. A., Lybrand, G. S., & Barry, K. J. (1988). Synthesis of phosphatidylethanol-a potential marker for adult males at risk for alcoholism. *Proceedings of the National Academy of Sciences, 85,* 9778–9782.

Mullan, M. J., Gurling, H. M. D., Oppenheim, B. E., & Murray, R. M. (1986). The relationship between alcoholism and neurosis: Evidence from a twin study. *British Journal of Psychiatry, 148,* 435–441.

Munjack, D. J., & Moss, H. B. (1981). Affective disorder and alcoholism in families of agoraphobics. *Archives of General Psychiatry, 38,* 869–871.

Murray, R. M., Clifford, C. A., & Gurling, H. M. D. (1983). Twin and adoption studies: How good is the evidence for a genetic role? In M. Galanter, (Ed.), *Recent Developments in Alcoholism,* (pp. 25–48) (Vol. 1). New York: Plenum Press.

Myers, R. D., & Oblinger, M. M. (1977). Alcohol drinking in the rat induced by acute intracerebral infusion of two tetrahydroisoquinolines and a b-carboline. *Drug and Alcohol Abuse, 2,* 469–483.

Nagoshi, C. T., & Wilson, J. R. (1987). Influence of family alcoholism history on alcohol metabolism, sensitivity, and tolerance. *Alcoholism: Clinical and Experimental Research, 11,* 392–398.

Naranjo, C. A., Sellers, E. M., Roach, C. A., Woodley, D. V., Sanchez-Craig, M., & Sykora, K. (1984). Zimelidine-induced variations in alcohol intake by nondepressed heavy drinkers. *Clinical Pharmacology and the Therapeutics, 35,* 374–381.

Nasrallah, H. A., Keelor, K., & McCalley-Whitters, M. (1983). Laterality shift in alcoholic males. *Biological Psychiatry, 18,* 1065–1067.

Newlin, D. B. (1985a). The antagonistic placebo response to alcohol cues. *Alcoholism: Clinical and Experimental Research, 9,* 411–416.

Newlin, D. B. (1985b). Offspring of alcoholics have enhanced antagonistic placebo response. *Journal of Studies on Alcohol, 46,* 490–494.

Newlin D. B. (1989). Placebo responding in the same direction as alcohol in women. *Alcoholism: Clinical and Experimental Research, 13,* 36–39.

O'Gorman, P. A. (1976). Self-concept, locus of control, and perception of father in adolescents from homes with and without severe drinking problems. *Dissertation Abstracts International, 36, 5156A.* (University Microfilms No. 76–4189).

O'Malley, S. S., Maisto, S. A. (1985). Effects of family drinking history and expectancies on responses to alcohol in men. *Journal of Studies on Alcohol, 46,* 289–297.

O'Neal, P., & Robins, L. N. (1958). The relation of childhood behavior problems to adult psychiatric status: A 30-year follow-up study of 150 subjects. *American Journal of Psychiatry, 114,* 961–969.

O'Sullivan, K., Whillans, P., Daly, M., Carroll, B., Clare, A., & Cooney, J. (1983). A comparison of alcoholics with and without coexisting affective disorders. *British Journal of Psychiatry, 143,* 133–138.

Parker, F. B. (1972). Sex-role adjustment in women alcoholics. *Quarterly Journal of Studies on Alcohol, 33,* 647–657.

Parker, D. A., & Harford, T. C. (1988). Alcohol-related problems, marital disruption and depressive symptoms among adult children of alcohol abusers in the United States. *Journal of Studies on Alcohol, 49,* 306–313.

Partanan, J., Bruun, K., & Markkanen, T. (1966). *Inheritance of drinking behavior. A study on intelligence, personality, and use of alcohol of adult twins.* Helsinki: Finnish Foundation for Alcohol Studies.

Peele, S. (1986). The implications and limitations of genetic models of alcoholism and other addictions. *Journal of Studies on Alcohol, 47,* 63–73.

Penick, E. C., Powell, B. J., Bingham, S. F., Liskow, B. I., Miller, N. S. & Read, M. R. (1987). A comparative study of familial alcoholism. *Journal of Studies on Alcohol, 48,* 136–145.

Penick, E. C., Read, M. R., Crowley, P. A., & Powell, B. J. (1978). Differentiation of alcoholics by family history. *Journal of Studies on Alcohol, 39,* 1944–1948.

Petrie, A. (1967). *Individuality in pain and suffering.* Chicago: University of Chicago Press.

Pihl, R. O., Young, S. N., Ervin, F. R., & Plotnick, S. (1987). Influence of tryptophan availability on selection of alcohol and water by men. *Journal of Studies on Alcohol, 48,* 260–264.

Pishkin, V., Lovallo, W. R., & Bourne, L. E. (1985). Chronic alcoholism in males: Cognitive deficit as a function of age of onset, age, and duration. *Alcoholism: Clinical and Experimental Research, 9,* 400–406.

Pitts, F. N., & Winokur, G. (1966). Affective disorder-VII: Alcoholism and affective disorder. *Journal of Psychiatric Research, 4,* 37–50.

Polich, J., & Bloom, F. E. (1988a). Event-related potentials in individuals at high and low risk for developing alcoholism: Failure to replicate. *Alcoholism: Clinical and Experimental Research, 12,* 368–373.

Polich, J., Burns, T., & Bloom, F. E. (1988b). P300 and the risk for alcoholism: Family history, task difficulty, and gender. *Alcoholism: Clinical and Experimental Research, 12,* 248–254.

Polich, J., Haier, R. J., Buchsbaum, M., & Bloom, F. E. (1988c). Assessment of young men at risk for alcoholism with P300 from a visual discrimination task. *Journal of Studies on Alcohol. 49,* 186–190.

Pollock, V. E., Teasdale, T. W., Gabrielli, W. F., Knop, J. (1986). Subjective and objective measures of response to alcohol among young men at risk for alcoholism. *Journal of Studies on Alcohol, 47,* 297–304.

Pollock, V. E., Volavka, J., Goodwin, D. W., Mednick, S. A., Gabrielli, W. F., Knop, J., & Schulsinger, F. (1983). The EEG after alcohol administration in men at risk for alcoholism. *Archives of General Psychiatry, 40,* 857–861.

Rathod, N. H., & Thomson, I. G. (1971). Women alcoholics. A clinical study. *Quarterly Journal of Studies on Alcohol, 32,* 45–52.

Reich, T., Clayton, P. J., & Winokur, G. (1969). Family history studies: V. The genetics of mania. *American Journal of Psychiatry, 125,* 1358–1369.

Reich, T., Cloninger, C. R., Van Eerdewegh, P., Rice, J. P., & Mullaney, J. (1988). Secular trends in the familial transmission of alcoholism. *Alcoholism: Clinical and Experimental Research, 12,* 458–464.

Rimmer, J., Reich, T., & Winokur, G. (1972). Alcoholism, V. Diagnosis and clinical variation among alcoholics. *Quarterly Journal of Studies on Alcohol, 33,* 658–666.

Robins, L. N. (1966). *Deviant children grown up: A sociological and psychiatric study of sociopathic personality.* Baltimore: Williams & Wilkins.

Robins, L. N. (1978). Sturdy childhood predictors of adult antisocial behaviour: Replications from longitudinal studies. *Psychological Medicine, 8,* 611–622.

Robins, L. N., Bates, W. M., & O'Neal, P. (1962). Adult drinking patterns of former problem children. In D. J. Pittman, & C. R. Snyder (Eds.), *Society, Culture, and Drinking Patterns* (pp. 395–412). New York: John Wiley & Sons.

Roe A. (1944). The adult adjustment of children of alcoholic parents raised in foster-homes. *Quarterly Journal of Studies on Alcohol, 5,* 378–393.

Rosenberg, C. M. (1969). Young alcoholics. *British Journal of Psychiatry, 115,* 181–188.

Sandel, A., & Alcorn, J. D. (1980). Individual hemisphericity and maladaptive behaviors. *Journal of Abnormal Psychology, 89,* 514–517.

Saunders G. R., & Schuckit, M. A. (1981). MMPI scores in young men with alcoholic relatives and controls. *Journal of Nervous and Mental Disease, 169,* 456–458.

Saunders, J. B., & Williams, R. (1983). The genetics of alcoholism: Is there an inherited susceptibility to alcohol-related problems? *Alcohol and Alcoholism, 18,* 189–197.

Savoie, T. M., Emory, E. K., & Moody-Thomas, S. (1988). Acute alcohol intoxication in socially drinking female and male offspring of alcoholic fathers. *Journal of Studies on Alcohol, 49,* 430–435.

Schachter, S. (1971). *Emotion, obesity, and crime.* New York: Academic Press.

Schaeffer, K. W., Parsons, O. A., Errico, A. L. (1988). Abstracting deficits and childhood conduct disorder as a function of familial alcoholism. *Alcoholism: Clinical and Experimental Research, 12,* 617–618.

Schaeffer, K. W., Parsons, O. A., & Yohman, J. R. (1984). Neuropsychological differences between male familial and nonfamilial alcoholics and nonalcoholics. *Alcoholism: Clinical and Experimental Research, 8,* 347–351.

Schandler, S. L., Brannock, J. C., Cohen, M. J., Antick, J., & Caine, K. (1988). Visuospatial learning in elementary school children with and without a family history of alcoholism. *Journal of Studies on Alcohol, 49,* 538–545.

Schandler, S. L., Cohen, M. J., & McArthur, D. I. (1988). Event-related potentials in intoxicated and detoxified alcoholics during visuospatial learning. *Psychopharmacology, 94,* 275–283.

Schooler, C., Zahn, T., Murphy, D. L., & Buchsbaum, M. S. (1978). Psychological correlates of monoamine oxidase activity in normals. *Journal of Nervous and Mental Disease, 166,* 177–186.

Schroeder, D., & Nasrallah, H. A. (1982). High alcoholism rate in patients with essential tremor. *American Journal of Psychiatry, 139,* 1471–1473.

Schuckit, M. A. (1973). Alcoholism and sociopathy-diagnositic confusion. *Quarterly Journal of Studies on Alcohol, 34,* 157–164.

Schuckit, M. A. (1980a). Self-rating of alcohol intoxication by young men with and without family histories of alcoholism. *Journal of Studies on Alcohol, 41,* 242–249.

Schuckit, M. A. (1980b). Alcoholism and genetics: Possible biological mediators. *Biological Psychiatry, 15*, 437–447.

Schuckit, M. A. (1980c). Biological markers: Metabolism and acute reactions to alcohol in sons of alcoholics. *Pharmacology, Biochemistry, & Behavior, 13*, 9–16.

Schuckit, M. A. (1981). Peak blood alcohol levels in men at high risk for the future development of alcoholism. *Alcoholism: Clinical and Experimental Research, 5*, 64–66.

Schuckit, M. A. (1982a). A study of young men with alcoholic close relatives. *American Journal of Psychiatry, 139*, 791–794.

Schuckit, M. A. (1982b). Anxiety and assertiveness in the relatives of alcoholics and controls. *Journal of Clinical Psychiatry, 43*, 238–239.

Schuckit, M. A. (1983a). Extroversion and neuroticism in young men at higher and lower risk for alcoholism. *American Journal of Psychiatry, 140*, 1223–1224.

Schuckit, M. A. (1983b). Alcoholic men with no alcoholic first-degree relatives. *American Journal of Psychiatry, 140*, 439–443.

Schuckit, M. A. (1984a). Differences in plasma cortisol after ingestion of ethanol in relatives of alcoholics and controls: Preliminary results. *Journal of Clinical Psychiatry, 45*, 374–376.

Schuckit, M. A. (1984b). Subjective responses to alcohol in sons of alcoholics and control subjects. *Archives of General Psychiatry, 41*, 879–884.

Schuckit, M. D. (1984c). Relationship between the course of primary alcoholism in men and family history. *Journal of Studies on Alcohol, 45*, 334–338.

Schuckit, M. A. (1985a). Ethanol-induced changes in body sway in men at high alcoholism risk. *Archives of General Psychiatry, 42*, 375–379.

Schuckit, M. A. (1985b). The clinical implications of primary diagnostic groups among alcoholics. *Archives of General Psychiatry, 42*, 1043–104.

Schuckit, M. A. (1986). Genetic and clinical implications of alcoholism and affective disorder. *American Journal of Psychiatry, 143*, 140–147.

Schuckit, M. A. (1988). Reactions to alcohol in sons of alcoholics and controls. *Alcoholism: Clinical and Experimental Research, 12*, 465–470.

Schuckit, M. A., & Duby, J. (1982). Alcohol-related flushing and the risk for alcoholism in sons of alcoholics. *Journal of Clinical Psychiatry, 43*, 415–418.

Schuckit, M. A., Engstrom, D., Alpert, R., & Duby, J. (1981). Differences in muscle-tension response to ethanol in young men with and without family histories of alcoholism. *Journal of Studies on Alcohol, 42*, 918–924.

Schuckit, M. A., & Gold, E. O. (1988). A stimultaneous evaluation of multiple markers of ethanol/placebo challenges in sons of alcoholics and controls. *Archives of General Psychiatry, 45*, 211–216.

Schuckit, M. A., Gold, E., & Risch, C. (1987). Serum prolactin levels in sons of alcoholics and control subject. *American Journal of Psychiatry, 144*, 854–859.

Schuckit, M. A., Goodwin, D. A., & Winokur, G. (1972). A study of alcoholism in half siblings. *American Journal of Psychiatry, 128*, 1132–1136.

Schuckit, M. A., Irwin, M., & Brown, S. A. (1990). The history of anxiety symptoms among 171 primary alcoholics. *Journal of Studies on Alcohol, 51*, 34–41.

Schuckit, M. A., Li, T. K., Cloninger, R., Deitrich, R. A. (1985). University of California, Davis-Conference: Genetics of alcoholism. *Alcoholism: Clinical and Experimental Research, 9*, 475–492.

Schuckit, M. A., & Morrissey, E. R. (1976). Alcoholism in women: Some clinical and social perspectives with an emphasis on possible subtypes. In M. Greenblatt & M. A. Schuckit (Eds.) *Alcoholism problems in women and children* (pp. 5–36). New York: Grune & Stratton.

Schuckit, M. A., & Morrissey, E. R. (1979). Psychiatric problems in women admitted to an alcoholic detoxification center. *American Journal of Psychiatry, 136*, 611–617.

Schuckit, M. A., O'Connor, D. T., Duby, J., Vega, R., & Moss, M. (1981). Dopamine-B-hydroxylase activity levels in men at high risk for alcoholism and controls. *Biological Psychiatry, 16,* 1067–1075.

Schuckit, M. A., Parker, D. C., & Rossman, L. R. (1983). Ethanol-related prolactin responses and risk for alcoholism. *Biological Psychiatry, 18,* 1153–1159.

Schuckit, M., Pitts, F. N., Reich, T., King, L., & Winokur, G. (1969). Alcoholism I. Two types of alcoholism in women. *Archives of General Psychiatry, 20,* 301–306.

Schuckit, M. A., & Rayses, V. (1979). Ethanol ingestion: Differences in blood acetaldehyde concentrations in relatives of alcoholics and controls. *Science, 203,* 54–57.

Schuckit, M., Rimmer, J., Reich, T., & Winokur, G. (1970). Alcoholism: Antisocial traits in male alcoholics. *British Journal of Psychiatry, 117,* 575–576.

Schuckit, M. A., Rimmer, J., Reich, T., & Winokur, G. (1971). The bender alcoholic. *British Journal of Psychiatry, 118,* 183–184.

Schuckit, M. A., Risch, S. C., & Gold, E. O. (1988). Alcohol consumption, ACTH level, and family history of alcoholism. *American Journal of Psychiatry, 145,* 1391–1395.

Schuckit, M. A., Shaskan, E., Duby, J., Vega, R., & Moss, M. (1982). Platelet monoamine oxidase activity in relatives of alcoholics. Preliminary study with matched control subjects. *Archives of General Psychiatry, 39,* 137–140.

Schuckit, M. A., & Sweeney, S. (1987). Substance abuse and mental health problems among sons of alcoholics and controls. *Journal of Studies on Alcohol, 48,* 528–534.

Schuckit, M. A., Sweeney, S., & Huey, L. (1987). Hyperactivity and the risk for alcoholism. *Journal of Clinical Psychiatry, 48,* 275–277.

Schulsinger, F. (1972). Psychopathy: Heredity and environment. *International Journal of Mental Health, 1,* 190–206.

Schulsinger, F., Knop, J., Goodwin, D. W., Teasdale, T. W., & Mikkelsen, U. (1986). A prospective study of young men at high risk for alcoholism. *Archives of General Psychiatry, 43,* 755–760.

Sher, K. J. (1985). Excluding problem drinkers in high-risk studies of alcoholism: Effect of screening criteria on high-risk versus low-risk comparisons. *Journal of Abnormal Psychology, 94,* 106–109.

Sher, K. J., & Levenson, R., W. (1982). Risk for alcoholism and individual differences in the stress-response-dampening effect of alcohol. *Journal of Abnormal Psychology, 91,* 350–367.

Sher, K. J., & McCrady, B. S. (1984). The MacAndrew Alcoholism scale: Severity of alcohol abuse and parental alcoholism. *Addictive Behaviors, 9,* 99–102.

Sher, K. J., & Walitzer, K. S. (1986). Individual differences in the stress-response-dampening effect of alcohol: A dose-response study. *Journal of Abnormal Psychology, 95,* 159–167.

Sigvardsson, S., Cloninger, C. R., Bohman, M., & von Knorring, A. L. (1982). Predisposition to petty criminality in Swedish Adoptees. *Archives of General Psychiatry, 39,* 1248–1253.

Sigvardsson, S., von Knorring, A. L., Bohman, M., & Cloninger, C. R. (1984). An adoption study of somatoform disorders I. The relationship of somatization to psychiatric disability. *Archives of General Psychiatry, 41,* 853–859.

Smith, V., & Chyatte, C. (1983). Left-handed versus right-handed alcoholics: An examination of relapse patterns. *Journal of Studies on Alcohol, 44,* 553–557.

Spilker, B., & Callaway, E. (1969). Effects of drugs on "augmenting/reducting" in averaged visual evoked responses in man. *Psychopharmacologia, 15,* 116–124.

Stabenau, J. R., & Hesselbrock, V. M. (1983). Family pedigress of alcoholic and control patients. *The International Journal of the Addictions, 18,* 351–363.

Stagner, B. H. (1986). The viability of birth order studies in substance abuse research. *International Journal of Addictions, 21,* 377–384.

Sullivan, J. L., Cavenar, J. O., Maltbie, A. A., Lister, P., & Zung, W. W. K. (1979). Familial biochemical and clinical correlates of alcoholics with low platelet monoamine oxidase activity. *Biological Psychiatry, 14,* 385–394.

Sullivan, J. L., Stanfield, C. N., Maltbie, A. A., Hammett, E., & Cavenar, J. O. (1978). Stability of low blood platelet monoamine oxidase activity in human alcoholics. *Biological Psychiatry, 13,* 391–397.

Swartz, C. M., Drews, V., & Cadoret, R. (1987). Decreased epinephrine in familial alcoholism. *Archives of General Psychiatry, 44,* 938–941.

Tanna, V. L., Wilson, A. F., Winokur, G., & Elston, R. C. (1988). Possible linkage between alcoholism and esterase-D. *Journal of Studies on Alcohol, 49,* 472–476.

Tarter, R. E. (1978). Etiology of alcoholism: Interdisciplinary integration. In P. E. Nathan, G. A. Marlatt, & T. Loberg (Eds.), *Alcoholism: New directions in behavioral research and treatment* (pp. 41–70). New York: Plenum Press.

Tarter, R. E., Alterman, A. I., & Edwards, K. L. (1985). Vulnerability to alcoholism in men: A behavioral-genetic perspective. *Journal of Studies on Alcohol, 46,* 329–356.

Tarter, R. E., & Edwards, K. (1988). Psychological factors associated with the risk for alcoholism. *Alcoholism: Clinical and Experimental Research, 12,* 471–480.

Tarter, R. E., Hegedus, A. M., & Gavaler, J. D. (1985). Hyperactivity in sons of alcoholics. *Journal of Studies on Alcohol, 46,* 259–261.

Tarter, R. E., Hegedus, A. M., Goldstein, G., Shelly, C., & Alterman, A. I. (1984). Adolescent sons of alcoholics: Neuropsychological and personality characteristics. *Alcoholism: Clinical and Experimental Research, 8,* 216–222.

Tarter, R. E., Jacob, T., & Bremer, D. A. (1989a). Cognitive status of sons of alcoholics. *Alcoholism: Clinical and Experimental Research, 13,* 232–235.

Tarter, R. E., Jacob, T., & Bremer, D. A. (1989b). specific cognitive impairment in sons of early onset alcoholics. *Alcoholism: Clinical and Experimental Research, 13,* 786–799.

Tarter, R. E., McBride, H., Buonpane, N., & Schneider, D. U. (1977). Differentiation of alcoholics: Childhood history of minimal brain dysfunction, family history, and drinking pattern. *Archives of General Psychiatry, 34,* 761–766.

Templer, D. I., Ruff, C. F., & Ayers, J. (1974). Essential alcoholism and family history of alcoholism. *Quarterly Journal of Studies on Alcohol, 35,* 655–657.

Utne, H. E., Hansen, V., Winkler, K., & Schulsinger, F. (1977). Alcohol elimination rates in adoptees with and without alcoholic parents. *Journal of Studies on Alcohol, 38,* 1219—1223.

Vaillant, G. E. (1980). Natural history of male psychological health: VIII. Antecendents of alcoholism and "orality". *American Journal of Psychiatry, 137,* 181–186.

Vaillant, G. E. (1983). *The natural history of alcoholism.* Cambridge: Harvard University Press.

Virkkunen, M., Nuutila, A., Goodwin, F. K., & Linnoila, M. (1987). Cerebrospinal fluid monoamine metabolite levels in male aronists. *Archives of General Psychiatry, 44,* 241–247.

Vogel-Sprott, M., & Chipperfield, B. (1987). Family history of problem drinking among young male social drinkers: Behavioral effects of alcohol. *Journal of Studies on Alcohol, 48,* 430–436.

Volavka, J., Pollock, V., Gabrielli, W. F., & Mednick, S. A. (1985). The EEG in persons at risk for alcoholism. In M. Galanter (Ed.), *Recent developments in alcoholism* (pp. 21–36). New York: Plenum Press.

Volicer, B. J., Volicer, L., & D'Angelo, N. (1983). Variation in length of time to development of alcoholism by family history of problem drinking. *Drug and Alcohol Dependence, 12,* 69–83.

von Knorring, L. (1976). Visual averaged evoked responses in patients suffering from alcoholism. *Neuropsychoobiology, 2,* 233–238.

von Knorring, A. L., Bohman, M., von Knorring, L., & Oreland, L. (1985). Platelet MAO activity as a biological marker in subgroups of alcoholism. *Acta Psychiatrica Scandanavia, 72,* 51–58.

von Knorring, A. L, Bohman, M., von Knorring, L, & Oreland, L. (1985). Platelet MAO activity as a biological marker in subgroups of alcoholism. *Acta Psychiatrica Scandanavia, 72,* 51–58.

von Knorring, L., Cloninger, C. R., Bohman, M., & Sigvardsson, S. (1983). An adoptive study of depressive disorders and substance abuse. *Archives of General Psychiatry, 40,* 943–950.

von Knorring, L., Palm, U., & Andersson, H. E. (1985). Relationship between treatment outcome and subtype of alcoholism in men. *Journal Studies on Alcohol, 46,* 388–391.

Weingartner, H., & Faillace, L. A. (1971). Verbal learning in alcoholic patients. *Journal of Nervous and Mental Disease, 152,* 407–416.

Weissman, M. M., Gershon, E. S., Kidd, K. K., Prusoff, B. A., Leckman, J. F., Dibble, E., Hamovit, J., Thompson, W. D., Pauls, D. L., & Guroff, J. J. (1984). Psychiatric disorders in the relatives of probands with affective disorders. *Archives of General Psychiatry, 41,* 13–21.

Weiss, G., Hechtman, L., Perlman, T., Hopkins, J., & Wener, A. (1979). Hyperactives as young adults. A controlled prospective ten-year follow-up of 75 children. *Archives of General Psychiatry, 36,* 675–681.

Wender, P. H., Reimherr, F. W., & Wood, D. R. (1981). Attention deficit disorder. ('Minimal brain dysfunction') in adults. *Archives of General Psychiatry, 38,* 449–456.

Whipple, S. C., Parker, E. S., & Noble, E. P. (1988). An atypical neurocognitive profile in alcoholic fathers and their sons. *Journal of Studies on Alcohol, 49,* 240–244.

Wilsnack, R. W., Wilsnack, S. C., & Klassen, A. D. (1986). Antecedents and consequences of drinking and drinking problems in women: Patterns from a U. S. national survey. In C. Rivers (Ed.), *Alcohol and Addictive Behaviro: Nebraska Symposium on Motivation.* Lincoln: University of Nebraska Press.

Wilson, J. R., & Nagoshi, C. T. (1987). One-month repeatability of alcohol metabolism, sensitivity and acute tolerance. *Journal of Studies on Alcohol, 48,* 437–442.

Wilson, J. R., & Nagoshi, C. T. (1988). Adult children of alcoholics: Cognitive and psychomotor characteristics. *British Journal of Addiction, 83,* 809–820.

Winokur, G. (1979). Unipolar depression. Is it divisible into autonomous subtypes? *Archives of General Psychiatry, 36,* 47–52.

Winokur, G., Behar, D., VanValkenburg, C., & Lowry, M. (1978). Is a familial definition of depression both feasible and valid? *Journal of Nervous and Mental Disease, 166,* 764–768.

Winokur, G., Cadoret, R., Dorzab, J., & Baker, M. (1971). Depressive disease. A genetic study. *Archives of General Psychiatry, 24,* 135–144.

Winokur, G., & Pitts, F. N. (1965). Affective disorder: VI. A family history study of prevalences, sex differences and possible genetic factors. *Journal of Psychiatric Research, 3,* 113–123.

Winokur, G., Reich, T., Rimmer, J., & Pitts, F. N. (1970). Alcoholism III. Diagnosis and familial psychiatric illness in 259 alcoholic probands. *Archives of General Psychiatry, 23,* 104–111.

Winokur, G., Rimmer, J., & Reich, T. (1971). Alcoholism IV: Is there more than one type of alcoholism? *British Journal of Psychiatry, 118,* 525–531.

Woerner, P. I., & Guze, S. B. (1968). A family and marital study of hysteria. *British Journal of Psychiatry, 114,* 161–168.

Wood, D. R., Reimherr, F. W., Wender, P. H., & Johnson, G. E. (1976). Diagnosis and treatment of minimal brain dysfunction in adults. *Archives of General Psychiatry, 33,* 1453–1460.

Wood, D. R., Wender, P. H., & Reimherr, F. W. (1983). The prevalence of attention deficit disorder, residual type, or minimal brain dysfunction in a population of male alcoholic patients. *American Journal of Psychiatry, 140,* 95–98.

Workman-Daniels, K. L., & Hesselbrock, V. M. (1987). Childhood problem behavior and neuropsychological functioning in persons at risk for alcoholism. *Journal of Studies on Alcohol, 48,* 187–193.

Yamane, H., Katoh, N., & Fujita, T. (1980). Characteristics of three groups of men alcoholics differentiated by age at first admission for alcoholism treatment in Japan. *Journal of Studies on Alcohol, 41,* 100–103.

Zabik, J. E. (1989). Use of serotonin-active drugs in alcohol preference studies. In M. Galanter (Ed.), *Recent developments in alcoholism* (Vol. 7), New York: Plenum Press.

Zabik, J. E., & Roache, J. D. (1983). 5-Hydroxytryptophan-induced conditioned taste aversion to ethanol in rat. *Pharmacology, Biochemistry, and Behavior, 18,* 785–790.

Zimberg, S. (1974). Two type of problem drinkers: Both can be managed. *Geriatrics, 29,* 135–139.

Zuckerman, M., Buchsbaum, M. S., & Murphy, D. L. (1980). Sensation seeking and its biological correlates. *Psychological Bulletin, 88,* 187–214.

II PHYSIOLOGY

Introduction

The section on the physiology of alcoholism is divided into five chapters. The first chapter begins with a discussion of alcohol's acute impact on some basic physiology. Included in the discussion are information on the absorption, distribution, and metabolism of alcohol. The initial impact on particular hormones and those areas of the brain that are most impacted are discussed. Specific alcohol related phenomena (intoxication, blackouts, coma, idiosyncratic intoxication, hangovers, alcohol withdrawal) are covered. An extended discussion of alcohol withdrawal is presented. Topics under discussion of alcohol withdrawal include seizures, alcoholic hallucinosis, delirium tremens, and a review of studies in which outpatient treatment for withdrawal has been evaluated.

Chapter 2 covers the long-term impact of heavy alcohol consumption. Rather than simply enumerating where damage is frequently apparent, the presentation focuses on understanding the physiological events which might account for the damage. The discussion is organized in terms of organ systems. The chapter begins with the liver since the effects of the liver have so many repercussions for other organ systems in the body. There is discussion of the effect of alcohol on the pancreas, the cardiovascular system, blood cell production, the skin, the kidneys, the lungs, the muscles, the bones, the endocrine glands, the male reproductive system, and the female reproductive system. The effects of alcohol on the gastrointestinal tract and resulting nutritional deficiencies are discussed. The effects of paternal and maternal drinking on the fetus are reviewed. Of course, there is a full discussion of the effects of alcohol on the nervous system.

The discussion of alcohol's impact on the nervous system is an extended one. Functional impact on the nervous system as manifested in mood and sleep disturbances is discussed. Structural damage to the autonomic, sensory, and voluntary nervous systems is separately considered. The recent controversies on whether the brain damage from alcoholism is qualitatively distinct from normal aging, whether CNS damage is confined to those who are already aging, and whether damage from alcohol occurs at social drinking levels (2–4 drinks per day) are discussed. Specific brain syndromes are identified. The chapter ends with some overarching questions and empirical findings on the nature of alcohol's toxicity. Some specific findings regarding damage from alcohol in women are shared. The elevated risk for accidents among alcoholics is discussed.

Chapter 3 concerns the topic of addiction. Tolerance and withdrawal are examined and theories that posit a common mechanism to explain both phenomena are reviewed. Recent data suggesting that tolerance and withdrawal are separate, independent processes are presented, and new theories that have been proposed to explain each phenomenon are discussed.

The fourth chapter concerns various pharmacological treatments for alcoholism that have been discussed and empirically evaluated in the literature. The review of drug treatments has been limited to those drugs for which a theoretical case for their utility can be made: We discuss lithium, serotonin agonists, stimulant drugs, and antabuse.

Chapter 5 concerns the topic of THIQs. The arguments presented in a widely distributed film featuring David Ohlms, which is seen by the patients in many treatment centers, are reviewed. Because many patients in treatment for alcoholism are exposed to this material, it is important for professionals to be aware of the perspective that is advanced. It is also important for professionals to know some of the empirical findings relevant to the THIQs. This chapter attempts to provide some of the bottom lines regarding what the research community knows about the THIQs. Topics of discussion include: In which populations are high levels of THIQs encountered? What functions might the THIQs subserve and at which neurotransmitter system might the THIQs operate? Is there evidence that they are addicting? Might they be neurotoxins? What are the findings regarding the induction of alcohol preference in animals?

7 Acute Effects of Alcohol

We begin with a discussion of the acute effects of alcohol on physiology. First, alcohol's absorption, distribution, and metabolism are delineated. Then, some of the acute effects of nervous system activity and glandular functions are discussed. In light of these findings, alcohol's classification as a drug is commented on. Some of the research on why alcohol can be used as a reinforcer for animals is reviewed.

Discussion then turns to specific alcohol induced phenomena that can occur given an acute episode of heavy drinking. The topics covered are: intoxication, blackouts, coma, idiosyncratic intoxication, hangover, and withdrawal. Discussion covers some explanations that have been proffered to account for these events. Several events (coma and withdrawal) can be treated medically. Those treatments that have been suggested in the literature are reviewed.

ABSORPTION, DISTRIBUTION, AND METABOLISM

When alcohol is consumed it is absorbed into the blood stream through the gastrointestinal tract. Twenty percent is absorbed through the stomach where the rate of absorption depends on the food content in the stomach and also decreases as a function of time. The other 80% is absorbed through the intestine. Absorption in the intestine is more rapid and occurs at a constant rate regardless of the presence of food. The rate of absorption in the stomach can be decreased by consuming food along with the alcoholic beverage. Milk or high protein foods are particularly good at decreasing rate of absorption. Beer retards stomach absorption. Hot beverages and carbonated beverages are absorbed most rapidly.

On average, it takes about 45 minutes to absorb two drinks, but absorption rate may last as long as 6 hours. Attempts to increase the rate of absorption by drinking quickly can backfire. Rapid consumption can cause the valve between the stomach and the intestine to spasm resulting in retention of the alcohol in the stomach where absorption is slower. Further, stomach mucous will be produced that will further retard absorption (Julien, 1978; Lee & Becker, 1982; Ritchie, 1980).

Alcohol is eliminated from the body by expiration (breathing) or the exocrine glands (sweating), through excretion in the urine, and through metabolism by the liver. Up to 90% of alcohol that is consumed is metabolized in the liver at a constant rate. Some authors report that larger livers will metabolize more rapidly (Ritchie, 1980). Despite slight variation due to individual liver size, the rate of metabolism is close to .5 oz of pure alcohol per 1.5 hrs. (A half oz. of alcohol is contained in a 1.25 shot of 80 proof whiskey, a 12 oz. can of 4 % beer, or a 4 oz. glass of 12% wine) (Julien, 1978). Alcoholics have increased the activity of their liver enzymes through a process called enzyme induction. As such, the rate of disappearance of alcohol for alcoholics is more rapid (Van Thiel, 1983).

At social drinking levels, up to 20% of the alcohol that is consumed can be metabolized by enzymes in the stomach. These stomach enzymes are less active in heavy drinkers and women, so for these groups, a greater percentage of the alcohol will be processed by the liver. Drugs such as tagamet (histamine 2 antagonists) can interfere with stomach enzymes thus inducing more extreme blood alcohol levels in those taking such drugs (Frezza et al., 1990; Lieber, 1988).

The metabolic fate of alcohol is a two-step process. The enzyme alcohol dehydrogenase breaks the alcohol down into acetaldehyde. The enzyme aldehyde dehydrogenase catalyzes the conversion of the acetaldehyde to acetate alone or water and acetic acid. Fructose will increase the rate of catabolism of alcohol by 25%, however large quantities of fructose are associated with additional problems (Sellers & Kalant, 1976). Protein consumption, food consumption in general, and stress will all increase the rate of liver catabolism (Lakshman, Chambers, Chirtel, & Ekarohita, 1988).

At very high levels of consumption an alternate metabolic pathway (MEOS pathway) for alcohol has been discovered. This second pathway also results in the production of acetaldehyde (Van Thiel, 1983). Recent evidence further suggests that yet another pathway involving P450 II E 1 is also induced in heavy consumers (Lieber, 1988). High levels of chronic alcohol exposure will result in a greater amount of acetaldehyde being produced relative to a constant amount of alcohol (Nuutinen, Lindros, & Salaspuro, 1983).

Alcohol is distributed throughout the body. It is soluble in both water and fat allowing it to be rapidly transported across cell membranes. Alcohol will achieve higher concentrations in muscle tissue than in fat tissue. Thus, a person with a great deal of tissue compared to a muscular individual of the same weight will achieve higher blood alcohol levels given consumption of an equivalent amount of alcohol (Julien, 1978).

Some specific comments should be noted for the pharmacodynamics of alcohol in women. Women absorb alcohol more rapidly from the stomach than do men (Lieber, 1988). Since women have more fat tissue relative to muscle tissue than men, more alcohol remains in the blood stream than is dispersed into the body tissues. The implication is that given the same amount of alcohol, women will achieve higher blood alcohol levels. Women have a more active hepatic alcohol dehydrogenase and their rate of metabolism will be faster than mens. The faster rate of metabolism offsets the higher blood alcohol level in women, thus the net effect is that women will clear a given amount of alcohol in about the same interval of time as men (Van Thiel & Gavaler, 1988).

Whereas men are fairly reliable in terms of the blood alcohol levels achieved given a constant amount of alcohol, women will vary as a function of the estrus cycle. At least part of the reason may be attributable to the fact that the rate of absorption through the stomach varies as a function of the estrus cycle in women (Van Thiel & Gavaler, 1988). The highest blood alcohol levels are achieved premenstrually and during ovulation (Jones & Jones, 1976). Women tend to spontaneously reduce consumption when estrogen levels are high but display relative increases when estrogen levels are low (as they are premenstrually) (Cicero, 1982; Van Thiel & Gavaler, 1988). This latter finding has been attributed to the fact that alcohol will act as an MAO inhibitor as will estrogen. Jones and Jones (1976) have speculated that women will increase their alcohol consumption when estrogen levels are low because they are spurred to inhibit MAO through some other means such as with alcohol.

PHYSICAL EVENTS OCCURRING GIVEN ACUTE CONSUMPTION

When a person drinks there are some notable physiological changes. Alcohol suppresses the pituitary release of anti-diuretic hormone (vasopressin) so that water is lost through urine excretion. Alcohol dilates the blood vessels on the surface of the skin, so flushing occurs, heat is lost through the skin, and body temperature drops. The decrease in body temperature is compounded through alcohol's effects on the central nervous system temperature regulating mechanism (Julien, 1978; Ritchie, 1980). Alcohol will decrease the coordination between the two eyeballs such that diplopia (double vision) redounds (Light, 1986). If alcohol is consumed with other drugs, alcohol will potentiate the effect of particular drugs, which include benzodiazepines, sedative hypnotics, and benadryl (Ritchie, 1980).

Alcohol impacts nerve cell functioning in the brain resulting in behavioral changes. Results of electrophysiological (EEG) studies suggest that the reticular activating system is more profoundly affected than the cortex (Blum, 1982). Results of EEG functioning in response to specific stimuli, suggest that the right brain is more heavily affected than the left brain (Chandler & Parsons, 1977; Kostandov et al., 1982; Porjesz & Begleiter, 1981; Rhodes, Obitz, & Creel, 1975).

There have been studies assessing regional blood flow during intoxication. During intoxication there is a general increase in blood flow to the grey matter. There is differentially less flow to the frontal region of the left hemisphere and more to the right hemisphere. Generally, blood flow to a region reflects differential activity. The increased blood flow to the right conflicts with EEG studies suggesting less right brain activity. Increased blood flow to an area usually suggests more and not less activity in a region. There has been some evidence suggesting that the increased blood flow to the right hemisphere found during intoxication does not reflect increased metabolism of glucose. It is believed that a metabolic uncoupling or change in the manner in which glucose is utilized may occur during intoxication (Risberg & Berglund, 1987, p. 66). This may explain the inconsistency.

EFFECTS ON HORMONE SECRETION

When people drink elevations in adrenal gland hormones (corticosteriods and adrenaline) occur. It is believed that the increase in corticosteroid secretions is achieved through alcohol's effects on the hypothalamus and secondarily the pituitary gland. The increase in corticosteriods may account for the mobilization of fats from storage in adipose tissue noted in imbibing individuals. The adrenaline may account for the rise in blood pressure and dilated pupils observed after consumption (Ritchie, 1980; Stokes, 1982).

Acutely, alcohol will increase prolactin, and melanocyte-stimulating hormones (Stokes, 1982). Luteinizing hormone levels in heavily drinking humans are generally found to be elevated (Cicero, 1982). There are inconsistencies in the literature with regard to the effect on thyroid stimulating hormones (Stokes, 1982; Cicero, 1982).

ALCOHOL'S CLASSIFICATION AS A DRUG

Alcohol is often categorized as a depressant drug (Julien, 1978; Ritchie, 1980). In the old literature, the well known reduction of inhibitions from alcohol and increase in some types of behavior observed during drinking have been attributed to a paradoxical process. Alcohol, it was believed, depresses the cortex leaving the emotional parts of the brain unopposed (Julien, 1978). Hence people will experience more behavioral freedom of expression when drinking. A review of the chapter on how alcohol effects mood and behavior (Chapter 14) will provide the impression that alcohol has both stimulating and depressing effects. At low doses, for rats and for people, it acts as a stimulant (Carlsson et al., 1972; Kastl, 1969; see Chapter 14 for additional references). Further, alcohol seems to preferentially affect the reticular activating system more than the cortex (Blum, 1982), again contradicting the old view. In light of new research, it is no longer clear how alcohol should be classified, but the old tradition still remains.

ALCOHOL AS A REINFORCER

Alcohol satisfies the definition of a reinforcer, i.e., it can be used to increase the performance of other behavior (Davis, Werner, & Smith, 1979). Researchers have sought to determine which areas of the brain are impacted such that a reinforcing effect is achieved. A number of norepinephrine antagonist drugs will block alcohol self-administration and preference for alcohol in rats. Aldomet, disulfiram, FLA-63, and propranolol (norepinephrine antagonists) will all block alcohol preference (Amit & Sutherland, 1975/76). Further, when norepinephrine nerve tracks are destroyed chemically, alcohol preference, but not morphine preference is block (Amit & Sutherland, 1975/76). Davis, Werner, and Smith (1979) performed an experiment further linking the reinforcing properties of alcohol to its impact on norepinephrine releasing nerves. Davis et al. employed alcohol as a primary reinforcer in conditioning a buzzer as a secondary reinforcer. When norepinephrine stores were destroyed chemically, alcohol no longer functioned as a primary reinforcer in the conditioning procedure, despite the fact that milk still operated as a primary reinforcer.

Whereas it has been argued that norepinephrine mediates the rewarding properties of alcohol, others have suggested that dopamine neurons in the limbic system are the sight of alcohol's rewarding effect (Wise & Bozarth, 1987). In fact, Wise and Bozarth as well as others (Di Chiara & Imperato, 1988) provide evidence that alcohol, as well as other drugs of abuse (nicotine, opiates, cocaine) all achieve their action at dopmaine synapses in the nucleus accumbens, the caudate nucleus, and the ventral tegmental area. Concomitant with the reinforcing effect are hypermotility, an enhanced attention to the environment, and a tendency to repeat stereotypic sequences of motoric patterns of behavior. Di Chiara and Imperato (1988) report that with low doses of alcohol, there is a positive correlation between the amount of activity the rat exhibits and the dopamine released in the accumbens area. Hence, there may be an association between the reinforcing effect and the behavioral activation. This may account for alcohol's excitatory effect and explains why animals will drink it. What is to explain alcohol's sedating property? Di Chiara and Imperato speculate that at high doses, alcohol impacts other regions of the brain exerting a depressing or sedating effect on behavior which predominates over the arousing effect at the dopaminergic areas. The observed effect will be sedation.

Theories suggesting that alcohol is reinforcing because it stimulates dopamine neurons where it arouses behavior are supported by data from other avenues of research. A study in which subjects were allowed to consume as much alcohol as they wished, found that heavy consumers, presumably finding more satisfaction in the achieved effect, more often characterized alcohol as an arouser (de Wit et al., 1987).

Findings from the rat genetic and human genetic literature suggest that for those inheriting a genetic risk factor, the arousing rather than the sedating effects of alcohol will predominate. Children of alcoholics are less impaired on cognitive tasks after drinking. They report fewer symptoms of intoxication. Hence for humans at genetic risk, alcohol is less sedating (Schuckit et al., 1985).

Human research is mirrored by findings from rat strains that have been bred to be alcohol preferrers. Rat strains which are bred to prefer alcohol, are more aroused by a low dose of alcohol (Schuckit et al., 1985). Further, they fail to develop tolerance to the arousing impact of alcohol (Li et al., 1989). Given a sedating dose, they sleep for a shorter period of time. They develop tolerance to the sedating effects more rapidly than nonpreferring rat strains (Schuckit et al., 1985). Perhaps the preferring rats are more strongly impacted at the areas of the brain where alcohol achieves both its reinforcing effect and its arousing effect.

Kornetsky et al. (1988) have discussed alcohol's role in sensitizing the dopamine area of the limbic system which is activated in self-stimulation studies. Given an electrode implanted in what is probably a dopamine nerve area, an animal will lever press for long duration. Alcohol can lower the threshold for the electrical charge required to induce self-stimulation. Kornetsky et al. suggest that in contrast to other abusable drugs, alcohol produces this effect in a much narrower region of the self-stimulation area. Hence, its impact on the reward centers in the brain may not be as robust as other drugs.

While bearing in mind that current theories of why alcohol is reinforcing reference alcohol's impact on brain reward centers which mediate behavioral arousal, there is a lack of consensus as to the nature of the circuitry in this brain-reward area. Wise and Bozarth (1987) discuss dopamine and endorphins. Others have adduced evidence that serotonin may be important in these areas as well (McBride, Murphy, Lumeng, & Li, 1989).

Research will continue into the question of "why is alcohol a reinforcer?", or alternatively asked, "why do people, or at least some people, like to drink?" There is evidence that strongly suggests that alcohol's activity augmenting properties may be heavily linked to what people find pleasurable in the experience of drinking.

INTOXICATION

At high doses of alcohol, speech becomes slurred, gait becomes ataxic, nystagmus develops, pupils dilate and become unresponsive to light (Knott, Beard, & Fink, 1987) and thinking becomes less precise (references in Chapter 14). The dosage at which these effects will occur vary with degree of tolerance, a topic addressed in a subsequent section.

A number of drugs have been found to decrease the intoxicant effect of alcohol. These drugs include lithium, which has been found to block alcohol's impairment on a sustained attention task but not on some other tasks including a copying task (Judd & Huey, 1984). Zimelidine, a serotonin agonist, will decrease alcohol induced memory impairment, although it has little impact on other signs of intoxication (Weingartner et al., 1983). Pretreatment prior to drinking with tryptophan will also reduce memory impairment during intoxication (Westrick et al., 1988). Prostaglandin synthesis inhibitors (e.g., aspirin) will diminish alcohol induced sedation (George & Collins, 1985). Drugs that inhibit phenylethanolamine N-methyltransferase, the chemical that converts norepinephrine to epinephrine, will block alcohol induced ataxia in rats (Mefford, Lister, Ota, & Linnoila, 1990).

Naloxone is a drug that displaces opiates from their receptor sites without stimuting the nerve to fire. Naloxone will also interfere with both alcohol and opiate depletion of calcium. In some ways naloxone will block intoxication. It will prevent visual nystagmus as well as alcohol induced antinociception, but will not reverse impairment on body sway (Boada, Feria, & Sanz, 1981; Jeffcoate et al., 1979; Mattila, Nuotto, Seppala, 1981). Reports are mixed as to impact on alcohol induced decrements in reaction time (Jeffcoate et al.; Mattila et al. 1981).

GABA (gamma-aminobutyric acid) synapses seem also to be involved in the mediation of alcohol intoxication, especially the loss of righting reflex (the inability of a supine rodent to turn over) exhibited by intoxicated rodents. It has been speculated that alcohol in some way enhances the sensitivity of GABA receptor sites resulting in an increased influx of chloride into GABA neurons. A drug that may operate in some unique way at benzodiazepine receptors on GABA neurons, the recently manufactured RO15-4513, will block the intoxicating effects of alcohol. Interestingly RO15-4513 will not alter the intoxicating effects of barbiturates and other drugs known to influence chloride influx at GABA neurons. Not all of alcohol's effects are blocked by RO15-4513, for example, respiratory depression is unaffected (Suzdak et al., 1986; Kolata, 1986).

Although the pharmacological literature suggests various chemicals that operate as amethystine agents, clinically chemical interventions are not recommended (Sellers & Kalant, 1976). Whereas there are a variety of chemical interventions that block specific signs of intoxication, other drugs will increase intoxication. These drugs include exogenous calicium (Harris, 1979) and pros-taglandin agonists (Wainright, Ward, & Molnar, 1985). Neurotensin will enhance ethanol induced anesthesia and hypothermia (Erwin, Jones, & Radcliffe, 1990).

SOME NEUROTRANSMITTER SYSTEMS THAT ARE AFFECTED BY ALCOHOL

Some drugs can be easily characterized in terms of the particular type of neuron that they affect. Alcohol is not one of these drugs. It impacts many neurotrans-mitter systems. Some crude statements can, however, be proffered. Alcohol decreases brain release of acetylcholine (Light, 1986). Low doses elevate GABA levels in the cerebellum and brain stem (Light, 1986). At low doses it will increase norepinephrine and dopamine turnover. The increase turnover in dopamine is probably secondary to release of endogenous delta-opiod agonists (Holman, 1987, p. 149). However, the effect generally is specific to particular brain regions (Holman, 1987). Chronic admisitration decreases both nor-epinephrine and dopamine (Light, 1986). Further, chronic alcohol administration will desensitize dopaminergic receptor sites to dopamine (Hunt, 1985). Hunt (1985, p. 112) concludes that firm conclusions cannot be drawn with regard to serotonin. Neurotensin levels are also affected by alcohol (Erwin, Jones, & Radcliffe, 1990).

Alcohol will increase the release of met-enkephalins and beta-endorphins (Ho & Allen, 1981; Tewari & Carson, 1982). Naloxone will block the increase in release of these transmitters by alcohol (Ho & Allen, 1981). Chronic alcohol consumption results in a depletion of brain endorphin levels (Blum, 1982). It takes approximately 2 weeks post drinking cessation for normal endorphin values to be restored (Tewari & Carson, 1982). In addition to affecting concentrations, alcohol will retard the binding affinity of enkephalin (sigma type endorphin receptors) but not morphine (mu type endorphin receptors) (Hiller, Angel, & Simon, 1981).

Statements about the impact of alcohol on particular neurotransmitters are difficult to make because many of the neurotransmitters are both increased or decreased depending on location, dosage, and duration of exposure. Further, Holman (1987) has noted that few studies have investigated alcohol's simul-taneous effect on multiple systems. It is probably safe to say that no one transmit-ter system can explain all the diverse effects of alcohol.

BLACKOUTS

At high blood alcohol levels, particularly when the blood alcohol level rises quickly, blackouts sometimes occur. Blackouts are a loss of memory for particu-lar periods of time despite the fact that the person may have functioned efficiently during the period of the blackout. State dependent memory effects describe the phenomenon of information learned under a particular mood state being better recalled during a similar mood state. Blackouts are not attributable to state dependent learning effects. Events occurring during a blackout will not be re-called when a person is next intoxicated (Ryback, 1971). During blackouts, cerebral blood flow is increased particularly in the frontal and fronto-temporal regions and less so in the parietal-occipital regions (Risberg & Berglund, 1987).

Attempts have been made to determine the biochemical mediators of a black-out. Branchey et al. (1985) examined alcoholics 2 weeks post detoxification. Alcoholics were grouped according to whether they had or had not experienced blackouts prior to detoxification. Those alcoholics who had experienced black-outs had lower plasma tryptophan values (a precursor to serotonin) than those who had not. Subjects did not differ on other amino acids.

Ryback (1971) reports that during a blackout, brain wave activity is similar to the activity of non-rapid-eye-movement sleep. It is known that if persons are awakened during non-rapid-eye-movement sleep, exposed to new material, but allowed to return to sleep prior to obtaining another brain wave state, such individuals will not remember the information to which they had been exposed. Ryback speculates that similar brain wave differences may underlie the blackout.

COMA

At high levels of alcohol consumption, the respiratory center in the medulla is depressed. This results in coma and possible death. Sellers and Kalant (1976) report that death has occurred at BALs (blood alcohol levels) of 4000 mg/liter but survival has been reported at 7000 mg liter. The LD 50 (amount lethal for half the sample) is 5000 mg per liter. Usual treatment consists of artificial respiration until enough of the alcohol has been metabolized so that breathing is no longer suppressed. Hemodialysis may be employed to rapidly lower BALs (Sellers & Kalant, 1976). Blood glucose levels as well as electrolytes should be monitored (Badawy, 1984).

Naloxone has been observed to reverse alcoholic coma (Jefferys, Flanangan, Volans, 1980). Naloxone reversibility seems limited to those individuals who display enhanced facial flushing to alcohol when they take chlorpropamide (Jeff-erys et al., 1980). (Chlorpropamide is an inhibitor of liver aldehyde dehydrogen-ase, the enzyme which catabolizes acetaldehyde.) Interestingly, individuals who respond to chlorpropamide are often noninsulin dependent diabetics. Leslie, Pyke, and Stubbs (1979) postulate that these individuals may be particularly sensitive to enkephalins, opiates, and naloxone.

Whereas it is true that naloxone blocks opiate receptor sites in the brain, it has other actions as well. For example, it is known that naloxone will interfere with depletion of brain calcium induced by alcohol or opiates (Ross, Medina, & Cardenas, 1974). It is not necessarily the case that naloxone reverses alcohol induced coma through action at opiate receptors. The particular mechanism through which naloxone blocks alcohol induced coma in some individuals has not yet been identified (Leslie, Pyke, & Stubbs 1979; Catley et al., 1981; Mattila, Nuotto, & Seppala, 1981).

IDIOSYNCRATIC INTOXICATION

At high blood alcohol levels in susceptible individuals, very aberrant behavior can be induced. Associated with this aberrant behavior is brain wave activity (temporal lobe dysrhythmia) suggestive of a seizure. The episode is terminated by sleep. Usually persons are amnesic for the period of aberrant behavior. This disorder is characterized by visual hallucinations, aggression, and paranoia (Knott, Beard, & Fink, 1987). Idiosyncratic intoxication has also been called pathological intoxication and is further discussed in Chapter 14.

HANGOVER

There has been surprisingly little scientific investigation of the common hangover. Studies suggest significantly more impairment than may be commonly recognized. Rydberg (1977) reports several phenomena that are more likely to be present during a hangover. During the hangover pulse rate, blood pressure, blood lactate levels, and urinary adrenaline are increased. Auditory brain evoked potentials are depressed and nystagmus is present. Alpha waves are decreased and theta waves are increased. Standing steadiness and hand steadiness as well as performance on tasks requiring speed and accuracy are impaired. Spatial performance is more affected than performance on verbal and inductive tasks. Persons generally are not cognizant of performance decrements during the hangover. They may report headache, nausea, drowsiness, dizziness, and thirst. Smoking in conjunction with drinking exacerbates hangover symptoms.

A particular experimental examination of the hangover yielded provocative findings (Yesavage & Leirer, 1986). Pilots were given 5 drinks between the hours of 5 to 7 PM and then tested at 9 AM the following morning. Assessment revealed that the pilots were less adept at establishing the proper angle for landing the plane. Similar findings have been reported by Swedish researchers concerned with traffic safety. After an experimenter party was given during which BALs averaged 147 mg/dL, subjects were tested the following morning. Tests were administered 3 hours after the subject's BAL had dropped to 0. Performance decrements were found on car breaking speed and ability to maneuver the car between pylons (Franck, 1983).

There are negative findings in the literature as well. Collins and Chiles (1980) failed to find performance decrements in subjects who had consumed 3.25 ml/kg of body weight of 100 proof beverage which raised BALs to an average of .093%. These subjects were compared to placebo subjects who had had equivalent amounts of sleep. Subjects were tested in the morning 8 hours after their last drink.

There has been speculation regarding whether hangovers are manifestations of the same process as withdrawal symptoms (Freund, 1980). Some have speculated that not all of the symptoms associated with a hangover are consequences of alcohol. Congeners are particular molecules that are found in some alcoholic beverages (whiskey, wines, but not vodka and beer). Cognitive deficits, nystagmus, and EEG changes associated with hangovers are correlated with the congener content of alcoholic beverages (Castaneda & Glanter, 1988; Feinman & Lieber, 1988).

ALCOHOL WITHDRAWAL

General Findings

Animals that have been exposed to alcohol continuously for a period of time will display withdrawal symptoms upon cessation of drinking. Continuous rather than intermittent exposure is required (Goldstein, 1972). An individual does not have to be an alcoholic to display withdrawal. Withdrawal symptoms have also been demonstrated in nonalcoholics who were induced to consume heavily for 48 to 87 days in the laboratory (Leroy, 1979; Tabakoff & Rothstein, 1983). Withdrawal is a function of both quantity and duration of exposure (Goldstein, 1972). If duration of exposure is held constant, a steeper rise in BAL will generally result in more severe withdrawal (Le Bourhis & Aufrere, 1983). Animals who have had a prior period of addiction display more severe withdrawal symptoms (Baker & Cannon, 1979; Ballenger & Post, 1978), although, in humans, even given heavy drinking in a person with a prior history of withdrawal does not ensure a second experience (Gross, Lewis, & Hastey, 1974).

Authors vary in terms of whether they divide the withdrawal process in 2 stages (Keeler & Miller, 1977; Tabakoff & Rothstein, 1983) or 3 stages (Knott, Beard, & Fink 1987). Initial symptoms may develop given a relative drop in blood alcohol levels. Withdrawal symptoms may decline by hours 72 to 96 (Knott, Beard, & Fink, 1987). Symptoms of withdrawal include tremors (intentional as opposed to resting), hyperreflexia, weakness, anxiety, diaphoresis, tachycardia, high blood pressure, hyperthermia, nausea, diarrhea, insomnia, and sleep disturbance. Throughout withdrawal, difficulties in articulation, ataxia, memory impairment, muscle cramps, internal tremors, paresthesias, tinnitus, and pruritus have been noted (Edwards & Gross, 1976; Feuerlein, 1974). If sleep occurs, vivid nightmares are likely (Gross et al., 1974). Fevers up to 101 degrees can be present and some develop superthermia (Gross et al., 1974). During withdrawal brain blood flow is reduced, although if hallucinations occur, there is usually increased blood flow to the sensory area of the brain mediating the activity (Risberg & Berglund, 1987).

Seizures

Grand mal seizures can occur during any of the stages of withdrawal including when alcohol is still in the system (Knott, et al., 1987). Grand mal seizures are generally not preceded by a prodromal aura (Gross et al., 1974). Knott et al., (1987) suggest that some seizure activity may be associated with alcohol induced intracellular accumulation of sodium in the CNS, changes secondary to respiratory alkalosis, or hypoglycemia. Knott et al. (1987) suggest that seizures generally are observed within the first 72–96 hours after intoxication, but Tabakoff and Rothstein (1983), basing their conclusions on a study by Victor and Wolfe, indicate more than 90% of seizures occur within 48 hours of withdrawal onset with peak occurrence at 24 hours. For obvious reasons, there has been little experimental research in this area. As the general state of health and nutritional deficiencies of alcoholics exhibiting withdrawal will vary enourmously, discrepancies might be expected.

Alcoholic Hallucinosis

Auditory hallucinations, delusions, and paranoid ideation are observed in alcoholic hallucinosis. The condition is usually associated with a clear sensorium. Autonomic hyperactivity and agitation may often be absent. Persons generally remember the phenomenon after the episode. Onset usually occurs 72–96 hours after blood alcohol levels decline, however, it may occur as late as 4 to 7 days after the last drink (Knott et al., 1987). Symptoms may occur intermittently throughout the withdrawal period (Tabakoff & Rothstein, 1983).

Delirium Tremens

Autonomic hyperactivity, delirium, disorientation, confusion, delusions, and visual hallucinations characterize the delirum tremens (Ballenger & Post, 1978; Freund, 1983; Knott, et al., 1987; Lewis & Femino, 1982). Delirium tremens begin between 60 to 80 hours after blood alcohol levels have declined and may last up to 120 hours (Keeler & Miller, 1977).

There is disagreement over whether chemical treatment of early withdrawal symptoms can avert delirium tremens (Lewis & Femino, 1982). It is estimated that around 5% of hospitalized alcoholics will progress to delirium tremens (Leroy, 1979). A mortality rate of 10–15% is associated with DTs (Gross et al., 1974; Leroy, 1979; Miller & Hester, 1980). Death is attributable to hyperthermia, peripheral circulatory collapse, and self-inflicted injuries (Gross et al.,

1974; Leroy, 1979). Death is usually preceded by marked clouding of sensorium although hallucinations are not necessarily prognostic (Gross et al., 1974).

Questions Regarding Withdrawal

There is some disagreement as to the time of onset of withdrawal relative to the last drink. There are reports of delirium occurring without evidence of drinking cessation (Gross et al., 1974), which is mirrored by similar findings in the animal literature (Goldstein, 1972). Withdrawal symptoms have been reported given a relative drop in blood alcohol levels. Those consuming up to 300 mg/100 ml may evidence severe withdrawal given a diminution to 100 mg/100 ml (Mendelson & Mello, 1979).

There are many physiological events that occur after drinking. Some of these phenomena may cause particular symptoms that are manifested during withdrawal. Particular effects are enumerated although their clinical significance is not yet known. Whereas alcohol initially suppresses vasopressin, when alcohol levels decrease in the body, a rebound increase in vasopressin occurs (Badaway, 1984). During the withdrawal process, calcium and magnesium are excreted whereas sodium and chloride ions are retained (Badaway, 1984; McIntyre, 1984). McIntyre (1984) indicates that decreased magnesium levels can lower potassium levels. Pitts and Van Thiel (1986a) indicate that cirrhosis can result in low sodium levels as well. Large doses of alcohol depress respiration, and during withdrawal hyperventilation can create respiratory alkalosis (Gross et al., 1974; Sellers & Kalant, 1982). One or another of these events may in some way mediate specific symptoms of withdrawal. Particular findings are available. Experimental work suggests that hypomagnesium and hypocalcemia may account for particular withdrawal symptoms. Muscular irritability, tetany, seizure susceptibility and hallucinations may well be attributable to low magnesium and low calcium although delirium tremens appear to be mediated through some other process (Badawy, 1984).

Treatment of Withdrawal

In terms of medical management, bezodiazepines are generally perscribed for reducing symptoms and decreasing the probability of a seizure. Achieving a maximal dosage by hour 10 to be maintained through hour 80 and then gradually reduced through the 120th hour is recommended dosage regimen (Keeler & Miller, 1977). Tabakoff and Rothstein (1983) recommend diazepam rather than chlordiazepoxide, because diazepam is absorbed more quickly and has a longer half life. Gallant (1990) suggests benzodiazepines whose catabolism does not occur in the liver (e.g., oxazepam or lorazepam) for those alcoholics in whom liver disease is suspicioned. Although no longer treatments of choice, paraldehyde, chloral hydrate, propranolol and barbiturates have also been employed

(Sellers & Kalant, 1976, 1982). Haloperidol has been recommended for hallucinations and delirium (Knott et al., 1987). However, Sellers and Kalant (1976, 1982) recommend against neuroleptics for other withdrawal symptoms because they lower seizure thresholds, can severely depress blood pressure, and have not been proven effective in preventing delirium tremens. A study by Robinson et al. (1989) evaluated clonidine as a treatment for withdrawal. Clonidine was not as effective as benzodiazepines in reducing initial symptoms. Further, Robinson et al. cautioned that there is a seizure risk associated with clonidine treatment.

Unless there is malnutrition, protracted vomiting, and diarrhea, treatment for dehydration during withdrawal is not likely to be necessary. In fact, superhydration may be the case. McIntyre (1984) reports a study in which withdrawal was attenuated through fluid restriction. Correction of acid-base disturbances may be necessary (Knott et al., 1987; Tabakoff & Rothstein, 1983). Patients being treated for hypoglycemia should be given thiamine before intravenous glucose, as glucose metabolism may deplete what may be an already limited supply of thiamine necessary for neuronal functions (Tabakoff & Rothstein, 1983). Seizures are best treated with benzodiazepines rather than phenytoin unless there is a prior history of seizure disorder (Sellers & Kalant, 1976).

The percentage of alcoholics expected to require medical management of withdrawal has been addressed. Schuckit, Zisook, and Mortola (1985) report that less than 5% of alcoholics entering treatment display severe withdrawal symptoms. Knott et al. (1987) indicate that the likelihood of withdrawal delirium is increased by a previous history of such events. A history of seizure disorder unrelated to alcoholism, poor health, and advanced age, all suggest a more difficult withdrawal process.

Whitfield et al. (1978) examined 1024 consecutive admitted patients who were not medicated. Of this group, 1 experienced delirium tremens, 12 experienced seizures. Feldman et al. (1975) evaluated 564 persons presenting for treatment in a public facility. Of this group, only 47% required medication for withdrawal and only 19% required inpatient care. Criteria for hospitalization were the presence of hallucinations, severe psychomotor agitation, convulsions, disorientation, marked elevation in blood pressure, emotional turmoil, or concomitant medical illness. Criteria for detoxification medication were psychomotor agitation, modest elevation in blood pressure, or somatic complaints.

Outpatient rather than inpatient detoxification has been utilized for the treatment of withdrawal symptoms. Webb and Unwin (1988) report that across studies between 40 to 83% of patients have been found to complete an outpatient detoxification regimen successfully without dropping out or needing hospitalization. Leroy (1979) recommends that patients who are outpatient detoxed be monitored daily.

Although inpatient detoxification may not be required to ensure the patient's medical safety, it is possible that there may be some beneficial impact associated with the drama of hospitalization. Hospitalization may impress upon the patient the dangers attendant with heavy drinking and may accentuate the necessity of treatment for the alcoholism. A study by Hayashida et al. (1989) found that patients were more likely to complete inpatient as opposed to outpatient detoxification, although there was no difference in subsequent admission to a rehabilitation program and there were no differences on drinking variables at 6 months. This study then fails to suggest that inpatient detox will increase patient motivation to participate in treatment or stay sober during the follow-up period. A study by Alterman et al. (1988) found that those patients who had been inpatient detoxified were more likely to complete a subsequent rehabilitation program and were more likely to be abstinent at 1 month, although differences were no longer apparent at 6 months. Hence, the latter study, suggests a modest impact of hospitalization on participation in treatment. Most studies suggest that detoxification without treatment, will do nothing to interrupt the process of alcoholism (Miller & Hester, 1980).

Wartenberg et al. (1990) have found that training physicians in the use of scales to assess alcohol withdrawal symptom severity will decrease the number of patients for whom benzodiazepines are prescribed. Whereas 73% of patients were medicated prior to training, only 13% were medicated after training. Foy, March, and Drinkwater (1988) have employed a modification of the CIWA (Clinical Institute Withdrawal Assessment discussed in Chapter 4 of Vol. I) to assess withdrawal symptomatology in a hospital population of detoxifying alcoholics. They identified a cutoff score above which the risk of later severe withdrawal (seizures, confusion, or hallucinations) was significantly elevated. Those scoring below their cutoff who later developed severe withdrawal were frequently found to be suffering from a separate medical condition (head injury, septicaemia, fractures, cirrhosis, etc.). Those scoring above their cutoff score who were medicated but for whom the benzodiazepine did not prevent severe withdrawal were also frequently found to be suffering from independent medical conditions.

Studies do seem to support the efficacy of outpatient treatment for the management of withdrawal symptoms. Some patients will require inpatient management, but the percentages will be low. It is well to remember that detoxification will do little to alter the progress of the alcoholic process. This requires another class of intervention discussed in the alcoholism treatment chapters.

8 The Long-Term Impact of Heavy Alcohol Consumption

Whereas the first chapter in this section discussed events that occur given acute ingestion of alcohol, the long-term consequence of heavy drinking are examined in this chapter. Discussion is organized according to organ system. The liver is discussed first because of profound effects on other systems in the body. By the end of the chapter, the reader will no doubt be impressed by alcohol's toxicity. At the end of the chapter, some thoughts on how alcohol exerts its toxic effect are provided. The chapter begins with a few comments on some general effects.

GENERAL EFFECTS

Alcohol is both fat and water soluble which means that it can gain rapid transport into all cells and can quickly cross the blood brain barrier. At a histological level there are changes in individual cells that can be observed. Intracellular edema, lipid droplets, excessive glycogen, abnormal mitochondria, deranged elements of the sarcoplasmic reticulum, and increased endoplasmic reticulum have been noted in muscle cells (Ferguson & Knochel, 1982; Watson et al., 1986). Histological observations suggest that cells have been altered in myriad ways. All of the ramifications for functioning are probably not yet apparent.

The incidence of cancer is higher in alcoholics. Many environmental carcinogens are too large to gain access into the cells of the body. Alcohol, however, provides a transport vehicle for carcinogens, thus increasing cancer risks (Tewari & Carson, 1982). Cancer risk is elevated for a variety of cancers. The greatest risk is for oropharyngeal and laryngeal cancer. Additional elevations include risk for esophageal, stomach, colon, liver, thyroid gland, liver cancer, pancreatic cancer, and malignant melanoma (Alcohol Health and Research World, 1981; Lowenfels, 1982).

Focus is now directed to specific organ systems of the body. The effects of alcohol on each organ system are discussed in turn.

LIVER

When alcohol is catabolized by the liver it changes the chemical environment in the liver, an organ which is responsible for the processing of various chemicals in the blood. A diagram is presented to refresh the reader's memory of the catabolism of alcohol. Most of the changes in liver function are explained by reference to the chemical process of alcohol's metabolism.

Accumulation of Estrogen

When large amounts of alcohol are consumed, due to alteration in the liver metabolism of estrogen and androgens, high blood levels of estrogen eventuate. Excess estrogen will cause palmar erythema (red palms) and spider angiomata (visible small blood vessels). Further manifestations include gynecomastia (breast development in males), feminine distribution of fat, feminine hair distribution, and decreased libido (Van Thiel, 1983; Van Thiel, Tarter, Rosenblum, & Gavaler, 1989).

Gout

When the liver metabolizes alcohol, two extra hydrogen atoms become available for each alcohol molecule catabolized. (These atoms on NADH+ that is, oxidized nicotinamide adenine dinucleotide). This surfeit of NADH+ disrupts the liver's production of glucose from amino acids. In the presence of excess NADH+, lactic acid rather than glucose is produced by the liver. The lactic acid enters the blood stream, is carried to the kidneys, and shifts kidney filtration such that increased blood uric acid levels accrue. High levels of uric acid may result in joint pain and inflammation, exacerbating the disease process of gout (Korsten & Lieber, 1982).

Usually the liver's inefficiency in producing blood glucose is not a major problem. Individuals with adequate diets have other sources of glucose, such as dietary carbohydrate. Further, the liver stores excess blood glucose as glycogen. The liver can convert glycogen back to glucose during hypoglycemia. Chronic alcoholics often do not have adequate diets, however, and fasting may have depleted stores of glycogen. Coma induced by hypoglycemia is a well recog-

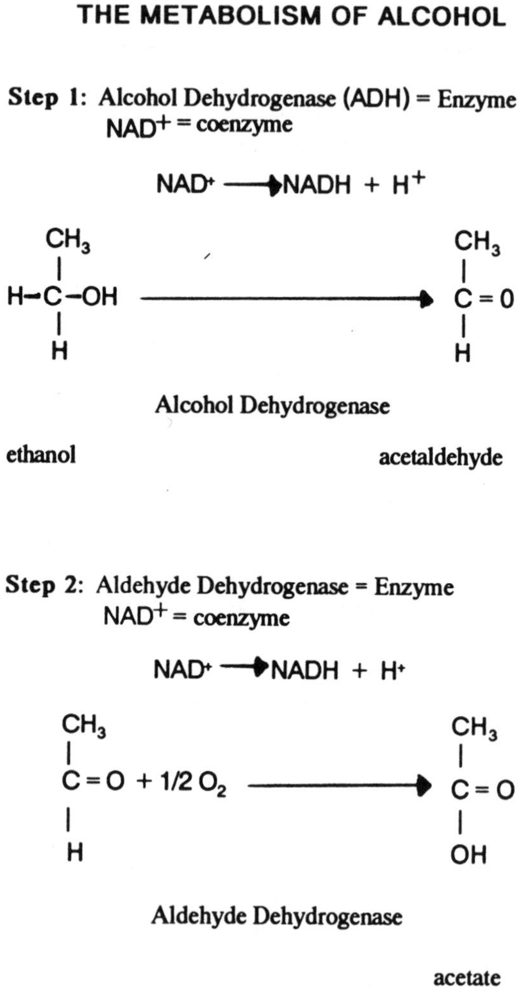

THE METABOLISM OF ALCOHOL

Step 1: Alcohol Dehydrogenase (ADH) = Enzyme
NAD^+ = coenzyme

$$NAD^+ \longrightarrow NADH + H^+$$

$$
\begin{array}{ccc}
CH_3 & & CH_3 \\
| & & | \\
H-C-OH & \longrightarrow & C=0 \\
| & & | \\
H & & H
\end{array}
$$

Alcohol Dehydrogenase

ethanol   acetaldehyde

Step 2: Aldehyde Dehydrogenase = Enzyme
NAD^+ = coenzyme

$$NAD^+ \longrightarrow NADH + H^+$$

$$
\begin{array}{ccc}
CH_3 & & CH_3 \\
| & & | \\
C=O + 1/2\, O_2 & \longrightarrow & C=O \\
| & & | \\
H & & OH
\end{array}
$$

Aldehyde Dehydrogenase

acetate

FIG. 8.1.   The chemical breakdown of alcohol.

nized problem in emergency rooms accommodating skid row populations (Arky, 1983/84). Beyond hypoglycemia, ketone acidosis can occur. The liver in the presence of alcohol increases its synthesis of ketones (Van Thiel, 1983). In response to low glucose, the body mobilizes fat in the form of ketone bodies. The mobilized ketones in addition to the surplus of ketones produced by the liver can result in alcoholic ketoneacidosis. The resultant blood pH changes can induce respiratory changes, confusion, and coma (Arky, 1983/84).

Increased Production of Fats and Ramifications of the Increased Production

An additional problem results from the excess hydrogen created in the metabolism of the alcohol. The hydrogen predisposes to increased liver production of triglycerides, ketone bodies, and lipoproteins (fats). These fats get spilled into the blood stream where they can be detected (Lieber, 1976; Van Thiel, 1983).

Fortuitously, some of the fats produced by an alcohol processing liver have a beneficial effect. High density lipoproteins (HDL) and low density lipoproteins (LDL) are categories of fats. LDL, known as to the lay person as cholesterol, predisposes to arteriosclerosis. HDLs cleanse the LDLs protecting against arteriosclerosis. Alcohol shifts toward an increase in the production of HDLs, thereby lowering cholesterol. The beneficial effects of drinking are achieved at about 3 drinks per day (Khetarpal & Volicer, 1981). At very high levels of drinking (in excess of 5 drinks per day), a bad HDL is produced, such that salubrious impact is lost (Hojnacki et al., 1988). The increase in HDLs observed in heavy consumers drops to normal ranges after about 2 weeks of abstention (Cushman, Barboriak, & Kalbfleisch, 1986).

Fatty Liver

Alcohol will create an excess of production of fat by the liver. Further, alcohol will increase catecholamine secretion from the adrenal glands which will mobilize fats from body storage. Finally, alcohol will impair the liver's breakdown of fats. All these factors contribute to the build up of fat in the liver called steatosis (Watson et al., 1986). A fatty liver is usually asymptomatic (Van Thiel, 1983). It is yet unknown whether a fatty liver predisposes to more omnious conditions, viz. cirrhosis and hepatitis (Van Thiel, 1983). Although a fatty liver may be benign in terms of the liver's ability to function, fat emboli liberated from the liver may create occlusions in the circulatory system (Bliven, 1982).

A fatty liver is detectable upon palpitation and is an early physical finding suggesting excessive alcohol consumption. The development of fatty liver occurs fairly rapidly. Lieber (1976) maintained subjects on 10 oz. of 86 proof alcohol per day and a low fat diet. By day 18, most had developed a fatty liver. Lieber (1976) cautions that drunkenness is not a prerequisite for the development of liver disease. A fatty liver is readily reversible given abstention (Knott et al., 1987).

Hepatic Insufficiency

The fact that inefficient liver functioning given heavy drinking occurs is a well established fact. Some of the compromised functions found in heavy drinkers are the following (Van Thiel, 1983):

First, the liver does not clear dead red blood cells (which are used in the production of bile salts) from the circulatory system. This results in a build up of bilirubin and manifests as a jaundiced appearance (yellow tinge).

Second, the blood, which moves directly from the gastrointestinal tract to the liver, is not purged of bacteria. Hence infections are more likely to occur.

Third, insufficient production of bile may occur. Bile is secreted into the stomach. Due to changes in bile production, dark urine and acholic (light) stools may occur. Bile is needed for gastric absorption of vitamin K. Without vitamin K, the liver cannot produce sufficient prothrombin necessary for blood clotting. Slow blood clotting, resulting in easy bruising, is frequently observed in heavy drinkers.

Fourth, the liver stores and processes vitamin A, C, D, and B-12. In the alcoholic, intake as well as storage and use of these vitamins is impaired.

Fifth, alcohol does inhibit liver production of certain proteins, blood clotting factors, and substances which aid the white blood cells in their attack on foreign elements.

Enzyme Induction

In some ways, the liver is induced to become more efficient as a result of the metabolism of large amounts of alcohol. Through a process called enzyme induction, liver enzymes are activated. The result is faster metabolism of alcohol as well as some other drugs (e.g., tranquilizers and anticoagulants) (Van Thiel, 1983). The implication is that heavy drinkers will require higher doses of particular drugs to produce the desired effect. The rule of thumb that more of a drug will be required to produce the same effect, cannot always be followed. Some drugs compete with alcohol to be broken down by alcohol dehydrogenase. Hence, while there is alcohol in the system, some drugs will accumulate in the blood (Lieber, 1976).

Another consequence of enzyme induction is that some chemicals that are benign prior to being processed, will be converted to a more hazardous compound. Many ordinarily harmless chemicals (particular carcinogens, acetaminophen, carbon tetrachloride) are harmful to alcoholics because of their more efficiently processing enzymes (Lieber, 1976, 1988). Lieber (1988) cautions that an alcoholic who has recently quit drinking may be particularly susceptible to the hepatotoxic effects of tylenol (acetaminophen). Drinking alcoholics are more vulnerable to vitamin A toxicity, although they may need vitamin A replenishment during protracted sobriety (Lieber, 1988).

Hepatitis and Cirrhosis

With continuation of heavy drinking other liver diseases develop. Hepatitis means liver inflammation. Although drinking contributes to this condition, a genetic predisposition may be necessary. Mortality rates for hepatitis are between

10–30% (Lieber, 1976). With or without hepatitis, formation of scar tissue in the liver (cirrhosis) can develop.

It is estimated that 10–30% of alcoholics develop cirrhosis (Goldstein, 1987). The probability of developing cirrhosis increases as the duration of heavy drinking continues. However, the relationship between duration of heavy drinking and probability of cirrhosis is not linear. Among persons consuming 160 grams of alcohol per day, 10% will develop cirrhosis by the fifth year, 40% will develop cirrhosis by the 10th year, the risk remains at 40% by the 15th year, and asymptotes at 80% by the 20th year (Skog, 1984). Based on population statistics, some authors have speculated that cirrhosis may be an all or nothing phenomenon, rather than a progressive process occurring at subclinical levels through the years. This implies that a heavy drinker who quits drinking prior to clinical manifestations, may have escaped permanent damage. Cirrhosis mortality rates are disproportionately high among Black males (Alcohol Health and Research World, 1981).

A cirrhotic liver is small and hard. Unlike a fatty liver, the scar tissue is irreversible. When enough of the liver tissue is replaced by scar tissue, liver failure will ensue. The complications of cirrhosis are a function of the structural problems created by scar tissue and the inability of the liver to perform its functions.

A scarred liver creates a plumbing problem. It is difficult for the blood to circulate through the scar tissue. Blood pressure in the afferent blood vessels around the liver builds up (portal hypertension). New circulatory routes are taken around the liver. Small blood vessels in the upper part of the body begin to break. One particularly nasty complication is esophageal varices, or varicose veins in the esophagus. These structures often break, resulting in hemorrhaging that is difficult to stem. Caput medusae is a spiral pattern of engorged blood vessels emanating from the navel that can emerge due to the circulatory pressure (Korsten & Lieber, 1982; Lieber, 1976). Not only does blood not flow properly through a scarred liver, but bile production routes are also congested, which can create jaundice and bile insufficiency. Persons with cirrhosis sometimes have very tan skin (Andreoli, Carpenter, & Plum, 1986).

When enough of the liver is replaced with scar tissue, vital liver functions are not performed. One particular liver function is the metabolism of protein. When proteins are not processed, ammonia builds up in the blood creating brain damage. In fact, positive correlations between serum ammonia and neurological deficits have been noted (Goldstein, 1987). Acute hepatic encephalopathy presents as alteration in functioning ranging from delirium to coma and finally death. There are unusual movement disorders (tension in the upper trunk, asterixis or tremor) and EEG abnormalities. Some patients are left with residual deficits in cognition or motor functioning (choreoathetosis, ataxia, tremor, dysarthria) even if they survive an acute episode of encephalopathy (McEvoy, 1982).

One of the proteins produced through processing in the liver is albumin.

Adequate levels of albumin are necessary to maintain osmotic pressure in the blood stream. Without adequate osmotic pressure, the fluid in the blood seeps out into the tissue. As ascites (fluid in the body cavity) develops, a person assumes a pregnant appearance. Anasarca (edema throughout the body) can occur. In persons with liver failure, kidney (renal) insufficiency may soon follow resulting in death (Pitts & Van Thiel, 1986c).

One intriguing complication of liver disease is Dupuytrens contracture of the fingers. A person with such a contracture cannot move his/her fingers (Korsten & Lieber, 1982). Other findings include splenomegaly (spleen enlargement secondary to the finding of excess immunoglobins which are insufficiently cleared by the liver or resulting from the portal hypertension) (Andreoli et al., 1986, p. 332; Pitts & Van Thiel, 1986b).

Serum Abnormalities of Hepatic Disease

When the liver is damaged and through the process of enzyme induction independent of tissue damage, particular enzymes are released into the blood stream. These enzymes include SGOT (serum glutamic oxaloacetic transaminase or AST, i.e., aspartate aminotransferase), SGPT (also called ALT or alanine aminotransaminase), and GGT (gamma glutamyl transferase) (Keso & Salaspuro, 1989; Korsten & Lieber, 1982). All three enzymes are often elevated in heavy drinkers. None of these laboratory findings are sensitive indices of the degree of liver damage. Values may be within normal range despite the occurrence of disease (Korsten & Lieber, 1982). Besides liver enzymes, there are characteristic findings in the blood signifying a change in liver metabolism induced by heavy drinking. The livers of heavily drinking individuals release more carbohydrate deficient transferrin (a protein produced by the liver) which can serve as a marker for heavy consumption (Lieber, 1988).

GASTROINTESTINAL TRACT

Heavy drinking is associated with characteristic changes throughout the digestive tract. Alcoholics often exhibit parotid gland enlargement although the exact cause is unknown (Van Thiel, 1983). Heavy drinking increases the risks for esophageal carcinoma and colon cancer. The presence of alcohol changes the operation of particular sphincters such that heart burn occurs (reflux esophagitis). Heavy drinking is associated with acute and chronic gastritis along with gastrointestinal bleeding. The stomach mucosa is destroyed by alcohol and may require between 6 to 9 months for recovery after abstention. A common cause of bleeding results from laceration of the gastric mucosa upon retching at the gastroesophageal junction (Mallory-Weiss syndrome) (Mezey, 1982). Alcohol's role in the creation of gastric ulcers remain controversial (Van Thiel, 1983).

In the presence of alcohol, many of the stomach enzymes to not operate effectively. Transport of many nutrients is impaired. Malabsorption despite adequate diet is common in heavy drinkers. D-xylose, thiamine, folic acid, vitamin B 12, calcium and vitamin A are among those substances most likely to be poorly absorbed (Mezey, 1982; Van Thiel, 1983). Whereas alcohol decreases the amounts of some substances that are absorbed into the blood stream, intestinal synthesis of fats (triglycerides, cholesterol, and phospholipids) is increased by alcohol and these fats are then absorbed by the blood in increased abundance. Enhanced intestinal motility contributes to diarrhea, which is a frequent clinical manifestation (Mezey, 1982).

NUTRITIONAL DEFICIENCIES

Some alcoholics with small incomes devote limited financial resources to alcohol rather than food. Some prefer to drink on an empty stomach to enhance absorption. High blood alcohol levels depress appetite (Feldman, 1982). Once established, diseases attributable to malnutrition can further depress appetite. For example, specific B vitamin deficiencies can result in anorexia and painful swallowing (dysphagia) and an enlarged glossitis. Folate deficiency contributes to malabsorption (Feldman, 1982).

Pellagra (niacin deficiency), scurvy (vitamin C deficiency), Wernicke-Korsakoff syndrome (thiamine deficiency), sideroblastic anemia (vitamin B-6 or pyridoxine deficiency), decreased sperm production, poor night vision (due to improper utilization of vitamin A), bone disease due to poor absorption and use of vitamin D, and beriberi (thiamine deficiency) are all found at higher rates in heavy drinkers. Further folate deficiencies contribute to anemia associated with larger red blood cells (Van Thiel, 1983; Watson et al., 1986).

Alcohol affects water, electrolyte, and mineral balance. Heavy drinkers retain sodium, iron, potassium, and chloride. Magnesium, calcium, and zinc are excreted in excess. Tachycardia and cardiac arrhythmias may be attributable to deficiencies of magnesium (Watson et al., 1986).

Studies suggest that because of the special metabolic pathways induced in the liver by heavy drinking, the calories in alcohol are not equivalent as those in other food sources for alcoholics. Alcoholics consuming calorically adequate diets plus alcohol do not gain weight (Leiber, 1988). In rats as well, it has been demonstrated that an alcohol diet, despite its caloric equivalent to a nonalcohol diet will result in weight loss. This attenuation in growth resulting from an alcohol diet seems to be moderated by the types of food consumed along with the alcohol in the diet. Increasing carbohydrates in conjunction with high alcohol consumption will attenuate the diminution in weight (Guthrie et al., 1990).

PANCREAS

Changes similar to those that occur in the liver also occur in the pancreas. The tissue becomes fatty, bloated, and full of pseudocysts. Interstitial edema, fibrosis, necrosis, inflammation, and atrophy are histological findings. Lesions are often distributed in a haphazard fashion. The ducts to the glands in the pancreas which secrete the enzymes necessary to break down food become calcified. Dissolving enzymes leak into the pancreatic tissue destroying surrounding tissue. Some theories posit a stimulatory role for alcohol in causing leakage of these caustic enzymes into the pancreatic tissue (Korsten & Lieber, 1982; Van Thiel, 1983).

In a pancreas in which there is gradual deterioration, there is a slow decline in functioning. The production of insulin and glucagon as well as stomach enzymes required for the absorption of fats, proteins, and vitamins B and D are diminished. A malfunctioning pancreas will result in poor absorption of fat and the excess fat is excreted in the feces (steatorrhea) (Mezey, 1982). Glandular deficiencies can be replaced through oral supplementation.

In addition to diminution in function, other more acute problems can develop. The pseudocysts can occlude other organs causing them to malfunction. Pancreatitis (an inflamed pancreas) can also occur. It is believed that genetic mediation may underlie some pancreatitis (Korsten & Lieber, 1982). An additional pancreatic condition can also occur in heavy drinking. If a duct to a stomach enzyme secreting gland becomes plugged, the balance between the inactivating substances in the gland and the stomach enzymes can be disrupted. Given too much active trypsin (the stomach enzyme) the pancreas can be dissolved (Guyton, 1981).

Pancreatitis is excruciatingly painful. It usually requires 10 to 15 years of heavy drinking before the condition emerges. Once established, further drinking can precipitate an episode. Severe attacks have a mortality rate of 30%. In those who continue drinking, expected longevity is about 10 years after an initial episode (Korsten & Lieber, 1982). In addition to the previously mentioned problems, pancreatic cancer is twice as likely in heavy drinkers as in nondrinkers (Van Thiel, 1983).

CARDIOVASCULAR EFFECTS

Effects on Vasculature

As mentioned previously, drinking in moderation is associated with a decrease in low density, lipoproteins and an increase in high density lipoproteins (Khetarpal & Volicer, 1981). It is known that HDL decreases the risk for arteriosclerosis whereas LDLs increase risk. Autopsy studies of alcoholics suggest that they manifest less arteriosclerosis than control populations (LaPorte et al., 1985). Studies with monkeys have demonstrated that drinking does decrease stenosis (fat occlusion of the arteries) (LaPorte et al., 1985) suggesting that alcohol may have a causal role. When alcoholics quit drinking, their HDL levels return to control levels within 2 weeks (Cushman et al., 1986; Flegal & Cauley, 1985).

As mentioned before, there is evidence that the salubrious impact of drinking on HDLs is lost at high consumption levels (Hojnacki et al., 1988). At higher consumption levels "bad" HDLs are produced as well as LDLs. High levels of alcohol use have been associated with venous conditions such as phlebitis and varicose veins (Alcohol Health and Research World, 1981).

Although the mechanism that accounts for the effect is yet unclear, drinking at moderate amounts has been associated with decreased risk for heart attacks and other problems associated with diminished blood flow (ischemic stroke) (Khetarpal & Volicer, 1981; Laporte et al., 1985; Stampfer et al., 1988). Even when those who quit drinking because of health problems are removed from the control group of nondrinkers, the moderately consuming drinkers exhibit lower rates of heart attacks (Laporte et al., 1985). Criqui (1986) speculates that a decrease in blood platelets (a consequence of drinking that we discuss later) may mediate the lower risk for heart attacks.

It may be the case that the vasculature of drinking individuals may be less obstructed with fatty lesions (stenosis) thereby diminishing the risk of ischemic episodes. It is also known that very high blood alcohol levels can induce spasms of the cerebral vasculature (Altura, Altura, & Gebrewold, 1983). Consistent with this finding is the fact that younger stroke victims are differentiated from older stroke victims on the variable of binge drinking (Taylor & Combs-Orne, 1985). Among heavy drinking males (those consuming over 30 drinks per week), an increased stroke risk has been noted (Gill et al., 1986). Males drinking over 30 drinks per week are at 4 times the risk for a stroke as nondrinkers, although light drinkers (those consuming 1 to 9 drinks per week) are at half the risk for stroke as are nondrinkers (Gill et al., 1986). There is evidence of extensive myocardial, small vessel deterioration even though large vessel deterioration is not observed (Knott et al., 1987). Further, in women, moderate drinking is associated with a slightly higher risk for subarachnoid hemorrhage, possibly due to decreased blood clotting ability (Stampfer et al., 1988). A positive correlation between hemorrhagic stroke and alcohol consumption has been noted (Shaw, 1987).

Acutely, alcohol is a dilator of the cutaneous vasculature yet reduces blood flow to muscles. The dilation of blood vessels to the skin is believed to be secondary to alcohol's effect on the sympathetic nervous system (Khetarpal & Volicer, 1981). Paradoxically, it has been demonstrated that if alcohol is infused intravenously it causes vasoconstriction in the skin and muscles (Knott & Beard, 1982). The dilated blood vessels in the skin may allow heat to escape resulting in hypothermia (Ryan, 1983/84). Whereas acute effects of alcohol are mediated through the nervous system, chronic drinking alters calcium and magnesium levels resulting in vasoconstriction (Altura & Altura, 1987).

Drinking in excess of 3 drinks per day has been associated with high blood pressure (Khetarpal & Volicer, 1981; Klatsky et al., 1977). The prevalence of high blood pressure is 2.3 times as high in alcoholic samples (Khetrapal & Volicer, 1981). Khetarpal and Volicer (1981) comment on the fact that in epidemiological studies, randomly timed blood pressure measurement most often serves as the dependent measure. The increased blood pressure could reflect acute or subacute withdrawal symptoms. In studies of alcoholics entering treatment, blood pressure decreases dramatically after a period of abstention (Flegal & Cauley, 1985).

Heart

The short-term functional impact of alcohol on the heart muscle is to decrease pumping strength (Knott & Beard, 1982; Van Thiel & Gavaler, 1985b). Imbalances in electrolytes associated with intoxication may disturb the pumping action. A phenomenon called "holiday heart" has been recognized. It refers to the arrhythmias and rapid heart beat that can be experienced at high blood alcohol levels and during withdrawal (Greenspon & Schaal, 1983; Van Thiel & Gavaler, 1985). There has been speculation as to whether the arrhythmias could be due to the increase in catecholamines occasioned by drinking or possibly acetaldehyde (Khetarpal & Volicer, 1981).

Cardiomyopathy has been well established as a consequence of chronic alcohol use. There is a correlation between injury to the heart and injury to skeletal muscles (Urbano-Marquez et al., 1989). Sustained heavy drinking over at least a decade is associated with enlarged heart (cardiomegaly), fatty infiltration, inflammation, and fibrosis of the heart muscle. Signs of cardiomyopathy include cardiac arrhythmias, lowered volume of blood being pumped, decreased oxygen extraction, and poor contractibility of the muscle fibers. Abnormalities of left ventricular function can be detected prior to the emergence of diagnosable disease (Khetarpal & Volicer, 1981; Knott et al., 1987). Later symptoms include dyspnea (shortness of breath) and palpitations. Congestive heart failure occurs when the pumping action is no longer sufficient to move the blood through the circulatory system. In addition to the direct role of alcohol in the development of cardiomyopathy, nutritional disturbances are associated with cardiac fibrosis and destruction of the heart tissue (Feldman, 1982).

BLOOD CELL PRODUCTION

As a result of nutritional deficiencies and changes in the bone marrow where blood cells are produced, there are some characteristic changes in blood cell production that occur. In terms of the red blood cells, larger red blood cells that are inefficient at carrying iron and nutrients are produced. This phenomenon is labeled macrocytic anemia. Due to altered use of vitamins, abnormal blood cells with characteristic iron rings are produced. This phenomenon is known as sideroblastic anemia. Abnormally shaped blood cells (spur cell anemia) may be present in those with malfunctioning livers. There may be an overall reduction in the production of red blood cells and a diminished number therefore in circulation (Van Thiel, 1983).

Fewer white blood cells are produced by heavily drinking persons. Liver disease results in less production of complement, a blood component needed to activate white blood cells to attack a foreign invader (Pitts & Van Thiel, 1986b). Further, alcohol interferes with the mobilization of white blood cells (Van Thiel, 1983). Alcoholics produce fewer blood platelets and those produced are slower to aggregate providing a second reason for poor blood clotting. Blood changes revert to normal within about a month of abstention (Chanarin, 1982).

SKIN

A variety of dermatological problems are created by heavy drinking. Further, heavy drinking will exacerbate most skin disease caused by other factors. In a sample of 355 alcoholic admissions to a public hospital, 44% suffered some type of skin condition (Rosset & Oki, 1971; Whitfield, 1982).

Heavy drinkers frequently exhibit facial edema, such that puffiness around the eyes is frequently observed. The edema may be attributable to increased vasopressin secretion which occurs during the plateau and fall curve of blood alcohol levels. Facial edema tends to resolve given one or two weeks of abstinence (Whitfield, 1982).

Skin redness can occur. Eyes can remain bloodshot (Van Thiel, 1983). The predisposition to develop the W. C. Fields nose (rhinophyma caused by lobular hypertrophy of the nose with reddish coloration) will be accelerated by drinking (Domonkos, Arnold, & Odom, 1982, p. 289). The W. C. Fields condition, which includes dilated blood vessels, and enlargement of sweat glands in the nose, and pustules, is called acne rosacea. Acne rosacea is attributable to alcohol's impact on vasculature which is in turn mediated by the peripheral endorphin release. It can be blocked by naloxone (Bernstein & Soltani, 1982).

Some dermatological manifestations are attributable to liver disease. High levels of bilirubin (the dead blood cells that are not cleared by the liver) cause itchiness. When proteins are not processed effectively by the liver, finger nail production is altered sometimes producing characteristic bands called semi-lunar (half moon) nails. Because of the liver's altered storage of iron along with other changes in the liver, the skin can assume a dark or greyish cast (Whitfield, 1982; Woeber, 1975).

KIDNEYS

Alcohol affects kidney filtration in characteristic ways. Vasopressin (antidiuretic hormone from the pituitary gland) is decreased by alcohol as it is building in the system (the ascending limb of the BAL) such that more free water is excreted. On the descending limb of BAL, vasopressin is increased. In heavy drinkers, renal hyperexcretion of zinc and magnesium occurs (Feldman, 1982). Whether enhanced urinary excretion of zinc results in insufficiency, has not been established (Van Thiel, 1983). Magnesium deficiency is in turn related to low serum calcium and potassium which are also decreased (Feldman, 1982).

The tissue of the kidneys is affected secondary to other conditions. When the liver fails, the resulting toxins create kidney failure despite the basic integrity of the kidneys themselves. Renal tissue can also be destroyed in conjunction with liver disease (Pitts & Van Thiel, 1986b). In alcoholics, bladder and kidney infections are more common due to the compromised immune system (Pitts & Van Thiel, 1986b).

LUNGS

Inhaled impurities are handled by the lungs in two ways. The cough reflex dislodges the impurities and the cilia on the lung's surface sweeps them away. Then white blood cells move in to phagocytize (gobble up and destroy) the impurities. Both these systems are compromised in the heavy drinker. The coughing reflex and ciliary activity are depressed. White blood cells are fewer in number and do not operate aggressively. The result is increased susceptibility to bronchitis, pneumonia, lung abesses, and very high rates of TB (Lyons, 1982). An additional complication occurs with aspiration. The very intoxicated individual can inhale food or vomit into the lung tissue with insufficient capacity to cough up the material (Chew & Rissing, 1982). If immediate death does not occur, infection may develop.

ENDOCRINE DISTURBANCES

The acute effect of alcohol is to stimulate the hypothalamic-pituitary-adrenocortical axis. The effect on the adrenal cortex glands (release of cortiosteroids) seems to be stimulated by changes in the hypothalamus. The chronic adjustment to high levels of these hormones disregulates the homostatic mechanisms in the hypothalamus. Alcoholics often exhibit an abnormal response to the dexamethasone suppression test (a test used to evaluate excessive adrenal gland secretion). Occasionally alcoholics present with Cushing's syndrome (an oversecretion of corticosteroids) which reflects the impact of alcohol on the adrenal glands and possibly inefficient metabolism of hormones by the liver (Stokes,

1982). (A malfunctioning liver will be inefficient in its catabolism of cortisol, aldosterone, and testosterone; although without liver failure, alcohol induces catabolizing enzymes for testosterone (Van Thiel, 1983). The Cushing's syndrome usually resolves within several weeks of abstention (Stokes, 1982).

There is speculation that alcohol's chronic stimulation of pituitary tropic hormones (prolactin for breasts; thyroid stimulating hormone; melanyocyte stimulating hormone for skin pigmentation) may be implicated in particular increased cancer rates for heavy drinkers. These increased cancer rates include thyroid cancer, breast cancer, and melanomas (Stokes, 1982).

Although alcohol has no direct effect on insulin secretion, when alcohol is ingested in combination with carbohydrates, alcohol will enhance the release of insulin in response to the carbohydrates. The increased insulin will result in a quicker clearing of blood glucose and ensuing hypoglycemia (Ryan, 1983/84). According to Ryan, the hypoglycemia may be experienced as an unpleasant after effect of drinking and can lead to dangerous mental impairment if one is operating a vehicle. In contrast to the more rapid clearing of glucose after drinking in normals, alcoholics exhibit an opposite reaction. Alcoholics, when sober, exhibit glucose intolerance. That is, if they are given a carbohydrate load, they will not exhibit the normal secretion of insulin and clearing of glucose (Sereny & Endrenyl, 1978). After weeks of sobriety, alcoholics regain their normal glucose tolerance. It has been speculated that the transient glucose intolerance is attributable to depleted insulin stores in alcoholic persons who may be continually exhausting their supplies (Sereny & Endrenyl, 1978).

Whereas acute alcohol ingestion will release insulin, it should also be noted that alcohol will induce adrenal gland secretion, that is epinephrine (adrenaline) will be released. Epinephrine will suppress pancreatic release of insulin and increase pancreatic release of glucagon. The increase of glucagon and decrease of insulin should have a hyperglycemic effect (Erwin & Towell, 1983). Further, it is known that alcohol will interfere with insulin's binding to receptor sites yielding a hyperglycemic effect (Singh et al., 1988).

Alcohol's effect on glucose regulation is complicated. Multiple mechanisms are involved often operating in opposition to each other. Predictions as to impact will vary as a function of the organisms prior state (hungry or fed; well nourished or not). Both hypoglycemic and hyperglycemic states are possible. Hypoglycemia caused by drinking may be superimposed upon hangover effects. Clinicians should be alert to the possible effects on blood sugar in both directions.

MALE REPRODUCTIVE SYSTEM

Over time alcohol decreases levels of testosterone. Testosterone decrease is attributable to four processes. First, alcohol stimulates the production of those liver enzymes which catabolize testosterone, thereby resulting in increased metabolism. Second, break-down products of alcohol influence cellular processes in the testes such that there is a decline in testosterone synthesis. Third, alcohol influences testosterone production through the hypothalamic-pituitary-gonadal axis. Alcohol alters release of the luteinizing hormone releasing factor from the hypothalamus such that down-regulation of the production of testosterone in the testes occurs (Cierco, 1983; Van Thiel 1983). Fourth, chronic heavy drinking destroys the cells in the testes, which synthesize testosterone such that hormonal changes will not resolve with abstinence (Alcohol Health and Research World, 1981).

As mentioned in the discussion of the liver, heavy drinking will result in an accumulation of estrogen. The combination of decreased testosterone and increased estrogen will result in feminization for males. Female fat and hair distribution, gynecomastia, spider angiomata, and palmar erythema, testicular atrophy, decreased libido, infertility, and impotence may occur. In terms of the rates, gynecomastia has been noted in 20% of alcoholics, palmar erythema and spider angiomata in 40 to 50% (Fadel & Hadi, 1982). Due to changes in the testes, sperm production is decreased and those produced may be of abnormal morphology (Stokes, 1982).

There has been recent attention focused on the impact of a heavy drinking father on the fetus. Statistics suggest a lower birth weight in those babies born to heavy consuming fathers after controlling for maternal behavior (Little, & Sing, 1986). The same findings have been found in animal research. Additionally in the rat literature, among rat pups conceived by heavy consuming male rats a decrease in rat pup activity and a decrease in active avoidance learning has been noted (Abel & Lee, 1988). Further, impaired immune responses have been noted (Berk, Montogomery, Hazlett, & Abel, 1989). It is speculated that free radicals produced by drinking may alter sperm such that lower birth weight is observed (Abel & Lee, 1988).

FEMALE REPRODUCTIVE SYSTEM

Heavy drinking women exhibit higher rates of menstrual disorders, infertility, and repeated miscarriages. Anovulation, luteal phase dysfunction, and amenorrhea may be observed (Mello et al., 1988). Some of the effects may be mediated through changes in pituitary hormones (Fadel & Hadi, 1982). Whereas males display increased feminization, females lose their secondary sex characteristics. There is loss of breast tissue and pelvic fat (Van Thiel, 1983).

There have been conflicting reports on the increased risk of breast cancer in female drinkers (Lowenfels & Zevola, 1989). One study suggested increased risk in women drinking 3.5 drinks per week (Schatzkin et al., 1987). After a meta analysis (statistical technique for evaluating findings from a number of studies) across 16 studies, Longnecker, Berlin, Orza, and Chalmers (1988) concluded that there was evidence of increased risk above 2 drinks per day. Harris and Wynder (1988) conclude that there are too many confounding variables to justify a definitive statement. Similarly, Lowenfels and Zevola (1989) conclude that the results across studies have not been consistent enough to justify recommendations. If any reduction in cancer risk from attenuation of alcohol consumption is to be realized, it can only be achieved through total abstention. In studies reporting positive findings, very modest levels of consumption have been found to be associated with increased risk.

Effects on the Fetus

Acutely, alcohol has long been used to interrupt labor pains which it does through its effect on the pituitary hormone, oxytocin (Fadel & Hadi, 1982). In the long run, heavy drinking women are at increased risk for spontaneous abortion and stillbirths (Tewari & Carson, 1982). In fact, increased risk for spontaneous abortion has been found in one study at one to two drinks per day and with two drinks twice a week (Alcohol Health and Research World, 1981). Fortunately, the rat and human literature suggests that women do spontaneously decrease their alcohol consumption during pregnancy (Van Thiel & Gavaler, 1988).

Fetal Alcohol Syndrome

Drinking through gestation produces the Fetal Alcohol Syndrome, a form of severe retardation associated with characteristic malformations (Rosett & Weiner, 1982). Babies born with fetal alcohol syndrome display particular malformations of the face. Characteristic findings include cleft palate, eye folds that are poorly defined, lower birth weight, poorer EEG function, and decreased head circumference (Russell & Skinner, 1988). Additional features of fetal alcohol syndrome include malformations of the cardiac, urogenital, and skeletal systems and failure to gain weight after birth (Alcohol Health and Research, 1981; Murcherjee & Hodgen, 1982).

The issue regarding whether there are critical periods of gestation during which the fetus is more at risk for particular types of damage has received attention. The first trimester may be a critical period for the establishment of alcohol's deleterious effect. During the first trimester, cells in the brain line up to form critical structures. Alcohol affects the migration of these cells, such that cells forming critical structures overshoot their appropriate destination. A disorganized brain results (Kotkoskie & Norton, 1988).

A child with fetal alcohol syndrome can be expected to display poor motor coordination, hypotonia (reduced muscle tone), irritability, tremulousness, and hyperactivity (Alcohol Health and Research World, 1981).

Alcohol's effect on sex hormones during gestation may result in feminization of male offspring (McGivern, Roselli, & Handa, 1988). The male fetus born to alcohol consuming animals exhibits feminization possibly attributable to hormonal changes in the intrauterine environment (McGivern, Roselli, & Handa, 1988). Unanswered questions concern the amount of alcohol that is sufficient for producing deleterious effects. Streissguth et al. (1989) found a mean IQ difference of 4.8 points in 4-year-olds whose mothers consumed 3 drinks and above per day during early pregnancy. To date research fails to support a critical value above which deleterious effects emerge, rather a continuous variable model better fits the data (Russell & Skinner, 1988).

In addition to structural anomalies attributable to drinking, high blood alcohol levels can induce spasm of the umbilical cord causing hypoxia in the developing fetus (Murcherjee & Hodgen, 1982). Alcohol reduces lactation and readily passes through mother's milk. Infant brain protein synthesis is impaired by alcohol ingested during nursing (Tewari & Carson, 1982). If alcohol is imbibed through mother's milk at sufficiently high dosages, a pseudo-Cushing's syndrome (too much adrenal gland release) can be produced in the infant (Alcohol Health and Research World, 1981).

MUSCLES

Nearly half of alcoholics display histological changes of muscle tissue. These changes include myofibrillar necrosis, inflammation, and interstitial fibrosis and abnormal mitochondria. Morphological examination have revealed intracellular edema, lipid droplets, excessive glycogen, and deranged myofibrillar elements. Muscle compostion changes include phosphorus deficiency, low magnesium content, depressed intracellular potassium, and increased intracellular sodium, chloride, and calcium. Clinically, muscle tissue is swollen and tender (Ferguson & Knochel, 1982). A history of muscle cramps and weakness is often reported (Van Thiel, 1983).

On a chronic basis, the muscle tissue wastes away. The decreased muscle mass occurs most notably in the hips and shoulders. The muscle wasting has been found to occur even under conditions of adequate nutrition. The acute condition is called rhabdomyolysis. As the muscle cells die, myoglobin is released into the blood stream. The myoglobin can impair kidney filtering and result in kidney failure. The myoglobin can impart a brown color to the urine (Ferguson & Knochel, 1982).

Consistent with the effects of alcohol on muscle tissue, it has been recognized that patients being treated for lower back pain are more likely to be alcohol abusers than the general population (Gorman et al., 1987).

BONES

Atrophy of bone (osteopenia) is often reported in heavy drinkers. The bone tissue decreases in density thus becoming brittle and more easily broken (Bliven, 1982). The bone changes may be attributable to loss of specific nutrients resulting from an inadequate diet or changes in kidney filtration.

Nontraumatic idiopathic osteonecrosis of the femoral head occurs when the blood supply to the head of the femur is restricted. A repair process ensues in which necrotic material is replaced by fibrous material. Gradually the head of the femur collapses. The disease is frequently bilateral with a later onset in the second hip. Fortunately its incidence is rare even in alcoholic populations (.3% in one study), although alcoholics constitute the largest group in whom the condition is encountered (Bliven, 1982).

THE NERVOUS SYSTEM

Functional Changes

Mood disturbances during periods of abstention are characteristic of heavy drinkers. When not drinking, alcoholics often report depression, oversensitivity, irritability, paranoia, agitation, lethargy, apprehension, anxiety, and poor concentration (Ron, 1987). Knott et al. (1987) describe an alcoholic paranoid state characterized by suspicion, distrust, jealousy, and paranoid delusions especially of marital infidelity. Ward environment studies attest to the fact that alcoholics become progressively more depressed as they continue to drink over a several day period (McNamee, Mello & Mendelsohn, 1968; Nathan et al., 1970; Tamerin & Mendelson, 1969). It is known that depression remits within several weeks of abstention (Overall et al., 1985).

Effect on Sleep

In persons who are not tolerant to alcohol, small amounts of alcohol can reduce the time to the onset of sleep. However, awakenings during the night are also increased and REM sleep is decreased until tolerance to the effect develops. Further, blood alcohol levels during sleep increase the probability of episodic parasomnias (bruxisms, sleepwalking, sleep talking) (Hartmann, 1982).

Studies of alcoholics allowed to consume high quantities of alcohol over a several day period have demonstrated that alcoholics can sleep for prolonged periods. When not drinking, alcoholics experience more sleep disturbance (arousals during the night and changes in the stage of sleep) and insomnia. After detoxification, sober alcoholics continue to exhibit sleep disturbances. There are onset insomnia, frequent awakenings, increased but fragmented rapid-eye-movement sleep. Insomnia with alterations in the sleep cycle and decreased slow wave sleep after detoxification may remain a problem for months (Hartmann, 1982; el-Guebaly, 1987). The incidence of sleep apnea is increased both during intoxication and after detoxification (Vitiello et al., 1990).

Tryptophan is frequently recommended for treating the insomnia of those in recovery (Hartmann, 1982). Schuckit (workshop attended by the author) cautions against treating insomnia with benzodiazepines. Tolerance to the soporific effects of benzodiazepine will develop in a short period of time such that no benefit is achieved. Establishing a regular bed time routine without daytime napping may be useful in hastening the resolution of insomnia.

Long-Term Changes in Structure

Alcohol effects nerves in a number of ways. The dietary deficiencies associated with drinking produce demyelination (destruction of the fat cells covering the nerve which allow faster conduction). Atrophy of axons and dentrites seems to be a direct effect of the alcohol. If the first two changes occur, the nerve cells can probably recover with abstention. However, alcohol is also associated with nerve cell death. A nerve cell cannot be replaced (Mayer & Khurana, 1982).

Damage to the nervous system is generally divided according to the type of nerve that is effected. The central nervous system (CNS) refers to nerves in the brain and spinal cord. The peripheral nervous system consists of all those nerves outside the CNS. One major division of the peripheral nervous system is the autonomic nervous system which regulate involuntary functions such as breathing, heart rate, digestion, etc. Other nerves in the peripheral system control motor and sensory activity. Alcohol impacts all systems. The effects on each system are now discussed.

Autonomic and Peripheral Nervous System

Damage to the autonomic nervous system can result in dysphagia (difficult swallowing), hoarseness, hypothermia, orthostatic hypotension, hypotension, anhidorsis, impotence, headaches, and incontinence. Damage to the voluntary nerves and sensory nerves outside the CNS is labeled peripheral neuropathy. Peripheral neuropathy is most often bilateral. Distal nerves are more commonly effected than proximal nerves. Sensory nerves are more effected than are motor nerves. Typical findings include complaints of burning or tingling of the extremities. There is often a loss of ability to feel things, explaining why alcoholics often have cigarette burns on their fingers (Mayer & Khurana, 1982). Red/green color blindness can occur. The retinal nerve is often damaged resulting in blurred vision. Some patients present with an inability to contract the muscle raising their foot (foot drop) (Mayer & Khurana, 1982).

Central Nervous System Effects

Alcoholism is the second most common cause of severe organic brain syndrome. It is preceded only by Alzheimer's disease. It accounts for 10% of all cases of organic brain syndrome (Eckhardt & Martin, 1986). Between 50–70% of all detoxified alcoholics display cognitive deficits (Eckhardt & Martin, 1986).

Cognitive deficits in alcoholic populations have been recorded on a number of assessment batteries. Typical findings include difficulty in breaking set after a series of problems of requiring the same cognitive strategy, poor performance on the block design and digit symbol of the WAIS (Wechsler Adult Intelligence Scale), slow reaction time, impaired short-term memory, slowed psychomotor speed, slower response to auditory and visual stimuli, and poor tactile recognition (McEvoy, 1982). More profound impairment is noted on spatial ability than on verbal ability. Performance IQ seems to be effected to a greater extent than verbal IQ. That is, deterioration of skills mediated by right brain functioning seem to be more apparent than deterioration of skills mediated by left brain functioning, although computed tomography scans reveal diffuse cortical atrophy (Miglioli et al., 1979; Miller & Orr, 1980; Risberg & Berglund, 1987; Tarter & Edwards, 1986). Reviewers of the literature have suggested that damage occurs in both hemispheres, although the tests for measuring damage are more sensitive to right hemispheric dysfunction (Ellis & Oscar-Berman, 1989). Socially, persons with alcoholic brain impairment will present with lack of concern, poor self-care, poor judgment, poor attention span, and generalized slowness (Goldstein, 1987, p. 229).

Functional deficits are consistent with anatomical findings and blood flow studies. Atrophy is visible on CAT (computerized axial tomography) scanning. The brain sulci are widened, there is frontal lobe atrophy, ventricular enlargement, and meningeal thickening (Ron, 1987; Lee, Moller, Hardt, Haubek, & Jensen, 1979). Concomitant with structural changes in the brain, there are changes in cerebral blood flow (Risberg & Berglund, 1987). Decreased blood flow to the frontal, parietal, anterior, and temporal regions have been documented (McEvoy, 1982; Risberg & Berglund, 1987). EEG abnormalities have been recorded (McEvoy, 1982). Under a microscope, neuronal loss, disruption of cortical laminae, pigmentary degeneration, and glial proliferation are visible (Ron, 1987).

Multiple mechanisms may be required to explain the diverse variety of deficits observed in alcoholics. Deterioration in the caudate and thalamic areas of the brain induced by thiamine deficiency may cause memory impairment. Decreased verbal fluency may be attributable to diminished frontal lobe density, itself caused by a more direct effect of alcohol exposure (Goldstein, 1987; Ron 1987). The noted correlation between GGT (liver enzyme) and neurological deficits has lead to the speculation that GGT may alter protein transport into neurons in a manner which impairs their function (Irwin et al., 1989).

With sobriety, improvement in cognitive functioning has been noted. Cognitive activity accelerates this improvement (Stringer & Goldman, 1988). Improvement in cognitive functioning is mirrored by increases in brain mass as noted on CAT scans and normalization of blood flow (Risberg & Berglund, 1987). Ron (1987) has speculated that the increase in brain mass may reflect rearborization of neurons. Increase in brain mass may continue over a 5-year period of sobriety (Donovan et al., 1987; Forsberg & Goldman, 1985). Older persons seem to exhibit less recovery than younger alcoholics (Forsberg & Goldman, 1985; Goldman, 1987).

Additional Questions

Beyond noting the nerve and brain damage that occurs, researchers have addressed questions pertaining to whether damage occurs at all ages and how drinking pattern and amount consumed corresponds with clinical findings. These questions are now discussed.

Is Alcoholic Brain Damage an Acceleration of Normal Aging and Does It Differentially Impair Older vs. Younger Persons?   Goldstein (1987) has concluded that damage due to drinking is qualitatively different than changes attributable to aging. Whereas both processes will produce atrophy of the cortex, third ventricle lesions are characteristic of alcohol damage. On memory tasks, alcoholics and older individuals display similar problems in retrieval, although unlike the elderly, alcoholics display problems with recognition as well. Further, alcoholics, unlike the elderly display problems in inhibiting irrelevant associations and impaired discriminations (Kramer, Blusewicz, & Preston, 1989).

There have been empirical attempts to assess whether alcohol only produces damage in those who are already aging rapidly (that is, accelerates normal aging) or whether deficits occur at all ages. Researchers have conducted experiments in which age is a variable and alcoholism is another variable. Studies have examined both dependent variables of performance and CAT scan findings. Results are mixed. There are reports in which damage has been documented in both the old and the young, or in the young in particular (Kramer et al., 1989; Lee et al. 1979; Noonberg, Goldstein, & Page, 1985). Sometimes damage can only be documented in older alcoholics (Parsons, 1987; Ryan, 1982).

Goldman (1987) speculates as to which factors might explain why alcoholic deterioration is sometimes only found among older persons. It may be that aging brains are more vulnerable to neurotoxicity. It may be that given the presence of a neurotoxin, older persons will be less able to metabolize and excrete the toxin, hence allowing for differential exposure. Perhaps the rate of damage due to alcohol may be constant across the life span, but a protracted period of damage is necessary in order to accumulate sufficient subclinical damage so as to be clinically observable. Finally, it may be that all ages experience that same degree of damage, but older persons, having depleted brain power due to normal aging, lack plasticity and capacity to compensate for dysfunction.

Are Particular Drinking Patterns More Damaging Than Others?   Investigators have compared binge drinkers with daily drinkers on cognitive tests. Sanchez-Craig (1980) found that daily drinkers were more impaired than binge drinkers. Unfortunately, Sanchez-Craig (1980) did not assess the amount consumed per occasion in the alcoholics in her study. It is possible that she was comparing daily bingers (those who consumed very heavily each day) with occasional bingers. Tarbox, Connors, and McLaughlin (1986) categorized drinkers as continuous or binge drinkers. Age was a factor in their study as was duration of heavy drinking. Results suggested that older alcoholics were more impaired that younger alcoholics; alcoholics who had sustained their alcoholic pattern over many years were more impaired than those who had sustained their pattern for a shorter duration of time; and daily drinkers were more impaired than binge drinkers.

How Many Years of Drinking Are Required For Damage To Occur?   Pishkin, Lovallo, and Bourne (1985) divided alcoholics into those with a long duration of heavy drinking vs. those with short duration of heavy drinking. Age was not a confounding factor in their study, as groups were equated on this variable. The duration for heavy drinking did relate to impairment of ability to learn a rule necessary for solving problems although it did not relate to impairment in the transfer of the rule once it was learned. Others have failed to find any association between degree of impairment and duration of heavy drinking or between degree of impairment and total amount of alcohol consumed over the life span (Eckhardt & Martin, 1986; Estrin, 1987; Forsberg & Goldman, 1985; Parson, 1987). Some have found that the amount of alcohol typically consumed per occasion seems to be more predictive of cognitive function than does frequency of consumption or overall years of drinking (Parsons, 1987, p. 155; Polich & Bloom, 1988). Oscar-Berman, (1987) suggests that heavy consumption is required for damage.

At What Level of Daily Consumption Is Risk For Brain Damage Incurred?   Whereas the prior studies have investigated cognitive impairment in alcoholics, others have investigated cognitive impairment in social drinkers. Researchers have pursued the question of whether moderate drinking (between 2–4 drinkers per day) is associated with deficit cognitive functioning. Results across studies have been inconsistent (see O. A. Parsons, 1986, for a review).

Studies in which poorer cognitive functioning in social drinkers is noted can not be used to infer the conclusion that moderate levels of drinking will cause brain damage. The comparison of social drinkers with teetotalers confounds a myriad of independent variables. The following points should be considered:

1. Parsons (1986) points out that in only one study was blood alcohol level assessed prior to testing cognitive functioning. Hence it is possible that some of the individuals in the social drinking group were under the influence at the time of assessment. Thus, studies in which drinkers were found to be more impaired than nondrinkers, might well reflect the effects of intoxication rather than cognitive damage.

2. Studies in which moderate drinkers were compared with teetotalers have not evaluated the time since last drink. It is possible that many of the moderate drinkers were assessed while they were hung over. It is known that cognitive deficits attributable to hangover/withdrawal are manifested as long as 3 weeks post drinking cessation (Goldman, 1987; McCrady & Smith, 1986). Hence differences between moderate drinkers and abstainers could reflect hang over rather than more permanent brain damage.

3. Moderate drinkers differ from abstainers in many ways. It is known that lower IQ individuals drink more per occasion. This may reflect the fact the lower IQ individuals gravitate to the subcultural groupings in which heavy alcohol consumption is encouraged (Emmerson, Dustman, Heil, & Shearer, 1988). Hence, differences between groups of drinkers vs. abstainers might reflect preexistent cognitive limitations rather than brain damage attributable to heavy drinking.

4. Bowden (1987) and Bowden, Walton, and Walsh (1988) take issue with the conclusion that moderate drinking (2 to 4 drinks per day) can induce cognitive deficits. Bowden (1987) argues that in those studies in which inferior cognitive performance was documented in the social drinking groups, the dependent measure was often the Shipley (a measure of intelligence). The Shipley is frequently insensitive to cognitive impairment in those with unequivocal alcoholism diagnoses. It can hardly be sensitive enough to detect slight impairment in social drinkers. Bowden argues that obtained group differences probably reflect the fact that less bright people are more likely to be frequent social drinkers.

Are Alcoholics With a Family History of Alcoholism More Likely to Develop Brain Damage as a Result of Their Alcoholism? The issue of whether FHPs (family history positive for alcoholism) are more vulnerable to brain damage than are FHN alcoholics has been addressed. Results of studies (Reed, Grant, & Adams, 1987; Schaeffer, Parsons, & Yohman, 1984) have failed to adduce evidence of differential sensitivity to brain damage in FHP alcoholics. Vulnerability to cirrhosis (Hrubec & Omenn, 1981) given heavy consumption appears to be genetically mediated. Vulnerability to Korsakoff's is also genetically mediated (Lishman, 1987, p. 492). However, vulnerability to brain damage from alcohol seems independent of the genetic risk for the development of alcoholism.

Specific Brain Syndromes

Beyond generalized cognitive impairment and brain atrophy attributable to heavy drinking, alcoholics display higher incidences of specific syndromes. The following brain syndromes are more likely to be found in alcoholic populations.

Wernicke-Korsakoff syndrome has been attributed to thiamine deficiency often associated with chronic alcoholism. The deficiency arises from lack of thiamine in the diet, impaired absorption through the gut, and impaired storage and utilization by the liver (Lishman, 1987, p. 492). Wernicke's encephalopathy manifests abruptly in response to dietary deficiency. It is characterized by confusion, ataxia, and ocular manifestations (paralysis of the eye muscle and nystagmus). In addition to the CNS findings, peripheral neuropathy also occurs. During an acute episode, encephalopathy stupor and hypothermia are common. Residual damage is referred to as Korsakoff's syndrome. In Korsakoff patients there is a profound loss of the ability to encode events into memory after the onset of the disorder. Confabulation (making up things) is a frequent coping device employed by patients as they attempt to function despite their loss of historical perspective. Patient often display apathy and indifference regarding symptoms. Despite impairment, patients are alert with adequate reasoning abilities. Attention to social amenities and attention to grooming is often preserved. Cerebellar ataxia can also be part of the syndrome. Genetic factors have been implicated in the development of the syndrome (McEvoy, 1982; Feldman, 1982; Goldstein, 1987).

Marchiafava–Bignamini labels a condition involving deterioration of the myelinated nerves of the corpus callosum (the area of the brain connecting the right and left cerebral hemispheres). Its development is insidious. It manifests as paranoia, mood disturbance, aphasia, seizures, apraxia, and progressive dementia (Freund, 1983; McEvoy, 1982).

Cerebellar deterioration can occur and will manifest as intentional tremor, wide based gait, dysarthria, and nystagmus (Freund, 1987; McEvoy, 1982).

Deficiency amblyopia occurs given demyelination of the optic nerves, chiasm and optic tracts. There is a progressive loss of vision over a several week period (McEvoy, 1982).

Central pontine myelinosis occurs with demyelination of the center of the pons. Symptoms involve spastic weakness, dysphagia, diminished cough and gag reflexes, and paralysis (Freund, 1987; McEvoy, 1982).

Chronic hallucinosis In up to 10% of alcoholics who have suffered hallucinosis in conjunction with withdrawal symptoms, the condition becomes chronic. This condition may be difficult to distinguish from schizophrenia. There may be ideas of reference and poorly systematized persecutory delusions (DSM-III).

Seizures Among heavy drinkers, there is an increased risk for unprovoked seizures. Statistical analyses suggest that these seizures are not related to withdrawal, as they are just as likely to occur after protracted abstinence as during drinking. Seizures have been noted in alcoholics who denied prior head injury (Neg et al., 1988).

SPECULATION REGARDING WHY ALCOHOL IS TOXIC

By now the reader has probably been convinced that alcohol is a toxic, damaging chemical. Researchers have puzzled over how the damage is done. Some have implicated acetaldehyde as the damaging factor. Against the acetaldehyde hypothesis is the fact that acetaldehyde is rapidly metabolized in the body. Further, metabolism of alcohol occurs in the liver but not substantially in other organs. There is no mechanism for producing high levels of acetaldehyde in organs other than the liver (Laposata & Lange, 1986). There have been, however, recent report of alcohol dehydrogenase (which converts alcohol to acetaldehyde) in specific brain areas (Kerr, Maxwell, & Crabb, 1989) and interest continues in the possibility of a role for acetaldehyde in mediating alcohol's toxicity (Kerr et al., 1989; Wickramasinghe et al., 1989). Another promising avenue in which interest has been awakened is the role of free radicals. It is known that alcohol will decrease free radical scavengers (Nordmann, 1987).

An intriguing study by Phillips and Cragg (1984), suggests that some particular damage that alcohol produces does not occur while body tissues are being exposed to alcohol, but rather the destruction occurs during the withdrawal process. Phillips and Cragg measured immunoglobins in the cerebrospinal fluid which they suggested might constitute a measure of cellular damage. They found that immunoglobins were elevated during the withdrawal process but not during intoxification. Further evidence corroborated their hypothesis of destruction occurring during the withdrawal process. Purkinje cells from the cerebellum in mice sacrificed while still intoxicated following a 4-month period of intoxication were intact. However, there was Purkinje cell death among those mice sacrificed after the withdrawal process. In mice among whom withdrawal symptoms were avoided by gradual reduction in alcohol intake, there was no evidence of cellular destruction. Similar findings, suggesting damage during the withdrawal process as opposed to during alcohol exposure have been reported (Cadete-Leite, Tavares, Alves, Uylings, & Paula–Barbosa, 1989). Whereas the foregoing is true, the fact that alcohol is injected into the axons of neurons in order to stop them from conducting pain impulses up the spinal column in individuals experiencing intractable pain suggests that alcohol is also directly cytotoxic (Walton, 1977, p. 177).

Beyond questions regarding the possible mediators of alcohol's destruction are questions regarding amounts necessary for destruction and whether patterns of consumption will make a difference. Polich and Bloom (1988) report that cognitive deficits correlate with typical amount consumed per occasion rather than frequency of consumption. Vaillant (1983, p. 113) in his book examining the natural history of alcoholism, indicates that in his male samples, both the socially and physically destructive effects of alcohol seemed to begin occurring at about 5 drinks per day. Rosalki (1984) cites findings of cirrhosis being induced in men with protracted drinking at 60–80 grams (6–8 drinks) per day. The level in women is about a third the amount required for men. High blood pressure can be induced at about the 3 drink per day level in men (Khetarpal & Volicer, 1981; Klatsky et al., 1977). The Royal College of Psychiatrists suggest that 60 grams per day is an upper limit for males and 30 grams per day is an upper limit for females (discussed in Rosalki, 1984).

SPECIFIC FINDINGS FOR WOMEN

With regard to the physical impact of drinking, special cautions need to be noted for women. Women appear to be more susceptible to liver disease (Van Thiel, 1983; Watson et al., 1986) and brain damage induced by heavy alcohol consumption (Gallant, 1987). Their longevity given a diagnosis of liver disease is shorter. Whereas males tend to die from complications of portal hypertension, women die from hepatocellular failure (Van Thiel & Gavaler, 1988).

ACCIDENTS

The risk of accident is definitely enhanced by intoxication. Fifty percent of persons sustaining minor or major traumas have been found to have a positive BAL at the time of hospital admission (Skinner et al. 1984). As many as 70% of the victims of fatal accidents have been found to be alcohol impaired at the time of the accident (Bliven, 1982). Fifty percent of fatal car accidents involve alcohol (Lowenfels, 1982). Thirty-six percent of regular drinkers report at least two accidental injuries per year, compared with an accident rate of only 8% in nondrinkers (Van Thiel, 1983). The occurrence of fractures in chronic alcoholics is 5–10 times higher than in control subjects (Peng et al., 1988). In fact, alcoholics are as likely to report a history of traumas as they are to suffer from alcohol related disease (Skinner et al., 1984).

Particular types of fractures are more characteristic of heavy drinkers. Heavy drinkers often exhibit fractures associated with intrinsic weakness of the bone rather than those induced by external pressure. In normals, hip fractures are very rare before the eighth decade, although they more frequently occur in alcoholics. Alcoholism is frequently implicated in persons sustain multiple fractures. Heavy alcohol consumption not only increases the probability of accidents, but also decreases the probability of timely treatment. Alcoholics often are neglectful of their injuries during recovery, putting weight on a limb prior to healing and failing to use crutches in the proper manner (Bliven, 1982).

Limb compression syndromes are a complication of intoxicated sleep. Normally, persons shift positions during sleep, preventing the loss of blood supply to any particular area. With extreme intoxication the probility of sleeping in a position which restricts blood supply to an area (usually the face, chest, or extremities) is enhanced. Necrosis of the skin and muscle tissue can occur (Bliven, 1982). Nerve compression can also occur, which will eventuate in slow conduction and demyelination (Mayer & Khurana, 1982).

It should be recalled that alcoholics often have blood that is compromised in its ability to clot. If bleeds occur, they are much more likely to result in serious complications. Subdural hematomas given a blow to the head are likely. Hemorrhagic strokes may be more serious.

Heavy drinking adds to the risk for surgery. Not only will deficient blood clotting ability create problems, but also cross tolerance to anesthesia is likely. Patients with liver disease will metabolize anesthetics more slowly and if the patient is intoxicated at the time of the operation, synergistic reactions may occur (Lowenfels, 1982).

CONCLUDING REMARKS

The long-term effects of alcohol on the body are profound. The level of alcohol consumption at which health is endangered has not been established. Certainly 6 drinks per day is too much. Safe drinking seems to vary with the organ being discussed. For women, the level of alcohol that is dangerous is probably well below the level of danger for men.

No organ system seems to be spared by alcohol. Organ function is impaired and long-term, irreversible damage, frequently occurs. The toll on longevity that alcohol takes was reviewed in the first chapter in the first volume of this work. Vaillant (1983, p. 162) also provides some summary statements. The death rate is 3 times what is expected among alcoholics 40 to 70; and exceeds the expected rate by 4 to 6 times among those who are younger than 40. Although the rates for suicide, accidents, and cirrhosis are an order of magnitude greater than the general population, over the life span heart disease, increased by a factor of two, among alcoholics accounts for a greater number of the excess deaths of alcoholics than do other causes. Suffice it to say here, that all studies indicate that life expectancy is shortened by heavy drinking.

9 Addiction

Alcohol has generally been regarded as an addicting drug (Jaffee, 1980). The pharmacological criteria for addiction require evidence of tolerance and withdrawal. Tolerance means that with continuing exposure to a drug, ever increasing amounts of the drug are needed to produce the effect that was initially produced on the first occasion of use. Withdrawal means that abrupt cessation of the drug will result in manifestations of physical and behavioral findings that are opposite to the direction of the pharmacological impact of the drug.

The concept of addiction has linked the causes of tolerance and withdrawal suggesting that they are manifestations of the same underlying process. The premise is that a homeostatic mechanism of some sort can account for both tolerance and withdrawal. The cells seek to maintain homeostasis or the baseline level of functioning that existed prior to exposure to the addicting drug. With exposure to the drug, the cells compensate for the presence of an addicting drug. Thus, more of the drug is required to offset the compensation of the cells. More of the drug is required to produce the effect achieved before the cells began to compensate. This is what is meant by tolerance. With the drug in the system, the cellular compensation is balanced by the effect of the drug. If the drug is abruptly removed from cells, the cells are still continuing to compensate for the presence of the drug. The cellular compensation should be observed unmasked, without counterbalancing by the pharmacological effect of the drug. The observed symptoms constitute withdrawal (Smith, 1981).

Researchers have sought to identify the mechanisms that can account for addiction. If some type of cellular change occurs given chronic exposure to alcohol, what is the nature of the change? One avenue of research has examined cellular changes that might account for the addiction phenomena of tolerance and withdrawal. In an entirely different vein, other research has challenged the basic premise of addiction. This research has suggested that tolerance and withdrawal may be separate phenomena that do not share a causal mechanism.

In Chapter 7, a description of the phenomena of tolerance and withdrawal were provided. In this chapter, these phenomena are discussed from a different perspective, and explanations for each are considered. Empirical findings speaking to the genesis of tolerance and withdrawal are reviewed, along with hypotheses that might account for the phenomena conjointly and separately.

TOLERANCE TO ALCOHOL

People who consume alcohol regularly become tolerant to many of its effects. Increased amounts of alcohol can be consumed before regularly consuming individuals display ataxia, hypothermia, slurred speech, or decrements in mental functioning. Tolerance is believed to develop rapidly. In fact, more behavioral impairment is observed when alcohol is increasing in the blood stream (ascending limb of the BAL), than when the amount of alcohol is decreasing in the system (descending limb of the BAL). Some believe that this difference in effect of alcohol, depending on whether the ascending and descending limb of consumption is occurring, constitutes an example of tolerance.

A few additional findings regarding tolerance are of interest. Tolerance will decay given time and abstention from alcohol. However, persons who abstain for a time, will build tolerance on a subsequent occasion more quickly than when they initially acquired the tolerance (Edwards & Gross, 1976). Persons who have developed a tolerance to alcohol will also display a tolerance to barbiturates, anesthetics, and the respiratory depressive effects of heroin (Ritchie, 1980; Siggins, Berger, French, Shier, & Bloom, 1982).

Some degree of tolerance development is attributable to an increase in hepatic enzymes which occurs as a result of exposure to alcohol. With an increase in liver enzymes, the alcohol is metabolized more rapidly. This type of tolerance is called metabolic tolerance. Interestingly, older persons or alcoholics who have suffered liver disease display decreased tolerance to alcohol because their livers no longer clear the alcohol as efficiently.

Recent evidence from the animal literature suggests that tolerance may fail to develop to alcohol's excitatory effects (Masur, De Souza, & Zwicker, 1986; Tabakoff & Kilanmaa, 1982). In fact, in the Masur et al. (1986) study increased sensitivity to the excitatory effect given exposure was demonstrated. Further research should be conducted on the issue of whether alcoholics develop tolerance to the excitatory effects of alcohol.

WITHDRAWAL

The previous chapter reviewed those symptoms that are manifested during the withdrawal process in humans. These symptoms include tremor, agitation, elevated blood pressure, increased heart rate, and seizures. Withdrawal symptoms in mice and rats that have consumed alcohol over a protracted period of time are similar. The animals are susceptible to seizures given any perturbation such as noise or handling.

EXPLANATIONS THAT LINK TOLERANCE AND WITHDRAWAL

As already discussed, early theories have linked the processes of tolerance and withdrawal. Some change in the cell was believed to occur given chronic exposure to alcohol. This cellular change was posited to account for both requiring more alcohol to achieve an effect and to account for the manifestation of excitability given abrupt cessation of alcohol intake. Researchers have examined physical changes at the cellular level in an attempt to identify the alterations that might explain addiction.

Cell Membrane Changes

Acute consumption of alcohol will cause a fluidization of the cell membrane. The increased fluidity of the membrane enhances the activity of Na+ and K+ ATPases, changing the propensity of the nerve cell to fire. Further, chemical interventions that alter membrane fluidity do block ethanol sedation (McCown, Frye, & Breese, 1986). It should be noted that many other small molecules whose intake similarly results in behavioral manifestations of intoxication or sedation exert a similar effect on the cell membrane. Most anesthetics produce a fluidizing effect on cell membrane activity. Changes in membrane fluidity are also produced by air pressure. When deep sea divers are subjected to increased air pressure, cell membranes are compressed, the membrane becomes less fluid, and seizures can be induced. The opposite phenomenon occurs in environments in which there is low air pressure (e.g., in the mountains). In low pressure environments, the cell membrane expands and the contents become more fluid. Ataxia, light headedness, eventual sedation occur (Winter & Miller, 1985).

Persons who are chronically exposed to alcohol or other sedative-hypnotic drugs become tolerant to the membrane fluidizing effects of these drugs. Some have sought to identify the specific changes at the cell membrane level which might account for tolerance to membrane fluidizing. One hypothesis holds that tolerance to the fluidizing effect is mediated by changes in the lipid composition of the cell membrane. This hypothesis has been challenged. It appears that the resistance of the cell membrane to becoming more fluid may be mediated by an increase in sialic acid and galactose concentration on the membrane surface (Beauge, Stibler, & Borg, 1985).

When a process is observed to occur, the question of the significance of the occurrence emerges. Cellular membrane changes in fluidity have been postulated to mediate tolerance and withdrawal (Lee, Friedman, & Loh, 1980). While there is little doubt that changes in membrane characteristics do occur given acute and chronic exposure to alcohol it is unclear which behavioral effects are mediated by membrane changes. Membrane phenomena have yet to be related to behavioral tolerance, specific symptoms of acute intoxication, behavioral changes in the sober behavior of alcoholics, or withdrawal symptoms. While there is little definitive support for membrane fluidity mediating tolerance and withdrawal, there are data against the hypothesis that cell membrane changes mediate behavioral tolerance to alcohol. Rats lose the tolerance to the membrane fluidizing effects of alcohol within a day after withdrawal, although the loss of tolerance to behavioral effects of alcohol takes considerably longer (Tabakoff & Hoffman, 1987).

Some have examined fluidity changes in cell membranes as a possible explanation for the phenomena of alcohol tolerance and withdrawal. Others have noted changes in the manner in which calcium is utilized (Dillon, Waters & Triggle, 1983; Leslie, 1986; Traynor et al., 1980). Calcium is integral to the process of a neuron's release of a neurotransmitter. Evidence is accumulating regarding the way in which alcohol alters how the brain utilizes calcium. Some of these alcohol induced changes in calcium utilization may mediate tolerance or withdrawal, although definitive conclusions are not yet possible.

At the cellular level then, a variety of specific changes have been observed when people drink. The acute effects of alcohol at the cellular level are distinct in persons who are accustomed to drinking. Although the molecular effects of alcohol are distinctive in persons experienced in drinking, none of these distinctive cellular processes have been demonstrated to account for withdrawal symptoms and behavioral tolerance. The significance of the changes in the manner in which the cell responds have yet to be delineated.

CHALLENGES TO EXPLANATIONS LINKING TOLERANCE AND WITHDRAWAL

Explanations linking tolerance and withdrawal as part of the same process have been challenged by recent evidence. If tolerance and withdrawal are reflections of the same process, they should co-occur. Further, a procedure that prevents the development of one, should also prevent the development of the other. (The word development is of course critical here, since it is possible to block a symptom of a process without preventing the process itself.)

Crabbe, Young, and Kosobud (1983) examined various strains of rats. They categorized the rat strains according to the magnitude and rapidity of the development of tolerance to the hypothermic effects of alcohol. They also measured the severity of withdrawal symptoms from alcohol in the rat strains. Crabbe et al, found no association between withdrawal and tolerance. Those rats who displayed few withdrawal symptoms, were the ones who rapidly developed tolerance. This challenged the notion of tolerance and withdrawal being inextricably linked. Others have also noted the independence of tolerance and withdrawal. Fish swimming in alcohol become tolerant without displaying withdrawal symptoms (Smith, 1981).

A number of procedures that block the development of tolerance do not interfere with withdrawal. Rat noradrenergic nerves have been ablated by intracerebroventricular administration of 6-OHDA. Ablated rats display withdrawal symptoms, but they do not display tolerance to the effect of alcohol (Tabakoff & Rothstein, 1983). The administration of chelating agents to the imbibing rat will attenuate withdrawal without effecting tolerance development (Abu-Murad & Nordmann, 1983).

Majchrowicz and Hunt (1976) have adduced evidence that the duration of alcohol exposure requisite for the establishment of the phenomena of tolerance and withdrawal are different. In animals, withdrawal was observed after 3–4 days, although 7 days of exposure to alcohol were required to witness tolerance. The decay time for the phenomena differed as well. Further a protracted exposure to low doses of alcohol induced tolerance although it failed to induce withdrawal.

A curious fact, inconsistent with the homeostatic explanation linking tolerance and withdrawal is the time frame for the occurrence of withdrawal symptoms. If the homeostatic explanation for alcohol addiction is viable, then the most intense withdrawal symptoms should be observed immediately upon the removal of alcohol from the system. This is what occurs when persons addicted to heroin are given a drug (naloxone) that displaces the heroin at the receptor site. The time frame for alcohol withdrawal symptoms do not conform to expectation. With alcohol, withdrawal symptoms build and the most dramatic effect can occur 3–4 days after the BALs have returned to O. Further, some authors report there is a considerable lag time between the clearance of alcohol from the system and the onset of withdrawal. Freund (1980) indicates that withdrawal manifestations begin up to 6 hours after alcohol is cleared from the system, although other authors report that withdrawal symptoms can occur given a relative fall in the blood alcohol level (Marjowitcz & Hunt, 1976; Mendelson & Mello, 1979). Further, dialysis, which rapidly removes alcohol from the system, will eliminate the development of withdrawal (Smith, 1981). None of these findings would be predicted from a homeostatic explanation.

Comment

A variety of findings suggest the independence of processes of tolerance and withdrawal. If they are independent events, those theories that link the two processes are called into question. Separate explanations for each process are required. Recent research has offered possible independent explanations for each phenomenon.

AN EXPLANATION FOR TOLERANCE

Research suggests that tolerance may be a learned phenomenon. In order to display tolerance to the disorienting effects of alcohol when running on a treadmill, rats must receive intoxicated practice with the treadmill. Merely giving rats exposure to intoxicating doses of alcohol provides the opportunity for the development of cellular tolerance (assuming there is such a phenomenon). However, rats given alcohol without an opportunity for practice on the treadmill while intoxicated, fail to display tolerance (Wenger, Tiffany, Bombardier, Nicholls, & Woods, 1981). Similar findings on other behavioral measures have been reported (Chen, 1972). Le, Poulous, and Cappell (1979) found that rats would only display tolerance to the hypothermic effect of alcohol, if the animal was given the alcohol in the cage in which the tolerance had developed. If given the alcohol in a distinctive environment, the animals failed to display the tolerance that they readily displayed in the environment in which they were accustomed to receiving alcohol. It is also the case that learning to compensate for a disorienting experience of any type will create tolerance to alcohol. Rats who are given practice in being spun around will display behavioral tolerance to both alcohol and benzodiazepines (Wenger et al., 1981).

Findings supportive of a learning explanation of tolerance have been reported for humans as well as animals. Drafters and Anderson (1982) demonstrated in humans that practice in a particular environment while intoxicated was necessary for the development of tolerance to alcohol on the dependent variable of tachycardia (increased heart rate). When a person who had developed tolerance to alcohol in one environment, was provided with alcohol in a novel environment, no tolerance was observed.

Pinel, Colborne, Sigalet, and Renfrey (1983) investigated tolerance to an effect of alcohol which would not ordinarily be thought to be effected by learning. Kindling is a process wherein rats are subjected repeatedly to a low level of electrical stimulation in their amygdalas. After repeated exposure, presentation of a small level of electrical stimulation will induce a seizure. It is known that giving alcohol to a rat that has been kindled, will confer resistance to the seizure that is ordinarily induced by the low level of electrical stimulation. If, however, the rat is frequently given alcohol, then resistance to the seizure induced by the low level of electrical stimulation will no longer be conferred by the alcohol. That is, for rats that have grown tolerant to alcohol, alcohol will not prevent the seizure. This is the manner in which alcohol effects kindling and how tolerance is displayed. Pinel's interesting discovery, however, was that the tolerance to the resistance to seizing which alcohol confers only develops when the alcohol is consumed during the kindling period (as the low level of electrical stimulation is presented). Rats that have frequently imbibed under different conditions, unrelated to the receipt of electrical stimulation, do not develop tolerance. Again, the findings may be consistent with a learning mechanism.

A further intriguing finding was made by Traynor, Schlapler, and Barondes (1980) working with single cells. Ordinarily alcohol will accelerate the decay of the postsynaptic potentiation in a nerve cell. Tolerance to this acceleration in decay will develop. This, however, will only occur if the nerve has been stimulated while in the alcohol bath. The mere presence of the alcohol bath, without giving the nerve an opportunity to "practice" will not result in tolerance.

Consistent with the learning explanations of tolerance are the observations that those interventions that impair learning block the development of tolerance. A list of drugs/procedures that impair learning, which have been demonstrated to block the development of tolerance include: drugs that impair protein synthesis, drugs that antagonize serotonin or norepinephrine, and ablation of the frontal cortex (Tabakoff & Rothstein, 1983). Assuming that extinction applies to tolerance just as it does to other learning phenomena, there is another consistent finding. Drugs that retard extinction (e.g., vasopressin) also diminish the disappearance of tolerance (Tabakoff & Rothstein, 1983).

The studies previously discussed were focused on demonstrating learning phenomenon that can account for tolerance. The second wave of research has gone in the opposite direction, that is, demonstrating some measure of tolerance beyond that which can be accounted for by learning. At this point some self-consciousness about types of learning is in order. The reader will recall that learning can be divided into associative learning (conditioning) and operant learning. Operant learning refers to learning caused by consequences which follow the behavior. The learned behavior is not dependent upon environmental cues for its occurrence. Associative learning is environment dependent. Associative learning occurs when stimuli that have been paired in time with presentation of a drug come to elicit reactions that occur upon consumption of the drug itself. With regard to associative learning, Newlin (1984, 1985) has demonstrated conditioned responses in experienced drinkers. An alcohol placebo will elicit autonomic responding which is opposite in direction to the autonomic reactions produced by the pharmacological impact of alcohol.

Melchoir and Tabakoff (1984) report that tolerance has been demonstrated in some paradigms that ruled out the effects of conditioning (associative learning) as an explanation for the tolerance. They exposed the animal to chronic alcohol in an environment that differed from the situation in which it was administered in the test situation. The animal still displayed alcohol tolerance despite the fact that associative learning was precluded. Further, specific chemical interventions disrupted the environment dependent tolerance (behavior presumably reflecting a conditioning phenomenon), but not the nonenvironment determined phenomenon. The authors concluded that intact norepinephrine systems were necessary for both environment dependent and independent tolerance to develop. Depleting the serotonin system enhanced the development of environment dependent tolerance but retarded the development of nonenvironment dependent tolerance. Another challenge to the idea that all tolerance is a function of learning came from Le, Kalant, and Khanna (1989). They demonstrated that at high doses of alcohol during the training sessions, intoxicated practice on a treadmill was less necessary for the subsequent display of tolerance. Tolerance to alcohol has also been demonstrated in disembodied organs. The heart muscle from rats that had been rendered tolerant to alcohol, continued to manifest tolerance when exposed (perfused) to alcohol outside of the living animal (Segel, 1988).

Studies that demonstrate that tolerance can or cannot be accounted for by learning will no doubt continue to appear in the literature. A problem with these studies is that there is little self-consciousness about where learning is and is not a possibility. For example, the Le, Kalant, and Khanna (1989) study found that intoxicated practice was unnecessary on a treadmill for tolerance to be developed. Although the authors eliminated practice on the treadmill in their study, the animal might have been practicing in other ways. Perhaps the animal was practicing maintaining equilibrium during intoxication in ways which were not immediately apparent to the experimenter. In those studies that preclude associative learning, the experimenters fail to rule out the possibility of operant learning. Presently, learning phenomenon have explained some degree of tolerance that has been demonstrated in the laboratory. Whether the procedures in which the nonlearning tolerance was ostensibly demonstrated totally ruled out the possibilities of operant and respondent conditioning is unclear. It is still unknown whether or not there is a type of tolerance that cannot be accounted for by learning.

HYPOTHESES EXPLAINING WITHDRAWAL

A number of processes have been advanced to account for the withdrawal symptoms observed following cessation of heavy drinking. It should be recalled that in the previous chapter a study (Phillips & Cragg, 1984) was discussed suggesting that the cell damaging effect of alcohol occurs during the withdrawal process but not during alcohol exposure. Thus, any explanation of withdrawal symptoms should also account for cellular damage. Some of the processes proffered to account for withdrawal are known to be toxic in their own right. Others do not provide mechanisms for why the withdrawal process might be the interval during which cellular damage is taking place. The processes that have been advanced to account for withdrawal are now reviewed. They include: the metabolism of methyl alcohol, increased cellular hydradation during the withdrawal process, kindling, perturbations in GABA neuron system, and changes in prostaglandins.

Methyl Alcohol Poisoning

Cedric Smith (1981) has suggested that a toxin (he did not speculate as to which one) may be the culprit in producing withdrawal symptoms. The Phillips and Cragg (1984) study had not yet been published when Smith proffered his speculation. The Phillips and Cragg (1984) data suggested that not only is a toxic process occurring during withdrawal, but in fact, much of the damage created by alcohol may occur during this toxic process of withdrawal. The unanswered question is what is there about withdrawal from alcohol that is toxic? Could a specific toxin be involved as Smith had implied? One possibility suggests itself.

It is known that methyl alcohol is consumed in conjunction with most alcoholic beverages (the highest percentages occurring in some of the spirits). Methyl alcohol is also produced endogenously as well as being present in some foods. People do encounter methyl alcohol in their diets and in other ways. There are then explanations for why people encounter methyl alcohol. In order to be implicated in alcohol withdrawal, there must be some process through which alcohol increases the threat posed by methyl alcohol which is encountered in daily living. Such a process can be hypothesized.

Alcohol and methyl alcohol compete for the same liver enzymes for their catabolism, the alcohol taking precedence. The methyl alcohol thus accumulates when both forms of alcohol are ingested (Pieper & Skeen, 1973). After alcohol exits the system, the accumulated methyl alcohol, larger in amount than would normally be encountered in common foods, awaits catabolism by the liver to formaldehyde. Could such heavy concentrations of methyl alcohol be the culprit creating alcohol toxicity?

There are a variety of findings that are suggestive. If methyl alcohol is the real culprit in the tissue damage produced by alcohol, then the pattern of damage produced by methyl alcohol consumption should be the same as the damage witnessed in heavy drinkers. In fact, the damage due to methyl alcohol poisoning on the various organ systems is similar to that produced by alcohol (Monte, 1984).

The time sequence for the occurrence of withdrawal symptoms is consistent with the possibility that methyl alcohol breakdown might produce withdrawal phenomena. The emergence of withdrawal occurs at a point in time at which enough of the alcohol is metabolized to allow for the initiation of the catabolizing of methyl alcohol. A diminution of blood methyl alcohol levels reflects catabolism of methyl alcohol to formaldehyde. Blood methyl alcohol levels begin to drop when blood ethanol levels decrease below 70–20 mg/100 ml (Majchrowitz & Mendelson, 1971; Pieper & Skeen, 1973). The blood alcohol level at which methyl catabolism begins roughly conforms to the point at which alcohol withdrawal emerges. A relative drop in blood alcohol level to about 100 mg/100 ml is the level at which withdrawal symptoms have been reported (Mendelson & Mello, 1979). The temporal initiation of withdrawal is consistent with a methyl alcohol mechanism. The time frame for the most severe symptoms from alcohol withdrawal is also consistent with a methyl alcohol mediator. Delirium tremens will occur about 3 days after alcohol has been cleared from the system. This is about the time required for methyl alcohol to be catabolized and for its metabolite, formaldehyde, to reach peak concentrations (Magrinat et al., 1973; Majchrowicz & Mendelson, 1971). The time frames for the initiation of methyl alcohol catabolism and the peak production of formaldehyde from methanol (methyl alcohol) do then conform respectively to the initiation of alcohol withdrawal symptoms and the emergence of the most severe withdrawal symptoms from alcohol.

There are a few additional curious facts. If methyl alcohol metabolism mediates alcohol withdrawal, then those procedures affecting alcohol withdrawal should also effect methyl alcohol levels. This is the case. Methyl alcohol poisoning, like alcohol withdrawal, is reversed by alcohol consumption (Majchrowicz & Mendelson, 1971). Dialysis will prevent alcohol withdrawal symptoms from occurring (Smith, 1981). It is known that methanol is dialyzable (Lee & Becker, 1982). All of these facts are certainly consistent with a role of methyl alcohol in toxicity during the alcohol withdrawal process.

Research designed specifically to test the hypothesis that methyl alcohol is the culprit toxin in alcohol withdrawal has been supportive. Majchrowicz and Steinglass (1973) measured the amount of methyl alcohol present in the blood stream of imbibing alcoholics prior to withdrawal. A correlation between methyl alcohol levels and severity of withdrawal symptoms was found. Further, over time, withdrawal symptoms were more closely associated with methyl alcohol concentrations in the blood than they were with the decreasing concentrations of blood alcohol levels (Majchrowicz & Steinglass, 1973).

Roine et al. (1989) have recently proposed that methyl alcohol levels in the blood be used as a mechanism for identifying heavy alcohol consumers. Although Roine did not speculate regarding the impact of methanol in the body of alcoholics, they did adduce evidence suggesting that the greater the level of alcohol consumption, the higher the methanol level. Roine et al. (1989) measured methanol levels in various populations. The mean methanol values in the plasma of the various samples differed significantly from each other with order being: populations of individuals presenting for detoxification, skid row inhabitants, drunken drivers, and social drinkers.

Perhaps future research will shed more light on the role of methanol in alcohol's toxicity. The findings are consistent with methanol involvement in producing withdrawal symptoms and possibly accounting for tissue damage. Other explanations for alcohol withdrawal symptoms are equally viable, however.

Super Hydration

Using NMR scanning, it has been shown that during withdrawal the brain is superhydrated (Besson, Glen, Foreman, MacDonald, Smith, Hutchison, Mallard, Ashcroft, 1981). The superhydration is probably attributable to plasma vasopressin, an antidiuretic hormone. Correlational data suggest that alcoholics exhibiting withdrawal have higher blood vasopressin concentrations than either alcoholics not exhibiting withdrawal or control subjects (Eisenhoffer, Whiteside, Lambie, & Johnson, 1982). Further, vasopressin will exacerbate withdrawal symptoms. Although there is no specific evidence that low levels of cellular hydration are damaging, Phillips and Cragg (1984) have questioned whether cellular hydration in some way mediates the manifestation of withdrawal and the cellular damage occurring during the withdrawal process.

Kindling

Kindling is a process whereby repeated electrical stimulation of the limbic system at levels which do not result in seizures, eventually will reliably come to elicit seizures at previously subthreshold levels of stimulation (Ballenger & Post, 1978). The time between electrical stimulation treatments is critical. A 24-hour schedule is optimal for kindling; massed treatments will retard kindling.

Ballenger and Post (1978) advance a kindling explanation to explain withdrawal seizures. They argue that a kindling process similar to the one induced via electrical stimulation occurs each time a person detoxes from alcohol. Findings are consistent with their hypothesis. During alcohol withdrawal, recordings of the electrical activity from the hippocampus, amygdala, thalamus, septal nucleus, and frontal cortex are similar to the recordings from limbic system structures during electrically stimulated kindling treatment.

Other findings are consistent with a kindling explanation. With kindling, repeated subthreshold levels of electrical stimulation render the occurrence of a seizure at low levels of stimulation more likely. If withdrawal constitutes a kindling procedure, one would expect to find seizures increasing in probability as a function of the number of times that an individual has experienced withdrawal symptoms. This is consistent with empirical findings from animal studies. Repeated withdrawal experiences increase the likelihood and severity of withdrawal symptoms. The severity of animal withdrawal symptoms is a function of the number of prior withdrawal experiences (Carrington, Ellinwood, & Krishnan, 1984). Further, rats previously exposed to electrical stimulation of kindling, display marked increase in severity of subsequent alcohol withdrawal reaction (Carrington et al., 1984).

Beyond accounting for withdrawal, kindling may explain some stereotypical alcoholic behavior. Ballenger and Post (1978) speculate regarding the interictal (between seizures) behavior of animals that have been kindled. Such animals display extreme emotional responding manifesting as increased aggression and fearfulness. Ballenger and Post draw parallels between these animal findings to the paranoia, religiosity, obsessions, and fearfulness which Jellinek contended are characteristic of sober alcoholics. (In fact, the reader will recall from the previous chapter that dysphoria is characteristic in alcoholics during early sobriety.) Perhaps the behavior of newly sober alcoholics reflects the effect of the kindling process.

If Ballenger and Post are correct in their hypothesis that alcohol withdrawal is a kindling process, the kindling literature with animals can be consulted to find ways of preventing the kindling. Those interventions that interdict kindling might also be expected to prevent withdrawal. Ballenger and Post (1978) cite findings that animals given valium during exposure to electrical stimulation will be resistant to kindling. A rat given a tranquilizer during the kindling process will be protected against long-term changes in brain function being established. Assuming that alcohol withdrawal is the same as the kindling process, implications for prevention are suggested. Provision of benzodiazepines (e.g., valium) during withdrawal may prevent kindling. Thus, personality changes would be prevented and the person would not be rendered more susceptible to a seizure given a second episode of alcohol detoxification.

GABA Depletion

GABA is one of the neurotransmitters that is increased while a person is drinking, but can be depleted by the drinking process (Goldman, Volicer, Gold, & Rotn, 1981; Lambie, Johnson, Vijayasenan, & Whiteside, 1980; Liljequist & Engel, 1980). Since GABA is an inhibitory transmitter that can prevent the occurrence of seizures, it is reasonable to assume that its depletion might result in seizures. This has been the logic for speculation that GABA depletion might account for withdrawal seizures and perhaps other withdrawal symptoms as well. Consistent with this speculation is the finding that those persons who experience withdrawal seizures display lower levels of GABA than those who do not (Goldman et al., 1981). Drugs with GABA agonist properties have the expected effect on withdrawal symptoms. Sodium valporate, intraventricular injection of GABA, amino oxyacetic acid, all of which are GABA agonists, will prevent withdrawal seizures (Goldman, Volicer, Gold, & Rotn, 1981; Lambie, Johnson, Vijayasenan, & Whiteside, 1980).

Decreased Prostaglandin

Horrobin (1987) has speculated regarding the role of prostaglandins in intoxication and the withdrawal process. During intoxication, prostaglandin turnover is increased. Drugs that decrease prostaglandin (e.g., aspirin, indomethacin,) will decrease the severity of intoxication on some but not all measures (Collins, Gilliam, & Miner, 1985). Although acute intoxication increases prostaglandin levels, sustained intoxication could deplete this neurotransmitter. Horribin speculates that drinking decreases the available stores of prostaglandin as well as interferring with particular metabolic pathways. Rotrosen, Mandio, and Segarnick (1980) have speculated on the implications of prostaglandin depletion. Perhaps low prostaglandin levels play a role in the withdrawal process. Prostaglandins have sedative and anticonvulsive properties. A prostaglandin depletion given the absence of the depressing effect of alcohol, could result in seizures. Consistent with this view is the fact that gamma linolenic acid and fatty acids (both of which are precursors to prostaglandin synthesis) will decrease withdrawal severity (Segarnick & Rotrosen, 1987).

Changes in Other Neurotransmitters Systems and Mineral Depletions

Tabakoff and Rothstein (1983) have reviewed the changes in various neurotransmitter systems (norepinephrine and acetylcholine) and the drop in magnesium levels that have been documented in the withdrawal process. Perturbations in these systems may mediate some withdrawal phenomena. Some recent studies have focused on the role of dopamine which is known to be depleted after heavy drinking (Modell, Mountz, & Beresford, 1990). Dopamine agonists have been used to attenuate the alcohol withdrawal symptoms of anxiety, restlessness, depression, tremor, sweating, and nausea (Borg & Weinholdt, 1980, 1982). Alcohol affects the body in many ways. As technology advances, a more precise catalog may become available. It may become possible to identify mediators of alcohol withdrawal.

SUMMARY AND COMMENT

A number of process have been advanced to account for withdrawal symptoms. The metabolism of methyl alcohol will occur at accelerated levels after the cessation of heavy drinking. The formation of formaldehyde (a metabolite of methyl alcohol) may cause tissue damage and withdrawal findings. The process of kindling has been advanced as a model that captures the relevant aspects of alcohol withdrawal. Changes in hydration, depletion of GABA, a decrease in prostaglandin, and alterations in electrolytes do occur concomitant with withdrawal and might be responsible for some the findings observed during the withdrawal process.

As researchers continue to make observations regarding how alcohol impacts the body during intoxication and withdrawal, there will no doubt be further documentation of changes in various neurotransmitters, electrolytes, and other chemistry. It is all too easy to postulate a casual relationship between a particular chemical change and the process of withdrawal. It is important to remember that a chemical change may reflect a consequence of a causal process in withdrawal. It may also reflect a consequence of exposure to alcohol which is independent of the withdrawal process. Whatever the cause of withdrawal, it will have to be capable of setting into motion the symptoms occurring during withdrawal. Further, it may have to explain the toxic impact of the withdrawal process.

None of the hypotheses regarding withdrawal that have been reviewed are contradictory. One would expect that a process like withdrawal which causes cellular damage and results in autonomic hyperactivity, hallucinations, seizures, and a process analogous to kindling, would have ramifications on a variety of neurotransmitter systems as well as on cellular chemistry. The real question is, which is the initial causal factor stimulating the entire sequence of events. Future research will surely provide a more detailed description of the biochemical processes which occur. Perhaps there will also be an answer pertaining to cause.

10 Drugs Used in the Treatment of Alcoholism

A variety of pharmacological interventions have been tested in the treatment of alcoholism including lsd and benzodiazepines (Sellers, Naranjo, & Peachey, 1981; Sinclair, 1987), antidepressants (Sellers et al., 1981; Viamontes, 1972), and dopamine agonists (Sinclair, 1987). In terms of utility for treatment of alcoholism, several classes of drugs may be more worthy of considerations in that a theoretical case can be advanced for their efficacy. These drugs are: lithium, serotonin agonists, stimulant drugs, and antabuse. There are theoretical reasons why each of these drug types might decrease the probability of relapse in recovering alcoholics. The mechanism by which each of these classes of drug could influence treatment outcome is different. A review of relevant outcome studies for these drugs is now presented.

LITHIUM

The inspiration for using lithium in the treatment of alcoholism came from several findings. Laboratory studies with rats demonstrated that lithium will decrease alcohol consumption (Ho & Tsai, 1976). Some investigators found that persons maintained on lithium are immune to the high usually produced by consumption of amphetamines (Judd et all, 1977; Pond et al., 1981). This has stimulated the hypothesis that the euphoric effects from alcohol ingestion might be similarly blocked. There was a rationale for why lithium might decrease the reinforcing effects of alcohol. Some experimental work set out to test the specific hypothesis.

Research investigating whether lithium would alter an individual's response to alcohol consumption was equivocal. An experiment by Judd et al. (1977) failed to find that lithium maintained nonalcoholic subjects responded any differently to alcohol than did placebo maintained subjects. Alcohol produced euphoria in both groups. In a similar later study with alcoholics, Judd and Huey (1984) found that the lithium group compared to control was not as cognitively impaired after drinking and they reported a diminution in the desire to continue drinking.

While some researchers were investigating issues of mechanisms for lithium's presumed efficacy in decreasing an alcoholic's alcohol consumption, other researchers focused on testing the efficacy question directly. Studies were conducted examining lithium's impact on enhancing abstention in alcoholics during a follow-up period. Early reports by Kline et al. (1974) and Merry et al. (1976) supported efficacy for depressed alcoholics. A report by Pendry (cited by Judd et al., 1977) suggested efficacy for binge alcoholics.

Several large N, random assignment studies appeared in literature. Fawcett et al. (1984) (N=84) and Fawcett et al. (1987) (N=104) demonstrated a decrement in the number of rehospitalizations, and more total abstention among those alcoholics given lithium. The follow-up period was a year in the first study and 18 months in the second study. Double blind conditions were observed. The efficacy demonstrated by Fawcett et al. (1987, 1984) was confined to the group that was compliant (assessed by lithium levels in the therapeutic range) with taking their medications as prescribed. The abstention rates in the lithium compliant group did exceed the rate in the group for which there was evidence that a placebo was being consumed as directed. Hence, the Fawcett et al. studies were supportive of lithium's efficacy in promoting abstention from alcohol.

Whereas the Fawcett et al. studies have suggested that lithium treatment is efficacious, there have been negative findings as well. A study by Pond et al. (1981) employing double blind methodology and a cross over design failed to demonstrate efficacy in a small N study. Another study (Powell et al, 1986) (N=100) demonstrated efficacy against a no drug treatment control group but no increment of efficacy as compared to a placebo drug treatment. Dorus conducted a large N study of 280 alcoholics followed for a year after treatment at a VA hospital. No differential efficacy was revealed for patients given lithium on measures of number of drinking days, alcohol related hospitalizations, or changes in severity of depression (reported by Bower, 1989).

Studies in which efficacy for lithium treatment has been demonstrated have explored why lithium might be effective in decreasing alcohol consumption. Findings rule against the interpretation that efficacy might be a function of reduction in depression. In the Fawcett et al. (1984) study, patients in the lithium treated group were not more depressed at intake than were those in the control group. At follow-up there was no difference in the incidence of depression in the lithium treated group than in the control group. Thus, the beneficial effect did not seem to be attributable to a reduction in depression. The question of whether lithium achieves its effects through the expectation of benefit in the patient has also been explored. The Fawcett et al. studies demonstrated efficacy for lithium against a placebo control although the Powell et al. (1986) did not demonstrate efficacy beyond placebo. Thus, the possibility that lithium's efficacy is achieved through the expectations inspired in the patient cannot be ruled out.

Beyond the efficacy of a drug in decreasing relapse, there are other considerations. Lithium treatment is associated with a long list of side effects. Without demonstrable efficacy, the gains may not offset the physical problems that are induced. Compliance with lithium is difficult to achieve and drinking among lithium maintained patients will enhance lithium toxicity (Sinclair, 1987). Certainly more research should be conducted into lithium's utility in the treatment of alcoholism. Presently, its efficacy has not yet been firmly established.

SEROTONIN AGONISTS

In the genetic section of this book, the hypotheses regarding serotonin irregularities as mediators of genetic risk were discussed. It is known that rat strains that prefer alcohol have lower brain levels of serotonin (Schuckit et al., 1985). Some studies have demonstrated decreased serotonin turnover in abstinent alcoholics as assessed by the CSF metabolites of serotonin (Ballenger et al., 1979). There is evidence that drinking will increase the rate of serotonin turnover (Badaway & Evans, 1983) and will increase platelet uptake of serotonin (Kent et al., 1983). It has been suggested that alcoholics are motivated to drink in order to enhance brain levels of serotonin. If serotonin deficits play a role in making alcohol more attractive, and if drinking helps to increase serotonin, then it is no surprise that interventions that might increase serotonin in other ways might be seen as worthy of consideration to decrease heavy drinking.

In fact, the evidence from animal subjects is promising in terms of suggesting that increasing serotonin can decrease alcohol consumption. Selective blockers of serotonin reuptake have been found to reduce alcohol consumption in laboratory animals (Sinclair, 1987). The human data is consistent with the animal findings. A human study (Naranjo et al, 1984) in which the impact of zimelidine, a drug that blocks the reuptake of serotonin at the synapse, was assessed on the consumption pattern of 13 heavy drinkers. In a double-blind design study in which drinkers received the drug during a 2-week period and then received placebo for a 2-week period, some efficacy for the serotonin agonist was demonstrated. During administration of zimelidine, drinkers consumed less per occasion and were abstinent on a greater number of days. In this study, the heavy drinkers were not attempting to maintain abstinence nor had they received treatment for alcoholism. In an additional study, Naranjo, Sellers, and Lawrin (1986) replicated the finding of a decrease in alcohol consumption employing a more specific serotonin reuptake blocker. The Naranjo et al. studies encourage optimism for the use of serotonin agonists in the treatment of alcoholism.

Consistent with studies suggesting some efficacy in prolonging sobriety for serotonin agonists is the data relating to diet. Yung, Gordis, and Holt (1983) found that patients who were sober for 50 days or more vs. those unable to stay sober were consuming more sugar, carbohydrates, and vitamins in their diets. It has long been recognized by clinicians that recovering alcoholics are heavy consumers of sugar. It is also known that high carbohydrate intake lacking in protein will increase brain level of serotonin (Wurtman, 1983). Although the causal chain is highly speculative, it may be that carbohydrates increase the probability of sobriety by increasing serotonin levels.

In light of positive findings, it seems likely that further work evaluating the efficacy of serotonin agonists in the treatment of alcoholism can be expected to appear in future literature.

STIMULANT DRUGS

In the section on genetics, those studies in which childhood hyperactivity was identified as a precursor to adult alcoholism were reviewed. There has been speculation as to whether hyperactivity is a life long condition. Wood, Wender, and Reimherr (1983) found that in a sample of adult alcoholics, one-third of their sample of 33 adult male alcoholics met the criteria for residual attention deficit disorder. Given the presence of attention deficit disorder, some have speculated that drugs that are effective in treating childhood hyperactivity might prove efficacious in the treatment of adult alcoholism. As discussed in the chapters on genetics, some have posited that alcoholics drink because alcohol can function as a stimulant drug. Similar to hyperactive children, alcoholics may function better when consuming a stimulant. If alcoholics drink to provide self-medication for hyperactivity, substituting a less harmful stimulant medication, should reduce their drinking.

The available research has evaluated the general efficacy of stimulant medication for attention deficit disorder in adults. Wood, Reimherr, Wender, and Johnson (1976) employed methylphenidate (ritalin) and pemoline in the treatment of adults manifesting minimal brain dysfunction (defined in terms of manifestations of hyperactivity and attention deficits). Twenty-seven percent of the sample met the criteria for alcoholism. The authors found a reduction in hyperactivity symptomotology in response to both methylphenidate and pemoline. Unfortunately the response on drinking variables for the alcoholics in the sample was not assessed. An N of one study by Turnquist, Frances, Rosenfeld, and Mobarak (1983) also supported a reduction in attention deficit disorder in a hyperactive alcoholic after treatment with pemoline.

The studies examining the impact of stimulants have not employed pure alcoholic samples. Further, the studies evaluating response to stimulant medications have failed to evaluate the impact on drinking variables. Perhaps, future research will evaluate the impact of stimulants on alcoholics with and without attention deficit symptoms. Dependent variables should include assessment of drinking.

ANTABUSE

Antabuse is a drug which will block the enzyme which degrades the first breakdown product of alcohol, acetaldehyde. Persons who drink while taking antabuse will experience an accumulation of acetaldehyde. High blood acetaldehyde levels induce an uncomfortable state. Hence, there is rationale for the belief that persons taking antabuse will avoid drinking lest they make themselves ill. There are other drugs that operate on aldehyde dehydrogenase (the enzyme which degrades acetaldehyde) in a similar manner to antabuse. Calcium carbimide is another drug which blocks aldehyde dehydrogenase. It is available in other countries, but is not marketed in the U. S. (Sinclair, 1987).

Antabuse has received more attention in the treatment of alcoholism than other drugs. Clinically, it is the more frequently used drug. The discussion of antabuse here will first focus on the specific physical symptoms of an alcohol/antabuse reaction. Then, side effects of antabuse are explained along with bottomlines from outcome studies. Speculation regarding mechanisms for efficacy are also examined.

The Physical Impact of Antabuse

The antabuse/alcohol reaction redounds as a consequence of increased acetaldehyde in the blood. High levels of acetaldehyde produce flushing, increased blood pressure, nausea, respiratory difficulties, sweating, thirst, chest pain, hypotension, headache, weakness, dizziness, blurred vision, and confusion (Ritchie, 1980). The more serious potentially lethal symptoms resulting from drinking on antabuse include marked respiratory depression, cardiovascular collapse, cardiac arrythmias, myocardial infarction, acute congestive heart failure, unconsciousness, and convulsions (Ritchie, 1980). A lethal delayed shock syndrome, not preceded by flushing has been reported (Kwentus & Major, 1979).

Sober individuals who consume antabuse do experience side effects. Among the listed side effects are rashes, orthostatic hypotension, lethargy, tremor, reduced sexual potency, urticaria, headaches, dizziness, a garlic or metallic taste, and mild gastrointestinal disturbances (Ritchie, 1980). More serious side effects include peripheral neuropathy, depression, and hepatitis (Ewing, 1982). Patients overdosing on antabuse may experience fever, lethargy, depression, EEG abnormalities, peripheral neuropathy, cerebellar dysfunction, Parkinson symptoms, and permanent intellectual impairment (Kwentus & Major, 1979).

Antabuse is contraindicated in those with liver disease, coronary disease, diabetes, hypothyroidism, and cerebral damage (Miller & Hester, 1980). It alters metabolism of drugs such as phenytoin, isoniazid, and warfarin. In combination with flagyl, psychotic reactions have occurred (Ewing, 1982).

In addition to blocking aldehyde dehydrogenase (the enzyme that catabolizes acetaldehyde), antabuse effects other enzymes as well. Antabuse will block the enzyme DBH which converts dopamine to norepinephrine. Some have speculated that the known side effects from antabuse, viz., seizures, schizophrenic psychosis may result from increased dopamine levels (Ewing, Mueller, Rouse, & Silver, 1977). Antabuse is a chelating agent and in patients with a low mineral diet, heart disease attributable to mineral deficits can result (Raloff, 1986). Antabuse is a known teratogen (Nora, Nora, & Blu, 1977) and carcinogen (Miller & Hester, 1980). In rat studies, increased alcohol consumption following cessation of antabuse administration has been noted (Sinclair, 1987). Hence, there is danger of a rebound phenomenon when alcoholics quit taking antabuse.

Patients taking antabuse are warned to avoid all alcohol containing products such as aftershave lotion and perfume. Any ingestion of vinegar, such as would occur with salsa or salad dressing, should also be avoided. In the body, the chemical reaction of conversion of acetaldehyde to vinegar or vinegar back to acetaldehyde will occur in both directions. Given acetaldehyde from any source such as from increased consumption of vinegar, when aldehyde dehydrogenase is blocked, elevated acetaldehyde levels will result (Ritchie, 1980).

Efficacy of Antabuse

Many studies evaluating the efficacy of antabuse in the treatment of alcoholism, have failed to establish random assignment or blind conditions. In the poorly controlled studies, those taking antabuse usually display better outcomes (Davies, Shepherd, & Myers, 1956; Hoff & McKeown, 1953). Of course, the positive findings from studies lacking random assignment may reflect the better motivation of those patients who are willing to accept antabuse, rather than the efficacy of the drug per se. Lundwall and Baekeland (1971) who reviewed the outcome literature available at the time, were unable to arrive at a conclusion regarding efficacy. They acknowledged that therapist enthusiasm for the new therapy was a confounding factor making it impossible to draw conclusions.

Some random assignment studies have been published. Rosenberg (1974) randomly assigned patient to receive no drug, vitamins, librium, or antabuse. Only the librium group produced a more favorable outcome. A study by Gallant et al. (1968) in which there was random assignment to group therapy, antabuse, group therapy plus antabuse, or no treatment, failed to detect outcome differences. In a large, double blind study (Fuller et al., 1986), in which patients were assigned to riboflavin placebo, low dose antabuse (included to control for the impact of the threat of a drinking reaction), or high dose antabuse, no differences were found in terms of percentage remaining totally abstinent or time to relapse. The high dose antabuse group, however, drank on fewer days than did those in the other conditions. In a study by Fuller and Williford (1980) patients were randomly assigned to antabuse or a control condition. Those taking antabuse evidenced increased rates of total abstention throughout the year follow-up interval. Hence, although there are some studies that support efficacy, strong support is lacking.

Assuming that antabuse is effective in reducing amount consumed during the follow-up period, the question of the factors that mediate efficacy remains. When antabuse was first introduced, it was believed that efficacy would be achieved through the first aversive alcohol/antabuse reaction the patient experienced. The patient would have to experience an aversive effect to instantiate the conditioning of a negative response to alcohol. Some have recommended an episode of drinking while taking antabuse under doctor directed conditions (Ewing, 1982). Findings on whether greater efficacy is achieved for those who have drunk on antabuse vs. those who have not, are not available.

Whereas some have suggested efficacy of antabuse through a punishment mechanism, there has been discussion of alternative mechanisms. Sinclair (1987) refers to findings suggesting that antabuse decreases alcohol craving. He has speculated that through its impact on DBH or brain aldehyde dehydrogenase, antabuse may change serotonin, norepinephrine, and dopamine metabolism. Such a change may mediate reduced craving or decreased reinforcement from drinking. It should be noted that not all investigators agree that antabuse will reduce cravings. Decreased alcohol consumption on antabuse is found in the animal literature and humans have reported a decrease in alcohol craving while on antabuse (Sinclair, 1987). However, Nirenberg et al. (1983) have argued that the daily ingestion of antabuse may serve as a reminder of one's desires for alcohol and thus increase cravings. Thus far, the question on overall impact on craving has not been sufficiently investigated to render a conclusion on the issue.

The results of some studies have suggested that medications of any type will increase patient retention in treatment. Gerrein, Rosenberg, and Manohar (1973) found that patients assigned to the antabuse condition vs. control were retained in treatment for a longer period of time. Powell and Viamontes (1974) have found that the provision of any medication (antabuse, tricyclics, or benzodiazepines) will increase attendance at aftercare. Hence, antabuse does seem to have indirect benefits beyond reducing drinking. It can be expected to increase aftercare and therapy involvement.

Even if antabuse's efficacy is assumed, there are problems with inducing patients to take the drug. Across studies between 20–95% refuse antabuse (O'Neil et al. 1982). Particular personality variables are associated with willingness to accept antabuse. Not surprisingly, persons who believe antabuse will help them stay sober and resist urges to drink are more likely to accept antabuse. Those who believe their families will be pleased with their antabuse acceptance are more likely to agree to the drug (Brubaker, Prue, & Rychtarik, 1987). O'Neil et al. (1982) failed to identify MMPI predictors of antabuse acceptance, save for high scores on the MF (feminine interest pattern) scale being related at a marginally significant level with antabuse acceptance. Obitz (1978) found that patients scoring in the external direction of the locus of control scale are more likely to accept antabuse. Vaillant (1983) reported that those who had been securely abstinent were less likely than those in early recovery to rely on antabuse. Generally then, only particular patients can be expected to accept antabuse. Even for those accepting antabuse, the drug seems to be a strategy for staying sober in early rather than late sobriety.

Some have experimented with methods for increasing patient acceptance of antabuse. Ewing (1982) recommended contracting as a mechanism for enhancing compliance, although he did not report empirical findings supporting efficacy. Kofoed (1987) demonstrated that a devise to measure antabuse in the blood did increase compliance with antabuse ingestion from 44.1% to 71.2%. Compliance with antabuse was unrelated to drinking outcome or participation in scheduled treatment, however.

Summary

Antabuse has been demonstrated to have some modest effects on decreasing drunk days during the follow-up interval in a large N study by Fuller et al. (1986). Most studies have not demonstrated superior efficacy and early studies in which favorable results were achieved suffered from lack of random assignment. Antabuse seems to be worth considering for those patients who are willing to take the drug. Even if it fails to increase sobriety directly, it may enhance retention in aftercare. Those people who do rely on antabuse seem to use it as a short-term strategy in early sobriety. Given antabuse's numerous side effects, it is probably best used as a short-term strategy.

11 The THIQ Hypothesis

In 1970, Davis and Walsh published an article linking alcohol dependence with opiate dependence. In the article, they described their research demonstrating that tetrahydropapaveroline could be synthesized in the brain in the process of alcohol metabolism. Davis and Walsh remarked upon the fact that tetrahydropapaveroline can be converted to morphine like alkaloid. Hence consuming alcohol could lead to the production of morphine like compounds. Such being the case, addiction to alcohol might be equivalent to addiction to the opiates.

The particular chemical process described by Davis and Walsh involved the synthesis of morphine like alkaloids from dopamine (a common neurotransmitter) and dihydroxyphenylacetic acid (the first breakdown product of the neurotransmitter dopamine). Davis and Walsh suggested that alcohol would enhance the formation of tetrahydropapaveroline by enabling more dopac (dihydroxyphenylacetic acid) to accumulate. Dihydroxyphenylacetic acid and acetaldehyde both compete for the same enzyme for catabolism. Hence, given alcohol consumption, acetaldehyde would saturate the enzymes catabolizing dihydroxyphenylacetic acid (dopac). Dihydroxyphenylacetic acid would accumulate. More dihydroxyphenylacetic acid would be available to participate in the formation of tetrahydropapaveroline.

Tetrahydropapaveroline is not the only compound of its class. It has been recognized that there are a wide variety of THIQ (tetrahydroisoquinoline) type alkaloids. These alkaloids are condensation products of amines (neurotransmitters such as norepinephrine, serotonin, and dopamine) and an aldehyde (e.g., acetaldehyde or dopac). If the initiating compound is a phenylethylamine (the amino acid precursor to dopamine) the alkaloid is a THIQ. If the initiating compound is an indolethylamine (amino acid forming serotonin) the alkaloid is a

167

tetrahydro-beta-carboline. Given alcohol consumption, there is reason to believe that all of them might be synthesized in greater abundance. (In this chapter, for the sake of brevity, THIQ will be used to refer to all of these alkaloids.)

In traditionally oriented treatment centers, there has been a great deal of attention devoted to the notion that the biochemical distinction between alcoholics and nonalcoholics is the presence or absence of THIQ alkaloids in the brain. The Davis and Walsh article inspired a film produced by Gary Whiteaker Co. featuring David Olhms, M.D. This film has been widely distributed and the opinions advanced have become coin of the realm in many traditionally oriented treatment programs. Because of the broad distribution this film has enjoyed, it is important for professionals in the field to be familiar with the notions popularized and to be apprised of the research supporting and contrary to the opinions advanced.

In the film, Olhms avers the following position: (1) THIQs are present in the brains of alcoholics and heroin addicts. They are not present in normals. THIQs are produced in the brains of alcoholics when they drink through the condensation of acetaldehyde and an amine. This condensation process does not occur in nonalcoholics. (2) THIQ alkaloids, once formed in the brain, remain present on a long-term basis. (3) THIQs perform two functions. They are highly addictive. Further, they induce a preference for alcohol which is enduring. (4) THIQs achieve their effect through interaction at opiate receptors.

Given that there are so many claims being advanced about the THIQs, some of the more relevant empirical data are now reviewed.

WHAT IS KNOWN ABOUT THIQS: IN WHICH POPULATIONS ARE THIQS FOUND? WHAT ALTERS THEIR PRODUCTION?

There is evidence to suggest that THIQs are found in the brain, cerebrospinal fluid, and the urine after drinking and under other conditions. That is, THIQs may be compounds found in many living things. Hamilton, Blum, and Hirst (1978) report finding salsolinol (condensation product of dopamine and acetaldehyde) in the brains of alcohol imbibing rats. Sjoquist, Eriksson, and Winblad (1982) performed autopsies on the brains of alcoholics and normals. They found salsolinol in both populations. Beck, Bosin, Holmstead, and Lundman (1982) report finding beta-carbolines (condensation product of an alkaloid and serotonin) in the urine of drinking alcoholics. Borg, Kvande, Magnuson, and Sjoquist (1980) measured the level of THIQs present in the cerebrospinal fluid of alcoholics after consumption of alcohol. THIQs were found.

There are conditions associated with lower levels of THIQs. Liver disease is associated with decreased levels of harman, a beta-carboline type of alkaloid (Rommelspacher et al., 1985). There have been inconsistent reports as to whether sober alcoholics produce greater amounts of THIQs or are possibly deficit in THIQ production. Faraj et al. (1989) found that sober alcoholics have greater amounts of salsolinol in the blood than normals. Brain autopsies of abstinent alcoholics reveal subnormal levels of THIQs (Sjoquist et al., 1982b). Sjoquist et al. (1982b) have speculated that alcoholics may drink to replenish their sober state, subnormal levels of salsolinol.

Some factors seems to enhance the levels of THIQs. Collins, Hannigan, Origitano, Moura, and Osswald (1982) report that chronic amphetamine consumption elevates the levels of THBCs (tetrahydro-beta-carbolines, formed from serotonin metabolites and tryptophan) found in the blood, brain, and adrenal glands. Elevated levels of phenylalanine, an amino acid, result in the accumulation of THIQs in the cerebellum and cortex in the rat (Lasada & Coscia, 1979). L-dopa (a drug used to treat Parkinson's disease) seems to increase the accumulation of THIQs (Cohen, 1976; Sandler, Glover, Armando, & Clow, 1982). Further, drinking alcohol seems to increase the production of the THIQs (Beck et al., 1982; Sjoquist, Eriksson, & Winblad, 1982a). Sandler, Glover, Armando, and Clow (1982) have found urinary THIQs to be highest at day five of withdrawal.

Although alcoholics are not the only persons who produce high levels of THIQs, there is some evidence that those who are genetically predisposed to alcoholism may produce THIQs in greater concentrations when they drink than normal populations. Schuckit (1984) reported preliminary findings from a pilot study. FHP (family history positive for alcoholism) individuals had higher levels of salsolinol (one of the THIQs) in the urine than did controls after drinking, although the small number of subjects precluded a statistical test. Rommelspacher et al. (1985) measured harman (a beta-carboline a subclass of alkaloid) in the urine and blood of detoxifying alcoholics. Those who were FHPs and those who had begun drinking at a younger age, exhibited higher harman levels as well as higher acetaldehyde levels in the blood.

Research comparing persons, who are not yet alcoholic but who have a family history of alcoholism, with a control population matched on extant drinking practices lends further support to the notion that THIQs may be differentially produced by persons at genetic risk for alcoholism. Schuckit and Rayses (1979) found that after alcohol consumption, family history positive individuals have twice the level of plasma acetaldehyde levels as control individuals. Acetaldehyde is an alkaloid that can participate in the condensation process forming THIQs. If more acetaldehyde is available, there is reason to believe that the production of THIQs will increase. In fact, experimental work does suggest that those producing higher acetaldehyde levels when drinking are higher in salsolinol production (Faraj et al., 1989).

In their 1989 publication, Faraj et al. speculated that salsolinol production in genetically predisposed alcoholics may be related to the way in which they catabolize dopamine, which might be in turn related to their low MAO (monoamine oxidase, the enzyme that catabolizes dopamine, serotonin, and norepinephrine). Faraj et al. cite documentation that MAO is low in both alcoholics and their relatives. As such, greater salsolinol production would be anticipated whether or not an alcoholic was consuming alcohol. Consistent with Faraj et al.'s speculation are some reports (cited by Faraj et al.) from alcoholic populations which suggest that their urinary levels of salsolinol remain elevated long into sobriety (2 to 10 years into sobriety). Faraj et al. (1989), themselves, found that blood levels of salsolinol were elevated in alcoholics after 3 weeks of sobriety.

Summary and Comment

Individuals who are family history positive for developing alcoholism produce higher levels of THIQs when they drink. The degree of production is relative. Everyone produces them; it is a question of amounts. It should be noted that THIQs do not remain in the body permanently. The levels of THIQs seem to fluctuate over time. The half lives of some THIQs have been measured. Salsolinol has a half life of 12 minutes and THP (condensation product of dopamine and its alkaloid metabolite, dopac) has a half life of 17 minutes when given as an intraventricular injection into the brain (Deitrich & Erwin, 1980).

WHAT DO THIQS DO?

The finding that family history positive individuals produce enhanced levels of THIQs after drinking has led investigators to ponder what functions the THIQs might subserve. Investigators have speculated whether the THIQs mediate symptoms of intoxication or are responsible for particular withdrawal symptoms. Further, if some alcoholics have deficit levels when abstinent, the deficit could mediate craving (Sjoquist et al., 1982a).

Given that a particular THIQ is a precursor to opium in the poppy, there has been speculation regarding the activity of the THIQs at opiate receptor sites. Binding studies have been performed. It is generally concluded that the THIQs do not bind as well to opiate receptor sites as codeine or morphine. Further, they bind more effectively to catecholamine receptor sites than to opiate receptor sites (Nimit, Schulze, Cashaw, Ruchirawat, & Davis, 1982). An additional problem with the notion that THIQs achieve their impact through interaction with opiate receptor sites, is the necessity of postulating a transport mechanism. THIQs are condensation products of alkaloids with a catecholamine or an indolamine (serotonin). Hence, they are probably produced near the nerve endings for these neurotransmitters. In order to be active at endorphin receptors, they would have to be transported to another area of the brain (Duncan & Deitrich, 1980).

Investigations into the pharmacological effects of the THIQs suggest a wide variety of activity at catecholamine releasing nerves. The THIQs are false trans-mitters for the catecholamines (Cohen, 1976). They compete for reuptake into the presynaptic nerve at catecholamine nerve terminals (Cohen, 1976; Deitrich & Erwin, 1980). They compete with serotonin, dopamine, and norepinephrine for enzymes that catabolize these neurotransmitters, viz., MAO and COMT (cate-chol-O-methyl transferase) (Collins, Cashaw, & Davis, 1973). Further, the me-tabolites produced by interaction with catabolizing enzymes are pharmacolog-ically active (Cohen, 1978). THIQs inhibit the enzyme (tyrosine hydroxylase) which synthesizes both dopamine and norepinephrine (Light, 1986). Given the large number of functions occurring at amine nerves, it seems likely that the behavioral effects of THIQs are achieved by activity at this type of terminal.

Alkaloids similar to the THIQs called beta-carbolines are condensation prod-ucts of alkaloids and indolamines or indolealkylamines (serotonin). (Actually, the tetrahydro-beta-carbolines do not belong under the superordinate of THIQs, however, the same type of condensation process is involved in their formation.) Braestrup and Nielsen (1982) report that beta-carbolines will bind at ben-zodiazepine receptor sites. Oakley and Jones (1980) report that beta-carbolines will lower the threshold for the production of seizures. Skolinck, Williams, Cook, Cain, Rice, Mendelson, Crawley, and Paul (1982) report that the beta-carbolines will antagonize the anti-convulsive, anxiolytic, and sedative hypnotic effects of sedative drugs. This suggests that the beta-carbolines are anxiety inducers. These findings have led researchers to speculate regarding the beta-carbolines as the searched for endogenous ligands of benzodiazepine receptors. Tetrahydo-b-carboline has also been found to increase the availability of brain serotonin possibly through blocking catabolism, although synthesis seems to be decreased (Buckholtz, 1982).

ARE THIQS ADDICTING?

One issue that has received surprisingly little attention in the literature is whether THIQs are addictive. Duncan and Dietrich (1980) claim that there is no evidence to suggest that they are. In their original paper, Davis and Walsh cite a 1961 article, which states, "By every criterion customarily used, degree and quality of morphinelike subjective effects, ability to suppress symptoms of abstinence from morphine, and severity of abstinence reaction after prolonged chronic admin-istration I-K-1 is a compound of very little or no addictiveness" (Fraser, Martin, Wolbach, & Isbell, 1961). Although evidence for addictive liability is lacking, THIQs are reinforcing. Rats will work for intraventricular injections of THIQs (Amit, Smith, Brown, & Williams, 1982). They will also work for intra-ventricular injections of acetaldehyde which may increase the endogenous pro-duction of THIQs (Kakihana & Butte, 1980).

THE QUESTION OF NEUROTOXICITY

THIQs are known neurotoxins (Melchoir, 1982). Lasada and Coscia (1979) speculate that the damage created in PKU victims (phenylketonuria, a form of retardation related to faulty catabolism of the amino acid phenylalanine) may be mediated by the high levels of THIQs found in the cortex and cerebellum, the areas that are most heavily damaged in PKU victims. Myers and Melchoir (1977) report that THP infusions results in wet dog shakes, licking behavior, weight loss, hypothermia, and piloerection. Duncan and Deitrich (1980) report THIQ induced seizures. These behavioral manifestations may all be reflections of neurotoxicity.

INDUCTION OF ALCOHOL PREFERENCE

One of the intriguing characteristics of THIQs, is that when supplied by intraventricular injection into the rat brain they will induce a long lasting preference for alcohol (Duncan & Deitrich, 1980; Myers & Melchoir, 1977; Myers & Oblinger, 1977). In these studies, the rat is typically exposed to alcohol during the THIQ infusion. The rat is later tested for amount of alcohol consumed after the THIQs are no longer being infused into the brain. Enhanced consumption is seen both during and after the infusion period. This enhanced preference is seen only when rat strains that are naturally nonpreferring are employed as subjects. Among rats that normally are heavy consumers, ordinarily drinking at rates equal to their abilities to metabolize the alcohol, THIQs will not increase drinking (Amit et al., 1982). In any case, the THIQ induced preference will not exceed the rat's capacity to metabolize, i.e., the alcohol will not accumulate in the rat's system (Duncan & Deitrich, 1980). Further, the relationship between the dosage of THIQs and induced alcohol preference is curvilinear. At high dose infusions, THIQs will decrease preference (Duncan & Deitrich, 1980; Myers & Melchoir, 1977).

Some of the findings in the rat have been replicated in the monkey (Myers, McCaleb, & Ruwe, 1982). THP infusions will increase the rate of alcohol consumed during the infusion. THe duration of the change has not been assessed. In the monkey, the level of consumption induced was found to exceed the animal's metabolic capacity to clear the alcohol. Again, a curvilinear relationship was noted, such that high doses of THP decreased drinking.

There has been speculation regarding the mechanism through which THIQs affect preference for alcohol. Some procedures have been found to abrogate the impact of the THIQs on preference. Rats given 6-OHDA (6-hydroxydopamine, a drug that destroys norepinephrine and dopamine neurons) will not respond to THIQs (Duncan & Deitrich, 1980). Alpha-methyl-tyrosine, a drug that impairs the synthesis of dopamine and norepinephrine, will block the THIQ induced preference for alcohol (Amit & Sutherland, 1975/1976). Further, naloxone (a drug that blocks opiate receptors) will attenuate the effect of THIQs on alcohol induced preference (Lin & Myers, 1978; Myers & Critcher, 1982).

The above findings seem to point to a catecholamine (norepinephrine or dopamine) mediator for the THIQ induced preference for alcohol. Only the naloxone finding suggests otherwise. Naloxone, while an opiate receptor antagonist, at larger doses is a GABA antagonist (Ho & Allen, 1981). Naloxone also will reverse the calcium depletion in brain tissue induced by a number of other drugs (e.g., morphine, salsolinol, and alcohol) (Cohen, 1976). Hence, the finding that naloxone moderates a particular effect does not necessarily implicate opiate receptors in the production of the effect.

Duncan and Deitrich (1980) suggest a particularly cogent criticism of the opiate mediation of THIQ induced alcohol preference. Apparently, the dosages of THIQs employed in the preference induction studies were lower than the concentrations required for interaction at the opiate receptor sites. Whereas opiate receptor action cannot be fully supported, the findings pertaining to drugs which modify the impact of THIQs on alcohol preference suggest catecholamine involvement.

Although the preceding would argue against the THIQ induced alcohol preference resulting from activity at opiate receptor sites, it is possible that THIQs in some way interact with opiate mediated events. A particular THIQ has been demonstrated capable of inducing a response at opiate receptor sites in the pig ileum (Hamilton, Marshall, Blum, & Hirst, 1976). THIQs share some of the properties of the opiates. THIQs, like opiates, are analgesic (Hannigan & Collins, 1979). THIQs will potentiate morphine analgesia (Blum, Futterman, Wallace, and Schwertner, 1977; Marshall, Hirst, & Blum, 1977). THIQs and morphine will deplete brain calcium (Ross, Medina, & Cardenas, 1974). THIQs, like the opiates, are reinforcing. This reinforcing property can be blocked by naloxine, although the dosage required exceeds the level required for interaction at opiate receptor sites (Bloom, 1982). Given that THIQs and morphine produce some common effects, it seems possible that they may possess some common pathways of operation. The possibility of mediation of alcohol preference through the opiate (endorphin/enkephalin) systems has not been ruled out (Myers, 1985).

WHAT EFFECTS OF ALCOHOL ARE CAUSED
BY THIQS?

An important question for present purposes is whether the THIQs mimick any of the effects of alcohol. An answer would suggest which manifestations of alcohol consumption can be attributed to the THIQs. The literature provides some answers. Rats taught to discriminate between alcohol and control substances could not distinguish between alcohol and intraventricular salsolinol (Altshuler, & Shippenberg, 1982). These rats, however, no longer responded to the salsolinol as if it were alcohol when they had been pretreated with naloxone. In these rats, alcohol retained its distinctive feature despite the naloxone. Salsolinol will produce its own narcosis and enhance alcohol narcosis (Blum, Futterman, Wallace, & Schwertner, 1977; Church, Fuller, & Dudek, 1976; Marshall & Hirst, 1976; Melchoir, 1982). Both alcohol and salsolinol create a depletion of calcium in the brain, and these effects are blocked by naloxone (Ross et al. 1974). Rats given intraventricular THIQ while they are developing dependence on alcohol, display enhanced withdrawal symptoms (Blum, Eubanks, Wallace, Schwertner, & Morgan, 1976; Cohen, 1976; Melchoir, 1982). It would seen that THIQs share a number of properties with alcohol as well as achieving additive effects on some events. There is one alcohol related phenomenon which is not potentiated by THIQ. Intraventricular administration of THP will block the development of tolerance to alcohol (Melchoir, 1982). Given that persons produce higher levels of THIQs when they drink, future research will probably reveal which of the changes manifested during intoxication and during withdrawal are attributable to the elevation in THIQs.

SUMMARY AND COMMENT

Although there are probably more unanswered questions regarding THIQs than extant information, available research does suggest a number of implications. First, there is good reason to believe that persons predisposed by genetics to the development of alcoholism produce higher levels of THIQs. Second, the supply of THIQs in the brain is in flux. Third, THIQs seem to enhance the consumption of alcohol. Although this may be attributable to some permanent physiological change induced by the THIQs in the brain, it also could result from a learning mechanism. That is, alcohol may be much more reinforcing when consumed with high brain levels of THIQs. The impact of the learning should endure for a time. Fourth, the nature of the alteration induced by THIQs rendering alcohol more attractive may involve the monoamine transmitters although an endorphin mechanism has not been ruled out. Fifth, the THIQs undoubtedly mediate some of the acute manifestations of alcohol intoxication, and perhaps withdrawal. Unfortunately, it is not yet clear which effects are mediated by the THIQs.

REFERENCES

Abel, E. L., & Lee, J. A. (1988). Paternal alcohol exposure affects offspring behavior but not body or organ weights in mice. *Alcoholism: Clinical and Experimental Research, 12,* 349–355.

Abu-Murad, C., & Nordmann, R. (1983). Reduction in severity of physical dependence on ethanol in mice caused by desferrioxamine administration. *Pharmacology, Biochemistry, and Behavior, 18,* 515–517.

Alcohol Health and Research World. (1981). Focus on the fourth special report to the U.S. congress on alcohol and health. U.S. Department of Health and Human Services, Rockville, MD.

Alterman, A. I., Hayashida, M., & O'Brien, C. P. (1988). Treatment response and safety of ambulatory medical detoxification. *Journal of Studies on Alcohol, 49,* 160–166.

Altshuler, H. L., & Shippenberg, T. S. (1982). Tetrahydroisoquinolines and opiod substrates of alcohol action. In F. Bloom, J. Barchas, M. Sandler, & E. Usdin (Eds.), *Beta-carbolines and tetrahydroisoqinolines* (pp. 329–344). New York: Alan R. Liss.

Altura, B. M., & Altura, B. T. (1987). Peripheral and cerebrovascular actions of ethanol, acetaldehyde and acetate: Relationship to divalent cations. *Alcoholism: Clinical and Experimental Research, 11,* 99–111.

Altura, B. M., Altura, B. T., & Gebrewold, A. (1983). Alcohol-induced spasms of cerebral blood vessels: Relation to cerebrovascular accidents and sudden death. *Science, 220,* 331–332.

Amit, Z., Smith, B. R., Brown, Z. W., & Williams, R. L. (1982). An examination of the role of the TIQ alkaloids in alcohol intake: Reinforcers, satiety agents or artifacts. In F. Bloom, J. Barchas, M. Sandler, & E. Usdin (Eds.), *Beta-carbolines and tetrahydroisoqinolines* (pp. 345–364). New York: Alan R. Liss.

Amit, Z. & Sutherland, E. A. (1975/1976). The relevance of recent animal studies for the development of treatment procedures for alcoholics. *Drug and alcohol dependence. 1,* 3–13.

Andreoli, T. E., Carpenter, C. C. J., & Plum, F. (1986). *Cecil essentials of medicine.* Philadelphia: Saunders.

Arky, R. A. (1983/1984). Alcohol use and the diabetic patient. *Alcohol Health and Research World. 8,* 8–13.

Badaway, A. A-B. (1984). Alcohol intoxication and withdrawal. In S. B. Rosalki (Ed.), *Clinical biochemistry of alcoholism* (pp. 95–116). Edinburgh: Churchill Livingstone.

Badaway, A. A-B, & Evans, M. (1983). Opposite effects of chronic administration and subsequent withdrawal of drugs of dependence on the metabolism and disposition of endogenous and exogenous tryptophan in the rat. *Alcohol & Alcoholism, 18,* 369–382.

Baker, T. B., & Cannon, D. S. (1979). Potentiation of ethanol withdrawal by prior dependence. *Psychopharmacology, 60,* 105–110.

Ballenger, J. C., Goodwin, F. K., Major, L. F., & Brown, G. L. (1979). Alcohol and central serotonin metabolism in man. *Archives of General Psychiatry, 36,* 224–227.

Ballenger, J. C., & Post, R. M. (1978). Kindling as a model for alcohol withdrawal syndromes. *British Journal of Psychiatry, 133,* 1–14.

Beague, F., Stibler, H., & Borg, S. (1985). Abnormal fluidity and surface carbohydrate content of the erythrocyte membrane in alcoholic patients. *Alcoholism: Clinical and Experimental Research, 9,* 322–326.

Beck, O., Bosin, T. R., Holmstedt, B., & Lundman, A. (1982). A GC-MS study on the occurrence of two tetrahydro-b-carbolines implicated in alcoholism. In F. Bloom, J. Barchas, M. Sandler, & E. Usdin (Eds.), *Beta-carbolines and tetrahydroisoquinolines* (pp. 41–55). New York: Alan R. Liss.

Berk, R. S., Montogomery, I. N., Hazlett, L. D., & Abel, E. L. (1989). Paternal alcohol consumption: Effects on ocular response and serum antibody response to pseudomonas aeruginosa infection in offspring. *Alcoholism: Clinical and Experimental Research, 13,* 795–798.

Bernstein, J. E., & Soltani, K. (1982). Alcohol-induced rosacea flushing blocked by naloxone. *British Journal of Dermatology, 107,* 59–62.

Besson, J. A. O., Glen, A. I. M., Foreman, E. I., MacDonald, A., Smith, F. W., Hutchison, J. M. S., Mallard, J. R., & Ashcroft, G. W. (1981). Nuclear magnetic resonance observations in alcoholic cerebral disorder and the role of vasopressin. *Lancet,* Oct. 24, 923–924.

Bliven, F. E. (1982). The skeletal system: Alcohol as a factor. In E. M. Pattison & E. Kaufman (Eds.), *Encyclopedic handbook of alcoholism* (pp. 215–224). New York: Gardner Press.

Bloom, F. W. (1982). Open questions: A summary of the workshop discussions. In F. Bloom, J. Barchas, M. Sandler, & E. Usdin (Eds.), *Beta-carbolines and tetrahydroisoqinolines* (pp. 401–410). New York: Alan R. Liss.

Blum, K. (1982). Neurophysiological effects of alcohol. In E. M. Pattison & E. Kaufman (Eds.), *Encyclopedic handbook of alcoholism* (pp. 105–134). New York: Gardner Press.

Blum, K. Eubanks, J. D., Wallace, J. E., Schwertner, H., & Morgan, W. W. (1976). Possible role of tetrahydroisoquinoline alkaloids in post alcohol intoxication states. *Annals of the New York Academy of Science. 273,* 234–246.

Blum, K., Futterman, S., Wallace, S., & Schwertner, H. A. (1977). Naloxone-induced inhibition of ethanol dependence in mice. *Nature, 265,* 49–51.

Boada, J., Feria, M., & Sanz, E. (1981). Inhibitory effect of naloxone on the ethanol-induced antinociception in mice. *Pharmacological Research Communications. 13,* 673–678.

Borg, S., Kvande, H., Magnuson, E., & Sjoqvist, B. (1980). Salsolinol and salsoline in cerebrospinal lumbar fluid of alcoholic patients. *Acta Psychiatrica Scandanavia Supplement, 62, suppl 286,* 171–177.

Borg, V., & Weinholdt, T. (1980). A preliminary double-blind study of two dopamine drugs, apomorphine and bromocriptine (parlodel), in the treatment of the alcohol-withdrawal syndrome. *Current Therapeutic Research, 27,* 170–177.

Borg, V., & Weinholdt, T. (1982). Bromocriptine in the treatment of the alcohol-withdrawal syndrome. *Acta Psychiatrica Scandanavia, 65,* 101–111.

Bowden, S. C. (1987). Brain impairment in social drinkers? No cause for concern. *Alcoholism: Clinical and Experimental Research, 11,* 407–410.

Bowden, S. C., Walton, N. H., Walsh, K. W. (1988). The hangover hypothesis and the influence of moderate social drinking on mental ability. *Alcoholism: Clinical and Experimental Research, 12.* 25–29.

Bower, B. (1989). Lithium dissolves as alcoholism treatment. *Science News, May 20,* p. 309.

Braestrup, C., & Nielsen, M. (1982). B-carboliines and benzodiazepine receptors. In F. Bloom, J. Barchas, M. Sandler, & E. Usdin (Eds.), *Beta-carbolines and tetrahydroisoqinolines* (pp. 227–232). New York: Alan R. Liss.

Branchey, L., Branchey, M., Zucker, D., Shaw, S., & Lieber, C. S. (1985). Association between low plasma tryptophan and blackouts in alcoholic patients. *Alcoholism: Clinical and Experimental Research, 9,* 393–395.

Brubaker, R. G., Prue, D. M., & Rychtarik, R. G. (1987). Determinants of disulfiram acceptance among alcohol patients: A test of the theory of reasoned action. *Addictive Behaviors. 12,* 43–52.

Buckholtz, N. S. (1982). Interaction of tetrahydro-beta-carbolines with brain serotonin metabolism. In F. Bloom, J. Barchas, M. Sandler, & E. Usdin (Eds.), *Beta-carbolines and tetrahydroisoqinolines* (pp. 183–190). New York: Alan R. Liss.

Cadete-Leite, A., Tavares, M. A., Alves, M. C., Uylings, H. B. M., & Paula-Barboas, M. M. (1989). Metric analysis of hippocampal granule cell dendritic trees after alcohol withdrawal in rats. *Alcoholism: Clinical and Experimental Research, 13,* 837–840.

Carlsson, A., Engel, J., & Svensson, T. H. (1972). Inhibition of ethanol-induced excitation in mice and rats by alpha-methyl-p-tyrosine. *Psychopharmacologia, 26,* 307–312.

Carrington, C. D., Ellinwood, E. H., & Krishnan, R. R. (1984). Effects of single and repeated alcohol withdrawal on kindling. *Biological Psychiatry, 19,* 525–537.

Castaneda, R., & Glanter, M. (1988). Ethnic differences in drinking practices and cognitive impairment among detoxifying alcoholics. *Journal of Studies on Alcohol, 49*, 335–339.

Catley, D. M., Jordan, C., Frith, C. D., Lehane, A. M., Rhodes, A. M., & Jones, J. G. (1981). Alcohol induced discoordination is not reversed by naloxone. *Psychopharmacology. 75*, 65–68.

Chanarin, I. (1982). Effects of alcohol on the hematopoietic system. In E. M. Pattison & E. Kaufman (Eds.), *Encyclopedic handbook of alcoholism* (pp. 281–292). New York: Gardner Press.

Chandler, B. C., & Parsons, O. A. (1977). Altered hemispheric functioning under alcohol. *Journal of Studies on Alcohol, 38*, 381–391.

Chen, C. S. (1972). A further note on studies of acquired behavioural tolerance to alcohol. *Psychopharmacologia, 27*, 265–274.

Chew, W. H., & Rissing, J. P. (1982). Infectious diseases and the alcoholic. In E. M. Pattison & E. Kaufman (Eds.), *Encyclopedic handbook of alcoholism* (pp. 263–274). New York: Gardner Press.

Church, A. C., Fuller, J., & Dudek, B. C. (1976). Salsolinol differentially affects mice selected for sensitivity to alcohol. *Psychopharmacologia. 1976, 47*, 49–52.

Cicero, T. J. (1982). Pathogenesis of alcohol-induced endocrine abnormalities. *Advances in Alcohol and Alcohol Abuse, 1*, 87–112.

Cohen, G. (1976). Alkaloid products in the metabolism of alcohol and biogenic amines. *Biochemical Pharmacology, 25*, 1123–1128.

Cohen, G. (1978). The synaptic properties of some tetrahydroisoquinoline alkaloids. *Alcoholism: Clinical and Experimental Research, 2*, 121–125.

Collins, A. C., Cashaw, J. L., & Davis, V. E. (1973). Dopamine-derived tetrahydroisoquinoline alkaloids-inhibitors of neuroamine metabolism. *Biochemical pharmacology. 22*, 2337–2348.

Collins, W. E., & Chiles, W. D. (1980). Laboratory performance during acute alcohol intoxication and hangover. *Human Factors, 22*, 445–462.

Collins, A. C., Gilliam, D. M., & Miner, L. L. (1985). Indomethacin pretreatment blocks the effects of high concentrations of ethanol. *Alcoholism: Clinical and Experimental Research, 9*, 371–376.

Collins, M. A., Hannigan, J. J., Origitano, T., Moura, D., & Osswald, W. (1982). On the occurrence, assay, and metabolism of simple tetrahydroisoquinolines in mammalian tissues. In F. Bloom, J. Barchas, M. Sandler, & E. Usdin (Eds.), *Beta-carbolines and tetrahydroisoqinolines* (pp. 155–166). New York: Alan R. Liss.

Crabbe, J. C., Young, E. R., & Kosobud, A. (1983). Genetic correlations with ethanol withdrawal severity. *Pharmacology, Biochemistry, and Behavior, 18*, 541–547.

Criqui, M. H. (1986). Alcohol consumption, blood pressure, lipids, and cardiovascular mortality. *Alcoholism: Clinical and Experimental Research, 10*, 564–569.

Cushman, P., Barboriak, J., & Kalbfleisch, J. (1986). Alcohol: High density lipoproteins, apolipoproteins. *Alcoholism: Clinical and Experimental Research, 10*, 154–157.

Davies, D. L., Shepherd, M., & Myers, E. (1956). The two year prognosis of fifty alcoholic addicts after treatment in the hospital. *Quarterly Journal of Studies on Alcohol, 17*, 484–502.

Davis, V. E., & Walsh, M. J. (1970). Alcohol, amines, and alkaloids: A possible biochemical basis for alcohol addiction. *Science, 167*, 1005–1007.

Davis, W., M., Werner, T. E., & Smith, S. G. (1979). Reinforcement with intragastric infusions of ethanol: Blocking effect of FLA 57. *Pharmacology, Biochemistry, & Behavior, 44*, 545–548.

Deitrich, R., & Erwin, V. (1980). Biogenic amine-aldehyde condensation products: Tetrahydroisoquinolines and tryptolines (b-carbolines). *Annual review of Pharmacological toxicology. 1980, 20*, 55–80.

de Wit, H., Uhlenhuth, E. H., Pierri, J., & Johanson, C. E. (1987). Individual differences in behavioral and subjective responses to alcohol. *Alcoholism: Clinical and Experimental Research, 11*, 52–59.

Diagnostic and statistical manual of mental disorders: Third edition. (1980). Washington, D. C.: American Psychiatric Association.

Di Chiara, G., & Imperato, A. (1988). Drugs abused by humans preferentially increase synaptic dopamine concentrations in the mesolimbic system of freely moving rats. *Proceedings of the National Academy of Sciences, 85,* 5274–5278.

Dillon, M. M., Waters, D. H., & Triggle, D. J. (1983). Demonstration of central nervous system tolerance to ethanol in mice: Consequent effects on smooth muscle in vitro. *Alcoholism: Clinical and Experimental Research, 7,* 349–356.

Domonkos, A. N., Arnold, H. L., & Odom, R. B. (1982). *Andrew's diseases of the skin: Clinical dermatology, Seventh Edition.* Philadelphia: Saunders.

Donovan, D. M., Walker, R. D., & Kivlahan, D. R. (1987). Recovery and remediation of neuropsychological functions: Implications for alcoholism rehabilitation process and outcome. In O. A. Parsons, N. Butters, & P. E. Nathan (Eds.), *Neuropsychology of alcoholism: Implications for diagnosis and treatment* (pp. 339–360). New York: Guilford.

Drafters, R., & Anderson, G. (1982). Conditioned tolerance to the tachycardia effect of ethanol in hymans. *Psychopharmacology, 78,* 365–367.

Duncan, C., & Deitrich, R. A. (1980). A critical evaluation of tetrahydroisoquinoline induced ethanol preference in rats. *Pharmacology, Biochemistry, & Behavior, 13,* 265–281.

Eckhardt, M. J., & Martin, P. R. (1986). Cognitive impairment in alcoholism: Clinical assessment of cognition in alcoholism. *Alcoholism: Clinical and Experimental Research, 10,* 123–127.

Edwards, G., & Gross, M. M. (1976). Alcohol dependence: Provisional description of a clinical syndrome. *British Journal of Medicine, 1,* 1058–1061.

el-Guebaly, N. (1987). Alcohol, alcoholism, and biological rhythms. *Alcoholism: Clinical and Experimental Research, 11,* 139–143.

Eisenhoffer, G., Whiteside, E., Lambie, D., & Johnson, R. (1982). Brain water during alcohol withdrawal.*The Lancet, 1,*Jan. 2, 50.

Ellis, R. J., & Oscar-Berman, M. (1989). Alcoholism, aging, and functional cerebral asymmetries. *Psychological Bulletin, 106,* 128–147.

Emmerson, R. Y., Dustman, R. E., Heil, J., & Shearer, E. E. (1988). Neuropsychological performance of young nondrinkers, social drinking, and long- and short-term sober alcoholics. *Alcoholism: Clinical and Experimental Research, 12,* 625–629.

Erwin, V. G., Jones, B. C., & Radcliffe, R. (1990). Low doses of ethanol reduce neurotensin levels in discrete brain regions from LS/Lbg and SS/Ibg mice. *Alcoholism: Clinical and Experimental Research, 14,* 42–47.

Erwin, V. G., & Towell, J. F. (1983). Ethanol-induced hyperglycemia mediated by the central nervous system. *Pharmacology, Biochemistry and Behavior, 18,* Supplement 1, 559–563.

Estrin, W. J. (1987). Alcoholic cerebellar degeneration is not a dose-dependent phenomenon. *Alcoholism: Clinical and Experimental Research, 11,* 372–375.

Ewing, J. A. (1982). Disulfiram and other deterrent drugs. In E. M. Pattison & E. Kaufman (Eds.), *Encyclopedidic handbook of alcoholism* (pp. 1033–1042). New York: Gardner Press.

Ewing, J. A., Mueller, R. A., Rouse, B. A., & Silver, D. (1977). Low levels of dopamine B-hydroxylase and psychosis. *American Journal of Psychiatry, 134.* 927–928.

Fadel, H. E., & Hadi, H. A. (1982). Alcohol effects on the reproductive function. In E. M. Pattison & E. Kaufman (Eds.), *Encyclopedic handbook of alcoholism* (pp. 293–300). New York: Gardner Press.

Faraj, B. A., Camp, V. M. Davis, D. C. Lenton, J. D., & Kutner, M. (1989). Elevation in plasma salsolinol sulfate in chronic alcoholics compared to nonalcoholics. *Alcoholism: Clinical and Experimental Research, 13,* 155–163.

Fawcett, J., Clark, D. C., Aagesen, C. A., Pisani, V. D., Tilkin, J. M., Sellers, D., McGuire, M., & Gibbons, R. D. (1987). A double-blind trial of lithium carbonate therapy for alcoholism. *Archives of General Psychiatry, 44,* 248–256.

Fawcett, J., Clark, D. C., Gibbons, R. D., Aagesen, C. A., Pisani, V. D., Tilkin, J. A., Sellers, D., & Stutzman, D. (1984). Evaluation of lithium therapy for alcoholism. *Journal of Clinical Psychiatry, 45,* 494–499.

Feinman, L., & Lieber, C. S. (1988). Toxicity of ethanol and other components of alcoholic beverages. *Alcoholism: Clinical and Experimental Research, 12,* 2–6.

Feldman, E. B. (1982). Malnutrition in the alcoholic and related nutritional deficiencies. In E. M. Pattison & E. Kaufman (Eds.), *Encyclopedic handbook of alcoholism* (pp. 255–262). New York: Gardner Press.

Feldman, D. J., Pattison, E. M., Sobell, L. C., Graham, T., & Sobell, M. B. (1975). Outpatient alcohol detoxification: Initial findings on 564 patients. *American Journal of Psychiatry, 132,* 407–412.

Ferguson, E. R., & Knochel, J. P. (1982). Myopathy in the chronic alcoholic. In E. M. Pattison & E. Kaufman (Eds.), *Encyclopedic handbook of alcoholism* (pp. 204–215). New York: Gardner Press.

Feuerlein, W. (1974). The acute alcohol withdrawal syndrome: Findings and problems. *British Journal of Addictions, 69,* 141–148.

Flegal, K. M., & Cauley, J. A. (1985). Alcohol consumption and cardiovascular risk factors. In M. Glanter (Ed.), *Recent developments in alcoholism,* (Vol. 3). New York: Plenum Press.

Forsberg, L. K., & Goldman, M. S. (1985). Experience-dependent recovery of functioning in older alcoholics. *Journal of Abnormal Psychology, 94,* 519–529.

Foy, A., March, S., & Drinkwater, V. (1988). Use of an objective clinical scale in the assessment and management of alcohol withdrawal in a large general hospital. *Alcoholism: Clinical and Experimental Research, 12,* 360–364.

Franck, D. H. (1983). 'If you drink, don't drive' motto now applies to hangovers as well. *Journal of the American Medical Association, 250,* 1657–1658.

Fraser, H. F., Martin, W. R., Wolbach, A. B., & Isbell, H. (1961). Addiction liability of an isoquinoline analgesic 1-(p-chlorophenethyl)-2-methyl-6,7-dimethoxy-1, 2, 3, 4-tetrahydroisoquinoline. *Clinical pharmacology and therapeutics. 2,* 287–299.

Freund, G. (1980). Comparison of alcohol dependence, withdrawal, and hangover in humans and animals. In K. Eriksson, J. D. Sinclair, & K. Kiianmaas (Eds.), *Animal models in alcohol research* (pp. 293–308). New York: Academic Press.

Freund, G. (1983). Neurologic diseases associated with chronic alcohol abuse. In B. Tabakoff, P. B. Sutker, & C. L., Randall (Eds.) *Medical and social aspects of alcohol abuse* (pp. 165–186). New York: Plenum.

Frezza, M., Di Padova, C., Pozzato, G., Terpin, M. Baraona, E., & Lieber, C. S. (1990). High blood alcohol levels in women: The role of decreased gastric alcohol dehydrogenase activity and first-pass metabolism. *New England Journal of Medicine, 322,* 95–99.

Fuller, R. K., Branchey, L., Brightwell, D. R., Derman, R. M., Emrick, C. D., Iber, F. L., James, K. E., Lacoursiere, R. B., Lee, K. K., Lowenstam, I., Maany, I., Neidershiser, Nocks, J. J., Shaw, S. (1986). Disulfiram treatment of alcoholism: A veterans administration cooperative study. *Journal of the American Medical Association, 256,* 1449–1455.

Fuller, R. K., & Williford, W. O. (1980). Life-table analysis of abstinence in a study evaluating the efficacy of disulfiram. *Alcoholism: Clinical and Experimental Research, 4,* 298–301.

Gallant, D. M. (1987). The female alcoholic: Early onset of brain damage. *Alcoholism: Clinical and Experimental Research, 11,* 190.

Gallant, D. M. (1990). Factors weighed in treating alcohol withdrawal syndromes. *Psychiatric Times, April,* 45–46.

Gallant, D. M., Bishop, M. P., Faulkner, M. A., Simpson, L., Cooper, A., Lathrop, D., Brisolara, A. M., & Bossetta, J. R. (1968). A comparative evaluation of compulsory (group therapy and/or antabuse) and voluntary treatment of the chronic alcoholic municipal count offender. *Psychosomatics, 9,* 306–310.

George, F. R., & Collins, A. C. (1985). Ethanol's behavioral effects may be partly due to increases in brain prostaglandin production. *Alcoholism: Clinical and Experimental Research, 9,* 143–146.

Gerrein, J. R., Rosenberg, C. M., & Manohar, V. (1973). Disulfiram maintenance in outpatient treatment of alcoholism. *Archives of General Psychiatry, 28,* 798–802.

Gill, J. S., Zezulka, A. V., Shipley, M. J., Gill, S. K., & Beevers, D. G. (1986). Stroke and alcohol consumption. *New England Journal of Medicine, 315,* 1041–1046.

Goldman, M. A. (1987). The role of time and practice in recovery of function in alcoholics. In O. A. Parsons, N. Butters, & P. E. Nathan (Eds.), *Neuropsychology of alcoholism: Implications for diagnosis and treatment* (pp. 291–321). New York: Guilford Press.

Goldman, G. D., Volicer, L., Gold, B. I., & Rotn, R. H. (1981). Cerebrospinal fluid GABA and cyclic nucleotides in alcoholics with and without seizures. *Alcoholism: Clinical and Experimental Research, 5,* 431–434.

Goldstein, D. B. (1972). Relationship of alcohol doese to intensity of withdrawal signs in mice. Journal of *Pharmacology and Experimental Therapeutics, 180,* 203–215.

Goldstein, G. (1987). Etiological considerations regarding the neuropsychological consequences of alcoholism. In O. A. Parsons, N. Butters, & P. E. Nathan (Eds.), *Neuropsychology of alcoholism: Implications for diagnosis and treatment* (pp. 227–247). New York: Guilford Press.

Gorman, D. M., Potamianos, G., Williams, K. A., Frank, A. O., Duffy, S. W., & Peters, T. J. (1987). Relationship between alcohol abuse and low back pain. *Alcohol & Alcoholism, 22,* 61–63.

Greenspon, A. J., & Schaal, S. F. (1983). The "holiday heart": Electrophysiologic studies of alcohol effects in alcoholics. *Annals of Internal Medicine, 98,* 135–139.

Gross, M. M., Lewis, E., & Hastey, J. (1974). Acute alcohol withdrawal syndrome. In B. Kissen & H. Beglieter (Eds.), *The biology of alcoholism* (pp. 191–263, Vol. 3). New York: Plenum Press.

Guthrie, G. D., Myers, K. J., Gesser, E. J., White, G. W., & Koehl, J. R. (1990). Alcohol as a nutrient: Interactions between ethanol and carbohydrate. *Alcoholism: Clinical and Experimental Research, 14,* 17–22.

Hamilton, M. G., Blum, K., & Hirst, M. (1978b). Identification of an isoquinoline alkaloid after chronic exposure to ethanol. *Alcoholism: Clinical and experimental research. 2,* 133–137.

Hamilton, M. G., Marshall, A. M., Blum, K., & Hirst, M. (1976). Effect of salsolinol on the field-stimulated guinea pig ileum. *Pharmacologist, 18,* 102.

Hannigan, J. J., & Collins, M. A. (1979). Tetrahydroisoquinolines and the serotonergic system. *Drug and Alcohol Dependence, 1,* 235–237.

Harris, R. A. (1979). Metabolism of calcium and magnesium during ethanol intoxication and withdrawal. In E. Majchrowicz & E P. Noble (Eds.), *Biochemistry and Pharmacology of Ethanol* (pp. 34–41, Vol. 2). New York: Plenum Press.

Harris, R. E., & Wynder, E. L. (1988). Breast cancer and alcohol consumption. *Journal of the American Medical Association, 259,* 2867–2871.

Hartmann, E. L. (1982). Alcohol and sleep disorders. In E. M. Pattison & E. Kaufman (Eds.) *Encyclopedic handbook of alcoholism* (pp. 180–193). New York: Gardner Press.

Hayashida, M. Alterman, A. I., McLellan, A. T., O'Brien, C. P., Purtill, J. J., Volpicelli, J. R., Raphaelson, A. H., & Hall, C. P. (1989). Comparative effectiveness and costs of inpatient and outpatient detoxification of patients with mild-to-moderate moderate withdrawal syndrome. *New England Journal of Medicine, 320,* 358–364.

Hiller, J. M., Angel, L. M., & Simon, E. J. (1981). Multiple optiate receptors: Alcohol selectively inhibits binding to delta receptors. *Science, 214,* 468–469.

Ho, A. K. S., & Allen, J. P. (1981). Alcohol and the opiate receptor: Interactions with the endogenous opiates. *Advances in alcohol and substance abuse. 1,* 52–74.

Ho, A. K. S., & Tsai, C. S. (1976). Effects of lithium on alcohol preference and withdrawal. *Annals of the New York Academy of Sciences, 273,* 371–377.

Hoff, E. C., & McKeown, C. E. (1953). An evaluation of the use of tetraehylthiuram disulfide in the treatment of 560 cases of alcohol addiction. *American Journal of Psychiatry, 109,* 670–673.

Hojnacki, J. L., Cluette-Brown, J. E., Mulligan, J. J., Hagan, S. M., Mahony, K. E., Witzgall, S. K., Osmolski, T. V., & Barboriak, J. J. (1988). Effect of ethanol dose on low density lipoproteins and high density lipoproteins subfractions. *Alcoholism: Clinical and Experimental Research, 12,* 149–154.

Holman, R. B. (1987). Specificity of ethanol's action in the CNS: Neurotransmitters and neuromodulators. *Alcohol and Alcoholism,* Supplement 1, 147–150.

Horrobin, D. F. (1987). Essential fatty acids, prostaglandins, and alcoholism: An overview. *Alcoholism: Clinical and Experimental Research, 11,* 2–9.

Hrubec, Z., & Omenn, G. S. (1981). Evidence of genetic predisposition to alcoholic cirrohosis and psychosis: Twin concordance to alcoholism and its biological end points by zygosity among male veterans. *Alcoholism: Clinical and Experimental Research, 5,* 207–215.

Hunt, W. A. (1985). *Alcohol and biological membranes.* New York: Guilford Press.

Irwin, M., Smith, T. L., Butters, N., Brown S., Baird S., Grant, I., & Schuckit, M. A. (1989). Graded neurpsychological impairment and elevated y-glutamyl transferase in chronic alcoholic men. *Alcoholism: Clinical and Experimental Research, 13,* 99–103.

Jaffe, J. H. (1980). Drug addiction and drug abuse. In A. G. Gilman, L. S. Goodman, & A. Gilman (Eds.), *The pharmacological basis of therapeutics* (pp. 535–584). New York: Macmillan Publishing.

Jeffcoate, W. J., Herbert, M., Cullen, M. H., Hastings, A. G., & Walder, C. P. (1979). Prevention effects of alcohol intoxication by naloxone. *Lancet,* December 1, 1157–1159.

Jeffreys, D. B., Flanagan, R. J., & Volans, G. N. (1980). Reversal of ethanol-induced coma with naloxone. *Lancet,* February 9, 308–309.

Jones, B. M., & Jones, M. K. (1976). Women and alcohol: Intoxication, metabolism, and the menstrual cycle. In M. Greenblatt & M. Schuckit (Eds.), *Alcoholism problems in women and children* (pp. 103–136). New York: Grune & Stratton.

Judd, L. L., Hubbard, B., Huey, L. Y., Attewell, P. A., Janowsky, D. S., & Takahashi, K. I. (1977). Lithium carbonate and ethanol induced "highs" in normal subjects. *Archives of General Psychiatry, 34,* 463–467.

Judd, L. L., & Huey, L. Y. (1984). Lithium antagonizes ethanol intoxication in alcoholics. *American Journal of Psychiatry, 141,* 1517–1521.

Julien, R. M. (1978). *A primer of drug action,* San Francisco: Freeman.

Kakihana, R., & Butte, J. C. (1980). Biochemical correlates of inherited drinking in laboratory animals. In K. Eriksson, J. D. Sinclair, & K. Kiianmaa (Eds.), *Animal models in alcohol research* (pp. 21–33). New York: Academic Press.

Kastl, A. J. (1969). Changes in ego functioning under alcohol. *Quarterly Journal of Studies on Alcohol, 30,* 371–383.

Keeler, M. H., & Miller, W. C. (1977). Selection among benzodiazepines for alcohol withdrawal. *Southern Medical Journal, 70,* 970–973.

Kent, T. A., Pazdernik, T. L., Gunn, W. H., Penick, E. C., Marples, B. W., Jones, M. P., & Goodwin, D. W. (1983). Platelet uptake of serotonin in ethanol intoxication: A preliminary study. *Biological Psychiatry, 18,* 929–933.

Kerr, J. T., Maxwell, D. S., & Crabb, D. W. (1989). Immunocytochemistry of alcohol dehydrogenase in the rat central nervous system. *Alcoholism: Clinical and Experimental Research, 13,* 730–736.

Keso, L., & Salaspuro, M. (1989). Laboratory markers as compared to drinking measures before and after inpatient treatment for alcoholism. *Alcoholism: Clinical and Experimental Research, 13,* 449–452.

Khetarpal, V. K., & Volicer, L. (1981). Alcohol and cardiovascular disorders. *Drug and Alcohol Dependence, 7,* 1–30.

Klatsky, A. L., Friedman, G. D., Siegelaub, A. B., & Gerard, M. J. (1977). Alcohol consumption and blood pressure: Kaiser-Permanente multiphasic health examination data. *New England Journal of Medicine, 296,* 1194–1200.

Kline, N. S., Wren, J. C., Cooper, T. B., Varga, E., & Canal, O. (1974). Evaluation of lithium therapy in chronic and periodic alcoholics. *American Journal of Medical Science, 268*, 15–22.

Knott, D. H., & Beard, J. D. (1982). Effects of alcohol ingestion on the cardiovascular system. In E. M. Pattison & E. Kaufman (Eds.), *Encyclopedic handbook of alcoholism* (pp. 332–342). New York: Gardner Press.

Knott, D. H., Beard, J. D., & Fink, R. D. (1987). Medical aspects of alcoholism. In W. M. Cox (Ed.), *Treatment and prevention of alcohol problems: A resource manual* (pp. 57–70). New York: Academic Press.

Kofoed, L. L. (1987). Chemical monitoring of disulfiram complaince: A study of alcoholic outpatients. *Alcoholism: Clinical and Experimental Research, 11*, 481–485.

Kolata, G. (1986). New drug counters alcohol intoxication. *Science, 234*, 1198–1199.

Kornetsky, C., Bain, G. T., Unterwald, E. M., & Lewis, M. J. (1988). Brain stimulation reward: Effects of ethanol. *Alcoholism: Clinical and Experimental Research, 12*, 609–616.

Korsten, M. A., & Lieber, C. S. (1982). Liver and pancreas. In E. M. Pattison & E. Kaufman (Eds.), *Encyclopedic handbook of alcoholism* (pp. 225–244). New York: Gardner Press.

Kostandov, A., Arsumanov, Y. L., Genkins, O. A., Restachikova, T. N., & Shostakovich, G. S. (1982). The effects of alcohol on hemispheric functional assymetry. *Journal of Studies on Alcohol, 43*, 411–426.

Kotkoskie, L. A., & Norton, S. (1988). Prenatal brain malformations following acute ethanol exposure in the rat. *Alcoholism: Clinical and Experimental Research, 12*, 831–836.

Kramer, J. H., Blusewicz, M. J., & Preston, K. A. (1989). The premature aging hypothesis: Old before its time? *Journal of Consulting and Clinical Psychology, 57*, 257–262.

Kewntus, J., & Major, L. F. (1979). Disulfiram in the treatment of alcoholism: A review. *Journal of Studies on Alcohol, 40*, 428–446.

Lakshman, M. R., Chambers, L. L., Chirtel, S. J., & Ekarohita, N. (1988). Role of hormonal and nutritional factors in the regulation of rat liver dehydrogenase activity and ethanol elimination rate in vivo. *Alcoholism: Clinical and Experimental Research, 12*, 407–411.

Lambie, D. G., Johnson, R. H., Vijayasenan, M. E., & Whiteside, E. A. (1980). Sodium valproate in the treatment of the alcohol withdrawal syndrome. *Journal of Psychiatry, 14*, 213–215.

LaPorte, R. E., Cauley, J. A., Kuller, L. H., Flegal, K., & Van Thiel, D. (1985). Alcohol, coronary heart disease, and total mortality. In M. Glanter (Ed.), *Recent Developments in Alcoholism* (pp. 157–163, Vol 3). New York: Plenum Press.

Laposata, E. A., & Lange, L. G. (1986). Presence of nonoxidative ethanol metabolism in human organs commonly damaged by ethanol abuse. *Science, 231*, 497–499.

Lasada, J. J., & Coscia, C. J. (1979). Accumulation of a tetrahydroisoquinoline in phenylketonuria. *Science, 203*, 283–284.

Le Bourhis, B., & Aufrere, G. (1983). Pattern of alcohol administration and physical dependence. *Alcoholism: Clinical and Experimental Research, 7*, 378–381.

Le, A. D., Kalant, H., & Khanna, J. M. (1989). Roles of intoxicated practice in the development of ethanol tolerance. *Psychophamacology, 99*, 366–370.

Le A. D., Poulos, C. X., & Cappell, H. (1979). Conditioned tolerance to the hypothermic effect of ethyl alcohol. *Science, 206*, 1109–1110.

Lee, N. M., & Becker, C. E. (1982). The alcohols, In B. G. Kartzung (Ed.), *Basic and Clinical Pharmacology* (pp. 231–238). Los Altos: Lange Medical Publications.

Lee, N. M., Friedman, H. J., & Loh, H. H. (1980). Effect of acute and chronic ethanol treatment on rat brain phospholipid turnover. *Biochemical Pharmacology, 29*, 2815–2818.

Lee, K., Moller, L., Hardt, F., Haubek, A., & Jensen, E. (1979). Alcohol induced brain damage and liver damage in young males. *Lancet, 2*, 759–761.

Leroy, J. B. (1979). Recognition and treatment of the alcohol withdrawal syndrome. *Primary Care, 6*, 529–539.

Leslie, S. W. (1986). Sedative-hynotic drugs: Interaction with calcium channels. *Alcohol and Drug Research, 6*, 371–377.

Leslie, R. D. G., Pyke, D. A., & Stubbs, W. A. (1979). Sensitivity to enkephalin as a cause of non-insulin dependent diabetes. *Lancet,* Feb. 17, 341–343.

Lewis, D. C., & Femino, J. (1982). Management of alcohol withdrawal. *Rational Drug Therapy, 16,* 1–5.

Li, T. K., Lumeng, L., McBride, W. J., Murphy, J. M., Froehlich, J. C., & Morzorati, S. (1989). Pharmacology of alcohol preference in rodents. In E. Gordis, B. Tabakoff, & M. Linnoila (Eds.) *Alcohol research from bench to bedside* (pp. 73–86). New York: Hawthorne Press.

Lieber, C. S. (1976). The metabolism of alcohol. *Scientific American,* March, 3–11.

Lieber, C. (1988). Biochemical and molecular basis of alcohol-induced injury to liver and other tissues. *New England Journal of Medicine, 319,* 25, 1639–1651.

Light, W. J. H. (1986). *Neurobiology of Alcohol Abuse.* Springfield, IL: Charles C. Thomas.

Liljequist, S., & Engel, J. (1980). Effect of ethanol on central gabaergic mechanisms. In K. Eriksson, J. D. Sinclair, 7 K. Kiianmaa (Eds.), *Animal models in alcohol research* (pp. 309–315). New York: Academic Press.

Lin, C. I., & Myers, R. D. (1978). Reversal of THP induced alcohol drinking in the rat by systemic naloxone and morphine. *Alcoholism: Clinical and Experimental Research, 2,* 188.

Lishman, W. A. (1987). *Organic psychiatry: The psychological consequences of cerebral disorder.* London: Blackwell Scientific Publications.

Little, R. E., & Sing, C. F. (1986). Association of father's drinking and infant's birth weight. *New England Journal of Medicine, 314,* 1644–1645.

Longnecker, M. P., Berlin, J. A., Orza, M. J., & Chalmers, T. C. (1988). A metaanalysis of alcohol consumption in relation to risk of breast cancer. *Journal of the American Medical Association, 260,* 652–656.

Lowenfels, A. B. (1982). Trauma, surgery, and anesthesia. In E. M. Pattison & E. Kaufman (Eds.), *Encyclopedic handbook of alcoholism* (pp. 343–353). New York: Gardner Press.

Lowenfels, A. B., & Zevola, S. A. (1989). Alcohol and breast cancer: An overview. *Alcoholism: Clinical and Experimental Research, 13,* 109–111.

Lundwall, L., & Baekeland, F. (1971). Disulfiram treatment of alcoholism. *Journal of Nervous and Mental Disease, 153,* 381–394.

Lyons, H. A. (1982). The respiratory system and specifics of alcoholism. In E. M. Pattison & E. Kaufman (Eds.), *Encyclopedic handbook of alcoholism* (pp. 325–331). New York: Gardner Press.

Magrinat, G., Dolan, J. P., Biddy, R. L., Miller, L. D., & Korol B. (1973). Ethanol and methanol metabolites in alcohol withdrawal. *Nature, 244,* 234–235.

Majchrowicz, E., & Hunt, W. A. (1976). Temporal relationship of the induction of tolerance and physical dependence after continuous intoxication and maximum tolerable doses of ethanol in rats. *Psychopharmacology, 50,* 107–112.

Majchrowicz, E., & Mendelson, J. H. (1971). Blood methanol concentrations during experimentally induced ethanol intoxication in alcoholics. *Journal of Pharmacology and Experimental Therapeutics, 179,* 293–300.

Majchrowicz, E., & Steinglass, P. (1973). Blood methanol, blood ethanol and alcohol withdrawal syndrome in humans. *Federal Proceedings,* Abstracts, *32,* 728.

Marshall, A., & Hirst, M. (1976). Potentiation of ethanol narcosis by dopamine and 1-DOPA based isoquinolines. *Experimentia, 32,* 201–203.

Marshall, A., Hirst, M., & Blum, K. (1977). Morphine analgesia augmentation by and direct analgesia with 3-carboxyl-salsolinol. *Experientia, 33,* 745–755.

Masur, J., De Souza, M. L. O., & Zwicker, A. P. (1986). The excitatory effect of ethanol: Absence in rats, no tolerance and increased sensitivity in mice. *Pharmacology, Biochemistry, and Behavior, 24,* 1225–1228.

Mattila, M. J., Nuotto, E., & Seppala, T. (1981). Naloxone is not an effective antagonist of ethanol. *Lancet, April,* 775–776.

Mayer, R. F., & Khurana, R. K. (1982). Periperal and autonomic nervous system. In E. M. Patterson & E. Kaufman (Eds.), *Encyclopedic handbook of alcoholism* (pp. 194–203). New York: Gardner Press.

McBride, W. J., Murphy, J. M., Lumeng, L., & Li, T. K. (1989). Serotonin and ethanol preference. In M. Galanter (Ed.), *Recent developments in alcoholism* (Vol. 7, pp. 187–209). New York: Plenum Press.

McCrady, B. S., & Smith, D. E. (1986). Implications of cognitive impairment for the treatment of alcoholism. *Alcoholism: Clinical and Experimental Research, 10*, 145–149.

McCown, T. J., Frye, G. D., & Breese, G. R. (1986). Evidence for site specific ethanol actions in the CNS. *Alcohol and Drug Research, 6*, 423–429.

McEvoy, J. P. (1982). The chronic neuropsychiatric disorders associated with alcoholism. In E. M. Pattison & E. Kaufman (Eds.), *Encyclopedic handbook of alcoholism* (pp. 167–179). New York: Gardner Press.

McGiven, R. F., Roselli, C. E., & Handa, R. J. (1988). Perinatal aromatase activity in male and female rats: Effect of prenatal alcohol exposure. *Alcoholism: Clinical and Experimental Research, 12*, 769–772.

McIntyre, N. (1984). The effects of alcohol on water, electrolytes, and minerals. In S. B. Rosalki (Ed.), *Clinical biochemistry of alcoholism* (pp. 117–134). Edinburgh: Churchill Livingstone.

McNamee, H. R., Mello, N. K., & Mendelson, J. H. (1968). Experimental analysis of drinking patterns of alcoholics: Concurrent psychiatric observations. *American Journal of Psychiatry, 124*, 1063–1069.

Mefford, I. N., Lister, R. G., Ota, M., & Linnoila, M. (1990). Antagonoism of ethanol intoxication in rats by inhibitors of phenylethanolamine N-methyltransferase. *Alcoholism: Clinical and Experimental Research, 14*, 53–57.

Melchoir, C. L. (1982). TIQs block the development of environment dependent tolerance to ethanol. In F. Bloom, J. Barchas, M. Sandler, & E. Usdin (Eds.), *Beta-carbolines and tetrahydroisoqinolines* (pp. 377–385). New York: Alan R. Liss.

Melchoir, C. L., & Tabakoff, B. (1984). A conditioning model of alcohol tolerance. In M. Galanter (Ed.) *Recent developments in alcoholism* (pp. 5–16, Vol. 4). New York: Plenum Press.

Mello, N. K., Mendelson, J. H., King, N. W., Bree, M. P., Skupny, A., & Ellingboe, J. (1988). Alcohol self-administration by female macaque monkeys: A model for study of alcohol dependence, hyperprolactinemia, and amenorrhea. *Journal of Studies on Alcohol, 49*, 551–560.

Mendelson, J. H., & Mello, N. K. (1979). Biologic concomitants of alcoholism. *New England Journal of Medicine, 301*, 912–921.

Merry, J., Reynolds, C. M., Bailey, J., & Coppen, A. (1976). Prophylactic treatment of alcoholism by lithium carbonate. *Lancet, 2*, 481–482.

Mezey, E. (1982). Effects of alcohol on the gastrointestinal tract. In E. M. Pattison & E. Kaufman (Eds.), *Encyclopedic handbook of alcoholism* (pp. 245–254). New York: Gardner Press.

Miglioli, M., Buchtel, H. A., Campanini, T., & De Riso, C. (1979). Cerebral hemispheric lateralization of cognitive deficits due to alcoholism. *Journal of Nervous and Mental Disease, 167*, 212–217.

Miller, W. R., & Hester, R. K. (1980). Treating the problem drinker: Modern approaches. In W. R. Miller (Ed.), *The addictive behaviors: Treatment of alcoholism, drug abuse, smoking, and obesity* (pp. 11–142). Oxford: Pergamon Press.

Miller, W. R., & Orr, J. (1980). Nature and sequence of neuropsychological deficits in alcoholics. *Journal of Studies on Alcohol, 41*. 325–337.

Modell, J. G., Mountz, J. M., & Beresford, T. P. (1990). Basal ganglia/limbic striatal and thalamocortical involvement in craving and loss of control in alcoholism. *Journal of Neuropsychiatry and Clinical Neurosciences, 2*, 123–144.

Monte, W. (1984). Methanol and the public health. *Journal of Applied Nutrition, 36,* 1, 42–54.

Murcherjee, A. B., & Hodgen, G. D. (1982). Maternal ethanol exposure induces transient impairment of umbilical circulation and fetal hypoxia in monkeys. *Science, 218,* 700–702.

Myers, R. D. (1985). Multiple metabolites theory, alcohol drinking and the alcogene. In M. A. Collins (Ed.), *Aldehyde adducts in alcoholism* (pp. 201–220). New York: Alan R. Liss.

Myers, R. D., & Critcher, E. C. (1982). Naloxone alters alcohol drinking induced in the rat by tetrahydropapaveroline (THP) inflused ICV. *Pharmacology, Biochemistry, & Behavior, 16,* 827–836.

Myers, R. D., McCaleb, M. L., & Ruwe, W. D. (1982). Alcohol drinking induced in the monkey by tetrahydropapaveroline (THP) infused into the cerebral ventricle. *Pharmacology, Biochemistry, & Behavior, 16,* 995–1000.

Myers, R. D., & Melchoir, C. L. (1977). Alcohol drinking: Abnormal intake caused by tetrahydropapaveroline in the brain. *Science, 196,* 554–556.

Myers, R. D., & Oblinger, M. M. (1977). Alcohol drinking in the rat induced by acute intracerebral infusion of two tetrahydroisoquinolines and a b-carboline. *Drug and Alcohol Dependence, 2,* 469–483.

Narajo, C. A., Sellers, E. M., & Lawrin, M. O. (1986). Modulation of ethanol intake by serotonin uptake inhibitors. *Journal of Clinical Psychology, 47,* Supplement 4, 16–22.

Naranjo, C. A., Sellers, E. M., Roach, C. A., Woodley, D. V., Sanchez-Craig, M. & Sykora, K. (1984). Zimeldine-induced variations in alcohol intake by nondepressed heavy drinkers. *Clinical Pharmacological Therapy, 35,*374–381.

Nathan, P. E., Titler, N. A., Lowenstein, L. M., Solomon, P., & Rossi, A. M. (1970). Behavioral analysis of chronic alcoholism. *Archives of General Psychiatry, 22,* 419–430.

Neg, S. K. C., Hauser, W. A., Brust, J. C. M., & Susser, M. (1988). Alcohol consumption and withdrawal in new-onset seizures.*New England Journal of Medicine, 319,* 666–673.

Newlin, D. B. (1984). The conditioned compensatory response to alcohol placebo in humans. *Psychophysiology, 21,* 590.

Newlin, D. B. (1985). The antagonistic placebo response to alcohol cues. *Alcoholism: Clinical and Experimental Research, 9,* 411–416.

Nimit, Y., Schulze, I., Cashaw, J. L., Ruchirawat, S., & Davis, V. E. (1982). In F. Bloom, J. Barchas, M. Sandler, & E. Usdin (Eds.), *Beta-carbolines and tetrahydroisoqinolines* (pp. 311–320). New York: Alan R. Liss.

Nirenberg, T. D., Sobell, L. C., Ersner-Hershfield, S., & Cellucci, A. J. (1983). Can disurlfiram use precipitate urges to drink alcohol? *Addictive Behaviors, 8,* 311–313.

Noonberg, A., Goldstein, G., & Page, H. A. (1985). Premature aging in male alcoholics: "Accelerated aging" or "increased vulnerability"? *Alcoholism: Clinical and Experimental Research, 9,* 334–338.

Nora, A. H., Nora, J. J., & Blu, J. (1977). Limb-reduction anomalies in infants born to disulfiram-treated alcoholic mothers. *Lancet,* Sept. 24, 664.

Nordmann, R. (1987). Oxidative stress from alcohol in the brain. *Alcohol and Alcoholism,* Supplement 1, 75–82.

Nuutinen, H., Lindros, K. O., & Salaspuro, M. (1983). Determinants of blood acetaldehyde levels during ethanol oxidation in chronic alcoholics. *Alcoholism: Clinical and Experimental Research, 7,* 163–168.

O'Neil, P. M., Roitzsch, J. C., Giacinto, J. P., & Miller, W. C. (1982). Disulfiram acceptors and refusers: Do they differ? *Addictive Behaviors, 7,* 207–209.

Oakley, N., & Jones, B. (1980). The proconvulsant and diazepam reversing effect of ethyl-B-carboline-3-carboxylate. *European Journal of Pharmacology, 68,* 381–382.

Obitz, F. W. (1978). Control orientation and disulfiram. *Journal of Studies on Alcohol, 39,* 1297–1298.

Oscar-Berman, M. (1987). Neuropsychological consequences of alcohol abuse: Questions, hypotheses, and models. In O. A. Parsons, N. Butters, & P. E. Nathan (Eds.), *Neuropsychology of alcoholism: Implications for diagnosis and treatment* (pp. 256–272). New York: Guilford Press.

Overall, J. E., Reilly, E. L., Kelley, J. T., & Hollister, L. E. (1985). Persistence of depression in detoxified alcoholics. *Alcoholism: Clinical and Experimental Research, 9,* 331–333.

Parson, O. A. (1986). Cognitive functioning in sober social drinkers: A review and critique. *Journal of Studies on Alcohol, 47,* 101–114.

Parsons, O. A. (1987). Neuropsychological consequences of alcohol abuse: Many questions-Some answers. In O. A. Parsons, N. Butters, & P. E. Nathan (Eds.), *Neuropsychology of alcoholism: Implications for diagnosis and treatment* (pp. 153–175). New York: Guilford Press.

Peng, T. C., Kusy, R. P., Hirsch, P. F., & Hagaman, J. R. (1988). Ethanol-induced changes in morpohology and strength of femurs of rats. *Alcoholism: Clinical and Experimental Research, 12,* 655–659.

Phillips, S. C., & Cragg, B. G. (1984). Alcohol withdrawal causes a loss of cerebellar Purkinje cells in mice. *Journal of Studies on Alcohol, 45,* 475–480.

Pieper, W. A., & Skeen, M. J. (1973). Changes in blood methanol concentrations in chimpanzees during periods of chronic ethanol ingestion. *Biochemical Pharmacology, 22,* 163–173.

Pinel, J. P. J., Colborne, B., Sigalet, J. P., & Renfrey, G. (1983). Learned tolerance to the anticonvulsant effects of alcohol in rats. *Pharmacology, Biochemistry, and Behavior, 18,* 507–510.

Pishkin, V., Lovallo, W. R., & Bourne, L. E. (1985). Chronic alcoholism in males: Cognitive deficits as a function of age of onset, age, and duration. *Alcoholism: Clinical and Experimental Research, 9,* 400–406.

Pitts, T. O., & Van Thiel, D. H. (1986a). Disorders in the serum electrolytes, acid-base balance, and renal function in alcoholism. In M. Galanter (Ed.), *Recent developments in alcoholism* (pp. 311–340, Vol. 4). New York: Plenum Press.

Pitts, T. O., & Van Thiel, D. H. (1986b). Urinary tract infections and renal papillary necrosis in alcoholism. In M. Galanter (Ed.), *Recent developments in alcoholism* (pp. 341–377, Vol. 4). New York: Plenum Press.

Pitts, T. O., & Van Thiel, D. H. (1986c). The pathogenesis of renal sodium retention and ascites formation in Laennec's cirrhosis. In M. Galanter (Ed.), *Recent Developments in Alcoholism* (pp. 379–440, Vol. 4). New York: Plenum Press.

Polich, J., & Bloom, F. E. (1988). Event-related brain potentials in individuals at high and low risk for developing alcoholism: Failure to replicate. *Alcoholism: Clinical and Experimental Research, 12,* 368–373.

Pond, S. M., Becker, C. E., Vandervoort, R., Phillips, M., Bowler, R. M., & Peck, C. C. (1981). An evaluation of the effects of lithium in the treatment of chronic alcoholism. I. Clinical results. *Alcoholism: Clinical and Experimental Research, 5,* 247–255.

Porjesz, B., & Begleiter, H. (1981). Human evoked brain potentials and alcohol. *Alcoholism: Clinical and Experimental Research, 5,* 304–317.

Powell, B. J., Penick, E. C., Liskow, B. I., Rice, A. S., & McKnelly, W. (1986). Lithium compliance in alcoholic males: A six month followup study. *Addictive Behaviors, 11,* 135–140.

Powell, B. J., & Viamontes, J. (1974). Factors affecting attendance at an alcoholic day hospital. *British Journal of Addiction, 69,* 339–342.

Raloff, J. (1986). Diet, metals, and hidden heart disease, *Science News,* Sept. 27, 201.

Reed, R., Grant, I., & Adams, K. M. (1987). Family history of alcoholism does not predict neuropsychological performance in alcoholics. *Alcoholism: Clinical and Experimental Research, 11,* 340–344.

Rhodes, L. E., Obitz, F. W., & Creel, D. (1975). Effect of alcohol and task on hemispheric asymmetry of visually evoked potentials in man. *Electroencephalography and Clinical Neurophysiology, 38,* 561–568.

Risberg, J., & Berglund, M. (1987). Cerebral blood flow and metabolism in alcoholics. In O. A.

Parsons, N. Butters, & P. E. Nathan (Eds.), *Neuropsychology of alcoholism: Implications for diagnosis and treatment* (pp. 64–75). New York: Guilford Press.

Ritchie, J. M. (1980.) The alphatic alcohols. A. G. Goodman, L. S. Goodman, & A. Gilmam. (Eds.), *The pharmacological basis of therapeutics* (pp. 376–390). New York: Macmillan.

Robinson, B. J., Robinson, G. M., Maling, T. J. B., & Johnson, R. H. (1989). Is clonidine useful in the treatment of alcohol withdrawal. *Alcoholism: Clinical and Experimental Research, 13,* 95–98.

Roine, R. P., Eriksson, J. P., Ylikahri, R., Penttila, A., & Salaspuro, M. (1989). Methanol as a marker of alcohol abuse. *Alcoholism: Clinical and Experimental Research, 13,* 172–175.

Rommelspacher, H., Damm, H., Schmidt, L., & Schmidt, G. (1985). Increased excretion of harman by alcoholics depends on events of their life history and the state of the liver. *Psychopharmacology, 87,* 64–68.

Ron, M. A. (1987). The brain of alcoholics: An overview. In O. A. Parsons, N. Butters, & P. E. Nathan (Eds.), *Neuropsychology of alcoholism: Implications for diagnosis and treatment* (pp. 1–20). New York: Guildford Press.

Rosalki, S. B. (1984). Alcoholism—an overview. In S. B. Rosalki (Ed.), *Clinical biochemistry of alcoholism* (pp. 3–19). Edinburgh: Churchill Livingstone.

Rosenberg, C. M. (1974). Drug maintenance in the outpatient treatment of chronic alcoholism. *Archives of General Psychiatry, 30,* 373–377.

Rosett, H. L., & Weiner, L. (1982). Effects of alcohol on the fetus. In E. M. Pattison & E. Kaufman (Eds.), *Encyclopedic handbook of alcoholism* (pp. 301–310). New York: Gardner Press.

Ross, D. H., Medina, M. A., & Cardenas, H. L. (1974). Morphine and ethanol: Selective depletion of regional brain calcium. *Science, 186,* 63–65.

Rosset, M., & Oki, G. (1971). Skin diseases in alcoholism. *Quarterly Journal of Studies on Alcohol, 32,* 1017–1024.

Rotrosen, J. (1987). Symposium: Interaction between alcohol and prostaglandins, essential fatty acids, and nonsteroidal antiinflammatory drugs. *Alcoholism: Clinical and Experimental Research, 11,* 1.

Rotrosen, J., Mandio, D., & Segarnick, D. (1980). Ethanol and prostaglandin E 1: Biochemical and behavioral interactions. *Life Sciences, 26,* 1867–1876.

Russell, M., & Skinner, J. B. (1988). Early measures of maternal alcohol misuse as predictors of adverse pregnancy outcomes. *Alcoholism: Clinical and Experimental Research, 12,* 824–830.

Ryan, C. (1982). Alcoholism and premature aging: A neuropsychological perspective. *Alcoholism: Clinical and Experimental Research, 6,* 22–30.

Ryan, K. (1983/84). Alcohol and blood sugar disorders: An overview. *Alcohol Health and Research World, 8,* 3–7.

Ryback, R. S. (1971). The continuum and specificity of the effects of alcohol on memory. *Quarterly Journal of Studies on Alcohol, 32,* 995–1016.

Rydberg, U. (1977). Experimentally induced alcoholic hangover. In C. M. Idestrom (Ed.), *Recent advances in the study of alcoholism: Proceedings of the first international Magnus Hull Symposium* (pp. 32–40). New York: Elsevier-Holland.

Sanchez-Craig, M. (1980). Drinking pattern as a determinant of alcoholics' performance on the Trail Making Test. *Journal of Studies on Alcohol, 41,* 1082–1090.

Sandler, M., Glover, V., Armando, I., & Clow, A. (1982). Pictet-Spengler condensation products, stress, and alcoholism: Some clinical overtones. In F. Bloom, J. Barchas, M. Sandler, & E. Usdin (Eds.), *Beta-carbolines and tetrahydroisoqinolines* (pp. 215–226). New York: Alan R. Liss.

Schaeffer, K. W., Parsons, O. A., & Yohman, J. R. (1984). Neuropsychological differences between male familial and nonfamilial alcoholics and non-alcoholics. *Alcoholism: Clinical and Experimental Research, 8* 347–351.

Schatzkin, A., Jones, D. Y., Hoover, R. N., Taylor, P. R., Brinton, L. A., Ziegler, R. G., Harvey,

E. B., Carter, C. L., Licitra, L. M., Dufour, M. C., & Larson, D. B. (1987). Alcohol consumption and breast cancer in the epidemiologic follow-up study of the first national health and nutrition survey. *New England Journal of Medicine, 316*, 1169–1173.

Schuckit, M. A. (1984). Biochemical markers of predisposition to alcoholism. In S. B. Roasalki (Ed.), *Clinical biochemistry of alcoholism* (pp. 20–47). Edinburgh: Churchill Livingstone.

Schuckit, M. A., Li, T. K., Cloninger, C. R., & Deitrich, R. A. (1985). University of California, Davis—Conference: Genetics of alcoholism. *Alcoholism: Clinical and Experimental Research, 9*, 475–492.

Schuckit, M., & Rayses, V. (1979). Ethanol ingestion: Differences in blood acetaldehyde concentrations in relatives of alcoholics and controls. *Science, 203*, 54–57.

Schuckit, M. A., Zisook, S., & Mortola, J. (1985). Clinical implications of DSM-III diagnoses of alcohol abuse and alcohol dependence. *American Journal of Psychiatry, 142*, 1403–1408.

Segarnick, D., & Rotrosen, J. (1987). Essential fatty acids, prostaglandins, and nonsteroidal antiinflammatory agents: Physiological and behavioral interactions. *Alcoholism: Clinical and Experimental Research, 11*, 19–24.

Segel, L. (1988). Tolerance to ethanol and cross-tolerance to pentobarbital by isolated hearts from chronic alcoholic rats. *Alcoholism: Clinical and Experimental Research, 12*, 523–530.

Sellers, E. M., & Kalant, H. (1976). Drug therapy: Alcohol intoxication and withdrawal. *New England Journal of Medicine, 294*, 757–762.

Sellers, E. M., & Kalant, H. (1982). Alcohol withdrawal and tremens. In E. M. Pattison & E. Kaufman (Eds.), *Encyclopedic handbook of alcoholism* (pp. 147–166). New York: Gardner Press.

Sellers, E. M., Narajano, C. J., Peachy, J. E. (1981). Drugs to decrease alcohol consumption. *New England Journal of Medicine, 305*, 1255–1262.

Sereny, G., & Endrenyl, L. (1978). Mechanism and significance of carbohydrate intolerance in chronic alcoholism. *Metabolism, 27*, 1041–1046.

Shaw, T. G. (1987). Alcohol and brain function: An appraisal of cerebral blood flow data. In O. A. Parsons, N. Butters, & P. E. Nathan (Eds.), *Neuropsychology of alcoholism: Implications for diagnosis and treatment* (pp. 129–149). New York: Guilford Press.

Siggins, G. R., Berger, T., French, E. D., Shier, T., & Bloom, F. E. (1982). Ethanol, salsolinol, and tetrahydropapaveroline after the discharge of neurons in several brain regions: comparison to opiod effects. In F. Bloom, J. Barchas, M. Sandler, & E. Usdin (Eds.), *Beta-carbolines and tetrahydroisoqinolines* (pp. 275–288). New York: Alan R. Liss.

Sinclair, J. D. (1987). The feasibility of effective psychopharmacological treatments for alcoholism. *British Journal of Addiction, 82*, 1213–1223.

Singh, S. P., Kumar, Y., Snyder, A. K., Ellyin, F. E., & Gilden, J. L. (1988). Effect of alcohol on glucose tolerance in normal and noninsulin-dependent diabetic subjects. *Alcoholism: Clinical and Experimental Research, 12*, 727–730.

Sjoquist, B., Eriksson, A., & Winbald, B. (1982a). Salsolinol and catecholamines in human brain and their relation to alcoholism. In F. Bloom, J. Barchas, M. Sandler, & E. Usdin (Eds.), *Beta-carbolines and tetrahydroisoqinolines* (pp. 57–67). New York: Alan R. Liss.

Sjoquist, B., Eriksson, A., & Winblad, B. (1982b). Brain salsolinol levels in alcoholism. *Lancet*, March, 675–676.

Skinner, H. A., Holt, S., Schuller, R., Roy, J., & Israel, Y. (1984). Identification of alcohol abuse using laboratory tests and a history of trauma. *Annals of Internal Medicine, 101*, 847–851.

Skog, O. J. (1984). The risk function for liver cirrhosis from lifetime alcohol consumption. *Journal of Studies on Alcohol, 45*. 199–208.

Skolnick, P., Williams, E. F., Cook, J. M., Cain, M., Rice, K. C., Mendelson, W. B., Crawley, J. N., & Paul, S. M. (1982). B-carbonlines and benzodiazepine receptors: Structure-activity relationships and pharmacologic activity. In F. Bloom, J. Barchas, M. Sandler, & E. Usdin (Eds.), *Beta-carbolines and tetrahydroisoqinolines* (pp. 233–252). New York: Alan R. Liss.

Smith, C. M. (1981). Pathophysiology of alcohol withdrawal syndrome. *Medical Hypothesis, 7,* 231–249.

Stampfer, M. J., Colditz, G. A., Willett, W. C., Speizer, F. E., & Hennekens, C. H. (1988). A prospective study of moderate alcohol consumption and the risk of coronary disease and stroke in women. *New England Journal of Medicine, 319,* 267–273.

Stokes, P. E. (1982). Endocrine disturbances associated with alcohol and alcoholism. In E. M. Pattison & E. Kaufman (Eds.), *Encyclopedic handbook of alcoholism,* (pp. 311–324). New York: Gardner Press.

Streissguth, A. P., Barr, H. M., Sampson, P. D., Darby, B. L., & Martin, D. C. (1989). IQ at age 4 in relation to maternal alcohol use and smoking during pregnancy. *Developmental Psychology, 25,* 3–11.

Stringer, A. Y., & Goldman, M. S. (1988). Experience-dependent recovery of block design performance in male alcoholics: Strategy training versus unstructured practice. *Journal of Studies on Alcohol, 49,* 406–411.

Suzdak, P. D., Glowa, J. R., Crawley, J. N., Schwartz, R. D., Skolnick, P., & Paul, S. M. (1986). A selective imidazobenodiazepine antagonist of ethanol in the rat. *Science, 234,* 1243–1247.

Tabakoff, B., & Hoffman, P. L. (1977). Ethanol tolerance and dependence. In H. W. Goedde & D. P. Aggarwal (Eds.), *Genetics and Alcoholism* (pp. 253–269). New York: Alan R. Liss.

Tabakoff, B., & Kilanmaa, K. (1982). Does tolerance develop to the activating, as well as the depressant effects of ethanol? *Pharmacology, Biochemistry, & Behavior, 17,* 1073–1076.

Tabakoff, B., & Rothstein, J. D. (1983). Biology of tolerance and dependence. In B. Tabakoff, P. B. Sutker, & C. L. Randall (Eds.), *Medical and social aspects of alcohol abuse* (pp. 187–222). New York: Plenum Press.

Tamerin, J. S., Mendelson, J. H. (1969). The psychodynamics of chronic inebriation: Observations of alcoholics during the process of drinking in an experimental group setting. *American Journal of Psychiatry, 125,* 886–899.

Tarbox, A. R., Connors, G. J. & McLaughlin, E. J. (1986). Effects of drinking pattern on neuropsychological performance among alcohol misusers. *Journal of Studies on Alcohol, 47,* 176–179.

Tarter, R. E., & Edwards K. L. (1986). Multifactorial etiology of neuropsychological impairment in alcoholics. *Alcoholism: Clinical and Experimental Research, 10,* 128–135.

Taylor, J. R., & Combs-Orme, T. (1985). Alcohol and stroke in young adults. *American Journal of Psychiatry, 142,* 116–118.

Tewari, S., & Carson, V. G. (1982). Biochemistry of alcohol and alcohol metabolism. In E. M. Pattison & E. Kaufman (Eds.), *Encyclopedic handbook of alcoholism* (pp. 83–104). New York: Gardner Press.

Traynor, A. E., Schlapfer, W. T., & Barondes, S. J. (1980). Stimulation is necessary for the development of tolerance to a neuronal effect of ethanol. *Journal of Neurobiology, 11,* 633–637.

Turnquist, K., Frances, R., Rosenfeld, W., & Mobarak, A. (1983). Pemoline in attention deficit disorder and alcoholism: A case study. *American Journal of Psychiatry, 140,* 622–624.

Urbano-Marquez, A., Estruch, R., Navarro-Lopez, F., Grau, J. M., Mont, L., & Rubin, E. (1989). The effects of alcoholism on skeletal and cardiac muscle. *New England Journal of Medicine, 320,* 409–415.

Vaillant, G. E. (1983). *The natural history of alcoholism: Causes, patterns, and paths to recovery.* Cambridge, MA: Harvard University Press.

Van Thiel, D. H. (1983). Effects of ethanol upon organ systems other than the central nervous system. In B. Tabakoff, P. B., Sutker, & C. L., Randall (Eds.), *Medical and social aspects of alcohol abuse* (pp. 79–132). New York: Plenum Press.

Van Thiel, D. H., & Gavaler, J. S. (1985). Myocardial effects of alcohol abuse: Clinical and physiologic consequences. In M. Galanter, (Ed.), *Recent developments in alcoholism* (pp. 181–187, Vol. 3). New York: Plenum Press.

Van Thiel, D. H., & Gavaler, J. S. (1988). Ethanol metabolism and hepatotoxicity: Does sex make a difference. In M. Galanter (Ed.), *Recent developments in alcoholism* (pp. 291–307, Vol. 6). New York: Plenum Press.

Van Thiel, D. H., Tarter, R. E., Rosenblum, E., & Gavaler, J. S. (1989). Ethanol, its metabolism and gonadal effects: Does sex make a difference? In E. Gordis, B. Tabakoff, & M. Linnoila (Eds.), *Alcohol research from bench to bedside* (pp. 131–169). New York: Haworth.

Viamontes, J. A. (1972). Review of drug effectiveness in the treatment of alcoholism. *American Journal of Psychiatry, 128,* 1570–1571.

Vitiello, M. V., Prinz, P. N., Personius, J. P., Vitalinao, P. P., Nuccio, M. A., & Koerker, R. (1990). Relationship of alcohol abuse history to nighttime hypoxemia in abstaining chronic alcoholic men. *Journal of Studies on Alcohol, 51,* 29–33.

Wainwright, P., Ward, G. R., & Molnar, J. D. (1985). Gaba-linolenic acids fails to prevent the effects of prenatal ethanol exposure on brain and behavioral development in B6D2F2 mice. *Alcoholism: Clinical and Experimental Research, 9,* 377–383.

Walton, J. N. (1977). *Brains diseases of the nervous system.* Oxford: Oxford University Press.

Wartenberg, A. A., Nirenberg, T. D., Liepman, M. R., Silvia, L. Y., Begin, A. M., & Monti, P. M. (1990). Detoxification of alcoholics: Improving care by symptom-triggered sedation. *Alcoholism: Clinical and Experimental Research, 14,* 71–75.

Watson, R. R., Mohs, M. E., Eskelson, C., Sampliner, R. E., & Hartmann, B. (1986). Identification of alcohol abuse and alcoholism with biological parameters. *Alcoholism: Clinical and Experimental Research, 10,* 364–385.

Webb, M., & Unwin, A. (1988). The outcome of outpatient withdrawal from alcohol. *British Journal of Addiction, 83,* 924–934.

Weingartner, H., Buchsbaum, M. S., & Linnoila, M. (1983). Zimeldine effects on memory impairments produced by ethanol. *Life Sciences, 33,* 2159–2163.

Wenger, J. R., Tiffany, T. M., Bombardier, C., Nicholls, K., & Woods, S. C. (1981). Ethanol tolerance in the rat is learned. *Science, 213,* 575–577.

Westrick, E. R., Shapiro, A. P., Nathan, P. E., & Brick, J. (1988). Dietary tryptoppan reverses alcohol-induced impairment of facial recognition but not verbal recall. *Alcoholism: Clinical and Experimental Research, 12,* 531–533.

Whitfield, C. L. (1982). Skin diseases associated with alcoholism. In E. M. Pattison & E. Kaufman (Eds.), *Encyclopedic handbook of alcoholism* (pp. 275–280). New York: Gardner Press.

Whitfield, C. L., Thompson, G., Lamb, A., Spencer, V., Pfeifer, M., & Browning-Ferrando, M. (1978). Detoxification of 1,024 alcoholic patients without psychoactive drugs. *Journal of the American Medical Association, 239,* 1409–1410.

Wickramasinghe, S. N., Clague, J. R., Barrison, I. G., Walker, J. G., Barden, G., & Aardner, B. (1989). Differences in the nature and kinetics of the ethanol-related circulating cytotoxic proteins in normal subjects and patients with alcohol-induced cirrhosis. *Alcoholism: Clinical and Experimental Research, 13,* 723–729.

Winter, P. M., & Miller, J. N. (1985). Anethesiology. *Scientific American,* April, 124–131.

Wise, R. A., & Bozarth, M. A. (1987). A psychomotor stimulant theory of addiction. *Psychological Review, 94,* 469–492.

Woeber, K. (1975). The skin in diagnosis of alcoholism. *Annals of the New York Academy of Sciences, 252,* 292–295.

Wood, D. R., Reimherr, F. W., Wender, P. H., & Johnson, G. E. (1976). Diagnosis and treatment of minimal brain dysfunction in adults: A preliminary report. *Archives of General Psychiatry, 33,* 1453–1460.

Wood, D., Wender, P. H., & Reimherr, F. W. (1983). The prevalence of attention deficit disorder, residual type, or minimal brain dysfunction, in a population of male alcoholic patients. *American Journal of Psychiatry, 140,* 95–98.

Wurtman, R. J. (1983). Nutrition: The changing scene. Behavioral effects of nutrients. *Lancet*, May 21, 1145–1147.

Yesavage, J. A., & Leirer, V. O. (1986). Hangover effects on aircraft pilots 14 hours after alcohol ingestion: A preliminary report. *American Journal of Psychiatry, 143*, 1546–1550.

Yung, L., Gordis, E., & Holt, J. (1983). Dietary choices and likelihood of abstinence among alcoholic patients in an outpatient clinic. *Drug and Alcohol Dependence, 12*, 355–362.

III

COGNITIVE AND ATTITUDINAL FACTORS IN DRINKING AND ALCOHOLOISM

Introduction

The section on cognitive and attitudinal factors in drinking is divided into 3 chapters. Whereas most of this book considers research on alcoholic individuals, much of the material in this section concerns cognitive and attitudinal factors in drinking among normal drinkers in addition to factors among alcoholics. The first chapter focuses on research findings from normal, nonproblem drinkers. Some statistics are presented on normative patterns of drinking in the general population. The influence of demographics on drinking patterns are discussed. The literature on how the attitudes of heavy drinkers differ from light drinkers is reviewed. The bottomlines on how expectancies regarding the effect of alcohol on mood and behavior differ between heavy and light drinkers are presented. There have been several studies in which persons have kept diaries, and analyses have been conducted to determine whether normal individuals increase drinking under stress. These studies are discussed. Then, studies are reviewed in which normal individuals have been brought into the laboratory, manipulated in various ways, and finally observed as they are allowed to drink. This literature has attempted to address basic questions such as will normal people drink more when they are angry? When they are scared? Will they drink more when they are happy? Will they drink more in the presence of heavy drinkers?

Chapter 13 examines cognitive and attitudinal factors in the development of alcoholism. Theories regarding why particular cultures and occupations seem to generate higher rates of alcoholism than others are presented. Sociologist's hypotheses regarding the relationship between the price of alcohol and the incidence of alcoholism are examined. Empirical findings on whether stress can produce alcoholism are summarized. Two variants of the hypothesis that stress causes alcoholism are discussed: Hull's hypothesis regarding self-consciousness and Jones' and Berglas' self-handicapping hypothesis. These theories along with pertinent empirical findings are reviewed. Finally, findings regarding expectations that alcoholics and their children hold for how alcohol will effect them are discussed; that is, what are their beliefs about how alcohol affects their mood and behavior?

The third chapter in this section considers the empirical literature on how alcohol actually affects mood and behavior. There is now a wealth of information pertinent to this questions. Most of this research was conducted on normal drinkers, although there are a few findings that are specific to the impact on consanguine family members of alcoholics. Answers to the question of whether alcohol is a good stress reducer, whether alcohol is a stimulant or depressant, and whether alcohol makes people happy have emerged. The literature on the specific ways in which alcohol increases aggression is reviewed. The literatures on the effects of alcohol on sex, altruism, yielding to influence, risk taking, self-consciousness, pain perception, smoking, self-evaluation, and self-disclosure are also reviewed. Chapter 14 ends with a discussion of two meta analyses on the effects of alcohol and why the authors of these two publications reached different conclusions. Finally, there is a discussion of Wise and Bozarth's hypothesis that people drink because alcohol stimulates the same area in the brain that is stimulated by other drugs of abuse.

12 Social and Cognitive Factors in the Drinking of the General Population

Population surveys have provided information on drinking patterns in this country. Sixty-eight percent of Americans drink at least once per year (Cahalan & Cisen, 1968). Rather than being normally distributed, drinking patterns fall into a trimodal distribution. A third of the adult population drinks minimally or abstains. A second third consumes less than 2 drinks per week. The final third is comprised of moderate drinkers (3–7 drinks per week) and heavy drinkers (2 drinks or more per day) (National Institute on Alcohol Abuse and Alcoholism, 1984). About 9% of the population consumes at least 2 drinks per day (Moskowitz, 1989). Broken down differently, 12% drink daily to weekly, 5 or more drinks per day (Cahalan & Cisen, 1968). A small segment of the population consumes much of the liquor that is produced. Fifty percent of the alcohol produced in this country is consumed by the 10% of the population whose intake is at the highest level of consumption (National Institute on Alcohol Abuse and Alcoholism, 1984).

A host of variables influence consumption level. Drinking patterns (frequency and location) and consumption levels vary as a function of age, socioeconomic status, sex, and ethnic identification. Persons under 25 drink the most per occasion but drink less frequently than older adults. Young males manifest the highest rate of drinking related antisocial behavior (barroom fights and public disturbances), drinking to get high, and frequent intoxications (Cutter & O'Farrell, 1984; Glynn, Lo Castro, Hermos, & Bosse, 1983; Mulford & Miller, 1960a; Vogel-Sprott & Barrett, 1984). Young males evidence the heaviest percentage of escape drinking, especially within lower SES levels (Cahalan & Cisen, 1968).

197

Older adults drink more frequently but drink less per occasion (Vogel-Sprott & Barrett, 1984). Blue collar persons drink less frequently but are more often intoxicated than white collar persons (Coleman & Strauss, 1983). Women of all ages drink less than men (Cahalan, Cisen, & Crossley, 1969); although in college populations trait masculinity is a better predictor of drinking than is sex (Chamok & Collins, 1987). Working class persons have the highest percentages of both abstainers and heavy drinkers; whereas among the middle class drinking habits tend to be homogeneous, most people exhibiting moderate drinking (Cahalan & Cisen, 1968). Professionals produce the highest percentages of persons who drink (82% vs. 53% among those with no high school). Professionals also have below average proportions of escape drinkers (Cahalan & Cisen, 1968). Persons from urban environments are more likely to be drinkers than persons from rural environments (Mulford, 1964; Mulford & Miller, 1960). Eighty-three percent of Catholic males drink and one-third of these are heavy drinkers. Ninety-two percent of Jews drink, but only 11% are heavy drinkers (Cahalan & Cisen, 1968). Single persons are more often drinkers or heavy drinkers than are married persons (Mulford, 1964).

Demographics do influence the conditions under which people drink as well as amount consumed. Women and older persons more often drink at home with relatives. Younger men tend to drink in public places with same sex peers (Martin & Casswell, 1987).

Characteristics of Persons at Various Levels of Consumption

There have been a number of investigations as to the prototypic individual at each of the levels of consumption. Several investigations have found that abstinent individuals are less psychologically well adjusted than those who drink in moderation (Jones, 1968, 1971; Vaillant, 1983). In a sample of lower class individuals, Vaillant (1983, pp. 114–116) found that abstinent males were less well adjusted as children, were less well adjusted as adults, and used prescription drugs more than moderate drinkers. In a sample of middle class females, female abstainers were found to have been more moody, anxious, and irritable as children than were female moderate and light drinkers. Goodwin, Johnson, Maher, Rappaport, and Guze (1960) found that abstinent males were more often single, had lower incomes, and were more often treated for psychiatric problems. The abstinent also have lower longevity than moderate drinkers (Vaillant, 1983, p. 118). In young samples, abstention is related to IQ. Among young people, on average, abstainers are lower in verbal IQ. However, within the drinking group a different picture of the relationship between IQ and drinking pattern emerges. Among young drinkers at all levels of socioeconomic status, low verbal IQ predicts dependency problems and alcohol related aggression, although it is not related to quantity and frequency of consumption (Windle & Blane, 1989).

The statistics suggesting better mental health among the moderate consumers as opposed to the abstainers are supported by additional findings. Among heavy drinkers and abstainers, stressful events are associated with increased symptomotology. That is, there is a positive association between noncatastrophic stressful life events and symptoms (mood and somatic complaints). The correlation suggesting that stressful occurrences will result in poor functioning is not found in moderate consumers. Apparently, moderate alcohol intake either buffers the impact of stress or moderate drinkers are just able to absorb stress due to some constitutional factor (Neff, 1985; Neff & Husaini, 1982.)

The finding of good mental health in heavy drinking but not problem drinking individuals has also been found in a female, middle class sample (Jones, 1971). (Heavy drinking was defined as daily drinking with occasional 5 to 6 drinks per drinking episode.) The heavy drinkers drank for social rather than compensatory reasons. They were judged as high in social skills, charm, expressiveness, and interest in the opposite sex. On the down side, they were also viewed as opportunistic, self-indulgent, and power oriented.

Alcoholics, defined as those for whom alcohol has created problems, do display greater depression, anxiety, and poor mental health. They are more likely than moderate alcohol consumers to use tranquilizers (Vaillant, 1983). However, heavy consumers for whom alcohol has not created problems, may resemble moderate drinkers more than alcoholics. In Vaillant's (1983) college sample there was a group of men who drank heavily (up to 5 drinks each evening) who did not exhibit problems. The characteristics of this group are heuristic. These males used less sick time than heavy problematic drinkers, they more often quit smoking, they did not use prescription drugs, they were rated as well adjusted in college and as adults, and reported more positive childhood experiences. Whereas mental health and childhood experiences were positive, this group was characterized as having unhappy adult home lives. This particular group came from a middle class sample. The finding of good mental health among the heavy, but not alcoholic, social drinkers was also found in Vaillant's (1983) lower class sample. The heavy social drinkers displayed good mental health scores, similar to the moderate social drinkers, and better than the problem drinkers.

Attitudes toward Drinking as Predictors of Behavior

Heavy drinkers do differ in their attitudes toward drinking from light to moderate drinkers. Heavy drinkers view other people's drinking more favorably, are less likely to view abstention favorably, are more likely to expect hosts to provide liquor, are more tolerant of intoxication, are more likely to be against social controls for drinking, and are more likely to view alcoholism as a disease (Huebner et al., 1976; Martin & Caswell, 1987; McCarty & Kaye, 1984; Orford, Waller, & Peto, 1974; Snortum, Kremer, & Berger, 1987; Veevers, 1972). One of the best predictors of level of alcohol consumption is the expectation of behavioral depression and cognitive impairment. The expectation is negatively associated with consumption. Heavy drinkers do not expect to be sedated (Leigh, 1989). Heavy drinkers expect more positive and fewer negative consequences as a result of drinking. Furthermore, when asked regarding the importance of the positive consequence, heavy drinkers value the positive consequences more than the light drinkers (McCarty, Morrison, & Mills, 1983). They perceive the deleterious consequences of drinking, both for self and others, less negatively (Leigh, 1987). Given a particular drinking behavior (intoxication, DWI, concern from relatives over drinking, etc.), it is more likely to be labeled as indicative of problem drinking by light consumers than by heavy consumers (Leavy & Dunlosky, 1989). The same behavior (intoxication, DWI, concern from relatives over drinking, etc.) is also more likely to be viewed as indicative of a problem by women than men (Leavy & Dunloskly, 1989).

As in other areas of attitude research, the link between attitude and behavior increases with increasing specificity of the attitude. McCarty et al. (1983) found that predictive link between attitude and behavior is enhanced when attitude is assessed with regard to amount in a particular context. Attitudes toward alcohol are more predictive of amount consumed than are attitudes toward alcoholism (McCarty et al., 1983).

In general population surveys, persons have been asked to endorse their reasons for drinking. Items are Guttmaned scaled, that is, some items are endorsed by almost all respondents but other items are endorsed by only the more heavily drinking, such that heavy drinkers tend to endorse more reasons than do light drinkers. Specific findings are the following: Everyone endorses drinking to be sociable. Heavy drinkers additionally endorse drinking to improve a bad mood or reduce tension, plus drinking to enhance involvement and stimulate arousal (Cooper, Russell, & George, 1988; Farber, Khavari, & Douglass, 1980; Jessor, Carmen & Grossman, 1968; Johnson et al., 1985; Martin & Casswell, 1987). With regard to the perceived impact of drinking, light drinkers tend to endorse those items pertaining to global effects (alcohol creates a party atmosphere; alcohol improves mood). Heavy drinkers additionally endorse items that suggest a personal effect from drinking (mood alteration; social ability facilitation; confidence building) (Cooper et al., 1988; Farber et al., 1980; Martin & Casswell, 1987 Mulford & Miller, 1960a). Problem drinkers reported imbibing to ameliorate negative affect or to enhance participation in masculine activities (Glynn et al., 1983).

In general, people expect alcohol to affect others more strongly than it will themselves (Rohsenow, 1983). A number of investigators have developed expectancy measures for assessing what individuals believe will be the effect of alcohol on their behavior (Brown, Goldman, Inn, & Anderson, 1980; Leigh, 1987; Southwick, Southwick & Critchlow, 1981). Farber et al. (1980) contributed a measure that assesses reasons for drinking. Consistent with other findings, heavy consumers endorsed more reasons for drinking and endorsed more escape reasons for drinking. Brown et al. (1980) developed the Alcohol Expectancy Questionnaire (AEQ) through factor analysis. The factor analysis yielded 6 Factors: a global positive expectancy factor, a social and physical pleasure factor, a sexual enhancement factor, an arousal, power, aggression factor, a social assertion factor, and a relaxation, tension reduction factor. In general population studies, everyone endorses the positive expectancy items. Those with longer drinking histories who also drink more additionally endorse items on the sexual enhancement and arousal factor (Brown et al., 1980). Southwick et al. (1981) developed an expectancy measure that yielded 3 factors: pleasure/disinhibition, stimulation/perceived dominance, and behavioral impairment. Both moderate and excessive drinkers as opposed to abstainers were more likely to endorse items on the first two factors. To summarize, results from the expectancy measures generally suggest that heavy drinkers expect to be stimulated and aroused by their drinking.

Among social drinkers, personality and sex are predictive of differences in reasons for drinking. Segal, Huba, & Singer (1980) examined these associations. Males report more sensation seeking/disinhibition reasons for drinking. Females report more relief drinking. Those lacking in self-esteem, report drinking to reduce shyness. Those with high needs for affiliation and social recognition, endorse coping with anger as a reason for drinking. Parker and Maattanen (1987) found that those males who report more frequent intoxication expect that alcohol will enhance their masculinity whereas those females who report more frequent intoxication expect alcohol to enhance their femininity.

Reasons for drinking are further related to the context in which people drink and whether they become intoxicated. Drinkers who endorse alleviation of depression as a reason for drinking are more likely to be solitary drinkers. Those who endorse drinking to get high and to produce pleasure report the highest frequencies of intoxication and the larger amounts consumed (Cutter & O'Farrell, 1984); although for women, intoxication is more strongly associated with relief drinking (Jessor et al., 1968).

UNDER WHAT CONDITIONS IS DRINKING MORE LIKELY TO OCCUR?

A number of methodological approaches have been brought to bear in addressing the question of when drinking is more likely to occur. Some have taken the more ecologically relevant approach, having subjects record their mood and life events for a period of time. That is, the subjects have kept diaries. By computing correlations between mood and drinking over time, researchers have assessed whether people drink more in particular moods. Most of the naturalistic studies have focused on the issue of stress induced drinking. By computing correlations between life events and drinking, researchers have assessed whether given a stressful event people will increase their drinking. In addition to naturalistic observation, data from laboratory studies are also available. The laboratory investigations have examined stress/dysphoria as a cause of drinking. They have examined additional variables (e.g., good mood, anger, presence of a drinking model) as well. Researchers have manipulated subject's mood or surrounding variables and then measured the impact on drinking. The manipulated variable research has allowed the generation of causal statements regarding whether particular mood or settings cause increased drinking.

This section reviews the literature relating to the conditions under which drinking is most likely to occur. Data collected under naturally occurring circumstances are reviewed first and then the manipulated research is discussed.

Natural Environment Observations on the Relationship Between Stress and Drinking

Subjects have kept logs of their daily mood and their drinking behavior. Among heavy drinking college students, drinking and intoxication were not found to covary with dysphoria or stressful events (Rohsenow, 1982b). Aneshensel and Huba (1983) assessed mood for the previous week and alcohol consumption at 4-month intervals throughout a year in the general population. Employing path analysis, they concluded that depression initially stimulates increased alcohol consumption but the long term depressed drink less.

When events that might be particularly stressful for a particular class of individuals are selected from a menu of heterogeneous stressors, covariation between the occurrence of the stressor and drinking has been noted. Pearlin and Radabaugh (1976) found an association between economic hardship and drinking to relieve stress among those with low self-esteem or a low sense of mastery. Hull, Young, and Jouriles (1986) found that persons high in self-consciousness drank more when experiencing ego threatening events. Chassin, Mann, and Sher (1988) found an association between bad grades and symptomatic drinking among the higher self-conscious male adolescents . It should be noted that these associations suggest those factors that will increase the drinking of particular individuals. They do not imply that the consumption of these individuals will be elevated when compared to others.

Sadava, Thistle, and Forseyth (1978) reported a positive association between stress and drinking among those who hold positive expectations for alcohol, although Rohsenow (1982c) examining college males who scored high on a scale suggesting the employment of alcohol to alter mood, found no covariation over time between mood and drinking. In contrast to Rohsenow (1982c), findings from a population of male homosexuals responding to a survey instrument in a newspaper support the association between stress and drinking for those who hold positive expectations for alcohol as a stress reliever. Among those who believed alcohol was a tension reducer and among those whose social life centered around bar room activities, there was an association between the frequently experienced negative mood (measured as a trait) and heavier alcohol consumption (McKiran & Peterson, 1988).

Related to the question of covariation between dysphoric mood and drinking, is whether trait depressed or anxious individuals display elevated consumption levels. If the drinking of trait anxious males is recorded over time, their consumption levels are less than the nontrait anxious (Holroyd, 1978; Rohsenow, 1982c). Trait anxious persons do not display elevated rates of alcoholism (Schuckit et al., 1990). Those male college students who are perhaps better adjusted as evidenced by increased social support for negative events, display high consumption levels (Rohsenow, 1982c). The higher consumers among college males score more highly on indices of masculinity (Rohsenow, 1982c). Orford et al. (1974) found that among college males, drinking frequency and drinking problems were more prevalent among the extroverted, adventurous, and pleasure seeking. Among adolescents, low self-consciousness rather than high self-consciousness is more predictive of drinking (Chassin et al., 1988). Cooper et al, (1988) found that in a community survey, abusive drinking was concentrated among those whose style was to directly express anger. Hingson et al. (1981) assessed satisfaction with life, a possible negative correlate of dysphoric/ anxious mood, and found it to be unrelated to average amount consumed per occasion, with expection of those unhappy with their romantic relationship tending to be higher consumers of alcohol. Most of the studies just presented then have found that those who are less dysphoric tend to be the heavier consumers. A study by Kalodner, Delucia, and Ursprung (1989) is an exception. Kalodner et al. found that trait anxious college students reported typical consumption levels that were elevated compared to the non-trait anxious college students.

Whereas the trait anxious have not consistently been found to consume more, they may hold specific beliefs about the impact of alcohol. Trait anxious college students expect alcohol to yield a stronger influence on their behavior than do the non-trait anxious (Brown & Munson, 1987; Orford et al., 1974).

The relationship between drinking and stress may be different among college student women. For women college students feeling bored or hopeless about the future has been found to covary with amount of drinking (Weschsler & Rohman, 1981). In college females an association between heavy drinking and high Beck depression inventory scores has been noted (Noel & Lisman, 1980). Of course, college women may be a very unusual group. They are likely to be less traditional than older women.

Summary of the Correlation Findings of the Relationship Between Stress and Alcohol Consumption

Heavy consumers do endorse a variety of self-descriptors, which suggest that they rely on alcohol to cope with stress. Heavy consumers say they use alcohol to cope. They do have fewer active coping skills relative to others. They hold positive expectations for alcohol's ameliorative impact on stress reduction. These associations suggest that heavy drinkers report employing alcohol to cope with stress. The findings do not imply, however, that stress or lack of mechanisms for coping with stress will necessarily cause the heavy drinking. These findings are correlational. Those most stressed out, viz., the trait anxious, are not distinguished as heavy consumers. In the general population, the occurrence of stress increases drinking in the short run but not the long run. Whereas, the self-report of heavy drinkers suggest they rely on alcohol as a coping mechanism for stress and perhaps have fewer alternative coping mechanisms, the correlational findings suggest they rely on alcohol for many other functions as well. Heavy consumers view alcohol as a power, arousal enhancer, a social facilitator, and a sexual stimulant. Etiology of heavy consumption is unclear.

LABORATORY STUDIES

The second approach to the question of when are people more likely to drink, has been the laboratory approach. Research assessing the impact of a variety of moods on alcohol consumption will be reviewed. A discussion of the impact of experimentally induced anxiety is presented first. Most of the research discussed concerns findings from human subjects. The discussion of whether experimentally induced anxiety results in increased consumption begins with a brief overview of the animal literature.

In the human literature, specific variables have been manipulated and then observations of the subjects consummatory behavior have been made. Studies have varied in terms of the ecological validity of the context in which the drinking occurs. Sometimes a gregarious, barroom atmosphere has provided the experimental context. Sometimes a wine tasting task, in which the amount consumed is measured as the solitary subjects make discriminations about the gustatory quality of the beverage has provided the context.

Several generic caveats can be proffered about this general area of research. First, the consumption of alcohol has been the prescribed response in the context of the experiment. In most studies, results do not speak to the issue of whether the subject would have sought out alcohol under particular conditions. Rather, the question addressed is will the subject, as a function of the independent variable, drink more when contexts prescribe some drinking. Second, in most of the experiments a control condition in which the available beverage was water rather than alcohol has been lacking. Such a control condition would have allowed for an inference as to whether the specific independent variable increased the rate of all consummatory behavior or whether the positive finding was specific to alcohol.

Anxiety and Drinking

Laboratory work in which the relationship between anxiety and drinking has been examined is now discussed. The animal literature is focused on first, followed by the human literature. The human work has offered a diverse variety of operationalizations of anxiety as an independent variable. These have included anticipation of shock, anticipation of evaluation by another individual, receipt of negative feedback for self-conscious subjects, anticipation of performance on a task upon which the subject has previously succeeded but is still uncertain about future ability, and being in the presence of a hyperactive youth. The results of the impact of these diverse operationalizations of anxiety have failed to yield consistent findings regarding the relationship between anxiety induction and alcohol consumption. This lack of consistency has allowed for the speculation regarding more complex functions of alcohol in anxiety provoking situations. The results of specific studies are reviewed followed by speculation regarding the meaning in the data.

Animal Literature

Experiments addressing the issue of alcohol consumption under stressful conditions have yielded inconsistent results (Pohorecky, 1981). Some have found that animals exposed to shock will increase their alcohol consumption (Mills, Bean, & Hutcheson, 1977; Wright, Pekanmaki, & Malin, 1971), although additional research suggests that the effect is particular to precise conditions. Cierco, Myers, and Black (1968) and Kinney and Schmidt (1979) report that rats increase their consumption when the shock is signaled and unavoidable but not when the shock is unsignaled and unavoidable. Other types of stressors also increase animal consumption (Derr & Lindbald, 1980). For example, stress immobilization and the presence of a dominant monkey as opposed to a subservient monkey or being alone will increase consumption (Altshueler, 1980; Derr & Lindbald, 1980). Increased consumption is specific to alcohol and not other beverages (Mills & Bean, 1978). The time of increase in consumption (days after the aversion exposure, at offset of shock, upon return to the home cage) have varied across studies (Pohorecky, 1981). As yet no conceptual explanations accounting for the association between animal stress and drinking has prevailed as the received view. Clear bottomlines are not available (Pohorecky, 1981).

Human Studies

Several experiments have arranged anxiety provoking experiences and then measured alcohol consumption. Higgins and Marlatt (1973) informed subjects that they would be subjected to inescapable painful shock. Prior to the anticipated shock, subjects participated in a wine tasting task. Results failed to yield support for the hypothesis that anxiety induced by shock anticipation would increase drinking. Similar results have been reported. Gabel, Noel, Keane, and Lisman (1980) faiied to detect increased consumption among subjects viewing slides of mutilated bodies. Subjects viewing erotic slides did, however, increase their consumption.

Whereas the Higgins and Marlatt (1973) experiment examined the impact of a non-ego-relevant stressor, others have created stress through inducing evaluation apprehension. An experiment by Collins, Parks, and Marlatt (1985) is consistent with the notion that subjects will drink more under stress. In this experiment, subjects drank more when interacting with a distant/aloof peer. Higgins and Marlatt (1975) allowed subjects to drink as they were or were not being rated on attractiveness by a confederate with whom they were interacting. The subjects who were being evaluated drank more than those in the control condition. Further, there was suggestion that the trait anxious were particularly susceptible to the increased consumption given evaluation apprehension. These two experiments then suggest that the stress of evaluation apprehension will increase alcohol consumption.

Rohsenow (1982a) investigated the question of whether providing the subjects with an opportunity to cope with anxiety apprehension would block the increase in drinking resulting from the stress. In one condition (the coping opportunity condition) the subjects were observed and believed that they would have an opportunity to rate their observer. In another condition, subjects were observed without the belief that they would have an opportunity to subsequently rate the observer. In a third condition (the control condition), subjects were not observed but believed they would be rating someone else. Rohsenow's experimental findings contradicted both anticipated results and prior findings. Subjects in whom evaluation apprehension was induced by an observing evaluator drank less than in control and coping conditions. Scrutiny of the precise difference in experimental procedure between those studies finding that evaluation apprehension increases drinking vs. Rohsenow's experiment, suggest the operation of a relevant moderator variable. In the Higgins and Marlatt procedure the subject was observed while answering questions about himself but his drinking during the taste testing task was not observed. In the Rohsenow procedure, the evaluator observed how much the subject had consumed. In the mind of Rohsenow's subjects being observed while drinking may have been a salient consideration in contributing to the evaluation. The interpolation of the coping procedure did have an effect. The restraint on drinking imposed through observation was lifted by the opportunity to cope. This particular difference between procedures in the Higgin and Marlatt vs. Rohsenow's procedure may account for differential results. Perhaps evaluation apprehension will only increase drinking when the drinking behavior itself is unobserved.

Others have interpolated interventions between the stressor and the opportunity to drink. Strickler, Tomaszewski, Maxwell, and Suib (1979) told male heavy drinkers that they would be delivering a speech to graduate students. Prior to the waiting period, subjects listened to a relaxation tape, a sensitization tape, or a neutral tape. They then were given an opportunity to drink while waiting prior to delivering the speech. The findings were that the sensitized subjects drank more than subjects in the relaxation condition, although other differences were not significant. Both the relaxation and the sensitization probably contributed to the obtained group difference, making it impossible to conclude that relaxation can erase the dissomanic impact of stress.

An Environmentally Relevant Stressor. Lang, Pelham, Johnston, and Gelernter (1989) examined a stressor that is likely to be present in the lives of alcoholics. These researchers examined the impact of interacting with a hyperactive child on drinking behavior. (Recall that increased rates of hyperactivity are found in alcoholic families.) Rather than using alcoholics as subjects, Lang et al. employed college students who were social drinkers. These researchers found that male subjects did drink more following interaction with a hyperactive child than did subjects who interacted with a well-behaved child. The findings were limited to the male subjects. The drinking of the female subjects was not increased by interacting with the hyperactive child.

Self-handicapping Strategy. Berglas and Jones (1978) proffered the notion of a self-handicapping strategy. Self-handicapping is a motivation for drinking that will be activated under specific conditions. According to Berglas and Jones, when an individual succeeds at a task but is uncertain of his/her ability to maintain the success in the future, that individual will seek to establish excuses for possible future failure. A handicap (e.g., "I was drinking") can constitute an excuse for failure. Failure can be blamed on the handicap. Any obtained success will suggest even greater ability as the individual has succeeded in spite of the handicap. Beglas and Jones reasoned that drinking constitutes a readily available handicap.

As support for their hypothesis, Berglas and Jones (1978) compared males who succeeded at a task that was insoluble such that these males could not be certain of their mastery of the task vs. males who succeeded at a soluble task. As predicted, the uncertain successful opted to ingest a performance impairing drug prior to an anticipated trial on a similar task. Tucker, Vuchinich, and Sobell (1981) brought the paradigm closer to the realm of motives for drinking. They replicated the Jones and Berglas finding in a procedure in which alcohol was the specific performance impairing drug that was available prior to the anticipated performance. The foregoing studies do suggest then that under certain conditions, people will opt to adopt the self-handicapping strategy of alcohol consumption. There has been a failure to replicate with female subjects. Despite the fact that the task was changed so as to be ego involving for the female subjects, Bordini, Tucker, Vuchinich, and Rudd (1986) failed to find that females choose to consume more following the fear arousal over the ability to maintain success.

Hull's Theory Regarding Why People Drink and When they Will be More Likely to Drink. Hull (1981) has advanced a theory of why people drink. According to Hull people drink to avoid a state of self-consciousness. The phenomenon of self-consciousness has received a great deal of attention in social psychology. It can be both a state and a trait. As a personality trait, it is called self-consciousness. As a state, it has been called Objective Self-Awareness (OSA). The state of Objective Self-Awareness can be aversive, particularly after failure. After failure, people will wish to decrease self-consciousness. Hull advances the case that alcohol will attenuate self-consciousness and hence is a mechanism for reducing the aversive state of self-focus. Hull avers that alcohol will decrease self-consciousness through its effect on cognitive processing. The established impact of alcohol on cognitive processing suggests that when drinking people will be less likely to encode information in terms of higher order concepts. One particular example of a higher order concept is the concept of the self. When drinking people will be less likely to access the higher order concept of self. They will thereby be less self-conscious. Hull, Levenson, Young, and Sher (1983) did adduce evidence supportive of a reduction in self-consciousness attributable to the pharmacological impact of alcohol. This research is reviewed in the chapter on alcohol's impact on mood and behavior (Chapter 14). Here, the findings pertinent to self-consciousness as an independent variable with increased consumption as the dependent variable are discussed.

There have been investigations demonstrating that those who are high in self-consciousness are particularly likely to drink given failure. Hull and Young (1983) exposed subjects high and low on self-consciousness to either positive or negative feedback on a test purported to measure IQ. According to theory, the trait highly self-conscious should drink more to attenuate their self-consciousness. Results were consistent with prediction. The high self-conscious subjects drank more after receiving the negative feedback than did subjects in the other 3 conditions. Although the high self-conscious subjects receiving the negative feedback, were significantly more dysphoric in mood than subjects in other conditions, only for the high self-conscious subjects receiving the negative feedback, did mood correlate with alcohol consumption. Hull and Young explained their results in terms of OSA. When information about the self is negative, people will avoid OSA. The dispositionally self-aware are particularly sensitive to such negative information and would be motivated to reduce OSA. In the particular paradigm, alcohol afforded a readily available mechanism for reducing the OSA.

As further support for their theory, Hull, Young, and Jouriles (1986) examined the real world consumption patterns of high and low self-conscious individuals as a function of negative life events in a population of posttreatment alcoholics and a population of college students. In both populations, data suggested that the high self-conscious drink more when they experience ego-threatening life events, although the drinking behavior of the low self-conscious is not associated with this type of negative event. Persons low in self-consciousness do not increase drinking given the experience of negative life events.

A study by Holroyd (1978) constitutes a failure to replicate a seminal relationship axiomatic to Hull's theory, viz., that the high self-conscious given ego threatening circumstance will drink more. Holroyd blocked subjects on the trait of high social anxiety. Then subjects were provided with feedback from a bogus personality test alleging that they were either socially adept or inept. Subsequent to receipt of the feedback, subjects were to interact and make a favorable impression, during which time they could consume alcohol. The results yielded two main effects. Subjects drank more after the positive feedback and the less socially anxious drank more. The Hull theory would have predicted increased consumption in the high socially anxious, negative feedback cell.

Studies That Have Contrasted the Impact of Anxiety Vs. a Good Mood on the Dependent Variable of Drinking.   The previously examined research has examined the impact of ego threatening stressors on drinking. There is support for the idea that a threat to the ego will result in increased alcohol consumption relative to a neutral mood state. That is, particular types of anxiety will increase drinking relative to a neutral mood state. There are several studies in which a state of ego threat has been contrasted with a good mood induced through positive feedback. Here, the studies suggest that a good mood is more impactful than a threatened ego in inducing increased consumption.

The previously discussed study by Holroyd (1978) illustrated that subjects who are given positive feedback from a personality test will subsequently drink more than subjects provided with negative feedback. Similar results were reported by Pihl and Yankofsky (1979) who gave subjects either positive or negative feedback from a bogus IQ test and then observed subsequent drinking under solitary conditions. Among heavy social drinkers, the positive feedback resulted in more drinking than the negative feedback. Although the Holroyd (1978) and Pihl and Yankofsky (1979) experiments did not include neutral mood conditions making it impossible to conclude whether good mood induction induces more drinking relative to a neutral mood, they do suggest that a positive mood is a more impactful way to increase drinking than is a negative mood.

Summary of the Findings Investigating Whether Anxiety is a Precipitant to Drinking.   The relationship between anxiety and drinking is complex. Clear bottom lines from the animal literature are unavailable. In the human literature, some operationalizations of anxiety result in increased drinking whereas others do not. Whereas shock anticipation has not been found to increase drinking, threats to the ego generally do increase drinking. Even given threats to the ego, drinking will only accelerate under particular conditions. For example if the drinking is observed by an evaluator, the person will fail to drink more.

The lack of consistency in the literature between anxiety as an independent variable on the dependent variable of drinking allows for the generation of hypotheses about the function served by drinking in an evaluation apprehensive, ego threatened individual. Alcohol is probably not being consumed for its general anxiety amelioration effect. That is, a dampening impact on some anxiety center in the brain probably does not constitute the motive for drinking. If such were the case, all types of anxiety might be expected to increase drinking. Only particular types of anxiety will result in increased alcohol consumption.

The self-consciousness studies by Hull and the self-handicapping studies both confirm that there are ego threatening conditions under which people will opt to consume more alcohol. These studies further offer motives for the drinking. Hull's theory suggests that ego threatened people will drink to decrease self-focus. The self-handicapping hypothesis suggests that people will drink to have an available excuse for anticipated failure. It would seem then that there are many functions served by drinking. Whether these functions are useful or attractive to certain individuals will probably vary according to the type of context in which they find themselves. Some effects of alcohol will be particularly attractive to individuals under certain types of ego threatening, anxiety provoking conditions.

Although empirical findings do allow for the conclusion that ego threats or evaluation apprehension types of anxiety inductions will increase drinking, other findings suggest that ego threats are not the most powerful way in which to create conditions that will accelerate consumption. Normal individuals will consume more given positive feedback than when self-doubts are induced.

Anger as a Precipitant

Marlatt, Kosturn, and Lang (1975) have evaluated the impact of anger with and without the opportunity for revenge on drinking. These researchers observed the drinking of subjects who were provoked, the drinking of subjects who were provoked and anticipated an opportunity for retaliation, and the drinking of subjects who were not provoked. Those subjects who were provoked and expecting an opportunity for retaliation, drank less on a taste testing task than did the subjects in the other two conditions. The results of this experiment are difficult to interpret. Although the authors concluded that assertion will negate the pressure to drink induced by anger, there was no evidence from the results that anger is a precipitant to increased drinking. Since the authors did not measure mood of subjects after their experimental manipulation, it is impossible to determine which mood was associated with the differential drinking behavior.

Depression

Noel and Lisman (1980) employed a learned helplessness induction which served to increase the hostility and depression scale scores of their female, college student subjects. Those exposed to the helplessness induction drank more beer but not more gingerale on a subsequent taste rating task. In a similar study, Bordini et al. (1987) found that women drank more after exposure to an insoluble as opposed to a soluble task.

In a study by Tucker, Vuchinich, Sobell, and Maisto (1980), the authors may have created a state capturing some of the features of depression. Subjects were compared after performance at a difficult or an easy task. The results were that subjects drank more both before and after performance at a difficult task as opposed to performance on an easy task.

Influence of a Preload

Inspired by the hypothesis in the obesity literature that the obese are motivated by external stimuli and insensitive to kinesthetic feedback, Young and Pihl (1982) evaluated the impact of an alcohol preload on drinking. All subjects were given a preload of alcohol. Next, they were asked whether they believed themselves to be more or less intoxicated than a partner with whom they were interacting. Then subjects were then informed that the preload was either a large or a small dose. The dependent variable of amount consumed was assessed as subjects continued to interact with their partners. Results suggested that those subjects told they had received a large preload drank less. Those who believed they were relatively less intoxicated drank more.

The Effect of the Presence of a Model

In experiments conducted in barroom type settings it has been demonstrated that subjects will drink more in the company of others than when alone (Strickler, Dobbs, & Maxwell, 1979). Subjects also drink more in the company of sociable heavy consuming model than a sociable light consuming model (Collins et al., 1985; Lied & Marlatt 1979). Heavy drinking models exert their influence when drinking simultaneously with the subject, but not when subjects drink alone subsequent to observation of the heavy drinking model (Collins & Marlatt, 1981). Male models have greater impact over the drinking of both male and female subjects (Collins & Marlatt, 1981; Cooper, Waterhouse, & Sobell, 1979).

These experimental findings conform to findings from the natural environment. People tend to drink more in bars than at home. They drink more with friends and relatives (Hartford, 1983). The rate of consumption in bars is not greater than when alone, however. People tend to drink for a longer duration of time in a bar than in other settings (McCarty, 1985, p. 259). Music with a slower beat will increase the rate of consumption (McCarty, 1985, p. 268). Bar waitresses approach solitary male patrons more frequently than they do couples (McCarty, 1985, p. 269), which tends to increase consumption rates.

Subject's Response to Drinking as an Influence on Consumption

A particularly clever investigation examined alcohol's impact on mood, and in turn, how the induced mood related to further consumption. De Wit et al. (1987) examined subject preference for alcohol or an inert substance, both of which were left unlabeled as to content. Subject's beverage selection was evaluated across a series of choice trials as they engaged in leisure activities in the company of others. Subjects responded to mood measures as they drank. Hence it was possible to examine choice as a function of the mood extant prior to the making of the next choice. Results revealed that those subjects who consistently chose the alcohol containing drink, reported more arousal, vigor, elation, and decreased fatigue on mood measures, although they did not differ from other subjects on mood measures prior to the experimental task. The alcohol choosers differed on personality measures as well. Those choosing the alcohol were higher on the sensation seeking scales, a state psychopathy scale, a boredom susceptibility scale, and a disinhibition measure.

SUMMARY

In this section some cognitive and situational factors associated with increased drinking among normal individuals were reviewed. Socioeconomic variables, age, and sex are all predictors of levels of consumption. Attitudes and expectancies are also associated with difference in consumption levels and patterns of alcohol use. Particular sets of cultural norms and attitudes either promotes or discourages drinking.

A number of diverse approaches have investigated the relationship between stress and drinking. Studies in which individuals are tracked over time do suggest that stresses can exert a short-term acceleration of drinking, however, this increase may not be sustained given a chronic stressful condition. Laboratory studies suggest that stresses of an interpersonal variety can increase drinking given a context in which drinking is a prescribed behavior. Aversive self-consciousness, evaluation apprehension, and uncertainty about ability to sustain success can increase drinking. It is well not to extrapolate too far from these findings. Although some types of anxiety will reliably increase drinking, this does not imply that those who are chronically anxious (the trait anxious) drink more than others. As discussed in Chapter 13, such is not the case. Further, positive mood inductions even in the laboratory, are stronger precipitants to drinking than are anxiety inductions.

Laboratory studies have identified additional mood inductions that will alter drinking. For women, depression may be a precipitant to drinking. Retaliation after anger provocation decreases drinking. The presence of a heavily drinking male model will increase drinking as well.

One study (de Wit et al., 1987) in the literature was unique in that it assessed degree of continued drinking as a function of the mood of the individual while drinking. This study found that those who were aroused, elated, and less fatigued as they drank opted to consume more. This study offers insights into the alcohol associated state which encourages drinking. It is also consistent with the expectations that those who drink more hold about the effects of drinking. Heavy consumers expect alcohol to exert an arousing effect.

13 Cognitive and Social Predictors of Alcoholism

The rate of alcoholism is estimated to be about 10% for males and 5% for females (Schuckit, 1986; Weissman, Myers, & Harding, 1980). Higher rates are found among non-Whites, Protestants, lower class persons, and persons who are divorced, separated, or single (Weissman, Myers, & Harding, 1980).

Not everyone is at equal risk for developing alcoholism. In the chapter on genetics, those inherited factors that might place an individual at risk were reviewed. Genetics is just one side of the picture. It is probably the case, that genetics will not have an opportunity to be expressed unless the proper set of environmental circumstances occur. In this section, theories and data are reviewed regarding which environmental circumstances and cognitive factors are conducive to the development of alcoholism.

Environmental factors can be divided along several lines. Some have recognized that particular subcultural groups have extraordinary rates of alcoholism. Other theorists have suggested that particular types of events may place individuals at risk for alcoholism. One particular stereotype that seems to prevail is that stress can lead to alcoholism. Research findings that address this issue are examined. Two variants on the theme that stress causes alcoholism have emerged in the social psychological literature: Berglas and Jones's self-handicapping and Hull's theory regarding self-consciousness. Both these theories were introduced in Chapter 12. Empirical findings relevant to alcoholism are reviewed here. Both theories offer specific predictions about types of stress for particular individuals that might motivate excessive drinking.

Another area of research has considered whether the belief systems of alcoholics regarding alcohol might be instrumental in the development of alcoholism. Some research findings from this literature are reviewed. After a review of the literature, some additional hypotheses as to the motivational road to excessive drinking are proffered.

CULTURAL FACTORS

It has long been recognized that the rates of alcoholism are higher in particular ethnic groups. The Irish have high rates of alcoholism (Vaillant, 1983). In Jellinek's (1960) day, Mediterranean cultures (Jews and Italians) displayed low rates, although recent data suggests that the rate of alcoholism among Italian Americans is high (Heien & Pompelli, 1987). In Vaillant's (1983, p. 55) longitudinal study, the variable in the regression analysis that was most predictive of future alcoholism was ethnicity (Mediterranean culture being low). Ethnicity had the largest weight in the regression analysis, although it was not significantly larger than the hereditary factor.

Sociologists have explained the high rates of alcoholism in terms of conflicting norms governing drinking behavior (Room, 1976). Subcultures that proscribe drinking, i.e., advocate abstinence, may produce lower rates of alcoholism, however, in such cultures when people do drink they are more likely to become socially disruptive. Often, high rates of abstention and high rates of alcoholism are found within the same cultural groups (Peele, 1987). Cultures that incorporate ritualistic drinking thereby prescribing moderate consumption levels and thereby providing moderate drinking models for children to observe, seem to avoid high rates of alcoholism (Linsky, Colby, & Strauss, 1986; Peele, 1987).

The adoption studies have identified a number of environmental factors that are associated with increased risk for alcoholism. Adopted out males seem to be at greater risk for development of alcoholism if they are raised in lower socioeconomic adoptive homes (Bohman et al., 1982; Cloninger, Bohman, & Sigvardsson, 1981). Adopted out females are at greater risk if raised in a rural, low socioeconomic adoptive home (Bohman et al., 1981). Adoptive parent drinking status was not found to influence the development of alcoholism in the adoptee in the Cloninger, Bohman, and Sigvardsson (1981) Swedish data base, however, it was predictive for Iowa adoptees (Cadoret et al., 1985; Cadoret et al., 1987). Alcoholism in the extended adoptive family, however, was most heavily associated with enhanced development in the Iowa sample (Cadoret et al., 1987). A study by Gabrielli and Plomin (1985) suggested that nuclear family environment does not contribute heavily to the development of alcoholism.

In the chapter on characteristics of family members of alcoholics (Vol. 1, Chapter 7), the impact of having been raised in an alcoholic home on the development of alcoholism in FHPs was discussed. A variety of findings suggest that the impact of being raised with an alcoholic parent is the promotion of teetotalism (Hall, Hesselbrock, & Stabenau, 1983a; Harburg, Davis, & Caplan, 1982; Lucero, Jensen, & Ramsey, 1971). Whereas abstinence is promoted, there is little evidence that being raised in an alcoholic home promotes emulation of the alcoholic pattern. In Goodwin et al.'s (1974) adoption study, FHPs raised at home compared to their FHP adopted out siblings produced lower rates of alcoholism, although this difference failed to reach significance. Further, studies suggest that a FHP is especially discouraged from repeating the paternal alcoholic pattern when the mother fails to hold the father in high esteem (McCord, 1988). A father who is openly intoxicated at family gatherings, and who fails to evoke disapproval is more often emulated (Wolin, Bennet, & Noonan, 1979).

The findings then suggest that culture, but not the independent effect of being raised in an alcoholic home, promote alcoholism. Cultural factors are probably linked with an increase in alcoholism through the attitudes toward drinking that are engendered through the culture. Having a positive attitude toward intoxication is associated with alcohol abuse as is association with heavily drinking friends (Kubicka, Kozeny, & Roth, 1990).

OCCUPATIONAL FACTORS

It has long been recognized that particular trades and occupations have higher rates of alcoholism. Persons in the armed forces, the liquor industry, in the fishing industry, the hotel business, and those who are executives, all display higher rates of cirrhosis (Plant, 1979; Slattery, Alderson, & Bryant, 1986). Plant (1979) lists the following characteristics as descriptive of high risk for alcoholism occupations: availability of alcohol at work, social pressure to drink at work, separation from the normal social or sexual relationships, freedom from supervision, very high or very low income levels, collusion on heavy drinking practices among colleagues, strains and stresses of heavy responsibilities, job insecurity, boredom, and recruitment of heavily drinking persons.

DOES THE PRICE OF ALCOHOL BEAR A CASUAL RELATIONSHIP TO ALCOHOLISM?

Many have noted a positive relationship between price and the consumption of alcohol in the population (Ornstein, 1980; Parker & Harman, 1978; Popham, Schmidt, & DeLint, 1976). Pattison (1982) suggests that when overall consumption by the entire populations increases, so does the number of individuals consuming at a level that will create health problems. As such, an increase in the general population level of consumption will be reflected in increased levels of alcoholism.

There has been some disagreement regarding whether an increase in price of alcohol will impact persons at all income levels and at all levels of consumption. Some argue that a limitation on supply will affect all drinkers (Horverak, 1983; Kendell, DeRoumanie, & Ritson, 1983). Supportive of this view, a relationship between price of alcohol and deaths from cirrhosis has been noted (Moskowitz, 1989). Specific studies suggest a fine grained statement of the relationship. In studies where geographic regions are the unit of analysis, price is related to alcohol distribution, but it is only weakly related to alcohol abuse (Gliksman & Rush, 1986; Rush, Gliksman, & Brook, 1986). For moderate and light consumers of alcohol, alcohol may be an elastic good. That is, price will effect the amount consumed. For those who are excessive drinkers, alcohol may not be an elastic good. That is, price will not effect consumption levels (Rush, et al., 1986).

The issue of raising the price of alcohol is germane for setting public policies which will prevent alcoholism. Consensus on the issue has not been reached (see Peele, 1987 and the response by Room, 1987). The relationship between price of alcohol and alcoholism might be indirect. Most problem drinkers will progress through the category of moderate drinker on their way to heavy drinking. Any price increase will be associated with fewer moderate consumers. Thus, fewer individuals will have an opportunity to enter an earlier stage of drinking and progress to full blown alcoholism. However, many factors will undoubtedly interact, such as cultural norms, which will naturally limit the amounts which people typically consume. Future research may provide a clearer picture of the concatenated relationship among these factors.

DOES STRESS CAUSE ALCOHOLISM?

Association of Alcoholism with Economic Indicators

Merton's (1957) theory of anomie holds that deviance has its roots in the disenfranchisement of individuals from the society's prescribed avenues to success. According to the theory, those groups experiencing more economic hardship and/or less opportunity for economic advancement should manifest higher rates of alcoholism. Results of an early investigation by Bales (1946) among the Irish, for whom norms allowed for consumption of alcohol as a stress relieving manuver, were consistent with Merton's hypothesis. In a more contemporary investigation, Linsky, Strauss, and Colby (1985) using states as their unit of analysis found that indices of alcoholism are directly related to statistical indicators of stress within the state population (business failures, mortgage loans foreclosed, number of persons applying for welfare, divorce rate, infant deaths, etc.). Heien and Pompelli (1987), using states as their unit of analysis, also found that the stress indicators of divorce and unemployment were related to cirrhosis deaths. It should be noted that the prior research was correlational making causation impossible to infer.

Findings from Longitudinal Studies on the Development of Alcoholism

Whereas the sociological studies in which geographic regions are the unit of analysis, provides correlational support for the notion that stress can lead to alcoholism, the longitudinal studies examining precursors to alcoholism fail to support this view. The longitudinal studies (discussed in the section of genetics) identify the personality traits of extroversion, high energy, and sensation seeking as the childhood precursors of adult alcoholism. Childhood depression was not related to adult alcoholism. Vaillant's (1983) study did find that familial disarray (frequent moves, less maternal surveillance and nurturance, general economic hardship) was predictive of offspring alcoholism. However, these variables were related through their association with paternal alcoholism, the genetic predictor.

Others have examined retrospectively the contribution of stress to the onset of alcoholism. In a population of women presenting to a detox center, Morrissey and Schuckit (1978) failed to identify a strong association between a variety of stressors and the onset of drinking related problems. Stressful events were precipitants to heavy consumption among problem drinking (those failing to reach criteria for alcoholism) females, however, Wilsnak, Wilsnak, and Klassen (1986) surveyed females. They failed to find an association between a list of stressful occurrence occurring 3 years prior to alcohol assessment and an increase in alcohol consumption or problems. However, specific stressful events (miscarriage, divorce, spouse's problem drinking, spouse's unemployment, and recent departure of child from home) were related. Current drinking was also associated with an absence of a partner confidant. Contrary to the idea of increased stress leading to alcoholism, in the Wilsnak et al. sample having less responsibility (that is, fewer roles such as parent, wife, wage earner) was associated with a higher probability of drinking. Thus, in females there is mixed support for a role of stress as a precursor to alcoholism.

Data from aging populations on the link between stress and alcoholism is also available. Finney and Moos (1984) investigating geriatric alcoholics failed to discern a relationship between stressful events and the onset of alcoholism, which for many in their population had begun later in life. They did suggest, however, that among those in a habit of heavy drinking, stress might constitute a press which could accelerate drinking across a threshold of alcoholism. In their review of the literature, Kushner, Sher, and Beitman (1990) concluded that social phobias and agoraphobia were more likely to precede alcoholism whereas general anxiety is more likely to follow a heavy drinking pattern.

Will Those at Risk Increase their Drinking in Response to Diverse Forms of Stress?   In the genetics section (Chapter 5) the stress dampening effect of alcohol was discussed. When subjects are exposed to a stress (e.g., being evaluated by someone whose opinion matters, anticipating shock), heart rate increases. This increase can be attenuated by alcohol. This stress dampening effect is derived to a greater degree by FHPs, high MacAndrew scorers, and those scoring low on the Socialization scale of the California Personality Inventory. These groups may carry a genetic diathesis for alcoholism. There is reason to believe that alcoholics may derive a stress dampening effect from alcohol. In Chapter 12, studies examining mood as an independent variable and drinking as a dependent variable were reviewed. In these studies in which the general population served as subjects, drinking did not increase for all diverse forms of anxiety inductions. Perhaps, if high MacAndrews or FHPs were selected, their drinking would be found to increase given all operationalizations of anxiety induction. It may be that all conditions that accelerate sympathetic activity (stress) may be particularly likely to increase drinking among those at genetic risk for alcoholism. It may also be the case that only particular types of events will accelerate sympathetic activity (be a stressor) in those at genetic risk for alcoholism. Specific research has not yet been conducted.

Self-Handicapping as an Etiological Factor in the Development of Alcoholism

Berglas and Jones (1978) have adduced evidence suggesting that normal males who are uncertain of their ability to continue to succeed after they have achieved in a particular domain, will choose to self-handicap. That is, they will choose to ingest a drug such as alcohol prior to performance so they have an excuse for failure. If they happen to succeed, even greater ability will be attributed to them by observers, because they have overcome their handicap.

In proposing their concept, Berglas and Jones suggested that the phenomenon of self-handicapping might be an etiological factor in the development of alcoholism. Wright and Obitz (1984) presented results that they suggested are consistent with a self-handicapping interpretation of the behavior of alcoholics. These researchers asked alcoholics and control subjects matched on SES (socioeconomic status) to project what would be their responsibility for hypothetical future negative and positive life events. The alcoholics envisioned less personal responsibility for both positive and negative events, although the differential between alcoholics and normals was larger for positive events than negative events. That is, the alcoholics were particularly likely to disavow responsibility for positive Events. Positive circumstances (not negative circumstances) constitute the situation in which Beglas and Jones have posited that alcoholics will be most desirous of eschewing responsibility, i.e., the circumstances under which they might most frequently seek a self-handicap.

The Wright and Obitz study does suggest that alcoholics will behave in a self-handicapping fashion. The study, however, does not establish that self-handicapping is relevant to the development of alcoholism. It may be that the alcoholism develops first, and then alcoholics learn to rely on external excuses for their behavior. In terms of etiology, data from adolescent populations may be particularly germane to the question of the development of alcoholism. Here the data are against the self-handicapping hypothesis. The self-handicapping theory predicts heavy consumption given success in those who lack confidence, (i.e., are uncertain of their ability to maintain success). Chassin et al, (1988) found low levels of drinking among those adolescents who might be particularly concerned about their ability to maintain success. Those who were high in self-consciousness and who obtained good grades displayed lower levels of consumption of alcohol than other groups. If self-handicapping is an etiological factor in adolescent alcohol abuse, the highly self-conscious who were achieving, should have consumed the most.

The Need for Reduction of Self-Consciousness as an Etiological Factor in the Development of Alcoholism

There are data suggesting that alcohol will reduce self-consciousness, i.e., the state in which a person focuses attention on himself/herself as a object. (The research supporting this statement is presented in Chapter 14.) Drawing upon this established consequence of drinking, Hull (1981) has advanced the hypothesis that individuals who are particularly in need of a reduction in self-consciousness will be especially prone to the development of excessive consumption of alcohol. Hull suggests that persons who are stylistically self-conscious will be particularly compelled to drink more heavily when their self-consciousness is most aversive for them. Data from the literature on self-consciousness (also called objective self-awareness), suggest that self-consciousness will be particularly aversive given failure or negative feedback. Drawing upon the objective self-awareness literature, Hull's theory makes predictions about who will be most likely to drink under which conditions. A motivation for excessive drinking is also imputed. Hull's theory predicts that the highly self-conscious will be most likely to drink under ego-threatening conditions in order to reduce their self-awareness.

In support of Hull's theory, are data from a laboratory study by Hull and Young (1983) that were discussed in Chapter 12. To refresh the reader's mind, in this experiment, groups of high self-conscious and low self-conscious subjects were given either positive or negative feedback from a bogus IQ test. (There were four experimental groups.) Of the four groups, the high self-conscious subjects, after receipt of the negative feedback were the most dysphoric. The group of highly self-conscious subjects after receiving the negative feedback, did drink more alcohol than subjects in the other groups.

As discussed previously in Chapter 12, the results of a similar experiment were not consistent with Hull and Young's (1983) results. Holroyd (1978) divided subjects into groups of high and low in social anxiety. Half the subjects in each group were told they were socially adept and the other half were told that they were socially inept. The results suggested two main effects. The positive feedback increased drinking for everyone. Those low in social anxiety drank more than those high in social anxiety regardless of type of feedback. Hull's theory would have predicted highest consumption for those high in social anxiety (assuming this trait is close to self-consciousness) when receiving the negative feedback.

In addition to the laboratory data, Hull also adduces support for his hypotheses from real world findings. Hull, Young, and Jouriles (1986) examined a sample of recovering alcoholics and a sample of college students. The alcoholic sample was asked about drinking relapse and life events during a 6 month follow-up interval. Students were assessed on typical consumption levels and grades. In each sample, the high self-conscious were particularly likely to drink given the occurrence of an ego threatening life event. Alcoholics high in self-consciousness drank more if they experienced negative life events. Students who were high in self-consciousness drank more if they received bad grades. Those low in self-consciousness did not seem to be impacted by the ego threatening events. Consistent with Hull et al.'s findings, Chassin et al. (1988) in a population of adolescents found a correlation between the receipt of bad grades and drinking among high self-conscious adolescents but not among low self-conscious adolescents.

Comment

Results from previously discussed studies do suggest that the highly self-conscious will drink more when their egos are threatened. Whereas these data are consistent with Hull's theory that the high self-conscious drink to reduce their self-consciousness, the results may simply reflect the positive relationship between negative events and increased drinking. The low self-conscious may not be perturbed by ego threatening feedback. Hence, receipt of bad grades or experience of negative events may impact their mood to a lesser degree than the high self-conscious. However, if one were to find a set of events that would induce a negative mood in the low self-conscious, their drinking might very well be increased. There is an additional problem with Hull's theory in explaining the development of alcoholism. For the Hull data to be germane to the etiology of alcoholism, it would have to be demonstrated that negative events which induce a negative mood are a factor inducing durable increase in consumption. Hull et al.'s studies have only documented a short-term increase in drinking.

Establishing that particular events can increase drinking for a particular group does not necessarily imply that a pathway to alcoholism has been discovered. In a general population survey study by Aneshensel and Huba (1983) negative events were found to increase drinking temporarily, but not over the long run. This study suggested that those factors that cause normal people to increase their consumption temporarily are not necessarily the path through which alcoholism develops.

Any pathway to alcoholism should be consistent with the longitudinal studies on childhood precursors to adult alcoholism. In the longitudinal studies the high sensation seeking, low self-conscious, high McAndrew scoring are identified as those most likely to develop alcoholism. Those scoring high on the MacAndrew scale are more outgoing, less socially reserved, and higher in energy (see Chapter 5). These are not the characteristics which Hull's theory predicts would lead to alcoholism.

Hull and Young (1983, p. 178) did specifically investigate what they believed is an index of self-consciousness in high MacAndrew subjects (recall, from Chapter 4, that the MacAndrew scale predicts future alcoholism). Based on their findings, Hull and Young imply that self-consciousness among high MacAndrew scores will be attenuated by alcohol and, by implication, might be a motive in the drinking of high MacAndrew scorers. Hull and Young's specific findings were the following. High MacAndrew subjects were observed to make more self-referential statements when sober than did low MacAndrew subjects. When drinking, high and Low MacAndrew Subjects did not differ in terms of frequency of self-referential statements. Hull and Young interpret these findings as consistent with their theory. Making more self-referential statements was interpreted as self-consciousness. That is, Hull and Young's operationalization of self-consciousness was a high rate of self-referential statements. Results suggested that high MacAndrews are more self-conscious than others under sober conditions and this exaggerated self-consciousness will be erased by drinking.

Hull and Young's interpretation hinges upon the meaning ascribed to a high frequency of self-referential statements. Hull and Young interpreted a high frequency of self-referential statements as an index of self-consciousness. There are other interpretations of the meaning of a high frequency of self-referential statements. Perhaps the measure used by Hull and Young tapped another construct besides self-consciousness. Perhaps a high frequency of self-referential statements in a sample of high MacAndrew scorers reflects conceit, rather than self-consciousness. It is known that alcohol will increase attention to external environment. Perhaps the high MacAndrews when drinking become more absorbed in external events, less self-absorbed, and less manifestly conceited. This increased absorption in external environment may account for the change in the behavior of the high MacAndrew scorers, rather than some effect on self-consciousness.

There is another finding against the Hull hypothesis. Hull theorizes that self-consciousness is a strong personality factor in the development of alcoholism. Sher and Walitwitz (1986) examined the impact of alcohol on those high in self-consciousness on another dependent variable. In their Study Sher and Walitwitz (1986) divided subjects into those high and low in self-consciousness. Then all subjects were subjected to a laboratory stressor. Whereas the autonomic response to the stress of the low self-conscious subjects was blocked by alcohol, no such ameliorative benefit was demonstrated for the high self-conscious. Similar results were obtained by Niaura, Wilson, & Westrick (1988) who found a stress dampening effect only among the low self-conscious, high Type A males. It would seem that part of the beneficial effect that Hull posits motivates the drinking in the high self-conscious should include dampened autonomic activity in response to stress. The Sher and Walitwitz findings and the Niaura et al. data, however, suggest that in terms of stress dampening effect, the high self-conscious are not benefited by alcohol.

Hull's data do establish that alcohol will decrease self-consciousness. He has further established that negative feedback can induce a negative mood in the self-conscious. This negative mood will increase drinking behavior. Although negative mood can temporarily increase drinking, there is little evidence that the effect will be sustained. Data from longitudinal studies exploring personality factors in the development of alcoholism, fail to suggest that the high self-conscious are at particular risk.

In many of the laboratory studies and the correlational studies, those traits identified as precursors to alcoholism in the longitudinal studies keep emerging as factors associated with heavy consumption. In their correlational study of an adolescent sample, Chassin, Mann, and Sher (1988) found that the low self-conscious persons are more likely to drink heavily and to drink symptomatically. The association between low self-consciousness and heavy drinking was particularly pronounced among children of alcoholics. In laboratory studies, the low self-conscious drink, high sensation seeking individuals compared to others drink the most (de Wit et al., 1987; Holroyd, 1978), although Hull's data suggest that the high self-conscious can be induced to rival the high self-conscious if made sufficiently dysphoric through ego deflation maneuvers. It would seem that in terms of personality factors predisposing to excessive consumption (i.e., alcoholism), the preponderance of data point to low self-conscious, high sensation seeking factors rather than a picture of the high self-conscious in pursuit of a method for decreasing their self-consciousness.

The Role of Stress Reduction in the Drinking of Established Alcoholics

Expectations of Alcoholics Regarding Stress Relieving Effects of Alcohol. There is evidence that alcoholics in contrast to normals do more often endorse the belief that alcohol will reduce tension (Farber et al., 1980). In contrast to nonexcessive drinkers, alcoholics are more likely to anticipate that alcohol will provide relief from dysphoria (Brown, Goldman, & Christiansen, 1985; Connors, O'Farrell, & Cutter, 1987; Deardorff et al., 1975). In terms of cognitions, alcoholics do associate alcohol with tension relief as well as arousal/stimulation (see next section in this chapter). Further, there is evidence that FHP individuals, that is, those who carry a genetic predisposition to alcoholism, derive an enhanced stress attenuating response as assessed on autonomic measures.

Given Established Alcoholism, Will the Occurrence of Stress Increase Alcohol Consumption? Several avenues of research converge to establish a connection between the occurrence of stress and alcohol consumption in alcoholics. Evidence for this connection comes from laboratory studies that have created stress and then allowed for alcohol consumption, ward drinking studies in which the ad lib consumption of alcoholics allowed to drink in a hospital setting has been tracked over a several day period, and studies in which alcoholics have been asked about the precipitants for relapse or asked to identify triggers for their drinking. Some relevant studies are now discussed.

Miller, Hersen, Eisler, Hilsman (1974) examined alcoholics vs. normals under stress. A role play of an assertion task after which subjects were berated for poor performance constituted the stressor. Although there was no difference on autonomic measures of stress response, the alcoholics drank more after the stressor than control conditions, whereas the reverse was true for normals. The Miller et al. experiment then suggested that alcoholics may drink more given stress than will normals.

Allman, Taylor, and Nathan (1972) observed ad lib drinking on a ward over a 32-day period. The alcoholics did drink more when stressed but only when drinking occurred under gregarious rather than solitary conditions. Generally convivial conditions increased drinking, whereas insolation suppressed drinking.

Hershenson (1965) explored which precipitants alcoholics would identify as triggers to drinking. The alcoholics indicated that the experience of self-doubt was a definite trigger, although work and interpersonal problems were not preceived to be as strongly related. Those who labeled themselves as definitely alcoholic as opposed to those who were uncertain about their alcoholic status more often believed that they would drink and drink to intoxication given the occasion of a trigger to drink.

Whereas the Hershenson data establishes that alcoholics predict that they will drink under some types of stressful circumstances, the relapse literature is supportive of the veridicality of the predictions. Studies have investigated those conditions that were present prior to the occurrence of drinking relapse. The findings from these studies are presented in the chapter on relapse in Volume I (Chapter 3). Suffice it to say here that stressors of diverse types are associated with drinking relapse.

There is evidence that alcoholics will use alcohol as a coping mechanism to deal with occasions of stress. They expect relief from tension/dysphoria from alcohol. They behave in accord with their expectations. Establishing that an individual with a long history of excessive alcohol consumption will rely on alcohol to cope with negative events does not speak to the issue of whether stress reduction was a causal factor in the onset of pathological drinking. There are findings that are more germane to this issue.

The Causal Significance of Expecting Alcohol to Relieve Dysphoria and Tension in the Development of Alcoholism

Alcoholics in contrast to normals do expect alcohol to relieve tension and dysphoria. They may derive an enhanced stress dampening response from alcohol which others do not experience. It is important not to ascribe causal significance to expectancies or the stress dampening response in the development of alcoholism. Expectancies may have developed after the onset of alcoholic drinking rather than before. Further, an alcoholics' relief drinking may have developed after the well established routine of heavy drinking.

There are some findings from the general population surveys which suggest that for the bulk of alcoholics the route to the development of excessive consumption was not through relief drinking. If problem drinking can be assumed to precede clinical alcoholism, then examination of those expectancies toward alcohol which differentiate the problem from nonproblem drinkers is relevant. (Note that problem drinking does not refer to quantity consumed but rather drinking associated with negative social behavior.) In fact, if nonclinical populations are examined, then problem drinkers are not differentiated from nonproblem drinkers in terms of drinking to relieve tension. In nonclinical populations, relief drinking (drinking to alter dysphoric mood or drinking to relieve tension) is a correlate of nonproblem, social drinking but not problem drinking (Orford, Waller, & Peto, 1974; Park, 1967). In college samples, thrill seeking reasons for drinking are more strongly associated with problem drinking than is relief escape drinking (McCarty & Kaye, 1984). These findings suggest that relief drinking is not a strong correlate of problem drinking.

Comment.   Different avenues of research suggest different answers to the question of whether stress and hardship cause alcoholism. The sociological inquiries suggest that hardship is related to alcoholism. The male longitudinal studies following a cohort throughout childhood and into adulthood, fail to support the view that those individuals who are more trait psychologically stressed are at higher risk for the development of alcoholism. If a population of clinically depressed individuals is selected, their rates of alcoholism do not surpass general population values (Lewis, Helzer, Cloninger, Croughman, & Whitman, 1982). In a population of clinically anxious, rates of alcoholism do not exceed general population values (Schuckit, Irwin, & Brown, 1990), however, the rates among agoraphobics and social phobics are higher (Kushner, Sher, & Beitman, 1990).

The scant longitudinal data for women does lend more support to stress/ dysphoria as a cause of alcoholism. Wilsnack et al. (1986) found that female alcoholics retrospectively report relatively elevated rates of depression and gynecological problems that had appeared prior to the onset of heavy drinking. Jones (1971) identified, in her longitudinal study, irritability, anxiety, pessimism, and sensitivity to criticism as female precursors to adult alcoholism.

Whereas most data are against the hypothesis that stress causes alcoholism in males, there is a group of alcoholics whom clinicians have suggested do develop alcoholism in response to stress. Schuckit (1986) identifies a group of primary depressives/secondary alcoholics who may have developed their excessive drinking in an attempt to relieve depression. Schuckit (1979) indicates that this type of alcoholic only accounts for about 5% of male alcoholism and about 25% of female alcoholism. Although stress induced alcoholism is represented as a pathway to alcoholism, it is by far the less frequent route. This route may be more frequently encountered in women.

TENTATIVE SUGGESTION OF AROUSAL ENHANCEMENT AS A MOTIVATING FACTOR IN ALCOHOLIC DRINKING

Personal Expectations Regarding Drinking and Personal Reasons for Drinking of Alcoholics

A research avenue for addressing the question of why people become alcoholic is to explore motivations for drinking. Perhaps alcoholics hold specific beliefs about what they can derive from alcohol that other people do not hold. That is, alcoholics might differ in their expectations for how alcohol will effect them. Some researchers have examined expectations and found that alcoholics do indeed report different expectations. Beyond the hypothesis that alcoholics vs. normals might hold differing expectations is the possibility that alcoholics might value the anticipated effects more than normals. Researchers have partially addressed the issues regarding expectations by comparing the reasons normals give for drinking with the reasons provided by alcoholics. If differences are found between the expectations of alcoholics vs. normals, these differences might reflect upon motivations in the development of excessive drinking patterns.

Relevant Data. As previously discussed, alcoholics are more likely than nondrinkers to view alcohol as a tension reducer (Farber et al., 1980) and as an escape mechanism from dysphoria (Brown et al., 1985; Connors et al., 1987; Deardorff et al., 1975). Beyond the negative reinforcement expectations for alcohol, there is considerable evidence that alcoholics expect alcohol to create positive moods. Clinical populations of alcoholics are distinguished by more favorable expectations for the impact of alcohol on their mood and behavior (Brown et al., 1985; Farber et al., 1980). They report as a reason for their drinking their belief that alcohol will enhance personal power (Deardorff et al., 1975). They expect heavy drinking to enhance their sense of being in charge (Connors et al., 1987) and to enhance their assertion (Parker, Gilbert, & Speltz, 1981). On Q-sort measure upon which alcoholics are requested to rate their (1) ideal, (2) sober, and (3) intoxicated selves, although the sober self is more similar to the ideal self overall, the drunk self is viewed as more assertive, arrogant, and non-self-effacing (MacAndrew & Garkinkel, 1962). Whereas alcoholics expect some positive effects from drinking, they anticipate less behavioral impairment than do nonproblem drinkers (Connors et al., 1987).

There are some data suggesting that the expectations that alcoholics hold for the impact of alcohol predates their alcoholism. In a group at high risk for the development of alcoholism, viz., children of alcoholics, expectations for the impact for alcohol have been found to be particularly positive. This is especially the case among high MacAndrew scoring, family history positive youth. They anticipate less behavioral impairment and more enhancement of functioning (Mann, Chassin, & Sher, 1987).

In addition to differential attitudes and expectancies toward alcohol that are particular to alcoholics, alcoholics consume alcohol in a different style. There are more likely to gulp drinks and drink at a more rapid pace (Schaefer, Sobell, & Mills, 1971; Sobell, Schaefer, & Mills, 1972; Williams & Brown, 1974). These patterns may be linked to a differential motivations for drinking.

WHAT MIGHT MOTIVATE EXCESSIVE DRINKING?

Alcohol affects mood and behavior in a myriad of ways. It is probably the case that human reasons for drinking will vary across individuals. Particular personality types will seek one or another effect of drinking. The depressed may drink to become more absorbed in a subsequent activity. Some will drink to fall asleep. Some will drink because they believe that alcohol will relieve tension.

There may be an association between the occasion of stress and drinking in alcoholics and FHPs. Alcoholics and FHPs may derive an enhanced stress dampening effect from alcohol. Whereas normals may drink only under specific types of stress, those at risk may drink in response to a broader range of stressors. What the data do not support is the idea that those who develop alcoholism were more frequently stressed than others prior to developing a heavy drinking routine. There also is little evidence that high MacAndrews (those at risk) will be inclined to respond to a broader range of events as stressful events.

Whereas the reasons for drinking are diverse, several areas of research suggest however that the motivation for excessive, that is alcoholic drinking, is to enhance arousal. Heavy drinkers do endorse alcohol as an arouser. They say they drink to feel in charge. They report less behavioral and cognitive impairment than do normal drinkers. The expectations of effects of alcohol that are reported by alcoholics are very similar to the effects expected by children of alcoholics. They expect less behavioral impairment and more enhancement of cognitive functioning. The laboratory findings (see Chapter 5) on how alcohol impacts family history positive young adults suggest that family history positive's expectations are consistent with behavioral reality.

The human findings are mirrored in the findings from rodent strains bred to prefer alcohol. The rodent preferring strains like children of alcoholics, are more hyperactive. When consuming alcohol, the rodent preferers display more excitation than the nonpreferers. They develop little tolerance to the excitatory effect. In contrast to the rodent nonpreferers, the preferers require more alcohol to induce sleep than do the nonpreferers. The preferers more quickly develop tolerance to the depressant effects than do the nonpreferers (Li et al., 1989).

Wise and Bozarth (1987) have suggested that alcohol achieves its pleasurable effect through action at the same area of the brain that is impacted by other abusable drugs. This is the ventral tegmental area. The effects of stimulating this area of the brain is to heighten arousal, increase attention, and accelerate motor behavior. Perhaps in the genetically predisposed, this area of the brain is differentially stimulated by alcohol or stimulation of this area exerts a more compelling effect on behavior.

A great deal of attention has been devoted to researching the hypothesis that excessive drinking develops through attempts to cope with negative mood states. Most of the longitudinal studies and some laboratory research point in another direction. Much of the research suggests that the bulk of excessive drinking cases eventuate through repeated opportunities to tap into alcohol's other beneficial capacity, that is its ability to enhance arousal.

It is well to remember that even given a motive for drinking in those who might be progressing down a path toward alcoholism, other factors beyond intrapersonal forces are important. The findings on social factors, suggests that cultural norms that permit or encourage excessive drinking are important in the development of alcoholism. It is probably the case that even given intrapersonal reasons to drink excessively, certain environmental variables are also needed before excessive drinking will emerge.

14   The Impact of Alcohol on Mood and Behavior

A great deal of research has accumulated examining the impact of alcohol on mood and behavior. This chapter reviews this literature. The research is summarized here, organized in terms of types of behaviors or moods that can be influenced by alcohol. There are several competing overarching theories of how alcohol affects behavior, each of which attempts to accommodate all the data. Overarching theories are examined at the end of the chapter. We begin with some comments regarding moderator conditions that can influence the impact of alcohol.

GENERAL MODERATOR VARIABLES

There are many conditions that will influence the impact that alcohol exerts on the behavior of drinkers. Situational context, the time of day, an individual's rate of metabolism of alcohol, the amount of alcohol ingested, and expectations of the drinker constitute powerful setting conditions which will shape the effect on any particular individual at a particular time. Each of these "moderator variables" are briefly considered before discussing the average effects of alcohol.

Context

Inconsistent findings in the literature have led to the recognition that the impact of alcohol will vary as a function of context. When the individual drinks while alone and without his/her focus being directed externally either by a task or social interaction, the individual will notice the impact of alcohol on physiologi-

228

cal events. Scales have been developed to measure these altered sensations. Persons typically report a sense of flushing and feeling more dizzy, more numb, less cognitively acute. If the individuals are engaged in an interpersonal context, however, they are less likely to notice kinesthetic events and more likely to report mood changes (O'Malley & Maisto, 1985).

Pliner and Cappell (1974) evaluated the impact of drinking when subjects were alone vs. when they were interacting with others. Some individuals imbibed alcohol or placebo while in a solitary context examining cartoons. Other individuals imbibed alcohol or placebo as they interacted in groups of three while rating the humor content of cartoons. In the solitary setting, the pharmacological effect of alcohol was to increase the drinker's report of feelings of aggression, dizziness, and nonclear thinking. In the social context, however, the effect of alcohol was an increase in the report of feelings of friendliness and euphoria. The results of the Pliner and Cappell experiment have lent force to the caveat that the impact of drinking will vary as a function of the context in which it occurs. One particular relevant variable along with context can vary is whether the situation is interpersonal or not.

Dosage

Of course, at high doses, alcohol will result in sedation and eventually a coma. The research reviewed in this chapter, examines the impact of alcohol at social drinking level doses, that is, doses yielding a blood alcohol level below .10. Subjects in most experiments were experienced social drinkers. Such subjects could be expected to display some tolerance, but certainly not the tolerance of an alcoholic.

Time of Day

Alcohol has a more profound effect on performance in the morning than in the evening. When consumed in the morning a greater subjective sense of lack of coordination has been observed. Subjects also display greater increases in their reaction times in the morning than at other times during the day (Lawrence, Herbert, & Jeffcoate, 1983).

Expectancy Effects

A more refined approach to the question of how alcohol impacts mood and behavior has been to determine whether any obtained effect is attributable to (a) the pharmacological effect of the drug, or (b) the effect of the belief that one is ingesting alcohol. In order to tease apart the two effects, Marlatt and Rohsenow

(1980) have advocated the use of the balanced placebo design. The balanced placebo design is a two-factor analysis with each factor having two levels represented (2 × 2). One factor is the beverage effect, i.e., whether the alcohol is or is not present in the beverage ingested. The other factor is expectancy factor, whether or not the subject is informed that he/she is drinking. If the behavior of persons who believe they are drinking is more heavily affected, then what people believe they are drinking is the critical factor. If the behavior of those persons who have received real alcohol rather than placebo is more heavily affected, then the pharmacological effect of alcohol becomes critical.

The balanced placebo design requires that those subjects told that they are ingesting alcohol but receiving water, and those subjects told that they are ingesting water but receiving alcohol, are actually deceived. Those procedures that incorporate tasks to distract the subject while the beverage is being absorbed are more successful at creating deception. Despite the fact that most experiments have included manipulation checks, even when the checks affirm a successful manipulation of the factor (suggesting that subjects have believed what they were told about the beverage), there is evidence that the results on the manipulation checks reflects the operation of demand characteristics (Knight, Barbaree, & Boland, 1986). Presently, there is no completely successful procedure for teasing apart the pharmacological from the cognitive impact of drinking. Nevertheless results from the balanced placebo design are probably suggestive of the relative impacts of expectation vs. pharmacology.

Researchers have recognized that being told that one is consuming alcohol will not carry the same meaning for all subjects in the particular condition. Subjects do vary in terms of their individually held expectations regarding the impact of alcohol on behavior. Being sensitive to this issue, some experimenters have measured individual subject's unique expectations for the effect of alcohol and have included subject's personal expectation as a factor in the design (see Crawford, 1984, for a list). This has allowed for a more sensitive assessment of the operation of expectancy on behavior.

Closely related to the impact of expectancy mediated through cognitions is the question of the impact of an alcohol placebo. Research evidence suggests that alcohol and alcohol placebos both elicit conditioned autonomic reactions, which are opposite in direction to the pharmacological effect of alcohol (Newlin, 1984, 1985). These conditioned reactions probably temper the impact of alcohol. Solomon (1980) has proffered the opponent process theory which avers that conditioned responses are of longer duration than the pharmacological impact of alcohol. These conditioned responses, opposite in direction to the pharmacological impact, may be uncomfortable and will stimulate the desire for continued consumption. As yet, most research findings have failed to measure and consider the impact of conditioned responses on the dependent variable under study. Such responses may be more intense for alcoholics than for social and irregular drinkers.

Tolerance

Persons with more prior exposure to alcohol vs. the naive are generally less affected by equivalent doses of alcohol (Tabakoff, 1980). (The explanations for tolerance are presented in Chapter 9.) There are some exceptions, however. Persson, Sjoberg, and Svensson (1980) found that within a social situation, regular drinkers derived more pleasure from consumption. Unfortunately, the Persson et al. (1980) study did not evaluate the pharmacological impact vs. the expectancy impact of alcohol. It may be that inexperienced drinkers anticipated alcohol induced impairment and became anxious when they believed they were drinking. (There are data suggesting that moderate consumers anticipate less impairment than light drinkers, (Leigh, 1989.) If such were the case, capacity for enjoyment might have been reduced through fear of impairment.

There is a phenomenon in the literature that is labeled acute tolerance. It refers to differences in the impact of alcohol on the ascending limb of blood alcohol level vs. the descending limb. The ascending limb occurs as alcohol is accumulating in the blood stream. The descending limb occurs as the blood alcohol level is diminishing after the dose is absorbed from the stomach and while that which is in the blood stream is metabolized. The impact of alcohol on behavior is more intense on the ascending limb as alcohol is being absorbed into the blood stream prior to the time that a significant quantity has been metabolized. Further, the steeper the rate of increase into the blood stream the more dramatic will be the effect on behavior (Connors & Maisto, 1979; Ekman et al., 1964). On the descending limb persons are more likely to be sleepy, fatigued, depressed, and less active. They are more likely to report they are sober despite notable blood alcohol levels (BALs) (Babor et al., 1983; Freed, 1978; Russell & Mehrabian, 1975). Most of the experiments presented in this section have assessed the impact of alcohol on the ascending limb.

Initial State of the Organism

There is evidence suggesting that the state of the organism will determine the effect that alcohol exerts on behavior. Animals and humans in whom anxiety has been induced prior to consumption of alcohol exhibit less alteration in their behavior (Frankenhaeuser et al., 1974; Pohorecky, 1981). Not only do animals who are anxious display less impairment given alcohol, but they more rapidly develop tolerance to the sedating impact of alcohol (Peris & Cunningham, 1987). Findings from single cell research are consistent with the notion that alcohol's effects will vary with the prior state of the organism. At the level of the single cell, initial arousal will determine alcohol's impact on cellular functioning (Pohorecky, 1981).

Having enumerated some of the major moderator variables that alter the impact that alcohol will exert on any given occasion of drinking, discussion now turns to the specific impact that alcohol exerts on specific types of behavior. The discussion begins with a brief examination of the effects on nervous system physiology and then turns to behaviors for which cognitive components play a larger role.

IMPACT ON THE CNS AND PERIPERAL NERVOUS SYSTEM

Electrophysiological readings suggest that the reticular activating system (RAS) is more heavily impacted by alcohol than is the cortex (Blum, 1982; Ho & Allen, 1981). Alcohol decreases discharge from the RAS and dampens the desynchronizing influence the RAS normally exerts on the cortex (Propping, 1978). In terms of electrical events possibly reflecting activity from subcortical areas, there are changes. Generally alpha wave production and slower waves, indicative of enhanced relaxation, are increased (Docter & Bernal, 1964; Docter, Naitoch, & Smith, 1966; Kalant, 1975). At low doses, higher frequency waves indicative of increased arousal have been noted (Kalant, 1975).

Electroencephalogram research suggests that alcohol has a more profound impact on the right side of the brain than the left (Chandler & Parsons, 1977; Rhodes, Obitz, & Creel, 1975). Imbibing subjects display greater decrement in electrical activity on the right as opposed to the left side. Electrical activity accompanying the reaction to visual input is slower in response to input processed on the right side of the brain than on the left side of the brain. Some have attributed the differential impact on the right brain to the more heavy integration of the right brain with the reticular activating system (Rhodes et al., 1975).

There are some caveats that should be stated regarding alcohol's greater impact on the right side of the brain. Although the right brain is differentially impaired on some dependent variables in normals, alcoholics when intoxicated have been found to perform better on viso-spatial tasks, which differentially tap right brain processes, than when sober. This effect has been attributed to a normalizing effect of alcohol on alcoholics. Both alcoholics and their non-alcoholic children display deficits on viso-spatial tasks when sober (Schandler, Cohen, & McArthur, 1988). Alcohol seems to decrease the relative deficits displayed in right brain processing in persons genetically related to alcoholics.

When drinking, sympathetic nervous system activity is increased, i.e., the body appears to be more aroused. Blood pressure increases but returns to baseline levels while alcohol remains in the system (Turkkan, Stitzer, & McCaul, 1988). Heart rate is increased (Dengerink & Fagan, 1978; Farkas & Rosen, 1976; Reed, 1980; Turkkan et al., 1988), although this effect may be confined to those who are family history positives or high MacAndrew scorers (Finn & Pihl, 1987; Levenson, Oyama, & Meek, 1987). Effects on Galvanic skin response have been inconsistent (Dengerink & Fagan, 1978). Cutaneous vasodilation occurs such that skin temperature increases (Turkkan et al., 1988). Core temperature is decreased. Cerebral blood flow is reduced. Peristalsis and gastric secretions are increased (Kalant, 1975).

In addition to direct effects on the nervous system, alcohol also exerts effects on the hormones regulated by the pituitary gland, which are in turn regulated by the hypothalamus. More beta-endorphins and ACTH are produced (Ho & Allen, 1981; Ng Cheong Ton et al., 1983). Urinary catecholamines, possibly suggestive of enhanced arousal somewhere in the body, are elevated (Pohorecky, 1981). Plasma non-esterized fatty acids and plasma cortisone also increase (Pohorecky et al., 1980). Vasopressin, a pituitary hormone that regulates kidney function such that more fluid is retained, is decreased (Stokes, 1982). The effect of decreased vasopressin is increased urination.

MOTOR AND COGNITIVE ACTIVITY

On some measures alcohol impairs functioning. Errors on reaction time tasks are manifested (Vuchinich & Sobell, 1978). Rote learning is impaired (Goodwin, Powell, Bremer, Hoine, & Stern, 1969; Parker, Birnbaum, & Nobel, 1976). Errors on arithmetic tasks are increased (Forney & Hughes, 1965). Generally, the more cognitive processing required to perform the task, the more impaired the performance (Williams, Goldman, & Williams, 1981).

The effects on memory have been inconsistent. Small doses have been found to improve memory (Ekman, et al., 1967). There is recent evidence that if a memory trace is encoded just prior to drinking low dose alcohol, the memory trace will be strengthened (Esposito, Parker, & Weingartner, 1984). Parker et al. (1981) speculate that this effect may be mediated through the brain's dopaminergic and enkephalin reward centers. Whereas low doses of alcohol can improve memory, at moderate doses immediate and short-term memory is impaired (Jones, 1973). Some maintain the data are consistent with an impairment of memory trace consolidation (Parker, Birnbaum, & Nobel, 1976). Both the storage and retrival processes of memory are impaired, and memory search involved in the retrival process is not as efficient (Gerrein & Chechile, 1977).

In drinking individuals, performance on tasks requiring coordination is affected. Performance on hand-eye coordination tasks deteriorates. Nystagmus is induced (Alkana & Malcolm, 1980). Both fine and gross motor activity become less precise (Levine, Kramer, & Levine, 1975; Vuchinich & Sobell, 1978). At low doses alcohol increases muscular strength, but at high doses strength is decreased (Boyatzis, 1983). Muscular activity (tested during resting) as measured by electromyogram lessens (Steffen, Nathan, & Taylor, 1974).

In social contexts, the conversation of drinking persons tends toward more philosophical questions (Kalin, McClelland, & Kahn, 1965). Time seems to pass more quickly (Ehrensing, et al., 1970). On locus of control measures, alcohol enhances the perceived predictability of the world but diminishes perceived controllability (Barling & Bolon, 1981). Alcohol has not been found to exert a change on moral reasoning assessed on Kohlberg type instruments (Graham, Turnbull, & LaRocque, 1979) or on measures of political conservatism (Barling & Fincham, 1979).

There have been attempts to identify the moderator variables influencing alcohol's impact. Some of the impairment on cognitive tasks is attributable to expectancy effects (Vuchinich & Sobell, 1978). Increasing motivation by punishing poor performance or rewarding favorable performance can attenuate alcohol induced impairment (Pohorecky, 1981). Stress created by telling subjects they will be shocked for poor performance can alleviate alcohol induced impairment (Frankenhaeusar et al., 1974), as can other forms of stress (Pohorecky, 1981). Inducing self-consciousness can counter alcohol induced performance decrements (Ross & Pihl, 1988).

INCREASED ACTIVITY

It is a well documented finding in the rat literature, that low dose drinking rats are more active (Carlsson, Engel, & Svensson, 1972; Goldman & Docter, 1966; Frye & Breese, 1981; Pohorecky, Rassi, Weiss, & Michalak, 1980); whereas high doses are sedating (Alkana & Malcolm, 1980).

People also display increased activity after low dose alcohol. On some measures there is evidence that alcohol increases cognitive activity. On cognitive tasks that request a spontaneous production of responses, drinking subjects produce more ideation, although the quality of the ideation is more conventional and not as complex (Kastl, 1969). Subjects requested to provide captions for humorous cartoons, devise more captions when drinking (Young & Pihl, 1982). Subjects requested to construct words from a given set of letters produce more words (Babor et al., 1983). Drinking subjects are able to sustain attention longer on repetitious tasks (Docter et al., 1966). Rapid eye movements in awake subjects, suggestive of accelerated cognitive activity, are increased (Docter & Bernal, 1964; Docter et al., 1966). When drinking occurs in a social context, alcohol increases verbal production (Babor et al., 1983). Impact on flicker fusion threshold is consistent with an excitation response (Parker et al., 1981).

PHYSICAL SENSATIONS

Adesso and Lauerman have developed a sensation scale to assess alterations of perceived internal events (see Connors & Maisto, 1979). The instrument yields six factors: anesthesia (e.g., face numb, relaxed), central stimulation (e.g., light headed, ringing, buzzing), impairment of functioning (e.g., impaired vision, difficulty with thinking), warmth/glow (e.g., cheeks warm, face flush), gastrointestinal alterations (e.g., nausea, stomach growling), and dynamic peripheral (e.g., breathing changes, body rushes). In general, alcohol is more likely to create a change that manifests on this scale when an individual is alone and undistracted by external events. Further, this scale is more subject to the impact of beverage alcohol and less effected by expectancy; whereas the opposite is true for mood (O'Malley & Maisto, 1985).

STRESS RESPONSE

The effects of alcohol on an organism's response to stress are complex. For some people the belief that one has been drinking produces effects that are the same as pharmacological effects. For other people the effects are opposite in direction. Because of the complexity, the discussion is broken into pharmacological effects and expectancy effects. First the pharmacological impact of alcohol on the stress response is explored. The animal literature, in which expectancy effects are not a contaminating factor, and the human data relevant to pharmacological impact are reviewed. Some of the hypotheses as to why pharmacologically, alcohol dampens stress (exerts a stress dampening effect) are examined. Then the expectancy effects are discussed.

Alcohol's Pharmacological Impact on Stress

Animal Literature.   Alcohol's impact on animals as they are exposed to stress has been the focus of numerous investigations. Alcohol has been noted to dampen the impact of stress on physiological variables as well as blocking the behavioral impact of stress. On autonomic nervous system responses (more specifically the sympathetic system), a drinking rat will display less reactivity to stressors. Drinking rats subjected to stress exhibit less increase in urinary catecholamines (Pohorecky, 1981). They display an attenuated increase in the usual rise in plasma cortisone, plasma catecholamines, and non-esterized fatty acids (Brick & Pohorecky, 1982; DeTurck & Vogel, 1982; Pohorecky et al., 1980). They display a diminished startle response (Pohorecky, Cagan, Brick, & Jaffe, 1976). The cardiotoxic impact on chronic stress is abrogated (Pohorecky, 1981).

An approach/avoidance paradigm has been recruited to explore how alcohol affects the behavioral impact of stress. The experimental situation is the following. The rat is first taught to lever press or run a goal box for food reinforcement but then is shocked when making the instrumental response. A sober rat will decrease lever pressing or running down a goal box for food when the rat is punished for the response. It is believed that the rat's anxiety will mediate its decrement in instrumental responding given punishment. Alcohol seems to decrease this anxiety mediated behavior in rats. Drinking animals within an approach avoidance situation will display less decrease in instrumental behavior (Goldman & Docter, 1966; Pohorecky, 1981; Vogel-Sprout, 1967).

Another paradigm in which a type of dysphoria/anxiety is believed to account for a change in behavior is an extinction paradigm. In an extinction paradigm, a rat will quit responding when it no longer receives reinforcement. This decrement in previously reinforced behavior has been attributed to a type of fatigue which sets in. Gray (1978) avers that this fatigue is mediated by neuronal activity in the anxiety centers of the brain. Alcohol does interfere with extinction. Within the context of an extinction paradigm, alcohol retards the process of extinction of conditioned responses (Cappell, LeBlanc, & Endrenyi, 1972).

Human Research

Many findings from the animal literature have been replicated in analogous findings in human functioning. A great deal of research has examined the impact of alcohol on the normal response to stress. As discussed previously, alcohol under baseline conditions has an arousing effect on sympathetic nervous system variables. When assessment is made on the same dependent variables under stress conditions, however, whereas sober subjects display a rapid increase in autonomic activity in response to stress, this increase is attenuated in drinking subjects. Alcohol diminishes the galvanic skin response spike (hand sweating) to a loud aversive noise (Carpenter, 1957; Greenberg & Carpenter, 1957); it decreases responsivity to affect ladden terms such that the usual increase in recognition time is not observed (Coopersmith, 1964); it attenuates the GSR (Galvanic skin response) increase in response to presentation of pictures of mutilated bodies (Garfield & McBrearty, 1970); it attenuates the increase in GSR created by a stress inducing social interaction (McDonnell & Carpenter, 1959); it attenuates the observable anxiety exhibited by the subject while being videotaped (Bradlyn, Strickler, & Maxwell, 1981); it attenuates the increase in heart rate and subjective anxiety displayed by male subjects (undifferentiated as to personality or FHP status) charged with the task of impressing a female confederate or awaiting shock (Levenson, Sher, Grossman, Newman, & Newlin, 1980; Sher & Walitzer, 1986). Alcohol will also decrease vicarious stress response. The rise in GSR displayed by subjects observing another receiving shock is attenuated in imbibing but not placebo subjects (Kilpatrick, Stuker, Best, & Allain, 1980). Additional research suggests that this stress dampening effect will occur at BALs somewhere above .03 (Wilson, Abrams, & Lipscomb, 1980).

In paradigms in which the dependent variable is cognitive functioning, alcohol has been found to attenuate some of the impact of stress. Alcohol reduces the performance decrement manifested by stressed subjects (Korman, Knopf, & Austin, 1960). It also seems to alter the manner in which information is processed. On tasks in which a subject is screening for aversive input, a tachycardia of attention is displayed; whereas when input is less aversive, a bradycardia of attention is exhibited. Drinking subjects are more likely to display bradycardia given a warning light prepatory to stimulus presentation (Lehrer & Taylor, 1974). Others have examined alcohol's capacity to reduce anxiety in snake phobics as they approach the feared object. At a BAL of .04, Rimm et al. (1981) demonstrated that alcohol consumption but not alcohol expectancy reduced subjective fear. In the Rimm et al. experiment, however, the pharmacological effect of alcohol did not alter approach behavior. Contrary to the Rimm et al. finding, Thyer and Curtis (1984) at BAl of .08 found no evidence of fear reduction for phobics on physiological, behavioral, or subjective measures. Thus, the findings regarding alcohol's effect on phobic behavior have not been consistent.

Further qualifications on the stress dampening effect. There are further qualifiers to the stress dampening effect. On heart rate measures, the stress dampening effect of alcohol may be more pronounced in or confined to those at high risk for developing alcoholism by virtue of their family history positive status or their high sensation seeking personalities (Finn & Pihl, 1987).

Theories Regarding Alcohol's Ability to Decrease Anxiety. There are two major hypotheses suggesting why pharmacologically alcohol will dampen the stress response. The first hypothesis avers that alcohol operates at the anxiety centers in the brain, making it more difficult to mount an anxiety response. This is the hypothesis that Gray (1978) has averred. Some recent data emerging from pharmacological research are supportive of this view. Research on particular drugs known to occupy specific neuronal cellular membrane sites has suggested some operation of alcohol at anxiety centers in the brain. It is believed that GABA neurons play an integral role in the production of anxiety. RO 4513 is a ligand (chemical which fits the receptor) for the beta subsites on GABA neurons. RO 4513 decreases the probability of the GABA neurons firing. That is, RO 4513 occupies the same sites as do the benzodiazepines (valium type drugs). Whereas valium type drugs enhance the activity of the GABA neurons, RO 4513 seems to increase rather than decrease anxiety. When rats are placed into an approach avoidance conflict and given alcohol, they fail to display a decrement in instrumental responding. When given RO 4513 and alcohol, the ameliorative impact of the alcohol on instrumental responding is blocked. That is, the rats appear to be anxious. They display the characteristic anxiety response. The conclusion that alcohol has some impact at some subunit of the GABA neuron that influences behavior in an approach avoidance conflict seems to be implied by this findings (Lister & Nutt, 1989). There is a caveat for this conclusion, however. Although the data do suggest that alcohol will interact with GABA neurons in some way, in order to support Gray's view, it must be unequivocally demonstrated that GABA neurons constitute an anxiety center. That is, more information is required to explicate GABA's exact role in the behavioral manifestations of anxiety.

Findings Which Call into Question the View that Alcohol Attentuation of the Stress Response is Mediated Through a Decrease in Anxiety.   In the animal literature, alcohol fails to decrease anxiety mediated behavior when alternative operationalizations of such behavior are employed. A rather complex test of the anxiety reducing hypothesis has called the tension reduction (stress dampening) hypothesis into question. When anxiety is operationalized as a increase in the speed of escape responding given a fear eliciting stimulus, alcohol enhanced rather than decreased the fear response (Cunningham & Brown, 1983). Further, alcohol will retard the extinction of avoidance responses that are presumably mediated by fear (Baum, 1969, 1970, 1971). Thus alcohol fails to decrease fear given diverse operationalizations, calling into question the tension reduction hypothesis. If the tension reducing hypothesis of alcohol's impact is rejected, other explanations for alcohol's effect in conflict situations are available. An intriguing possibility is that the faster running speeds in an approach avoidance paradigm, the closer approach to the goal box, and the lack of suppression of instrumental responding in an approach avoidance paradigm may be attributable to the known excitatory effect of alcohol (Frye & Breese, 1981; Goldman & Docter, 1966).

Human research also suggests that alcohol fails to decrease anxiety responses under all conditions. In contrast to the positive findings suggesting that alcohol dampens the usual response to stress, there is evidence that when shock is certain to occur and definitely anticipated, alcohol increases the rise in GSR and heart rate in response to stress (Dengernick & Fagan, 1978).

An alternative possibility.   The possibility exists that in those experimental situations in which alcohol has been found to decrease anxiety or the response to stress, the effect may be mediated by alcohol's impact on cognitive processing. It is possible that drinking organisms fail to become anxious under stressful situations, because they are less able to process information regarding the stressor. Simply put, they just fail to notice the aversive stimulus. Information processing may also account for the animal data. Perhaps animals fail to respond to punishment in an approach/avoidance situation because they learn less well. Perhaps they fail to decrease behavior in an extinction paradigm because they are less aware of changes in their environment (Pohorecky, 1981). There is an additional experiment in the human literature that supports this view.

Steele and Josephs (1988) compared subjects who either drank alcohol or placebo when anticipating having to deliver an anxiety arousing speech. The dependent measure was subjective anxiety. The critical independent variable was the presence or absence of a distracting task. Drinking subjects who performed the distracting task evidenced decreased anxiety over time. Drinking subjects without the distracting task evidenced increased anxiety over time and enhanced anxiety relative to the control group. Steele and Josephs' (1988) explanation was that alcohol limits attentional capacity. When a person cannot focus on a stressor, he/she does not become anxious. When a drinking person is allowed to focus on the stressor, alcohol enhances the experience of anxiety. This experiment does support the attentional capacity view.

The Impact of Believing You are Drinking on Anxiety.   The issue of expectancy effect on behavior is a complex one because there are many expectations that people hold about alcohol. Whereas alcohol is commonly believed to be an anxiety reducer, most people also believe it will impair performance. Given an experimental context incorporating both anxiety induction and cognitive functioning, preditions regarding the impact of the *belief* that one has imbibed will differ depending upon the particular expectancy that is most salient for the subject. Individuals for whom the stress dampening expectation is salient, should display less subjective anxiety and should improve functioning in an anxiety eliciting performance context. Those for whom the performance impairment expectancy is most salient, should display performance decrements and an increase in subjective anxiety.

In fact, person variables predict which groups will be more heavily effected by the expectation that alcohol will decrease tension and which groups will be more effected by the expectation of impaired performance. It has been documented that inexperienced drinkers are more likely to hold the expectation that alcohol will impair performance (Leigh, 1989). Inexperienced male drinkers and women, as a group more likely to be inexperienced, should be more heavily effected by the expectation that alcohol will impair their performance. In a drinking situation, especially when they are being evaluated, the belief that alcohol has been imbibed should create more anxiety. For experienced drinkers, the expectation that alcohol will allay anxiety should be more salient. For experienced drinkers, the belief that alcohol has been consumed, should decrease their anxiety. In fact, experimental data support these predictions.

The balanced placebo design has been recruited to evaluate the pharmacological vs. the expectancy effect associated with alcohol on stress. Bradlyn et al. (1981) found that both expectancy and the pharmacological properties of alcohol were instrumental in decreasing subjective anxiety as male social drinkers made a videotape which was to be later evaluated. Woolfolk, Abrams, Abrams, and Wilson (1979) found that male subject's belief that alcohol had been consumed decreased female observer ratings of anxiety and inhibition and increased observer ratings of subject's dominance. Wilson and Abrams (1977) also found that belief that alcohol had been consumed, although not the beverage itself, decreased heart rate acceleration in male social drinkers charged with the task of creating a favorable impression on a female confederate.

Logue et al. (1978) measured anxiety as subjects performed various tasks. Alcohol increased the anxiety of subjects as they performed their tasks. A correlation between the belief that performance was impaired and anxiety was noted. Poliy, Schueneman, and Carlson (1976) found that for light social drinkers belief that alcohol was being consumed increased subjective anxiety in the context of a reaction time task. Keane and Lisman (1980) also report no evidence that alcohol reduced anxiety in shy males as they tried to impress a female confederate. These studies then suggested that subjective anxiety is increased in particular groups (shy males and light social drinkers) for whom the performance impairing expectation of alcohol's effect is probably most salient.

Females also seem to display increased anxiety and performance impairment when they believe that they have consumed alcohol. Sutker et al. (1982) found differential expectancy effects for men and women. Given a stressor (being shocked for errors on a word list memory task), women increase in subjective anxiety when they believe they are drinking, whereas for men expectation does not effect the response. Abrams and Wilson (1979) showed an expectancy effect on heart rate acceleration and observer ratings of anxiety, for females. Belief that alcohol had been consumed increased anxiety for the female subjects as they tried to create a favorable impression on a male confederate.

The preceding studies conform fairly well to the hypotheses suggested at the beginning of this section. Inexperienced drinkers, women, shy men probably all hold the belief that alcohol will impair their performance. Given the assumption that they are consuming, their performance should manifest anxiety. Experiments suggest that this is the case. Experienced, male drinkers subscribe more heavily to the tension reduction belief and anticipate less performance impairment from alcohol. Given the assumption that they are consuming, they should manifest less anxiety. This hypothesis has also been supported by the data.

ALCOHOL'S IMPACT ON MOOD

The impact of alcohol on mood can vary as a function of context. In friendly, relaxed, gregarious contexts, anxiety and depression decrease and friendliness, involvement, happiness, and euphoria increase (Pliner & Cappell, 1974; Smith, Parker, & Noble, 1975b). These findings are consistent with animal research which finds that playful activity is increased in primates by drinking (Alkana & Malcolm, 1980). When persons are interacting with a stranger, decreased activity, decreased friendliness, increased depression, increased confusion, and increased fatigue have been reported (Warren & Rayes, 1972).

Findings as to the impact of alcohol on solitary drinkers have not been consistent. Warren and Rayes (1972) found increased dysphoria among those drinking alone. Solitary subjects reading the National Geographic and other magazines have been found to exhibit increases in their subjective levels of social affection, egotism, social affection and surgency (Connors & Maisto, 1979; McCollam et al., 1980). Subjects given alcohol intravenously in a hospital have been found to initially respond with euphoria and energy followed by depression and sleepiness on the descending limb (Hartocollis, 1962).

Some researchers have manipulated mood as an independent variable and then assessed the alcohol's capacity to alter the preexisting mood. Steele, Southwick, and Pagano (1986) induced a negative mood state in their subjects. They manipulated mood by telling subjects that they had performed poorly on an IQ test. Then subjects were given water or alcohol to drink followed by a period of sitting quietly or involvement in an engrossing task. Only the negative mood of the drinking subjects who engaged in the engrossing task was ameliorated. Those subjects who drank without the distracting task did not change, i.e., there was no evidence that the alcohol alone ameliorated their bad mood or that it further enhanced their bad mood. The results of the Steele et al. experiment failed to support the view that alcohol per se will make people feel better. Rather, alcohol ameliorates a bad mood by making it easier to become engrossed in a task. The task then has an opportunity to erase the negative mood.

The results of the Steele, Southwick, and Pagano (1986) study fail to provide support for the notion that alcohol per se will improve a negative mood. Other researchers anticipating that subject variables would influence alcohol's mood altering properties have examined the impact of alcohol on depressed vs. normal persons. Although contrary findings have been reported (Majczakk, cited by Pohorecky, 1981), in some investigations a greater positive change in mood has been noted for depressed as opposed to normal subjects (Mayfield, 1968; Mayfield & Allen, 1967). The Mayfield results suggest that alcohol may have more impact as a mood ameliorator than as an inducer of a good mood. The differential results depending on the subject's initial mood may, however, simply reflect a ceiling effect among normal subjects.

Ward studies investigating ad lib consumption among alcoholics allows for preliminary conclusions on the effect of alcohol consumed continuously over several days duration. Over time, alcohol results in increased irritability, anxiety, and depression (see Pohorecky, 1981).

Summary.   Alcohol's effect on mood is hard to characterize because it varies with the context. In comfortable surroundings, a positive mood is usually induced. However, subjective discomfort is magnified if the context is uncomfortable. The general principle is that alcohol creates greater responsivity to context. For persons in a bad mood initially, alcohol will help them to derive relief from a soothing activity. They too will be more responsive to situational context. For those who binge, alcohol will induce a unique phenomenon always associated with dysphoria, anxiety, and bad feeling.

EVALUATION OF FACIAL EXPRESSIONS

Drawing on the literature suggesting that alcohol impairs a variety of cognitive processing, Tucker and Vuchinich (1983) predicted that alcohol would impair the correct recognition of facial emotions in others. Consistent with the prediction, subjects who had been imbibing (BAL = .05), especially when they believed they had been consuming, were less often correct in labeling the emotion depicted by the expressive faces in photographs. A similar investigation replicated these findings (Borrill, Rosen, & Summerfield, 1987). In the Borrill et al. experiment, males were particularly impaired in their recognition of the expression of anger.

The impairment of ability to discern emotions in others has real world implications. Drinking individuals may lack access to the feedback from others necessary for regulating their behavior in interpersonal situations. A lack of feedback could account for inappropriate responding sometimes found in drinking persons.

IMPACT ON ALTRUISM

An experiment by Steele, Critchlow, and Liu (1985) demonstrated that imbibing subjects will volunteer to complete a larger proportion of a boring task in order to help out an experimenter than will nonimbibing subjects. The results from the balanced placebo design suggested that the effect was attributable to the pharmacological impact rather than the expectancy effect of alcohol. Further, the lack of correlation between mood enhancement and helping suggested that the effect was not mediated through alcohol's enhancement of good mood, which is known to increase altruism.

HUMOR

A number of experiments have demonstrated that drinking persons will display more overt amusement to cartoons (Weaver et al., 1985; Young & Pihl, 1982). Weaver et al. (1985) found that the enhanced amusement was limited to slap stick comedy rather than subtle humor. Further, Weaver et al. found that although subjective amusement rating increased in the alcohol condition, the correlation between amusement as manifested in facial expression and subjective amusement ratings was decreased in the alcohol condition as compared to the sober condition. This latter finding suggested that drinking persons fail to code their emotional responses into overt facial emotional expression as effectively.

Vuchinich, Tucker, and Sobell (1979) investigated a more complex issue regarding alcohol's effect on humor. These researchers examined whether persons drinking alcohol would act similarly to the subjects in the classic Schachter and Singer experiment. In the Schachter and Singer experiment, subjects who were given adrenaline and informed of the effect that the drug would have on their behavior, failed to act in an emotional manner when placed in a humor eliciting situation. Vuchinich et al. (1979) wondered whether subjects who experienced greater arousal after drinking would decide that the alcohol and not the situation had produced the arousal. Perhaps the subject's having the drug alcohol available as an explanation for their merriment would fail to display emotional behavior. In the Vuchinich et al. experiment, some subjects were correctly told that they had received alcohol. Other subjects were given alcohol but told that the beverage they had consumed was a medicine. The impact on the subjects behavior varied according to how the alcohol was labeled. Persons who believed they were drinking alcohol, as opposed to persons drinking alcohol but believing they were ingesting a medicine, rated themselves as more amused by a comedy record and displayed more overt manifestation of amusement.

Apparently, subjects expect alcohol to enhance their reactions and behave in accordance with expectation. Unlike subjects in the Schachter and Singer experiment, drinking subjects acted in an emotional manner even though they had a chemical explanation for their internal feelings. However, when subjects were asked whether the comedy record or the beverage produced their reaction, the subjects who believed they had consumed alcohol attributed their amusement to the alcoholic beverage. In some respects then drinking persons are like Schachter and Singer's subjects: they know their enhanced reaction is caused by the alcohol rather than the stimulus. Unlike the Schachter and Singer subjects, however, their behavior follows their expectation

YIELDING TO INFLUENCE

An Asch paradigm provides a vehicle for exploring yielding to influence. In the Asch paradigm, a subject is seated in a group of experimental stooges. All members of the group are asked for their assessments of the length of a line. The stooges provide inaccurate estimates. The dependent variable is whether or not the subject will amend his/her estimate to conform with the stooge's judgments, thus being influenced by the others in the group. In an Asch paradigm drinking subjects have been found to less often amend their judgments when their judgments fail to correspond with the judgments of others in the group (Bostrom & White, 1979; Smith, 1974). However, in other contexts, drinking seems to increase willingness to yield. Some have arranged the Asch paradigm so that male college students subjects discuss with female college students partners (the stooges) their judgments about the length of a line. Under these conditions, the male students more often yield to the judgment of the female partners when they have been drinking alcohol vs. placebo (Gustafson, 1988). Perhaps it is not just suggestibility that is being measured here.

An experiment by Lubin (1977) in which subjects were given feedback on their performance and were then asked for a self-evaluation, suggested that the drinking subjects relied more heavily on the external feedback in formulating their own evaluations.

The data are mixed as to whether people become more or less susceptible to influence when drinking. It may be that yielding to influence is determined by a number of situational variables. Sometimes faith in one's own ability is measured in the particular experimental context. Sometimes desire to affiliate and respond congenially is being measured. Sometimes a desire to avoid exerting the thinking effort required to make a judgment is being measured. These diverse factors may all interact to determine whether an individual will yield to influence. Alcohol may fail to influence these diverse factors in the same way. Hence lack of consistency in yielding to influence can be expected across various situational contexts.

RISK TAKING

As would be predicted from the behavior of cocktail waitresses at Las Vegas, alcohol does increase risk taking. In a procedure in which subjects are asked to place bets on outcomes with varying probabilities of success, a curvilinear association with alcohol was found. At high dose (BAL = .67) subjects are less risky. At a low dose (BAL = .42), they are more risky (Sjoberg, 1969). Goodwin, Powell, and Stern (1971) assessed risk taking defined as reaction time for committing self to an incorrect answer vs. reaction time for committing self to a correct answer. (They assumed that on incorrectly answered questions subjects should be less certain and therefore these responses should take more time in order to reduce risk.) Results suggested that subjects consuming a low dose of alcohol were more risky, that is they took less time to commit to a wrong answer. Teger, Katlin, and Pruitt (1969) found that subjects with BALs at .08 asked to recommend a course of action to a business, recommended the more risky ventures. Increased risk taking has been demonstrated in yet another situation. On a driving simulation task, the subject's belief that he/she has been drinking increases the frequency of passing other drivers and the duration of high speed driving (McMillen & Wells-Parker, 1987) especially among those who are high sensation seekers (McMillen et al., 1989).

Data support the case that alcohol will increase risk taking.

SMOKING

Observations of social drinkers (Mello, Mendelson, & Palmieri, 1987; Mintz et al., 1985) and observations of alcoholics on ad lib drinking schedules on a hospital ward (Griffiths, Bigelow, & Liebson, 1976) both indicate that cigarette consumption increases in drinking subjects. Puffs are faster and those puffs that are taken are stronger (Mintz et al., 1985). The alcohol induced increase in smoking is more pronounced in alcoholics than in social drinkers (Henningfield, Chait, & Griffiths, 1984).

PAIN PERCEPTION

Subject variables predict the impact of alcohol on pain perception at low doses. Those whose pain is reduced by alcohol endorse the belief that alcohol helps to forget problems, alcohol enhances self-satisfaction, and alcohol improves self-confidence (Cutter, Jones, Maloof, & Kurtz, 1979). Cutter, Maloof, Kurtz, and Jones (1976) found that alcoholics displayed attenuated responses to a cold pressor test when imbibing alcohol whereas normals did not. Brown and Cutter (1977) found that reduced pain perception given alcohol was associated with a pattern of barroom drinking, larger typical consumption levels, and greater frequency of drinking.

Further work by Cutter and O'Farrell (1987) suggests that for those who hold positive expectancies for alcohol, both alcohol and alcohol placebo will reduce pain perception. Cutter and O'Farrell (1987) speculate that diminished pain may be a conditioned opponent process response. These authors demonstrated that the diminished pain perception can be blocked by naloxone.

SELF-CONSCIOUSNESS

Hull (1981) has argued that alcohol will reduce self-consciousness. Hull begins his argument by referencing alcohol's impact on cognitive processing: Alcohol does interfere with higher order cognitive processing. Encoding information about the self is a higher order cognitive process that should be vitiated by the consumption of alcohol. Hull adduces evidence in support of alcohol's reduction of self-consciousness.

Hull, Levenson, Young, and Sher (1983) demonstrated that drinking subjects vs. subjects who had consumed an alcohol placebo acted in what might be construed as a less self-conscious manner. Drinking subjects in the context of giving a speech about "what I like and dislike about my body" used fewer first person pronouns and exhibited a diminished frequency of self-focused statements.

Hull, Levenson, Young, and Sher (1983) also demonstrated that alcohol would alter the behavior of trait highly self-conscious individuals to be more like the behavior of trait low self-conscious individuals. In their experiment, high self-conscious types and low self-conscious types were examined when drinking alcohol and when drinking alcohol placebo. The dependent measure was an operationalization of self-consciousness, recall of self-relevant word. All subjects were given the task of rating adjectives along particular dimensions. Later, subjects were tested to determine their memory for self-descriptive adjectives vs. non-self-relevant adjectives. The prediction was that the low self-conscious would never display a penchant for recall of self-relevant adjectives. High self-conscious individuals, would recall more self-relevant adjectives, unless their self-consciousness had been erased by drinking. The results of the experiment were hypothesis consistent. The memory for self-descriptive words of the low self-conscious did not vary in terms of whether they were imbibing. The recall of self-relevant words of the low self-conscious individuals was lower relative to high self-conscious, sober individuals. However, the high self-conscious, drinking individuals did not differ from the low self-conscious when imbibing. That is, the personality differences were washed out by the alcohol.

Hull has argued that many of the other findings specific to how alcohol impacts behavior may be a function of decreased self-consciousness. It is known that when people become less self-focused, their inhibitions are reduced. Their values exert less force over their behavior. Perhaps the disinhibition observed in drinking subjects (which will be further discussed during the discussion of the impact of alcohol on aggression and deviant sexual arousal) is attributable to reduced self-consciousness.

There has been controversy in the literature over the issue of whether alcohol decreases attention to the self. A reduction in self-consciousness has not been demonstrated in women (Wilson et al., 1989). Wilson (1983) has cited failures to replicate the finding that drinking subjects are less self-conscious as evidenced by their use of first person pronouns and ratio of self-referenced statements to other verbal productions (see Frankenstein & Wilson, 1984). Hull and Reilly (1983) have countered that there were too many self-referential cues present in the experimental situation in the Frankenstein and Wilson experiment thus precluding differences between conditions. However, Hull does not address why his original experiment (Hull, Levenson, Young, & Sher, 1983) in which subjects were asked to make a speech about their bodies did not furnish an equivalent degree of self-referential cues. Much of the controversy may be a function of the fact that a particular operationalization may vary across experimental procedures in terms of what underlying construct is being measured. Depending upon the context, increased self-reference could reflect diminished self-consciousness. It could also reflect a release from the inhibition of concern not to appear conceited or self-indulgent. Self-focused attention (self-consciousness) seems to be a difficult construct to measure. Firm conclusions are not yet available. Hopefully, future experiments will endeavor to find better ways to measure self-consciousness.

COGNITIVE DISSONANCE

When people are induced to make positive statements about something they hate, they are moved to a more positive view (attitude) on the subject. The explanation is that when a person voluntarily chooses to say something positive about that which he/she hates, a bad feeling is experienced. One way for the person to erase the bad feeling is to decide that he/she held a positive view all along. Maybe, on second thought, the object of derision was not so bad. Thus a change in attitude is realized. The cognitive dissonance refers to the bad feeling that promotes the change.

An experiment by Steele, Southwick, and Critchlow (1981) demonstrated that drinking subjects fail to display dissonance induced attitude change. Whereas this is a fairly esoteric topic for most people, cognitive dissonance has significance for clinicians. In the chapter on relapse prevention, the importance of the role played by cognitive dissonance in accounting for continuation of a relapse was discussed. Knowledge of the impact of alcohol on cognitive dissonance is therefore important.

Persons concerned about cognitive dissonance theory will be interested in the explanations proffered for why alcohol inhibits cognitive dissonance changes. Steele et al. speculated regarding possible explanations for alcohol's blocking of cognitive dissonance attitude change. They decided that the evidence was against a general arousal of positive energy as positive energy does not correlate with decreased dissonance change generally. They ruled out a misattribution explanation. (Misattribution occurs when the arousal is attributed to the chemical so that the subject ignores the arousal. As such there is no pressure for the subject to change.) Steele et al. cited an experiment in which coffee was substituted for alcohol. The coffee similarly allowed an opportunity for misattribution. The coffee, however, did not erase cognitive dissonance attitude change effects. Therefore, a misattribution mediator of alcohol's impact on cognitive dissonance was discounted by the authors. The authors, through a process of elimination of potential explanations, suggested that alcohol might vitiate dissonance induced change by reducing tension. Another explanation which the authors failed to consider is that alcohol interferes with cognitive dissonance, by virtue of its reduction of self-consciousness (that is, objective self-awareness). The cognitive dissonance literature suggests that some degree of objective self-awareness may be required for dissonance change to occur (Laird et al., 1982). Perhaps the reduction in self-consciousness/objective self-awareness is the explanation for alcohol's interference with cognitive dissonance.

VOLUBILITY/SELF-DISCLOSURE/FREEDOM OF EXPRESSION

As discussed in the sections on impact on activity level and impact of cognitive activity, a number of investigations have found that people talk more when drinking (Frankenstein & Wilson, 1984; Kalin, McClelland, & Kahn, 1965). Drinking subjects are more likely to make a contribution to posters full of graffiti (Korytnyk & Perkins, 1983). In cocktail party contexts, they are more likely to expound on philosophical concerns and to increase sexual references (Kalin et al., 1965). The depth of intimacy of the information disclosed increases (Rohrberg,

Sousa, & Poza, 1976; Wilson, Abrams, & Lipscomb, 1980). In the context of a cooperative tasks, negative remarks to a partner increase (Young & Pihl, 1982).

Caudill, Wilson, and Abrams (1987) evaluated expectancy effects as well as pharmacological impact of alcohol. For men, low dose alcohol (BAL = .03) increased self-disclosure, as did belief that self and partner were imbibing. Although Caudill et al. did not evaluate the pharmacological impact of alcohol on women, they did find that for women, the belief that alcohol had been consumed decreased self-disclosure. Again, women are observed to be effected differently by the belief that alcohol has been consumed.

SELF-EVALUATION

A rather elaborate experiment by Yankofsky, Wilson, Adler, Hay, and Vrana (1986) suggested that individuals when drinking are more charitable in their self-evaluations and place a great deal of confidence in these self- evaluations. These researchers instructed male subjects to interact with a female confederate (an experimenter stooge) with the goal of creating a favorable impression. A balanced placebo design was employed. The researchers arranged the situation to be maximally discouraging for their male subjects. In all conditions, the female confederate appeared bored and aloof during the interaction. The results suggested that although the drinking subjects noticed that the confederate appeared aloof, they did not conclude, as did the sober subjects, that the confederate had responded to them unfavorably. (This was a pharmacological effect.) The drinking subjects and those who believed they had consumed alcohol rated their interaction more favorably. Also, during observation of a videotape of their performance, although the drinking subjects stopped the tape to indicate evaluative comments as frequently as sober subjects, drinking subjects more often made favorable evaluative comments when stopping the tape. On a measure tapping confidence in their judgments, the drinking subjects seemed more self-assured. Drinking subjects were more often willing to engage in a subsequent interaction with the confederate in which they were to stake money on their ability to impress the confederate.

Other research supports the view that drinking subjects will be more charitable in their self-evaluations. Wilson et al. (1989) found that alcohol increased belief that one would be able to behave in a positive manner (self-efficacy) in a situation requiring assertion in women. Berg (1971) demonstrated that the discrepancy between self and ideal self-concept is reduced when alcoholics are drinking. When asked for to complete a Q-sort measure while under the influence alcoholics indicate that they are more clever, clear thinking, and outspoken. Lang, Verret, and Watt (1984) examined alcohol's impact on social drinking males. They used a balanced placebo design. Subjects were given the Torrence test of

Creative Thinking and then asked to evaluate their performance. Those subjects who believed they had imbibed rated their creativity more favorably, although actual performance did not differ among the cells. Whereas those subjects who believed they were drinking evaluated their product more favorably, they did not take more personal credit for the production. Those subjects who believed they had imbibed more often attributed their performance to luck rather than to ability.

An experiment by Keane and Lisman (1980) yielded some contrary findings on the issue of whether people when drinking will be more charitable towards themselves. Keane and Lisman (1980) recruited shy subjects for a dating skills training session. The procedure called for subjects to imbibe or not depending upon condition, before interacting with a female confederate. Results indicated that the imbibing subjects evinced more negative self-statements during the task. Although this result could be interpreted as increased negative self-evaluation when drinking, Hull (1983) has argued that it reflects increased self-disclosure, i.e., willingness to admit to negative self-statements.

Konovsky and Wilsnack (1982) observed couples in a contrived party type atmosphere. For males, drinking improved self-satisfaction as assessed by the Tennessee Self-Concept scale. Women, particularly those endorsing traditional sex roles, evidenced a decrease in self-esteem when drinking.

The preceding experiments suggest that both belief that one is drinking and the pharmacological effect of drinking can enhance self-evaluation. The effect may be limited to males. Women, who possibly anticipate that alcohol will impair their performance, can display increased negativity regarding themselves after drinking.

SEX

Animal Literature

The bottom line from the animal literature is that alcohol decreases performance although interest is not diminished. Alcohol, at doses insufficient to impair motor behavior, has been found to decrease copulatory behavior in male rats (Dewsbury, 1967) and decrease lordosis response in female rats (Merari et al., 1973). Latency to erection is increased and the duration of erection is decreased (Teitelbaum & Gantt, 1958). An attenuation of sexual interest has not been found to accompany diminished responding (Alkana & Malcolm, 1980; Carpenter & Armenti, 1972). Some have investigated the physiological basis for the diminished sexual response. Impairment of spinal cord reflexes rather than events mediated through higher cortical structures seems to underlie the diminished sexual response (Hart, 1969; Merari et al., 1973). Whereas most of the effects of alcohol on animal sexual responses are depressing, for neurotic dogs, alcohol enhances erection relative to baseline levels (Carpenter & Armenti, 1972).

Human Literature

Response to Nondeviant Stimuli.   Both sexes believe that alcohol will enhance sexual arousal (Briddel et al., 1978; Crowe & George, 1989). This expectation is reflected in the sexual responses of subjects who imbibe an alcohol placebo. Males drinking an alcohol placebo display greater penile tumescence when exposed to arousing material (Wilson & Lawson, 1976a). Although greater sexual arousal on physical measures was not demonstrated in response to heterosexual material in women drinking alcohol placebo, there was a positive association between female subject's subjective perception of intoxication and subjective measures of arousal after exposure to arousing material (Wilson & Lawson, 1978).

On measures of subjective arousal, beverage alcohol, in some experiments not disguised as to content, has been shown to increase sexual responsivity. Generally, drinking males perceive themselves as more sexually aroused and outwardly behave that way. Kalin et al. (1965), whose subjects were aware that they were drinking, found that sexual references on TAT cards increased among drinking subjects. McCarty, Diamond, and Kaye (1982) found that beverage alcohol, especially when subjects were unaware they were consuming, increased subjects' appraisal of the arousal value of erotic slides.

Whereas the preceding discussion focused on alcohol's impact on subjective arousal, there is also data on alcohol's impact on physiological sexual responses. At low doses of alcohol, physiological findings conform to subjective perceptions. There is some increase in penile tumescence in males exhibiting BALs lower than .025 (Farkas & Rosen, 1976). At higher levels of alcohol consumption, sexual physiological responding is diminished. Experiments have been conducted measuring males penile tumescence as they are exposed to erotic material following ingestion of alcohol. Above BAL of .025 there is a linear decline in amplitude of erection, reaction time of response, and duration of response (Briddel & Wilson, 1976; Farkas & Rosen, 1976; Rubin & Henson, 1976). Similar findings are available for women. Imbibing women experience less vaginal blood while viewing erotic films (Wilson & Lawson, 1976b, 1978). For both sexes then, the pharmacological effect of high to moderate doses of alcohol is a decrease in physical signs of sexual arousal.

Whereas alcohol seems to be a depressor of physiological sexual arousal, drinking persons also have less control over their responding. Drinking males who are requested to suppress their erections while listening to an arousing tape are less effective at doing so (Rubin & Henson, 1976; Wilson & Niaura, 1984).

Response to Deviant Material

Statistics indicate that 30–50% of all rapes are committed by persons who are under the influence (Barbaree et al ,1983; Rada,1975). These statistical associations have prompted investigations into how alcohol increases deviant sexual behavior. One area of investigation has pursued the issue of whether increased deviant sexual behavior occurs because pharmacologically alcohol is disinhibiting or because the belief that alcohol has been consumed provides an excuse for disinhibition.

Most of the experimental literature supports the view that belief that alcohol has been consumed is sufficient to increase deviant responding (see Crowe & George, 1989, for a more complete review). Several investigations have found that the belief that one has imbibed will increase response to deviant scenes. An effect of the pharmacological impact of alcohol on increasing arousal to deviant material has received equivocal support. Wilson & Lawson (1976a) found that belief that alcohol was consumed, but not the beverage itself, increased penile tumescence in response to homosexual scenes. Briddell et al. (1978) found that belief that alcohol was consumed, particularly when the beverage consumed *was* alcohol, increased penile tumescence in response to rape scenes (Briddell et al., 1978). Further, in the Briddell et al. investigation, subjects were requested to produce an erection without benefit of an erotic tape. Those subjects who believed they had imbibed more often fantasized the rape scene material to which they had been previously exposed to produce the erection. Others have shown that the belief that alcohol has been consumed will increase interest in deviant material. Subjects of George and Marlatt (1986) who believed they had imbibed alcohol displayed an increase in the time spent viewing erotic and violent/erotic slides. The support for an expectancy effect increasing sexual response to deviant material has been found in both sexes. In women subjects, Wilson and Lawson (1978) supported an expectancy effect (the belief that one has imbibed) for arousal to homosexual material.

The expectancy effect findings suggest that alcohol may increase sexual arousal to deviant material by providing people with an excuse for their behavior such that they are willing to engage in what they might regard as negative behavior. Lang, Searles, Lauerman, and Adesso (1980) advanced further support for this hypothesis in finding that believing alcohol had been consumed affected the behavior of males high in sex guilt (those for whom an excuse might influence behavior) but not those low in sex guilt (those who do not need an excuse). Those high in sex guilt viewed an erotic slide longer and rated it as more stimulating and as less pornographic when they believed they had ingested alcohol.

Lansky and Wilson (1981) attempted to identify the mediator through which the belief that alcohol had been imbibed increases arousal. They reasoned that perhaps knowing that alcohol has been imbibed would free subjects to attend more to the stimulus and the enhanced attention would then redound in greater arousal. They found no support for the notion that increased attention to the stimulus is responsible for the enhanced arousal.

Summary

Alcohol does influence sexual behavior. Both sexes believe that alcohol will enhance their sexual response. Drinking an alcohol placebo has been found to increase sexual responsiveness to erotic, nondeviant material. Actual drinking does increase interest in sexual material, however the physical response is attenuated. The impact of alcohol on deviant sexual material requires an elaborate explanation. Belief that alcohol has been consumed does increase sexual interest and response to deviant material. The effect seems to occur because alcohol provides people with an excuse for their behavior.

AGGRESSION

Animal Literature

The animal literature provides a complex picture of alcohol's impact on aggression. Miczek and Thompson (1983) draw attention to the problem of definition of aggression when referring to animal behavior. Whereas behavior must be intended to inflict pain to satisfy the criteria for human aggression (Carpenter & Armenti, 1973), intent is not a relevant consideration for animal aggression. Animal aggression is more instinctual, i.e., it is elicited by specific stimuli and proceeds according to a patterned sequence. The function of the sequence is probably both communicative as well as destructive.

A study by MacDonnell and Ehmer (1969) suggests that alcohol enhances the magnitude of provoked aggressive responses in animals, although not necessarily impacting the threshold for the responses. MacDonnell and Ehmer (1969) aroused anger in cats by electrically stimulating their hypothalamuses. Animals that were pretreated with alcohol differed from those that had not been pretreated, in that the former required more stimulation for display of aggressive behavior, took longer to complete the attack, but bit other animals with greater force. Other studies have been less exact in separating whether threshold for eliciting the response or magnitude of the response is being measured. Alcohol has been found to increase stress induced (foot shock or forced isolation) fighting (Alkana & Malcolm, 1980). A low dose of alcohol has been found to increase frequency of attack in isolated mice, and increases frequency of territorial attacks in fish (Miczek & Thompson, 1983). Further, the usual decrease in aggression displayed by rats in unfamiliar cages, does not occur when the rat has been drinking (Miczek & Thompson, 1983). It should be noted that the previously cited studies pertain to the impact of low dose alcohol. At high doses, alcohol decreases all activity including aggressive displays, probably due to its sedating effects (Alkana & Malcolm, 1980).

Whereas the studies reporting an increase in aggression given low dose alcohol have observed behavior in response to a stimulus, a decrease in aggression has been noted under particular baseline conditions. For example, rooster aggression toward chicks is decreased (Alkana & Malcolm, 1980). As with humans, alcohol affects the behavior of targets of aggression as well as the behavior of the aggressor. A subordinate, alcohol-fed rat will more often be attacked by a dominant, sober rat (Miczek & Thompson, 1983).

Human Data

Crime Statistics

Statistics suggest that alcohol is associated with aggression. Sixty percent of murders and comparably high levels of assault, robbery, and domestic violence are committed by intoxicated individuals (Spieker, 1983). Between 58 to 72% of incarcerated persons report having imbibed at the time of the perpetration of the crime (Mayfield, 1976; Shupe, 1954). Fifty percent of a sample of rapes were committed by an intoxicated perpetrator (Rada, 1975). Forty-four percent of self-injury incidents are committed by drinking persons (Frankel, Ferrence, Johnson, & Whitehead, 1976). Not only are acts of violence often perpetrated by drinking persons, but victims of violence are also likely to have been drinking. Across studies between 19 to 66% of victims of violence have been found to have been intoxicated at the time of the event (Spieker, 1983).

More refinement of these general population statistics are provided by investigations of the association of drinking and violence within particular groups. The relationship between alcohol consumption and violent crime occurs for those who are acute consumers. Chronic heavy alcohol consumption is not correlated with commission of violent crimes in criminal populations (Collins & Schlenger, 1988). When intoxication in a family member is heavy and almost continual, the probability of violence is no longer high (Coleman & Strauss, 1983). The relationship between alcohol and family violence is stronger in blue collar than in white collar families (Coleman & Strauss, 1983). The finding of intoxication at the time of crime commission is most likely among young, poorly educated, and unemployed (Spieker, 1983). These statistics suggest that whether drinking results in violence will be greatly influenced by the particular subgroup norms and attitudes governing drunken comportment within particular contexts (Levinson, 1983).

Controlled Observations

Investigators have assessed alcohol's impact on hostile expression in informal conversation, in role plays, or in response to TAT cards. Kruetzer, Schneider, and Myatt (1984) found that both beverage alcohol and the belief that alcohol was being imbibed increased hostile expression during a role play. Alcohol also resulted in more profanity. An increase in sexual and aggressive responses to TAT card responses has been noted (Babor et al., 1983; Kalin, McClelland, & Kahn, 1965). Takala (cited by Carpenter & Armenti, 1972) found an increase in aggressive reference among the drinking engaged in discussion groups. Hostile interruptions during discussions are increased in those who are drinking as well (Babor et al., 1983). Observation of subjects engaged in competitive games in a barroom atmosphere suggests that alcohol levels below a BAL of .10 increases aggressive expression (Boyatzis, 1974). A field experiment in which persons were observed in a barroom type atmosphere indicated that increased aggressive expression may be particular to certain individuals. Boyatzis (1975) found that low scorers on a measure of social integration were most likely to display aggression while drinking as they played a competitive game in a bar.

Whereas the above studies examined aggression as it might occur under real world circumstances, other researchers have examined aggression given a contrived situation in which an aggressive response is required by the researchers. The laboratory procedure has prompted aggression. The researchers have asked whether alcohol will increase the magnitude of the experimenter demanded aggressive response. Many of these studies have attempted to tease apart expectancy effects from pharmacological effects. An expectancy effect could suggest that alcohol increases aggression by providing an excuse. An excuse could eradicate the inhibiting impact of anticipated guilt. Alcohol could be blamed for the aggression, rather than the self. Hence, the belief that the excuse is available would be sufficient to release aggression. In contrast to an expectancy effect, some pharmacological feature of the alcohol might increase aggression. Finding that consumption of alcohol, regardless of what the subject believed he/she had consumed increases aggression, would suggest that some pharmacological feature of alcohol mediated the increased aggression.

Evidence for Pharmacological Effects

In the lab, alcohol has been demonstrated to increase aggression on a variety of measures. The typical laboratory paradigm has engaged subjects in competitive tasks in which there is a series of trials. On each trial the winner is allowed to determine the magnitude of an aversive consequence for his partner. Across experiments, researchers have used shock, an aversive noise, or subtracting money from a partner's earnings as the method for measuring aggression (the dependent variable). In shock paradigms, the experimenters have examined both the intensity level and duration of the shock.

Studies in which a drinking subject has been in competition with a partner have found that beverage alcohol will increase aggression. Shuntich and Taylor (1972) and Taylor, Schmutte, and Leonard (1977) found that consuming alcohol as opposed to placebo, resulted in a subject's selection of a higher level of shock for a partner. Bond and Lader (1986) reported similar results when the dependent variable was the level of noise selected to annoy the partner. Cherek, Steinberg, & Manno (1985) allowed subjects a choice of neutral responding, aggression in the form of subtracting money from a partner's earning, or aggression in the form of delivery of an aversive noise. Drinking subjects relative to placebo subjects subtracted more money but did not deliver more aversive noise. The results of these three studies suggest that the pharmacological component of alcohol does increase aggression. A further qualifier was provided by an experiment by Taylor and Gammon (1975) in which it was demonstrated that low dose alcohol (1 drink) decreases aggression, but 3 drinks will increase it.

the aversive tone was related to their prior behavior and when it was randomly determined. A similar experiment by Taylor and Gammon (1976) produced evidence that drinking subjects, although responsive to the behavior of the confederate opponent, are not as responsive as sober subjects.

In a study by Zeichner and Pihl (1980) the partner in the experiment was either particularly nasty, setting very high aversive tones for the subject, or tone values were set by the experimenter thus depriving the subject of information regarding the intent of his/her opponent. (The actual tone intensity experienced by the subjects did not vary between conditions.) Both sober subjects and drinking subjects responded by increasing the intensity of the shock delivered when the confederate was particularly nasty of his own volition. However, the differential was greater for the sober subjects. The sober subjects in contrast to the drinking subjects were much more responsive to the information provided in the situation. There was also evidence in this experiment that drinking subjects are less able to modulate their behavior in response to the behavior of an opponent even when they might have made a cognitive decision to do so. Whereas the drinking subjects were differentially responsive on the variable of shock setting selected for the opponent as a function of whether the opponent was volitionally nasty, no difference on duration of suppression of shock button were obtained between the two conditions. Depressing the shock button is probably a difficult response to regulate when drinking.

Zeichner, Pihl, Niaura, and Zacchia (1982) sought to further investigate how a drinking subject's attention to his/her opponent might mediate his/her enhanced aggression. Zeichner et al. (1982) manipulated subjects' attention to the pain of the victim. Some subjects drank alcohol whereas other received placebo. Some subjects were instructed to record the level of pain experienced by the victim during the course of the experiment. Other subjects were purposefully distracted from attending to the victim by working on math problems in between trials. On the dependent variable of shock intensity levels, there were no differences among any of the conditions. On the variable of shock duration, no difference was found in the behavior of those who drank alcohol vs. placebo. All subjects provided more shock (longer duration but not greater intensity of shock) when they were forced to attend. This experiment was difficult to interpret. It may be that forcing subjects to record their partners level of pain frustrated them. This frustration may have been manifested in sloppier responding as evidenced by their depression of the shock button, although not in a purposeful choice to aggress, which would have been manifested on their selection of a higher level of shock intensity.

Although the Taylor and Gammon (1976) study, and the Zeichner and Pihl studies (1979, 1980) suggest that subjects who are under the influence are not as sensitive in their behavioral response to changes in the behavior of their competitors, there is experimental data that at the grosser extremes, even drinking subjects will respond according to the situation when the situational cues are strong. A study by Taylor, Schmutte, Leonard, and Cranston (1979) demonstrated that gross differences in the behavior of the partner will be differentially responded to by drinking individuals. Taylor, Schmutte, Leonard, and Cranston (1979) compared the behavior of (1) a drinking subject whose partner was particularly nasty (shock values set by the partner were of the highest intensity), (2) a drinking subject whose partner set medium shock values, and (3) a sober subject responding to a particularly nasty opponent. The drinking subjects on shock intensity did respond differentially when the opponent was particularly malicious. A study by Taylor and Gammon (1976) examined whether subjects under the influence would respond to advice from an observer-advisor to be lenient toward the target of aggression. The drinking subjects did respond to the pleas for leniency.

The bottom lines on this series of experiments does support the view that alcohol, the beverage, increases aggression through its impairment of cognitive processing. Drinking subjects respond only to the manifest aspects of the situation. They fail to account for intention in the behavior of a competitor. They are less able to regulate their motoric responses.

A Caveat

Although there are data suggesting that pharmacologically, alcohol may increase aggression through its effect on information processing, other explanations have been proffered as well. Cicero (1983) discusses hormonal explanations that might account for alcohol's increase in both sex and aggression. Alcohol does have definite impact on the hypothalamus, pituitary, adrenal, and gonadal hormones. Some of the effects are not linear. For example, testosterone is initially decreased and then followed by a short-term rebound. Further, nicotine, likely to be consumed concomitant with alcohol also, impacts hormones. Thus predictions are difficult to make regarding alcohol's precise effect on hormone levels. Further complicating the issue is the fact that clear relationships between particular hormonal levels and sex and aggression have not been established. Although hormonal effects probably contribute to alcohol's effects on sex and aggression, mechanisms have yet to be articulated and substantiated. There is no doubt, however, that such effects exist.

Interest in and Response to Aggressive Material. Beyond the situations that have been reviewed, alcohol can also increase interest in aggressive material among those who harbor latent hostility. Hetherington and Wray (1964) presented college students who had been assessed on need for aggression and need for approval with a series of cartoons either of a nonaggressive nature or a hostile nature. Half the subjects were given enough alcohol to attain BALs around .035. Others consumed 7-up. No instruction regarding beverage content was provided. Subjects were then requested to rate the amusement value of each cartoon. Drinking increased the humor ratings for all cartoons. However, there was a differential response for particular subjects to the hostile cartoons. Those subjects both high in need for aggression and high in need for approval, found the hostile cartoons more humorous after imbibing. Apparently, among those subjects who were inhibiting a need to display aggression, (as evidenced by their high need for social support) alcohol changed their behavior.

Expectancy Effects on Aggression

Support for expectancy, i.e., increased aggression due to believing one has consumed alcohol, has also been reported (Lang, Goeckner, Adesso, & Marlatt, 1975; Pihl, Zeichner, Niaura, Nagy, and Zacchia, 1981; Zeichner & Pihl, 1980). Interestingly, in the Lang et al. (1975) experiment, expectation of drinking resulted in increased aggression toward a nonprovocative learner who was not in a competitive role. There has been support for the belief that one has consumed increasing aggression in an assertion task (Kreutzer, et al., 1984) and on selection of shock intensity (Lang et al., 1975; Zeichner & Pihl, 1980) and duration of shock (Lang et al., 1975).

George and Marlatt (1986) employed a balanced placebo design and examined the impact on attention to violent material. Neither the belief that alcohol had been consumed nor the pharmacological impact of the alcohol increased time spent viewing non-sexual violent material. Alcohol expectancy did effect time viewing the sexually violent material, however. Belief of consumption increased the time spent viewing rape scenes.

There is also suggestion that the belief that one has consumed alcohol may result in a decrease in aggression on some measures. Rohsenow and Bachorowski (1984) arranged for subjects to receive a negative evaluation on their personality from a partner who was to then be evaluated by the subject. Those subjects who believed they had consumed alcohol were more charitable than those who believed they were consuming water. The increased charitability seemed to be confined to those subjects who expected alcohol to increase happiness.

Summary

The pharmacological impact of alcohol will increase aggression. There are qualifications to this statement. The increased aggression occurs after provocation. It is most likely to be observed on measures that tap a loss of modulation in self-control. Drinking individuals are not necessarily more acrimonious toward the targets of their aggression. Rather than making people mean, alcohol seems to disrupt information processing. Because information processing is impaired, drinking individuals are less likely to consider mitigating circumstances and to modulate their behavior in response to the intention of a provoker.

Belief that one has consumed, can also increase aggression. Unfortunately, experiments have not investigated whether the permission giving effect is more likely to impact those who harbor a great deal of hostility but who under ordinary conditions restrain their aggression. Competing expectancies for alcohol's effect on aggressive behavior exist. Research also suggests that expectancies can lead to less verbal aggression as well. The expectation that alcohol will create a rosy glow on the world is commonly held. Among those who hold this expectation, belief that alcohol has been consumed seems to engender more charitable behavior toward others under some circumstances.

PATHOLOGICAL INTOXICATION

This discussion has pertained to the effect of alcohol on aggression at BALs around .100. The DSM-III identifies a condition referred to as pathological intoxication. Pathological intoxication constitutes a discontinuous, distinct response to alcohol: a phenomenon in its own right. Maletsky (1976, p. 1227) suggests the following description: "An acute brain syndrome manifested by psychotic behavior after alcohol intake, and characterized by delusions, hallucinations, disorientation with or without inappropriate expressions of rage, prolonged sleep following the episode, and amnesia for the episode thereafter."

Demonstrations of the viability of the phenomenon have been attempted. Bach-y-Rita, Lion, and Ervin (1970) selected subjects with a history of violent behavior while under the influence. He failed to elicit the phenomenon in those subjects given an infusion of alcohol. Maletzky employed doses of alcohol three to four times the dosages infused by Bach-y-Rita et al. (1970). Approximately two-thirds of his subjects, all of whom had been selected for a prior history of such response, exhibited either violence or psychosis when, unbeknown to the subjects, they were infused with alcohol.

Questions regarding the phenomenon of pathological intoxication still exist. Maletzky speculates that the disorder probably only occurs in persons who are predisposed. He discounts the possibility that sufficiently high levels of alcohol will create the phenomenon in most persons. Since Maletzky's patients were in a neutral mood prior to infusion, the data mitigate against the idea that a predisposing mood is required to induce the state. The range of dosage employed by Maletzky was wide (400 cc to 1200 cc of 25% alcohol solution). However, since Bach-y-Rita at lower doses, failed to elicit the syndrome, there is reason to believe that moderately high dosages of alcohol are required to elicit the condition.

There has been speculation as to the neuroendocrinological events that might underlie the disorder of pathological intoxication. Mayfield (1983) lists three possibilities: an increase in testosterone, perturbations in EEG (electroencephalogram), and release of catecholamines. He dismisses the first possibility because alcohol generally has the acute effect of decreasing testosterone levels. Of course, without empirical investigation of the testosterone levels of those persons who display the idiosyncratic reaction assessed during the experience, the possibility cannot be dismissed.

Another possible mediator of pathological intoxication is seizure activity. In terms of the possibility that pathological intoxication may be related to seizure type activity, there has been some attempt to correlate EEG (electroencephalogram) changes with expression of pathological intoxication syndrome. Maletzky's subjects did exhibit EEG changes during expression of the syndrome. Evidence for a clear on-to-one correspondence between the manifestation and the EEG changes was, however, lacking. In characterizing the quality of the EEG changes, Maletzky reported that the induced waves are not characteristic of seizure activity. (The waves were slow and dysynchronized, with occasional spiking.) Interestingly, these waves also are characteristic of blackouts and blackouts generally are part of the syndrome of pathological intoxication. Despite interesting preliminary findings, extant empirical data does not allow conclusions regarding whether EEG changes are causal or merely correlated events.

A final hypothetical cause of pathological intoxication is release of catecholamines. There is ample evidence that alcohol does result in the acute release of norephinephrine, dopamine, and serotonin (see Blum, 1982). It is also known that drugs increasing the release of catecholamines (e.g., cocaine, amphetamines) can precipitate aggression, paranoia, and psychosis. Whether catecholamine release plays a causal role in the manifestation of pathological intoxication is undetermined, but a plausible hypothesis.

META ANALYSES

Perhaps the overarching goal of all the research on alcohol's impact has been to generate a definitive statement regarding alcohol's general effect. Several meta analyses have been published attempting to categorize domains of behavior in meaningful ways such that a definitive statement can be derived. Steele and Southwick (1985) published the first meta analysis. They categorized behaviors as either high in conflict or low in conflict. High conflict behaviors are those for which there are both strong pressure inducing performance and strong inhibiting forces. They include aggression, human conflict, drinking, eating, gambling, risk taking, self-disclosure, and sexual interest in those high in sex guilt. Low conflict behaviors include assertion, mirth, moral judgment, normal sexual interest in those low in sex guilt and yielding. The results of the Steele and Southwick meta analysis suggested that alcohol's pharmacological effect impacts high conflict behaviors more than low conflict behaviors. The effect of believing one had imbibed did have a significant impact on all behavior but did not differentially effect high- and low-conflict behaviors.

Hull and Bond (1986) published a second meta analysis. They categorized behavioral domains in a manner similar to but not the same as Steele and Southwick. Their dichotomy was behaviors that are socially discouraged which might be released should one have an excuse (sexual arousal, alcohol consumption, aggression, and ignoring requests for help) vs. behaviors that are socially neutral for which excuse availability is not relevant (physical sensations, mood, attentional focus, locus of control, motor performance, information processing, physiology). Hull and Bond limited their analysis to those studies that utilized the balanced placebo design allowing evaluation of both expectancy and beverage effects.

For those behaviors that were socially neutral, Hull and Bond's meta analysis suggested that the expectancy effects on these behaviors were minimal and the pharmacological impact of alcohol was significant. Conducting individual meta analyses for the behaviors of particular types, Hull and Bond (1986) concluded that there was support for a pharmacological impact of alcohol on memory, internal sensations, and on performance. The impact on mood and humor depended on the context of the behavior, such that alcohol increased both good mood and humor in congenial but not anxiety provoking milieus.

For socially discouraged behaviors (sexual arousal, alcohol, consumption, aggression and refusing to be helpful), Hull and Bond found a significant expectancy effect. In terms of the pharmacological effects of alcohol on socially discouraged behaviors, Hull and Bond concluded that across domains, pharmacology does not have much impact on these behaviors. This conclusion contradicted the meta analysis of Southwick and Steele, which concluded that there is a significant pharmacological effect of alcohol on the performance of high conflict behaviors.

Apparent Contradictions between Results of the Two Meta Analyses

The contradictions between the conclusions yielded by Hull and Bond and Steele and Southwick all derive from the fact that overlapping but different domains were lumped together in each analysis. The contradictions are the following:

(1) Both Hull and Bond and Southwick and Steele find an expectancy effect on socially discouraged behaviors (i.e., behaviors whose expression is effected by excuse availability, which overlaps with Southwick and Steele's high conflict behaviors). The two meta analyses differed in the magnitude to the expectancy effect. Whereas Steele and Southwick reported their results as suggesting an effect size of .38 of a standard deviation; Hull and Bond's results suggested an effect size for expectancy of 2.32 standard deviations. The discrepancy between the two analyses is attributable to differences in the dependent variable. For example, Hull and Bond examine the impact of expectancy on decreasing al-

truism. Steele and Southwick do not examine the particular study that Hull and Bond included nor do they examine altruism.

(2) Hull and Bond conclude that beverage alcohol does not affect socially discouraged behaviors. Southwick and Steele conclude that alcohol does affect high conflict behavior. The fact that there are differences in the conclusions between the analyses regarding overlapping behavioral domains is again attributable to differences in the behaviors examined. Hull and Bond classified normal sexual response as a socially discouraged behavior. Southwick and Steele classified normal sexual interest as a low conflict behavior. Such discrepancy should and do drastically influence the results obtained.

The subanalyses presented by Hull and Bond for each domain of behavior are illuminating. On sex arousal, the pharmacological impact of alcohol is to decrease arousal, which is opposite in direction to any impact alcohol might have through a release of inhibition mechanism. On increase in alcohol consumption (the dependent variable), there is very little pharmacological impact of alcohol. Hull and Bond conclude that there is little pharmacological effect of alcohol on increasing further consumption of alcohol. For aggression, Hull and Bond conclude there is a pharmacological effect in the direction of increased aggression.

(3) Another major discrepancy between the analyses concerns the conclusions regarding another aspect of expectancy effects. Hull and Bond suggest that expectancy effects interact with type of behavior (socially discouraged or neutral behavior); Southwick and Steele suggest that expectancy affects both high conflict and low conflict behavior but find no evidence of an interaction. Again the conflict occurs because the dichotomies proffered by the two meta analyses overlap but are not the same such that different results should be expected. For drawing conclusions as to the impact of expectancy for any particular type of behavior, specific research in that area should be consulted.

Agreement between the two meta analyses: The Hull and Bond and the Steele and Southwick analyses do generate the same conclusion in one area. Both analyses rule against the explanation that alcohol achieves its major impact solely through a general arousal mechanism. All authors make the assumption that if arousal could account for the effect of alcohol on all behaviors, then all behaviors would be impacted by alcohol to the same degree, i.e., no interaction would be obtained. However, alcohol affects behavior differentially depending upon the degree to which the behavior is normally inhibited. According to the authors, results of meta analyses that find an interaction rule against an arousal mediation.

Although the authors of both meta-analyses agree about discounting arousal as a fundamental explanatory mechanism for alcohol's effect, they may be wrong. It may be that arousal will differentially impact socially discouraged behaviors vs. neutral behavior. It may be that aroused persons are more willing to engage in socially discouraged behavior because the consequences seem less intimidating or less probable. Hence arousal could effect the expression of socially discouraged behavior through an additional avenue beyond enhancement of activity in general. Thus, arousal could exert more impact on socially discouraged vs. socially neutral behavior. Until there are more data available on how arousal impacts socially discouraged vs. socially neutral behaviors, arousal should not be ruled out as a mediator of the effect of alcohol.

ALL THINGS CONSIDERED

Alcohol influences behavior through its phamacology. The belief that alcohol has been consumed also influences behavior. Regardless of what a person believes he/she is consuming, alcohol will increase aggression given a context that provokes aggression, it will increase cognitive activity as well as verbal output, it will dampen the magnitude of the physical sexual response while increasing interest in sexual material, it will increase altruism, it will dampen the individual's response to stress if the situation allows the individual to turn his/her attention elsewhere. The belief that alcohol has been consumed also influences behavior. Belief of consumption can lead to more charitable views of other people, particularly among those who hold that expectation that alcohol improves disposition. In performance contexts, those who believe alcohol impairs performance become more anxious when they believe they have consumed alcohol. Belief of consumption results in enhanced aggression when aggression is provoked and an enhanced sexual response to erotic material especially to deviant erotic material. For those behavioral domains in which inhibition decreases the probability of behavior (aggression, deviant arousal), both beverage effects and expectancy effects have been demonstrated. Alcohol is disinhibiting.

Alcohol does influence behavior and mood in a variety of ways. There are several theories that strive to account for alcohol's effect in general. Specific hypotheses seek to account for alcohol's disinhibiting effect and alcohol's pleasure enhancing effect. In order to explain the disinhibition, Hull (1981) advances the idea that by decreasing cognitive processing individuals will be less self-conscious. Decreasing self-consciousness is known to exert a disinhibiting effect. When self-consciousness is decreased, people are less likely to comply with their own attitudinal standards. Gray (1978) advances another explanation for alcohol's disinhibiting effects. Gray believes that alcohol dampens anxiety centers. When anxiety is dissipated, conscience, which is based on anticipatory anxiety, may exert less of a break on behavior. These two hypotheses speak to why alcohol as a drug might disinhibit behavior. The belief that alcohol has been consumed, even when the beverage was inert, also disinhibits behavior. The availability of an excuse provided by the belief that alcohol has been consumed will decrease personal responsibility for the intended behavior. Without responsibility for behavior, the retraints of the conscience are decreased and behavior is disinhibited. All of these hypotheses have received experimental support. It should be noted that these three hypotheses are not mutually exclusive. The Gray and Hull hypotheses explain why the pharmacological effect of alcohol is disinhibiting. The excuse hypothesis explains why belief that alcohol has been consumed will disinhibit behavior. Future research may provide further clarification regarding the circumstances under which each explanation is most germane.

Wise and Bozarth (1987) have considered why alcohol is pleasurable. They have averred that people find alcohol pleasurable because alcohol stimulates the same area in the brain that is stimulated by other abusable drugs, the ventral tegmental area. They argue that when this area in the brain is activated, increased pleasure and behavioral activity occur. Hence, the pleasurable effects of alcohol are correlated with the arousing effects. Wise and Bozarth's idea is intriguing. The reader will recall the de Wit et al. (1987) study discussed in the first chapter of this section. In this study, subjects were given a beverage that they did not know was alcohol. Those subjects who reported greater arousal drank the most during the course of the experiment. At least in this study, the link between arousal and reinforcement was demonstrated. The Wise and Bozarth hypothesis speaks to alcohol's pleasurable effect and alcohol's increase in activity. It makes no attempt to account for alcohol's other effects on behavior.

Others have sought to advance theories regarding alcohol's general effect on many domains of behavior, including disinhibition. MacAndrew and Edgerton (1969) have argued that each culture maintains particular beliefs about how alcohol will alter behavior. People learn the rules about how they are supposed to act when drinking. Hence, many of the effects that are observed in drinking individuals constitute a kind of self-fulfilling prophecy with drinking individuals living up to what they believe is expected of them. The MacAndrew and Edgerton (1969) explanation of alcohol's effect probably accounts for some of the expectancy effects of alcohol (e.g., on sex and aggression) that have been demonstrated in the literature. The MacAndrew and Edgerton hypothesis is an explanation about the effect of belief that alcohol has been imbibed rather than an explanation regarding the phamacological effect of alcohol.

Consistent with Wise and Bozarth's thoughts, there is support for the fact that alcohol is a stimulant drug. Wise and Bozarth linked arousal from alcohol with pleasure derived from drinking. However, arousal probably has other ramifications for behavior not considered by Wise and Bozarth. Because of its arousal property, alcohol can be expected to influence behavior in a wide variety of domains. The effects of arousal are protean. Arousal increases cognitive activity and should result in more talking. Arousal should also impact emotion. Schachter and Singer's classic experiment (Schachter, 1971) suggests that given arousal from a chemical stimulant, persons will behave in an emotional manner, although the situational context will determine which emotion is manifested. The effect of the arousal is to make emotional behavior of some type more likely and to increase the intensity of the emotional display. In fact, alcohol has been demonstrated to have diverse consequences in terms of its effect on mood. It will intensify the display of provoked anger. Drinking people respond with greater jocularity to slap stick entertainment. Sometimes alcohol enhances a good mood providing the individual is in a comfortable context. If a person focuses on a fearful stimulus alcohol can intensify anxiety. Perhaps the principle that can account for these diverse, almost contradictory effects, is to recall that alcohol is an arousing drug. The predictions given arousal is that whatever feeling is elicited by the context will be displayed with greater force. It is the context that determines the quality of the emotion displayed. The drug provides the intensity.

Although there is evidence that alcohol is an arousing drug at low doses, at high doses it is sedating. This too is difficult to explain. Is the same area of the brain responsible for both the arousal and the sedation? Perhaps this is not the case. Wise and Bozarth (1987) suggest that alcohol may affect more than one center in the brain. It is possible that each of the affected centers may exert an opposite effect on behavior. It is further possible that each center will be activated at different doses of alcohol. For example, the arousing center of the brain may be activated by low dose alcohol, whereas at higher doses of alcohol, the sedating centers of the brain are turned on. At higher doses of alcohol, the sedating centers would eclipse the arousing centers. This could explain the contradictions that are observed.

All of the overarching explanations for the beverage and expectancy impact of alcohol are still alive. Because these explanations are not mutually exclusive, it may be that more than one of these theories will be supported by future research. Future study may suggest those particular circumstances for which particular explanations are specifically relevant.

REFERENCES

Abrams, D. B., & Wilson, G. T. (1979). Effects of alcohol on social anxiety in women: Cognitive versus physiological processes. *Journal of Abnormal Psychology, 88,* 161–173.

Alkana, R. L., & Malcolm, R. D. (1980). Comparison of the effects of acute alcohol intoxication on behavior in humans and other animals. In K. Eriksson, J. D., Sinclair, & K. Kiianmaa (Eds.), *Animal models in alcohol research.* New York: Academic Press 193–269.

Allman, L. R., Taylor, H. A., & Nathan, P. E. (1972). Group drinking during stress: Effects on drinking behavior, affect, and psychopathology. *American Journal of Psychiatry, 129,* 669–678.

Altshuler, H. L. (1980). Intragastric self-administration of ethanol: A subhuman primate model of alcoholism. In K. Eriksson, J. D., Sinclair, & K Kiianmaa (Eds.), *Animal models in alcohol research* (pp. 179–183). New York: Academic Press.

Aneshensel, C. S., & Huba, G. J. (1983). Depression, alcohol use, and smoking over one year: A four-wave longitudinal causal model. *Journal of Abnormal Psychology, 92,* 134–150.

Babor, T. F., Berglas, S., Mendelson, J. H., Ellingboe, J, & Miller, K. (1983). Alcohol, affect and the disinhibition of verbal behavior. *Psychopharmacology, 80,* 53–60.

Bach-y-Rita, G., Lion, J. R., & Ervin, F. R. (1970). Pathological intoxication: Clinical and electroencephalographic studies. *American Journal of Psychiatry, 127,* 698–703.

Bales, R. F. (1946). Cultural difference in rates of alcoholism. *Quarterly Journal of Studies on Alcohol, 6,* 480–499.

Barbaree, H. E., Marshall, W. L., Yates, E., & Lightfoot, L. (1983). Alcohol intoxication and deviant sexual arousal in male social drinkers. *Behavior Research and Therapy, 21,* 365–373.

Barling, J., & Bolon, K. (1981). Effects of alcohol, expectancies, sex and social setting on locus of control. *Journal of Studies on Alcohol, 42,* 680–684.

Barling, J., & Fincham, F. (1979). The effects of alcohol on psychological conservatism. *Journal of Social Psychology, 107,* 129–130.

Baum, M. (1969). Paradoxical effect of alcohol on the resistance to extinction of an avoidance responses in rats. *Journal of Comparative and Physiological Psychology, 69,* 238–240.

Baum, M. (1970). Effect of alcohol on the acquisition and resistance-to-extinction of avoidance responses in rats. *Psychological Reports, 26,* 759–765.

Baum, M. (1971). Effect of alcohol, on the resistance-to-extinction of an avoidance response: Replication in mice. *Physiology and Behavior, 6,* 307–309.

Bennett, R. M., Buss, A. H., & Carpenter, J. A. (1969). Alcohol and human physical aggression. *Quarterly Journal of studies on Alcohol, 30,* 870–877.

Berg, N. L. (1971). Effects of alcohol intoxication on self-concept. *Quarterly Journal of Studies on Alcohol, 32,* 442–453.

Berglas, S., & Jones, E. E. (1978). Drug choice as a self-handicapping strategy in response to noncontingent success. Journal of Personality and Social Psychology, 36, 405–417.

Blum, K. (1982). Neurophysiological effects of alcohol. In E. M. Pattison & E. Kaufman (Eds.), *Encyclopedic handbook of alcoholism* (pp. 105–134). New York: Gardner Press.

Bohman, M., Cloninger, C. R., Sigvardsson, S., and von Knorring, A. L. (1982). Predisposition to petty criminality in Swedish adoptees I. Genetic and environmental heterogeneity. *Archives of General Psychiatry, 39,* 1233–1241.

Bohman, M., Sigvardsson, S., & Cloninger, C. R. (1981). Maternal inheritance of alcohol abuse. *Archives of General Psychiatry, 38,* 965–969.

Bond, A., & Lader, M. (1986). The relationship between induced behavioral aggression and mood after the consumption of two doses of alcohol. *British Journal of Addiction, 81,* 65–75.

Bordini, E. J., Tucker, J. A., Vuchinich, R. E., & Rudd, E. J. (1986). Alcohol consumption as a self-handicapping strategy in women. *Journal of Abnormal Psychology, 95,* 346–349.

Borrill, J. A., Rosen, B. K., & Summerfield, A. B. (1987). The influence of alcohol on judgment of facial expressions of emotion. *British Journal of Medical Psychology, 60,* 71–77.

Bostrom, R. N., & White, N. D. (1979). Does drinking weaken resistance. *Journal of Communications, 29*, 73–80.

Boyatzis, R. E. (1974). The effect of alcohol consumption on the aggressive behavior of men. *Quarterly Journal of Alcohol, 35*, 959–972.

Boyatzis, R. E. (1975). The predisposition toward alcohol-related interpersonal aggression in men. *Journal of Studies on Alcohol, 36*, 1196–1207.

Boyatzis, R. E. (1983). Who should drink what, when, and where if looking for a fight. In E. Gottheil, K. A. Druley, T. E. Skolada, & H. M. Waxman (Eds.), *Alcohol, drug abuse and aggression* (pp. 314–329.) Springfield IL: C. C. Thomas.

Bradlyn, A. S., Strickler, D. P., & Maxwell, W. A. (1981). Alcohol, expectancy and stress: Methodological concerns with the expectancy design. *Addictive Behaviors, 6*, 1–8.

Brick, J., & Pohorecky, L. A. (1982). Ethanol-stress interaction: Biochemical findings. *Psychopharmacology, 77*, 81–84.

Briddell, D. W., Rimm, D. C., Caddy, G. R., Krawitz, G., Sholis, D., & Wunderlin, R. J. (1978). Effects of alcohol and cognitive set on sexual arousal to deviant stimuli. *Journal of Abnormal Psychology, 87*, 418–430.

Briddell, D. W., & Wilson, G. T. (1975). Effects of alcohol and expectancy set on male sexual arousal. *Journal of Abnormal Psychology, 85*, 225–234.

Brown, R. A., & Cutter, H. S. G. (1977). Alcohol, Customary drinking behavior, and pain. *Journal of Abnormal Psychology, 86*, 179–188.

Brown, S. A., Goldman, M. S., & Christiansen, B. A. (1985). Do alcohol expectations mediate drinking patterns of adults? *Journal of Consulting and Clinical Psychology, 53*, 512–519.

Brown, S. A., Goldman, M. S., Inn, A., & Anderson, L. R. (1980). Expectations of reinforcement from alcohol: Their domain and relation to drinking patterns. *Journal of Consulting and Clinical Psychology, 48*, 419–426.

Brown, S. A., & Munson, E. (1987). Extroversion, anxiety, and perceived effects of alcohol. *Journal of Studies on Alcohol, 48*, 272–276.

Cadoret, R. J., O'Gorman, T. W., Troughton, E., & Heywood, E. (1985). Alcoholism and antisocial personality. Interrelationships, genetic and environmental factors. *Archives of General Psychiatry, 42*, 161–167.

Cadoret, R. J., Troughton, E., & O'Gorman, T. W. (1987). Genetic and environmental factors in alcohol abuse and antisocial personality. *Journal of Studies on Alcohol, 48*, 1–8.

Cahalan, D., & Cisin, I. H. (1968). American drinking practices: Summary of findings from a national probability sample: I. Extend of drinking by population subgroups. *Quarterly Journal of Studies on Alcohol, 29*, 130–151.

Cahalan, D., Cisin, I. H., & Crossley, H. M. (1969). *American Drinking Practices.* New Brunswick, NJ: Rutgers Center of Alcohol Studies.

Carlsson, A., Engel, J., & Sevensson, T. H. (1972). Inhibition of ethanol-induced excitation in mice and rats by alpha-methyl-p-tyrosine. *Psychopharmacologia, 26*, 307–312.

Cappell, H., LeBlanc, A. E., & Endrenyi, L. (1972). Effects of cholordiazepoxide and ethanol on the extinction of a conditioned taste aversion. *Physiology and Behavior, 9*, 167–169.

Carpenter, J. A. (1957). Effects of alcoholic beverages on skin conductance: An exploratory study. *Quarterly Journal of Studies on Alcohol, 18*, 1–18.

Carpenter, J. A., & Armenti, N. P. (1972). Some effects of ethanol on human sexual and aggressive behavior. In B. Kissen & H. Begleiter (Eds.), *The biology of alcoholism* (pp. 509–543 Vol. 2). New York: Plenum Press.

Caudill, B. D., Wilson, G. T., & Abrams, D. B. (1987). Alcohol and self-disclosure: Analyses of interpersonal behavior in male and female social drinkers. *Journal of Studies on Alcohol, 48*, 401–409.

Chamok, S., & Collins, R. L. (1987). Relationship between sex-role behaviors and alcohol consumption in undergraduate men and women. *Journal of Studies on Alcohol, 48*, 194–201.

Chandler, B. C., & Parsons, O. A. (1977). Altered hemispheric functioning under alcohol. *Journal of Studies on Alcohol, 38,* 381–391.

Chassin, L., Mann, L. M., & Sher, K. J. (1988). Self-awareness theory, family history of alcoholism, and adolescent alcohol involvement. *Journal of Abnormal Psychology, 97,* 206–217.

Cherek, D. R., Steinberg, J. L., & Manno, B. R. (1985). Effects of alcohol on human aggressive behavior. *Journal of Studies on Alcohol, 46,* 321–328.

Cicero, T. J. (1983). Behavioral significance of drug-induced alterations in reproductive endrocrinology in the male. In E. Gottehil, K. A. Druley, T. E. Skoloda, & H. M. Waxman (Eds.), *Alcohol, drug abuse, and aggression* (pp. 203–226). Springfield, IL: Charles C. Thomas.

Cicero, T. J., Myers, R. D., & Black, W. C. (1968). Increase in volitional ethanol consumption following interference with a learned avoidance response. *Physiology and Behavior, 3,* 657–660.

Cloninger, C. R., Bohman, M., & Sigvardsson, S. (1981). Inheritance of alcohol abuse. Cross-fostering analysis of adopted men. *Archives of General Psychiatry, 38,* 861–868.

Coleman, D. H., & Strauss, M. A. (1983). Alcohol abuse and family violence. In E. Gottehil, K. A. Druley, T. E. Skoloda, & H. M. Waxman (Eds.), *Alcohol, drug abuse, and aggression.* Springfield, IL: Charles C. Thomas.

Collins, R. L., Marlatt, G. A. (1981). Social modeling as a determinant of drinking behavior: Implications for prevention and treatment. *Addictive Behavior, 6,* 233–239.

Collins, R. L., Parks, G. A., & Marlatt, G. A. (1985). Social determinants of alcohol consumption: The effects of social interaction and model status on the self-administration of alcohol. *Journal of Consulting and Clinical Psychology, 53,* 189–200.

Collins, J. J., & Schlenger, W. E. (1988). Acute and chronic effects of alcohol use on violence. *Journal of Studies on Alcohol, 49,* 516–521.

Connors, G. J., & Maisto, S. A. (1979). Effects of alcohol, instructions, and consumption rate on affect and physiological sensations. *Psychopharmacology, 62,* 261–266.

Connors, G. J., O'Farrell, T. J., & Cutter, H. S. G. (1987). Dose-related effects of alcohol among male alcoholics, problem drinkers, and nonproblem drinkers. *Journal of Studies on Alcohol, 48,* 461–466.

Cooper, M. L., Russell, M., & George, W. H. (1988). Coping, expectancies, and alcohol abuse: A test of social learning formulations. *Journal of Abnormal Psychology, 97,* 218–230.

Cooper, A. M., Waterhouse, G. J., & Sobell, M. B. (1979). Influence of gender on drinking in a modeling situation. *Journal of Studies on Alcohol, 40,* 562–570.

Coopersmith, S. (1964). The effects of alcohol on reactions to affective stimuli. *Quarterly Journal of Studies on Alcohol, 25,* 459–475.

Crowe, L. C., & George, W. H. (1989). Alcohol and human sexuality: Review and integration. *Psychological Bulletin, 105,* 374–386.

Cunningham, C. L., & Brown, J. S. (1983). Escape from fear under alcohol: Fear inhibits alcohol-enhanced responding. *Physiological Psychology, 11,* 81–86.

Cutter, H. S. G., Maloof, B. A., Kurtz, N. R., & Jones, W. C. (1976). Pain as a joint function of alcohol intake and customary reasons for drinking. *International Journal of Addiction, 14,* 173–182.

Cutter, H. S. G., Jones, W. C., Maloof, B. A., & Kurtz, N. R. (1979). "Feeling no pain": Differential responses to pain by alcoholics and nonalcoholics before and after drinking. *Journal of Studies on Alcohol, 37,* 273–277.

Cutter, H. S. G., & O'Farrell, T. J. (1984). Relationship between reasons for drinking and customary drinking behavior. *Journal of Studies on Alcohol, 45,* 321–325.

Cutter, H. S. G., & O'Farrell, T. J. (1987). Experience with alcohol and endogenous opiod system in ethanol analgesia. *Addictive Behavior, 12,* 331–344.

Deardorff, C. M., Melges, F. T., Hout, C. N., & Savage, D. J. (1975). Situations related to drinking alcohol: A factor analysis of questionnaire responses. *Journal of Studies on Alcohol, 36,* 1184–1195.

Deer, R., & Lindbald, S. (1980). Stress induced consumption of ethanol by rats. *Life Sciences, 27,* 2183–2186.

Dengerink, H. A., & Fagan, N. J. (1978). Effect of alcohol on emotional responses to stress. *Journal of Studies on Alcohol, 39,* 525–539.

DeTurck, K. H., & Vogel, W. H. (1982). Effects of acute ethanol on plasma and brain cate-cholamine levels in stressed and unstressed rats: Evidence for an ethanol-stress interaction. *Journal of Pharmacology and Experimental Therapeutics, 223,* 348–354.

de Wit, H., Uhlenhuth, E. H., Pierri, J., & Johnson, R. H. (1987). Individual differences in behavioral and subjective responses to alcohol. *Alcoholism: Clinical and Experimental Research, 11,* 52–59.

Dewsbury, D. A. (1967). Effects of alcohol ingestion on copulatory behavior in male rats. *Psychopharmacologia, 11,* 276–281.

Docter, R. F., & Bernal, M. E. (1964). Immediate and prolonged psychophysiological effects of sustained alcohol intake in alcoholics. *Quarterly Journal of Studies on Alcohol, 25,* 438–450.

Docter, R. F., Naitoh, P., & Smith, J. C. (1966). Electroencephalographic changes and vigilance behavior during experimentally-induced intoxication with alcoholic subjects. *Psychosomatic Medicine, 28,* 605–615.

Ehrensinig, R. H., Stokes, P. E., Pick, G. R., Goldstone, S., & Lhamon, W. T. (1970). Effect of alcohol on auditory and visual time perception. *Quarterly Journal of Studies on Alcohol, 31,* 851–860.

Ekman, G., Frankenhaeuser, M., Goldberg, L., Hagdaill, R., & Myrsten, A. L. (1964). Subjective and objective effects of alcohol as functions of dosage and time. *Psychopharmcologia, 6,* 399–409.

Esposito, R. U., Paker, E. S., & Weingartner, H. (1984). Enkephalinergic "reward" pathways: A critical substrate for the stimulatory, euphoric and memory-enhancing actions of alcohol-a hypothesis. *Substance and Alcohol Actions/Misuse, 5,* 111–119.

Farber, P. D., Khavari, K. A., & Douglass, F. M. (1980). A factor analytic study of reasons for drinking: Empirical validation of positive and negative reinforcement dimensions. *Journal of Consulting and Clinical Psychology, 48,* 780–781.

Farkas, G. M., & Rosen, R. C. (1976). Effect of alcohol on elicited male sexual response. *Journal of Studies on Alcohol, 37,* 265–272.

Finney, J. W., & Moos, R. H. (1984). Life stressors and problem drinking among older adults. In M. Galanter (Ed.), (*Recent Developments in Alcoholism* (pp. 267–288, Vol. 2). New York: Plenum Press.

Finn, P. R., & Pihl, R. O. (1987). Men at high risk for alcoholism: The effect of alcohol on cardiovascular response to unavoidable shock. *Journal of Abnormal Psychology, 96,* 230–236.

Forney, R. B., & Hughes, F. W. (1965). Effect of caffeine and alcohol on performance under stress of audiofeedback. *Quarterly Journal of Studies on Alcohol, 26,* 206–212.

Frankel, B. G., Ferrence, R. G., Johnson, F. G., Whitehead, P. C. (1976). Drinking and self-injury: Toward untangling the dynamics. *British Journal of Addictions, 71,* 299–306.

Frankenhaeuser, M., Dunne, E., Bjurstrom, H., & Lundberg, U. (1974). Counteracting depressant effects of alcohol by psychological stress. *Psychopharmacologia, 38,* 271–278.

Frankenstein, W., & Wilson, G. T. (1984). Alcohol's effects on self-awareness. *Addictive Behaviors, 9,* 323–328.

Freed, E. X. (1978). Alcohol and mood: An updated review. *The International Journal of Addictions, 13,* 173–200.

Frye, G. D., & Breese, G. R. (1981). An evaluation of the locomotor stimulating action of ethanol in rats and mice. *Psychopharmacology, 75,* 372–379.

Gabel, P. C., Noel, N. E., Keane, T. M., & Lisman, S. A. (1980). Effects of sexual versus fear arousal on alcohol consumption in college males. *Behavior Research and Therapy, 18,* 519–526.

Gabrielli, W. F., Jr., & Plomin, R. (1985). Drinking behavior in the Colorado adoptee and twin sample. *Journal of Studies on Alcohol, 46,* 24–31.

Garfield, Z. H., & McBrearty, J. F. (1970). Arousal level and stimulus response in alcoholics after drinking. *Quarterly Journal of Alcohol Studies, 31,* 832–838.

George, W. H., & Marlatt, G. A. (1986). The effects of alcohol and anger on interest in violence, erotica, and deviance. *Journal of Abnormal Psychology, 95,* 150–158.

Gerrein, J. R., & Chechile, R. A. (1977). Storage and retrieval processes of alcohol-induced amnesia. *Journal of Abnormal Psychology, 86,* 285–294.

Gliksman, L., & Rush, B. R. (1986). Alcohol availability, alcohol consumption and alcohol-related damage. II. The role of sociodemographic factors. *Journal of Studies on Alcohol, 47,* 11–18.

Glynn, R. J., LoCastro, J. S., Hermos, J. A., & Bosse, R. (1983). Social contexts and motives for drinking in men. *Journal of Studies on Alcohol, 44,* 1011–1025.

Goldman, P. S., & Docter, R. F. (1966). Facilitation of bar pressing and "suppression" of conditioned suppression in cats as a function of alcohol. *Psychopharmacologia, 9,* 64–72.

Goodwin, D. W., Johnson, J., Maher, C., Rappaport, A., & Guze, S. B. (1969). Why people do not drink: A study of teetotalers. *Comprehensive Psychiatry, 10,* 209–214.

Goodwin, D. W., Powell, B., Bremer, D., Hoine, H., & Stern, J. (1969). Alcohol and recall: State-dependent effects in man. *Science, 163,* 1358–1360.

Goodwin, D. W., Powell, B., & Stern, J. (1971). Behavioral tolerance to alcohol in moderate drinkers. *American Journal of Psychiatry, 127,* 1651–1653.

Goodwin, D. W., Schulsinger, F., Moller, N., Hermansen, L., Winokur, G., & Guze, S. B. (1974). Drinking problems in adopted and nonadopted sons of alcoholics. *Archives of General Psychiatry, 31,* 164–169.

Graham, K., Turnbull, W., & La Rocque, L. (1979). Effects of alcohol on moral judgment. *Journal of Abnormal Psychology, 88,* 442–445.

Gray, J. (1978). The neuropsychology of anxiety. *British Journal of Psychology, 69,* 417–434.

Greenberg, L. A., & Carpenter, J. A. (1957). The effect of alcoholic beverages on skin conductance and emotional tension: I. Wine, whiskey, and alcohol. *Quarterly Journal of Studies on Alcohol, 18,* 190–204.

Griffiths, R., Bigelow, G., & Liebson, I. (1976). Facillitation of human tobacco administration by ethanol: A behavioral analysis. *Journal of Experimental Analysis of Behavior, 25,* 279–292.

Gustafson, R. (1988). Effects of alcohol on power in social interaction between man and woman. *Journal of Studies on Alcohol, 49,* 78–84.

Hall, R. L., Hesselbrock, V. M., & Stabenau, J. R. (1983a). Familial distribution of alcohol use: I. Assortative mating in the parents of alcoholics. *Behavior Genetics, 13,* 373–382.

Harburg, E., Davis, D. R., & Caplan, R. (1982). Parent and offspring alcohol use: Imitative and aversive transmission. *Journal of Studies on Alcohol, 43,* 451–458.

Hart, B. L. (1969). Effects of alcohol on sexual reflexes and mating behavior in the male rat. *Psychopharmacologia, 14,* 377–382.

Hartford, T. C. (1983). A contextual analysis of drinking events. *International Journal of Addictions, 18,* 825–834.

Hartocollis, P. (1962). Drunkeness and suggestion: An experiment with intravenous alcohol. *Quarterly Journal of Studies on Alcohol, 23,* 376–389.

Heien, D., & Pompelli, G. (1987). Stress, ethnic and distribution factors in a dichotomous response model of alcohol abuse. *Journal of Studies on Alcohol, 48,* 450–455.

Henningfield, J. E., Chait, L. D., Griffiths, R. R. (1984). Effects of ethanol on cigarette smoking by volunteers without histories of alcoholism. *Psychopharmacology, 82,* 1–5.

Hershenson, D. B. (1965). Stress-induced use of alcohol by problem drinkers as a function of their sense of identity. *Quarterly Journal of Studies on Alcohol, 26,* 213–222.

Hetherington, E. M., & Wray, N. P. (1964). Aggression, need for social approval, and humor preferences. *Journal of Abnormal and Social Psychology, 68,* 685–689.

Higgings, R. L., & Marlatt, G. A. (1973). Effects of anxiety arousal on the consumption of alcohol by alcoholics and social drinkers. *Journal of Consulting and Clinical Psychology, 41,* 426–433.

Higgins, R. L., & Marlatt, G. A. (1975). Fear of interpersonal evaluation as a determinant of alcohol consumption in male social drinkers. *Journal of Abnormal Psychology, 84,* 644–651.

Hingson, R., Scotch, N., Barrett, J., Goldman, E., & Mangione, T. (1981). Life satisfaction and drinking practices in the Boston metropolitan area. *Journal of Studies on Alcohol, 42,* 24–37.

Ho, A. K. S., & Allen, J. P. (1981). Alcohol and the opiate receptor: Interactions with the endogenous opiates. *Advances in Alcohol and Substance Abuse, 1,* 52–74.

Holroyd, K. A. (1978). Effects of social anxiety and social evaluation on beer consumption and social interaction. *Journal of Studies on Alcohol, 39,* 737–743.

Horverak, E. (1983). The 1978 strike at the Norwegian wine and spirits monopoly. *British Journal of Addiction, 78,* 51–66.

Huebner, R. B., Slaughter, R. E., Goldman, R. D., & Caddy, G. R. (1976). Attitudes toward alcohol as predictors of self-estimated alcohol consumption in college students. *International Journal of Addictions, 11,* 377–388.

Hull, J. G. (1981). A self-awareness model of causes and effects of alcohol consumption. *Journal of Abnormal Psychology, 90,* 586–600.

Hull, J. G., & Bond, C. F. (1986). Social and behavioral consequences of alcohol consumption and expectancy: A meta-analysis. *Psychological Bulletin, 99,* 347–360.

Hull, J. G., Levenson, R. W., Young, R. D., & Sher, K. J. (1983). Self-awareness reducing effects of alcohol consumption. *Journal of Personality and Social Psychology, 44,* 461–473.

Hull, J. G., & Reilly, N. P. (1983). Self-awareness, self-regulation, and alcohol consumption: A reply to Wilson. *Journal of Personality and Social Psychology, 92,* 514–519.

Hull, J.G.., & Young, R. D. (1983). The self-awareness-reducing effects of alcohol: Evidence and implications. In J. Suls & A. G. Greenwald (Eds.), *Psychological perspectives on the self* (pp. 159–190, Vol. 2). Hillsdale, NJ: Lawrence Erlbaum Associates.

Hull, J. G., Young, R. D., & Jouriles, E. (1986). Applications of the self-awareness model of alcohol consumption: Predicting patterns of use and abuse. *Journal of Personality and Social Psychology, 51,* 790–796.

Jellinek, E. M. (1960). *The disease concept of alcoholism.* New Brunswick, NJ: Hillhouse Press.

Jessor, R., Carman, R. S., & Grossman, P. H. (1968). Expectations of need satisfaction and drinking patterns of college students. *Quarterly Journal of Studies on Alcohol, 29,* 101–116.

Johnson, R. C., Schwitters, S. Y., Wilson, J. R., Nagoshi, C. T., & McClearn, G. E. (1985). A cross-ethnic comparison of reasons given for using alcohol, not using alcohol, or ceasing to use alcohol. *Journal of Studies on Alcohol, 46,* 283–288.

Jones, B. M. (1973). Memory impairment on the ascending and descending limbs of the blood alcohol curve. *Journal of Abnormal Psychology, 82,* 24–32.

Jones, M. C. (1968). Personality correlates and antecends of drinking patterns in adult males. *Journal of Consulting and Clinical Psychology, 32,* 2–12.

Jones, M. C. (1971). Personality antecedents and correlates of drinking patterns in women. *Journal on Consulting and Clinical Psychology, 36,* 61–69.

Kalant, H. (1975). Direct effects of ethanol on the nervous system. *Federation Proceedings, 34,* 1930–1941.

Kalin, R., McClelland, D. C., & Kahn, M. (1965). The effects of male social drinking on fantasy. *Journal of Personality and Social Psychology, 1,* 441–452.

Kalodner, C. R., Delucia, J. L., & Ursprung, A. W. (1989). An examination of the tension reduction hypothesis: The relationship between anxiety and alcohol in college students. *Addictive Behaviors, 14,* 649–654.

Kastl, A. J. (1969). Changes in ego functioning under alcohol. *Quarterly Journal of Studies on Alcohol, 30,* 371–383.

Keane, T. M. & Lisman, S. A. (1980). Alcohol and social anxiety in males: Behavioral, cognitive, and physiological effects. *Journal of Abnormal Psychology, 89,* 213–223.

Kendell, R. E., De Roumanie, M., & Ritson, E. B. (1983). Influence of an increase in excise duty on alcohol consumption and its adverse effects. *British Medical Journal, 287,* 809–811.

Kilpatrick, D. G., Sutker, P. B., Best, C. L., & Allain, A. N. (1980). Acute alcohol intoxication and vicarious emotional responsiveness. *Addictive Behaviors, 5,* 191–198.

Kinney, L., & Schmidt, H. (1979). Effect of cued and uncued inescapable shock on voluntary alcohol consumption in rats. *Phamacology, Biochemistry, and Behavior, 11,* 601–604.

Knight, L. J., Barbaree, H. E., & Boland, F. J. (1986). Alcohol and the balanced-placebo design: The role of experimenter demands in expectancy. *Journal of Abnormal Psychology, 95,* 335–340.

Konovsky, M., & Wilsnack, S. C. (1982). Social drinking and self-esteem in married couples. *Journal of Studies on Alcohol, 43,* 319–333.

Korman, M., Knopt, I. J., & Austin, R. B. (1960). Effects of alcohol on serial learning under stress conditions. *Psychological Reports, 7,* 217–220.

Korytnyk, N. X., & Perkins, D. V. (1983). Effects of alcohol versus expectancy for alcohol on the incidence of graffiti following an experimental task. *Journal of Abnormal Psychology, 92,* 382–385.

Kreutzer, J. S., Schneider, H. G., & Myatt, C. R. (1984). Alcohol, aggression, and assertiveness in men: Dosage and expectancy effects. *Journal of Studies on Alcohol, 45,* 275–278.

Kubicka, L., Kozeny, J., & Roth, Z. (1990). Alcohol abuse and its psychosocial correlates in sons of alcoholics as young men and in the general population of young men in Prague. *Journal of Studies on Alcohol, 51,* 49–58.

Kushner, M. G., Sher, K. J., & Beitman, B. D. (1990). The relation between alcohol problems and the anxiety disorders. *American Journal of Psychiatry, 147,* 685–695.

Laird, J. D., Wagener, J. J., Halal, M., & Szegda, M. (1982). Remembering what you feel: Effects of emotion on memory. *Journal of Personality and Social Psychology, 42,* 646–657.

Lang, A. R., Goeckner, D. J., Adesso, V. J., & Marlatt, G. A. (1975). Effects of alcohol on aggression in male social drinkers. *Journal of Abnormal Psychology, 84,* 508–518.

Lang, A. R., Pelham, W. E., Johnston, C., & Gelernter, S. (1989). Levels of adult alcohol consumption induced by interactions with child confederates exhibiting normal versus externalizing behaviors. *Journal of Abnormal Behavior, 98,* 294–299.

Lang, A. R., Searles, J., Lauerman, R., & Adesso, V. (1980). Expectancy, alcohol, and sex guilt as determinants of interest in and reaction to sexual stimuli. *Journal of Abnormal Psychology, 89,* 644–653.

Lang, A. R., Verret, L. D., & Watt, C. (1984). Drinking and creativity: Objective and subjective effects. *Addictive Behaviors, 9,* 395–400.

Lansky, D., & Wilson, G. T. (1981). Alcohol, expectations, and sexual arousal in males: An information processing analysis. *Journal of Abnormal Psychology, 90,* 35–45.

Lawrence, N. W., Herbert, M., & Jeffcoate, W. J. (1983). Circadian variation in effects of ethanol in man. *Pharmacology, Biochemistry, & Behavior, 18,* 555–558.

Leavy, R. L., & Dunlosky, J. T. (1989). Undergraduate student and faculty perceptions of problem drinking. *Journal of Studies on Alcohol, 50,* 101–107.

Lehrer, P. M., & Taylor, H. A. (1974). Effects of alcohol on cardiac reactivity in alcoholics and nonalcoholics. *Quarterly Journal of Studies on Alcohol, 38,* 1044–1052.

Leigh, B. C. (1987). Beliefs about the effects of alcohol on self and others. *Journal of Studies on Alcohol, 48,* 467–475.

Leigh, B. C. (1989). In search of the seven dwarves: Issues of measurement and meaning in alcohol expectancy research. *Psychological Bulletin, 105,* 361–373.

Leonard, K. E. (1984). Alcohol consumption and escalatory aggression in intoxicated and sober dyads. *Journal of Studies on Alcohol, 45,* 75–80.

Levenson, R. W., Oyama, O. N., & Meek, P. S. (1987). Greater reinforcement from alcohol for those at risk: Parental risk, personality risk, and sex. *Journal of Abnormal Psychology, 96,* 242–253.

Levenson, R. W., Sher, K. J., Grossman, L. M., Newman, J., & Newlin, D. B. (1980). Alcohol and stress response dampening: Pharmacological effects, expectancy, and tension reduction. *Journal of Abnormal Psychology, 89,* 528–538.

Levine, J. M., Kramer, G. G., & Levine, E. N. (1975). Effects of alcohol on human performance: An integration of research findings based on an abilities classification. *Journal of Applied Psychology, 60,* 285–293.

Levinson, D. (1983). Social setting, cultural factors, and alcohol-related aggression. In E. Gottheil, K. A. Druley, T. E. Skoloda, & H. M. Waxman (Eds.), *Alcohol, drug abuse, and aggression* (pp. 41–58). Springfield, IL: Charles C. Thomas.

Lewis, C. E., Helzer, J., Cloninger, C. R., Croughan, J., & Whitman, B. Y. (1982). Psychiatric diagnostic predispositions to alcoholism. *Comprehensive Psychiatry, 23,* 451–461.

Li, T. K., Lumeng, L., McBride, W. J., Murphy, J. M., Froehlich, J. S., & Morzorati, S. (1989). Pharmacology of alcohol preference in rodents. In E. Gordis, B. Tabakoff, & M. Linnoila (Eds.), *Alcohol research from bench to bedside* (pp. 73–86). New York: Hawthorne.

Lied, E. R., & Marlatt, G. A. (1979). Modeling as a determinant of alcohol consumption: Effect of subject sex and prior drinking history. *Addictive Behaviors, 4,* 47–54.

Linsky, A. S., Colby, J. P., & Strauss, M. A. (1986). Drinking norms and alcohol-related problems in the United States. *Journal of Studies on Alcohol, 47,* 384–393.

Linsky, A. S., Straus, M. A., Colby, J. P. (1985). Stressful events, stressful conditions, and alcohol problems in the United States: A partial test of Bale's theory. *Journal of Studies on Alcohol, 46,* 72–80.

Lister, R. G., & Nutt, D. J. (1989). RO 15–4513 and its interaction with ethanol. In E. Gordis, B. Tabakoff, & M. Linnoila (Ed.) *Alcohol research from bench to bedside* (pp. 119–124). New York: Hawthorne.

Logue, P. E., Gentry, W. D., Linnoila, M., & Erwin, C. W. (1978). Effect of alcohol consumption on state anxiety changes in male and female nonalcoholics. *American Journal of Psychiatry, 135,* 1079–1081.

Lubin, R. A. (1977). Influences of alcohol upon performance and performance awareness. *Perceptual and Motor Skills, 45,* 303–310.

Lucero, R. J., Jensen, K. F., & Ramsey, C. (1971). Alcoholism and teetotolism in blood relatives of abstaining alcoholics. *Quarterly Journal of Studies on Alcohol, 32,* 183–185.

MacAndrew, C., & Edgerton, R. B. (1969). *Drunken comportment: A social explanation.* Chicago: Aldine.

MacAndrew, C., & Garfinkel, H. (1962). A consideration of changes attributed to intoxication as common-sense reasons for getting drunk. *Quarterly Journal of Studies o. ` Alcohol, 23,* 252–266.

MacDonnell, M. F., & Ehmer, M. (1969). Some effects of ethanol on aggressive behavior in cats. *Quarterly Journal of Studies on Alcohol, 30,* 312–319.

Maletzky, B. M. (1976). The diagnosis of pathological intoxication. *Journal of Studies on Alcohol, 37,* 1215–1228.

Mann, L. M., Chassin, L., & Sher, K. J. (1987). Alcohol expectancies and the risk of alcoholism. *Journal of Consulting and Clinical Psychology, 55,* 411–417.

Marlatt, G. A., Kosturn, C. F., & Lang, A. R. (1975). Provocation to anger and opportunity for retaliation as determinants of alcohol consumption in social drinkers. *Journal of Abnormal Psychology, 84,* 652–659.

Marlatt, G. A., & Rohsenow, D. J. (1980). Cognitive processes in alcohol use: Expectancy and the balanced placebo design. In N. K. Mello (Ed.), *Advances in substance abuse: Behavioral and biological research* (pp. 159–199). Greenwich, CT: JAI Press.

Martin, C., & Casswell, S. (1987). Types of male drinkers: A multivariate study. *Journal of Studies on Alcohol, 48,* 119–123.

Ma, .ield, D. G. (1968). Psychopharmacology of alcohol. I. Affective change with intoxication, drinking behavior and affective state. *Journal of Nervous and Mental Disease, 146,* 314–321.

Mayfield, D. (1976). Alcoholism, alcohol intoxication and assaultive behavior. *Diseases of the Nervous System, 37,* 288–291.

Mayfield, D. (1983). Substance abuse and aggression: A psychopharmacological perspective. In E.

Gottheil, K. A. Druley, T. E. Skolada, & H. M. Waxman (Eds.), *Alcohol, drug abuse and aggression* (pp. 139–149). Springfield, IL: C. C. Thomas.

Mayfield, D., & Allen, D. (1967). Alcohol and affect: A psychopharmacological study. *American Journal of Psychiatry, 123,* 1346–1351.

McCarty, D. (1985). Environmental factors in substance abuse: The microsetting. In M. Galizio & S. A. Maisto (Eds.), *Determinants of substance abuse: Biological, psychological, and environmental factors* (pp. 247–281. New York: Plenum Press.

McCarty, D., Diamond, W., & Kaye, M. (1982). Alcohol, sexual arousal, and the transfer of excitation. *Journal of Personality and Social Psychology, 42,* 977–988.

McCarty, D., & Kaye, M. (1984). Reasons for drinking: Motivational patterns and alcohol use among college students. *Addictive Behaviors, 9,* 185–188.

McCarty, D., Morrison, S., & Mills, K. C. (1983). Attitudes, beliefs and alcohol abuse. *Journal of Studies on Alcohol, 44,* 328–341.

McCollam, J. B., Burish, T. G., Maisto, S. A., & Sobell, M. B. (1980). Alcohol's effects on physiological arousal and self-reported affect and sensations. *Journal of Abnormal Psychology, 89,* 224–233.

McCord, J. (1988). Identifying developmental paradigms leading to alcoholism. *Journal of Studies on Alcohol, 49,* 357–362.

McDonnell, G. J., & Carpenter, J. A. (1959). Anxiety, skin conductance, and alcohol: A study of the relation between anxiety and skin conductance and the effect of alcohol on the conductance of subjects in a group. *Quarterly Journal of Studies on Alcohol, 20,* 38–52.

McKiran, D. J., & Peterson, P. L. (1988). Stress, expectancies, and vulnerability to substance abuse: A test of a model among homosexual men. *Journal of Abnormal Psychology, 97,* 461–466.

McMillen, D. L., Smith, S. M., & Wells-Parker, E. (1989). The effects of alcohol, expectancy, and sensation seeking on driving risk taking. *Addictive Behaviors, 14,* 477–484.

McMillen, D. L. & Wells-Parker, E. (1987). The effect of alcohol consumption on risks-taking while driving. *Addictive Behaviors, 12,* 241–248.

Mello, N. K., Mendelson, J. H., & Palmieri, S. L. (1987). Cigarette smoking by women: interactions with alcohol use. *Psychopharmacology, 93,* 8–15.

Merari, A., Ginton, A., Heifez, T., & Lev-Ran, T. (1973). Effects of alcohol on mating behavior of the female rat. *Quarterly Journal of Studies on Alcohol, 34,* 1095–1098.

Merton, R. K. (1957). *Structure.* Glencoe, IL: The Free Press.

Miczek, K. A., & Thompson, M. L. (1983). Drugs of abuse and aggression: An ethopharmacological analysis. In E. Gottheil, K. A. Druley, T. E. Skolada, & H. M. Waxman (Eds.), *Alcohol, drug abuse and aggression* (pp. 164–188). Springfield, IL: C. C. Thomas.

Miller, P. M., Hersen, M., Eisler, R. M., & Hilsman, G. (1974). Effects of social stress on operant drinking of alcoholics and social drinkers. *Behavior Research and Therapy, 12,* 67–72.

Mills, K. C., & Bean, J. W. (1978). The caloric and intoxicating properties of fluid intake as components of stress induced ethanol consumption in rats. *Psychopharmacology, 57,* 27–31.

Mills, K. C., Bean, J. W., & Hutcheson, J. S. (1977). Shock inducted ethanol consumption in rats. *Pharmacology, Biochemistry, and Behavior, 6,* 107–115.

Mintz, J., Boyd, G., Rose, J. E., Charuvastra, V. C., & Jarvik, M. E. (1985). Alcohol increases smoking: A laboratory investigation. *Addictive Behaviors, 10,* 203–208.

Morrissey, E. R., & Schuckit, M. A. (1978). Stressful life events and alcohol problems among women seen at a detoxification center. *Journal of Studies on Alcohol, 39,* 1559–1576.

Moskowitz, J. M. (1989). The primary prevention of alcohol problems: A critical review of the research literature. *Journal of Studies on Alcohol, 50,* 54–88.

Mules, J. E., Hague, W. H., & Dudley, D. L. (1977). Life change, its perception, and alcohol addiction. *Journal of Studies on Alcohol, 38,* 487–493.

Mulford, H. A. (1964). Drinking and deviant drinking, U.S.A., 1963. *Quarterly Journal of Studies on Alcohol, 25,* 634–650.

Mulford, H. A., & Miller, D. E. (1960a). Drinking in Iowa, III. Drinking and alcoholic drinking. *Quarterly Journal of Studies on Alcohol, 21,* 267–278.

National Institute on Alcohol Abuse and Alcoholism. *Alcohol and health. Fifth special report to the U.S. Congress.* DHHS Publication No. (ADM) 84–1291. Washington: Government Printing Office, 1984.

Neff, J. A. (1985). Evaluating the stress-buffering role of alcohol consumption variation by type of event and type of symptom. *Alcohol and Alcoholism, 29,* 391–401.

Neff, J. A., & Husaini, B. A. (1982). Life events, drinking patterns, and depressive symptomatology. *Journal of Studies on Alcohol, 43,* 301–318.

Newlin, D. B. (1984). The conditioned compensatory response to alcohol placebo in humans. *Psychophysiology, 21,* 590.

Newlin, D. B. (1985). The antagonistic placebo response to alcohol cues. *Alcoholism: Clinical and Experimental Research, 9,* 411–416.

Ng Cheong Ton, M. J. Brown, Z., Michalakeas, A., & Amit, Z. (1983). Stress induced suppression of maintenance but not of acquisition of ethanol consumption in rats. *Pharmacology, Biochemistry, and Behavior, 18,* 141–144.

Niaura, R., Wilson, G. T., & Westrick, E. (1988). Coronary-prone behavior, self-awareness, and the stress response dampening effects of alcohol. *Psychosomatic Medicine, 50,* 360–380.

Noel, N. E., Lisman, S. A. (1980). Alcohol consumption by college women following exposure to unsolvable problems: Learned helplessness or stress induced drinking? *Behavior Research and Therapy, 18,* 429–440.

O'Malley, S. S., & Maisto, S. A. (1985). Effects of family drinking history and expectancies on responses to alcohol in men. *Journal of Studies on Alcohol, 46,* 289–297.

Orford, J., Waller, S., & Peto, J. (1974). Drinking behavior and attitudes and their correlates among University students in England. I. Principal components in the drinking domain. II. Personality and social influence. III. Sex differences. *Quarterly Journal of Studies on Alcohol, 35,* 1316–1374.

Ornstein, S. I. (1980). Control of alcohol consumption through price increases. *Journal of Studies on Alcohol, 41,* 807–818.

Park, P. (1967). Dimensions of drinking among male college students. *Social Problems, 14,* 473–482.

Park, P. (1974). Dimensions of drinking among male college students. *Social Problems, 14,* 473–482.

Parker, E. S., Birnbaum, I. M., & Noble, E. P. (1976). Alcohol and memory: Storage and state dependency. *Journal of Verbal Learning and Verbal Behavior, 15,* 691–702.

Parker, J. C., Gilbert, G., & Speltz, M. L. (1981). Expectations regarding the effects of alcohol on assertiveness: A comparison of alcoholics and social drinkers. *Addictive Behaviors, 6,* 29–33.

Parker, D. A., & Harman, M. S. (1978). The distribution of consumption model of prevention of alcohol problems. *Journal of Studies on Alcohol, 39,* 377–399.

Parker, D. A., & Maattanen, K. (1987). Intoxication and self-orientations during alcohol use: An empirical assessment of the relationship and of its determinants among employed men and women. *Journal of Studies on Alcohol, 48,* 443–449.

Parker, E. S., Morihisa, J. M., Wyatt, R. J., Schwartz, B. L., Weingartner, H., & Stillman, R. C. (1981). The alcohol facilitation effect on memory: A dose-response study. *Psychopharmacology, 74,* 88–92.

Pattison, E. M. (1982). Alcohol use: Social policy. In E. M. Pattison & E. Kaufman (Eds.), *Encyclopedic handbook of alcoholism* (pp. 490–514). New York: Gardner Press.

Pearlin, L. I., & Radabaugh, C. W. (1976). Economic strains and coping functions of alcohol. *American Journal of Sociology, 82,* 652–663.

Peele, S. (1987). The limitation of control-of-supply models for explaining and preventing alcoholism and drug addiction. *Journal of Studies on Alcohol, 48,* 61–77.

Peris, J., & Cunningham, J. L. (1987). Stress enhances the development of tolerance to the hypotheramic effect of ethanol. *Alcohol and Drug Research, 7,* 187–193.

Persson, L. O., Sjoberg, L., & Svensson, E. (1980). Mood effects of alcohol. *Psychopharmacology, 68,* 295–299.

Pihl, R. O., Zeichner, A., Niaura, R., Nagy, K., & Zacchia, C. (1981). Attribution and alcohol-mediated aggression. *Journal of Abnormal Psychology, 90,* 468–475.

Pihl, R. O., Zacchia, C., & Zeichner, A. (1982). Predicting levels of aggression after alcohol intake in men social drinkers; A preliminary investigation. *Journal of Studies on Alcohol, 43,* 599–602.

Pihl, R. O., & Yankofsky, L. (1979). Alcohol consumption in male social drinkers as a function of situationally induced depressive affect and anxiety. *Psychopharmacology, 65,* 251–257.

Plant, M. A. (1979). Occupations, drinking patterns, and alcohol-related problems: Conclusions from a follow-up study. *British Journal of Addiction, 74,* 267–273.

Pliner, P., & Cappell, H. (1974). Modification of affective consequences of alcohol: A comparison of social and solitary drinking. *Journal of Abnormal Psychology, 83,* 418–425.

Pohorecky, L. A. (1981). The interaction of alcohol and stress: A review. *Neuroscience and Biobehavioral Reviews, 5,* 209–229.

Pohorecky, L. A., Cagan, M., Brick, J., & Jaffe, L. S. (1976). The startle response in rats: Effect of ethanol. *Pharmacology, Biochemistry, & Behavior, 4,* 311–316.

Pohorecky, L. A., Rassi, E., & Weiss, J. M., & Michalak, V. (1980). Biochemical evidence for an interaction of ethanol and stress: Preliminary studies. *Alcoholism: Clinical and Experimental Research, 4,* 423–426.

Polivy, J., Schueneman, A. L., & Carlson, K. (1976). Alcohol and tension reduction: Cognitive and physiological effects. *Journal of Abnormal Psychology, 85,* 595–600.

Popham, R. E., Schmidt, W., & De Lint, J. (1976). The effects of legal restraint on drinking. In B. Kissen & H. Begleiter (Eds.) *The biology of alcoholism: Social aspects of alcoholism* (pp. 579–625, Vol. 4). New York: Plenum Press.

Propping, P. (1978). Genetic aspects of alcohol action on the electroencephalogram (EEG). In H. Begleiter (Ed.), *Biological effects of alcohol advances in experimental medicine and biology* (pp. 589–623). New York: Plenum Press.

Rada, R. T. (1975). Alcoholism and forcible rape. *American Journal of Psychiatry, 132,* 444–446.

Reed, T. E. (1980). Change in heart rate and "normalization" of heart rate as indicators of acute alcohol response in mice and humans. In K. Eriksson, J. D., Sinclair, & K. Kiianmaa (Eds.), *Animal models in alcohol research* (pp. 93–96). New York: Academic Press.

Rhodes, L. E., Obitz, F. W., & Creel, D. (1975). Effect of alcohol and task on hemispheric asymmetry of visually evoked potentials in man. *Electroencephalography and Clinical Neurophysiology, 38,* 561–568.

Rimm, D., Briddell, D., Zimmerman, M., & Caddy, G. (1981). The effects of alcohol and the expectancy of alcohol on snake fear. *Addictive Behaviors, 6,* 47–51.

Rohrberg, R. G., & Sousa-Poza, J. F. (1976). Alcohol, field dependence, and dyadic self-disclosure. *Psychological Reports, 39,* 1151–1161.

Rohsenow, D. J. (1982a). Control over interpersonal evaluation and alcohol consumption in male social drinkers. *Addictive Behaviors, 7,* 113–121.

Rohsenow, D. J. (1982b). The alcohol use inventory and predictor of drinking by male heavy social drinkrs. *Addictive Behaviors, 7,* 387–395.

Rohsenow, D. J. (1982c). Social anxiety, daily moods, and alcohol use over time among heavy social drinking men. *Addictive Behavior, 7,* 311–315.

Rohsenow, D. J. (1983). Drinking habits and expectancies about alcohol's effects for self versus others. *Journal of Consulting and Clinical Psychology, 51,* 752–756.

Rohsenow, D. J., Bachorowski, J. (1984). Effects of alcohol and expectancies on verbal aggression in men and women. *Journal of Abnormal Psychology, 93,* 418–432.

Room, R. (1976). Ambivalence as a sociological explanation: The case of cultural explanations of alcohol problems. *Sociological Review, 4,* 1047–1065.

Room, R. (1987). Alcohol control, addiction and processes of change: Comment on "The limitations of control-of-supply models for explaining and preventing alcoholism and drug addiction. *Journal of Studies on Alcohol, 48,* 78–83.

Ross, D. F., & Pihl, R. O. (1988). Alcohol, self-focus, and complex reaction-time performance. *Journal of Studies on Alcohol, 49,* 115–125.

Rubin, H. B. & Henson, D. E. (1976). Effects of alcohol on male sexual responding. *Psychopharmacology, 47,* 123–134.

Rush, B. R., Gliksman, L., Brook, R. (1986). Alcohol availability, alcohol consumption and alcohol-related damage. I. The distribution consumption model. *Journal of Studies on Alcohol, 47,* 1–10.

Russell, J. A., & Mehrabian, A. (1975). The mediating role of emotions in alcohol use. *Journal of Studies on Alcohol, 36,* 1508–1534.

Sadava, S. W., Thistle, R., & Forsyth, R. (1978). Stress, escapism, and patterns of alcohol and drug use. *Journal of Studies on Alcohol, 39,* 725–735.

Samsonowitz, V., & Sjoberg, L. (1981). Volitional problems of socially adjusted alcoholics. *Addictive Behaviors, 66,* 385–398.

Schachter, S. (1971). *Emotion, obesity, and crime.* New York: Academic Press.

Schaefer, H. H., Sobell, M. B., & Mills, K. C. (1971). Baseline drinking behaviors in alcoholics and social drinkers: Kinds of drinks and sip magnitude. *Behavior Research and Therapy, 9,* 23–27.

Schandler, S. L., Cohen, M. J., & McArthur, D. L. (1988). Event-related brain potentials in intoxicated and detoxified visuospatial learning. *Psychopharmacology, 94,* 275–283.

Schmutte, G. T., Leonard, K. E., & Taylor, S. P. (1979). Alcohol and expectations of attack. *Psychological Reports, 45,* 163–167.

Schuckit, M. A. (1979). *Drug and Alcohol Abuse: A Clinical Guide.* New York: Plenum Medical Books.

Schuckit, M. A. (1986). Genetic and clinical implications of alcoholism and affective disorder. *American Journal of Psychiatry, 143,* 140–147.

Schuckit, M. A., Irwin, M., & Brown, S. A. (1990). The history of anxiety symptoms among 171 primary alcoholics. *Journal of Studies on Alcohol, 51,* 34–41.

Segal, B., & Huba, G. J., & Singer, J. L. (1980). Reasons for drug and alcohol use by college students. *International Journal of Addictions, 15,* 489–498.

Sher, K. J., & Walitzer, K. S. (1986). Individual differences in the stress-response-dampening effect of alcohol: A dose-response study. *Journal of Abnormal Psychology, 95,* 159–167.

Shuntich, R. J., & Taylor, S. P. (1972). The effects of alcohol on human physical aggression. *Journal of Experimental Research in Personality, 6,* 34–38.

Shupe, L. M. (1954). Alcohol and crime: A study of the urine alcohol concentration found in 882 persons arrested during or immediately after the commission of a felony. *Journal of Criminal Law Criminological Political Science, 44,* 661–664.

Sjoberg, L. (1969). Alcohol and gambling. *Psychopharmacologia, 14,* 284–298.

Slattery, M., Alderson, M. R., & Bryant, J. S. (1986). The occupational risks of alcoholism. *International Journal of the Addictions, 21,* 929–936.

Smith, R. C. (1974). Alcohol and the acceptance of social influence: An experimental study. *Psychopharmacologia, 36,* 357–366.

Smith, R. C., Parker, E. S., & Noble, E. P. (1975). Alcohol and affect in dyadic social interaction. *Psychosomatic Medicine, 37,* 25–40.

Snortum, J. R., Kremer, L. K., & Berger, E. D. (1987). Alcoholic beverage preference as a public statement: Self-concept and social image of college drinkers. *Journal of Studies on Alcohol 48,* 243–251.

Sobell, M. B., Schaefer, H. H., Mills, K. C. (1972). Differences in baseline drinking behavior between alcoholics and normal drinkers. *Behavior Research and Therapy, 10,* 257–267.

Solomon, R. L. (1980). The opponent-process theory of acquired motivation: The cost of pleasure and the benefit of pain. *American Psychologist, 35*, 691–712.

Southwick, C. M., Southwick, L. L., & Critchlow, B. (1981). Dissonance and alcohol: Drinking your troubles away. *Journal of Personality and Social Psychology, 41*, 831–846.

Spieker, G. (1983). What is the linkage between alcohol abuse and violence? In E. Gottheil, K. A. Druley, T. E. Skoloda, & H. M. Waxman (Eds.), *Alcohol, drug abuse, and aggression* (pp. 125–138). Springfield, IL: Charles C. Thomas.

Steele, C. M., Critchlow, B., & Liu, T. J. (1985). Alcohol and social behavior II: The helpful drunkard. *Journal of Personality and Social Psychology, 48*, 35–46.

Steele, C. M., & Josephs, R. A. (1988). Drinking your troubles away II: An attention-allocation model of alcohol's effect on psychological stress. *Journal of Abnormal Psychology, 97*, 196–205.

Steele, C. M., & Southwick, L. (1985). Alcohol and social behavior II: The psychology of drunken excess. *Journal of Personality and Social Psychology, 48*, 18–34.

Steele, C. M., & Southwick, L. L., & Critchlow, B. (1981). Dissonance and alcohol: Drinking tour troubles away. *Journal of Personality and Social Psychology, 41*, 831–846.

Steele, C. M., Southwick, L., & Pagano, R. (1986). Drinking your troubles away: The role of activity in mediating alcohol's reduction of psychological stress. *Journal of Abnormal Psychology, 95*, 173–180.

Steffen, J. J., Nathan, P. E., & Taylor, H. A. (1974). Tension-reducing effects of alcohol: Further evidence and some methodological considerations. *Journal of Abnormal Psychology, 83*, 542–547.

Stokes, P. E. (1982). Endocrine disturbances associated with alcohol and alcoholism. In E. Pattison, & E. Kaufman (Eds.), *Encyclopedic handbook of alcoholism* (pp. 311–323). New York: Gardner Press.

Strickler, D. P., Dobbs, S. D., & Maxwell, W. A. (1979). The influence of setting on drinking behaviors: The laboratory vs. the barroom. *Addictive Behaviors, 4*, 339–344.

Strickler, D. P., Tomaszewski, R., Maxwell, W. A., & Suib, M. R. (1979). The effects of relaxation instructions on drinking behavior in the presence of stress. *Behavior Research and Therapy, 17*, 45–51.

Sutker, P. B., Allain, A. N., Brantley, P. J., & Randall, C. L. (1982). Acute alcohol intoxication, negative affect, and autonomic arousal in women and men. *Addictive Behaviors, 7*, 17–25.

Tabakoff, B. (1980). Alcohol tolerance in humans and animals. In K. Eriksson, J. D., Sinclair, & K. Kiianmaa (Eds.), *Animal models in alcohol research* (pp. 271–291). New York: Academic Press.

Taylor, S. P., & Gammon, C. B. (1975). Effects of type and dose of alcohol on human physical aggression. *Journal of Personality and Social Psychology, 32*, 169–175.

Taylor, S. P., & Gammon, C. B. (1976). Aggressive behavior of intoxicated subjects: The effect of third-party intervention. *Journal of Studies on Alcohol, 37*, 917–930.

Taylor, S. P., Gammon, C. B., & Capasso, D. R. (1976). Aggression as a function of the interaction of alcohol and threat. *Journal of Personality and Social Psychology, 34*, 938–941.

Taylor, S. P., Schmutte, G. T., & Leonard, K. E. (1977). Physical aggression as a function of alcohol and frustration. *Bulletin of Psychonomic Society, 9*, 217–218.

Taylor, S. P., Schmutte, G. T., Leonard, K. E., & Cranston, J. W. (1979). The effects of alcohol and extreme provocation on the use of a highly noxious electric shock. *Motivation and Emotion, 3*, 73–81.

Teger, A. I., Katkin, E. S., & Pruitt, D. G. (1969). Effects of alcoholic beverages and their congener content on level and style of risk taking. *Journal of Personality and Social Psychology, 11*, 170–176.

Teitelbaum, H. A., & Gantt, W. H. (1958). The effect of alcohol on sexual reflects and sperm count in the dog. *Quarterly Journal of Studies on Alcohol, 19*, 394–398.

Thyer, B. A., & Curtis, G. C. (1984). The effects of ethanol intoxication on phobic anxiety. *Behavior Research and Therapy, 22,* 599–610.

Tucker, J. A., & Vuchinich, R. E. (1983). An information processing analysis of the effects of alcohol on perceptions of facial emotions. *Psychopharmacology, 79,* 215–219.

Tucker, J. A., Vuchinich, R. E., & Sobell, M. B. (1981). Alcohol consumption as a self-hand-icapping strategy. *Journal of Personality and Social Psychology, 90,* 220–230.

Tucker, J. A., Vuchinich, R. E., Sobell, M. B., & Maisto, S. A. (1980). Normal drinkers' alcohol consumption as a function of conflicting motives induced by intellectual performance stress. *Addictive Behaviors, 5,* 171–178.

Turkkan, J. S., Stitzer, M. L., & McCaul, M. E. (1988). Psychophysiological effects of oral ethanol in alcoholics and social drinkers. *Alcoholism: Clinical and Experimental Research, 12,* 30–38.

Vaillant, G. E. (1983). *The natural history of alcoholism: Causes, patterns, and paths to recovery.* Cambridge, MA Harvard University Press.

Veevers, J. E. (1972). Drinking attitudes and drinking behavior: An exploratory study. *Journal of Social Psychology, 85,* 103–109.

Vogel-Sprott, M. (1967). Alcohol effects on human behaviour under reward and punishment. *Psychopharmacologia, 11,* 337–344.

Vogel-Sprott, M., & Barrett, P. (1984). Age, drinking habits, and the effects of alcohol. *Journal of Studies on Alcohol, 45,* 517–521.

von Wright, J. M., Pekanmaki, L., & Malin, S. (1971). Effects of conflict and stress on alcohol intake in rats. *Quarterly Journal of Studies on Alcohol, 32,* 420–433.

Vuchinich, R. E., & Sobell, M. B. (1978). Empirical separation of physiologic and expected effects of alcohol on complex perceptual motor performance. *Psychopharmacology, 60,* 81–85.

Vuchinich, R. E., Tucker, J. A., & Sobell, M. B. (1979). Alcohol, expectancy, cognitive labeling, and mirth. *Journal of Abnormal Psychology, 88,* 641–651.

Warren, G. H., Raynes, A. E. (1972). Mood changes during three conditions of alcohol intake. *Quarterly Journal of Studies on Alcohol, 33,* 979–989.

Weaver, J. B., Masland, J. L., Kharazmi, S. & Zillman, D. (1985). Effect of alcoholic intoxication on the appreciation of different types of humor. *Journal of Personality and Social Psychology, 49,* 781–787.

Wechsler, H., & Rohman, M. (1981). Extensive users of alcohol among college students. *Journal of Studies on Alcohol, 42,* 149–155.

Weissman, M. M., Myers, J. K. & Harding, P. S. (1980). Prevalence and psychiatric heterogeneity of alcoholism in a United States urban community. *Journal of Studies on Alcohol, 41,* 672–681.

Williams, R. J., & Brown, R. A. (1974). Differences in baseline drinking behavior between New Zealand alcoholics and normal drinkers. *Behavior Research and Therapy, 12,* 227–294.

Wilsnack, R. W., Wilsnack, S. C., & Klassen, A. D. (1986). Antecedents and consequences of drinking and drinking problems in women: Patterns from a U. S. national survey. In P. C. Rivers (Ed.), *Alcohol and addictive behavior: Nebraska symposium on motivation* (pp. 85–158). Lincoln: University of Nebraska Press.

Wilson, G. T. (1983). Self-awareness, self-regulation, and alcohol consumption: An analysis of J. Hull's model. *Journal of Abnormal Psychology, 92,* 505–513.

Wilson, G. T., & Abrams, D. (1977). Effects of alcohol on social anxiety and physiological arousal: Cognitive versus pharmacological processes. *Cognitive Therapy and Research, 1,* 195–210.

Wilson, G. T., Abrams, D. B., & Lipscomb, T. R. (1980). Effects of intoxication levels and drinking pattern on social anxiety in men. *Journal of Studies on Alcohol, 41,* 250–264.

Wilson, G. T., Brick, J., Alder, J., Cocco, K., & Breslin, C. (1989). Alcohol and anxiety reduction in female social drinkers. *Journal of Studies on Alcohol, 50,* 226–235.

Wilson, G. T., & Lawson, D. M. (1976a). Effects of alcohol on sexual arousal in women. *Journal of Abnormal Psychology, 85,* 489–497.

Wilson, G. T., & Lawson, D. M. (1976b). Expectancies, alcohol, and sexual arousal in male social drinkers. *Journal of Abnormal Psychology, 85,* 587–594.

Wilson, G. T., & Lawson, D. M. (1978). Expectancies, alcohol and sexual arousal in women. *Journal of Abnormal Psychology, 87,* 358–367.

Wilson, G. T., & Niaura, R. (1984). Alcohol and the disinhibition of sexual responsiveness. *Journal of Studies on Alcohol, 45,* 219–224.

Windle, M., & Blane, H. T. (1989). Cognitive ability and drinking behavior in a national sample of young adults. *Alcoholism: Clinical and Experimental Research, 13,* 43–48.

Wise, R. A., & Bozarth, M. A. (1987). A psychomotor stimulant theory of addiction. *Psychological Review, 94,* 469–492.

Wolin, S. J., Bennett, L. A., & Noonan, D. L. (1979). Family rituals and the recurrence of alcoholism over generations. *American Journal of Psychiatry, 136,* 589–593.

Woolfolk, A. E., Abrams, L. M., Abrams, D. B., & Wilson, G. T. (1979). Effects of alcohol on the nonverbal communication of anxiety: The impact of beliefs on nonverbal behavior. *Environmental Psychology and Nonverbal Behavior,* summer, 205–217.

Wright, M. H., & Obitz, F. W. (1984). Alcoholics' and nonalcoholics' attributions of control and future life events. *Journal of Studies on Alcohol, 45,* 138–143.

Yankofsky, L., Wilson, G. T., Adler, J. L., Hay, W. M., & Vrana, S. (1986). The effect of alcohol on self evaluation and perception of negative interpersonal feedback. *Journal of Studies on Alcohol, 47,* 26–33.

Young, J. A., & Pihl, R. O. (1982). Alcohol consumption and response in men social drinkers: The effects of causal attributions concerning relative response control. *Journal of Studies on Alcohol, 43,* 334–351.

Zeichner, A., Pihl, R. O. (1978). Responsiveness of social drinkers to aversive tone stimulation. *Psychological Reports, 42,* 48.

Zeichner, A., & Pihl, R. O. (1979). Effects of alcohol and behavior contingencies on human aggression. *Journal of Abnormal Psychology, 88,* 153–160.

Zeichner, A., & Pihl, R. O. (1980). Effects of alcohol and instigator intent on human aggression. *Journal of Studies on Alcohol, 41,* 265–276.

Zeichner, A., Pihl, R. O., Niaura, R., & Zacchia, C. (1982). Attentional processes in alcohol-mediated aggression. *Journal of Studies on Alcohol, 43,* 714–724.

Author Index

Subject Index